Lecture Notes
in Business Information Processing   504

Series Editors

Wil van der Aalst ⓘ, *RWTH Aachen University, Aachen, Germany*
Sudha Ram ⓘ, *University of Arizona, Tucson, AZ, USA*
Michael Rosemann ⓘ, *Queensland University of Technology, Brisbane, QLD, Australia*
Clemens Szyperski, *Microsoft Research, Redmond, WA, USA*
Giancarlo Guizzardi ⓘ, *University of Twente, Enschede, The Netherlands*

LNBIP reports state-of-the-art results in areas related to business information systems and industrial application software development – timely, at a high level, and in both printed and electronic form.

The type of material published includes

- Proceedings (published in time for the respective event)
- Postproceedings (consisting of thoroughly revised and/or extended final papers)
- Other edited monographs (such as, for example, project reports or invited volumes)
- Tutorials (coherently integrated collections of lectures given at advanced courses, seminars, schools, etc.)
- Award-winning or exceptional theses

LNBIP is abstracted/indexed in DBLP, EI and Scopus. LNBIP volumes are also submitted for the inclusion in ISI Proceedings.

Ewa Ziemba · Witold Chmielarz ·
Jarosław Wątróbski

Editors

Information Technology for Management: Solving Social and Business Problems Through IT

ITBS 2023 Main Track and ISM 2023
Thematic Track, Held as Part of FedCSIS 2023
Warsaw, Poland, September 17–20, 2023
Extended and Revised Selected Papers

 Springer

Editors
Ewa Ziemba (iD)
University of Economics in Katowice
Katowice, Poland

Witold Chmielarz (iD)
University of Warsaw
Warsaw, Poland

Jarosław Wątróbski (iD)
University of Szczecin
Szczecin, Poland

ISSN 1865-1348   ISSN 1865-1356 (electronic)
Lecture Notes in Business Information Processing
ISBN 978-3-031-61656-3   ISBN 978-3-031-61657-0 (eBook)
https://doi.org/10.1007/978-3-031-61657-0

This Springer imprint is published by the registered company Springer Nature Switzerland AG
The registered company address is: Gewerbestrasse 11, 6330 Cham, Switzerland

If disposing of this product, please recycle the paper.

Preface

Eight volumes have appeared in this series in recent years:

- *Information Technology for Management* in 2016 (LNBIP 243);
- *Information Technology for Management: New Ideas or Real Solutions* in 2017 (LNBIP 277);
- *Information Technology for Management: Ongoing Research and Development* in 2018 (LNBIP 311);
- *Information Technology for Management: Emerging Research and Applications* in 2019 (LNBIP 346);
- *Information Technology for Management: Current Research and Future Directions* in 2020 (LNBIP 380);
- *Information Technology for Management: Towards Business Excellence* in 2021 (LNBIP 413);
- *Information Technology for Management: Business and Social Issues* in 2022 (LNBIP 442);
- *Information Technology for Management: Approaches to Improving Business and Society* in 2023 (LNBIP 471).

The COVID-19 pandemic underscored the critical role of IT in maintaining societal functions during global threats. Remote work, remote teaching, remote entertainment, e-commerce and electronic banking, as well as organizational restrictions forced by the circumstances meant that, even in the face of the growing number of illnesses, economic and social life continued, albeit at a slightly slower pace. Naturally, this period also resulted in a rapid, dynamic development of IT applications, almost increasing by leaps and bounds since the beginning of the pandemic. Consequently, we found it imperative to release another publication in this series, focusing on the latest IT advancements post-pandemic.

The Conference on Computer Science and Intelligent Systems, FedCSIS, serves as a platform for scientists to share and discuss their findings, acting as a forum for the exchange of ideas and their applications within the computer science community. It invites researchers and practitioners from around the world to contribute their research results focused on emerging topics in the field. Since 2012, the Proceedings of FedCSIS have been indexed in the Thomson Reuters Web of Science, Scopus, IEEE Xplore Digital Library, and the DBLP Computer Science Bibliography.

The present book includes extended and revised versions of a set of selected papers submitted to the Main Track titled Information Technology for Business and Society (ITBS 2023) and two Thematic Tracks: Information System Management (ISM 2023) and Knowledge Acquisition and Management (KAM 2023), held in Poland, Warsaw, September 17–20, 2023.

ITBS addresses the most recent innovations, current trends, professional experiences, and new challenges in designing, implementing, and using information systems and technologies for business, governments, education healthcare, smart cities, and sustainable development.

ISM concentrates on various issues of planning, organizing, resourcing, coordinating, controlling, and leading management functions to ensure the smooth, effective, and high-quality operation of information systems in organizations.

KAM discusses approaches, techniques, and tools in knowledge acquisition and other knowledge management areas with a focus on the contribution of artificial intelligence to improving human-machine intelligence and facing the challenges of this century.

For our field of activity, we received 60 papers from 19 countries on all continents. The quality of the papers was carefully evaluated by the members of the Program Committees by taking into account the criteria for papers: relevance to conference topics, originality, and novelty. The single-blind review method was used. Each paper was reviewed by 2 to 5 reviewers. After extensive reviews, only 15 papers (25%) were accepted as full papers and 11 (18%) – as short papers, yielding an acceptance rate of average 22%. Finally, 13 papers of the highest quality (50% of full and short papers) were carefully reviewed and chosen by the Chairs of our field, and the authors were invited to extend their research and submit the new extended papers for consideration for this LNBIP publication. Our guiding criteria for including papers in the book were the excellence of the paper as indicated by the reviewers, the relevance of the subject matter for improving management by adopting information technology, as well as the promise of the scientific contributions and the implications for practitioners. The selected papers reflect state-of-the-art research work that is often oriented toward real-world applications and highlights the benefits of information systems and technologies for business and public administration, thus forming a bridge between theory and practice.

The papers selected to be included in this book contribute to understanding relevant trends of current research on and future directions of information systems and technologies for improving and developing business and society. The book's first part focuses on the role and place of IT in improving management systems, the second part presents approaches to improving social problems, and the third part explores methods of solving business problems.

On behalf of the authors, we would like to express the hope that the presented publication is an expression of a new look at the current and future developments and problems in the use of computer science. For representatives of practice, this publication should offer new information on the issues discussed, while for the world of science it may prove to be motivation, guidance, and even inspiration to undertake new research in the field of computer science and its applications.

We hope it will provide the necessary knowledge and enable better understanding of the "IT reality" that surrounds us. It will also be useful for students of economic and technical faculties at universities where subjects related to computer science and its applications are taught. In this spirit and belief, we submit the volume, which is the result of the authors' intellectual effort, to the final judgment of the Readers.

We are always open to discussion on the issues raised in this publication, and we also await polemical or even critical opinions regarding the content and shape of future publications in this area. They will allow us to improve our work in the coming years and better transfer the knowledge necessary to function properly in a complex reality increasingly dominated by information technology.

We would like to express our thanks to everyone who made our scientific meeting successful. First of all, to our authors for offering very interesting research and submitting their new findings for publication in LNBIP. We express our appreciation to the members of the Program Committees for taking the time and effort necessary to help us with their expertise and diligence in reviewing the papers and providing valuable insights for the authors. The high standards followed by them enabled the authors to ensure the high quality of the papers. The excellent work of the Program Committee members and the authors enabled us to ensure the high quality of the conference sessions and valuable scientific discussion. We acknowledge the Chairs of FedCSIS 2023, i.e., Maria Ganzha, Marcin Paprzycki, Dominik Ślęzak, and Leszek A. Maciaszek, for building an active international community around the FedCSIS conference. Last but not least, we are indebtedto the team of Springer-Verlag, without whom this book would not have been possible.

We cordially invite you to visit the FedCSIS website at https://fedcsis.org and join us at future conferences.

March 2024   Ewa Ziemba
                                                                   Witold Chmielarz
                                                                 Jarosław Wątróbski

Organization

Roisin Mullins	University of Wales Trinity Saint David, UK
Alexander Oppermann	Physikalisch-Technische Bundesanstalt, Germany
Grażyna Paliwoda-Pękosz	Cracow University of Economics, Poland
Amit Rechavi	Ruppin Academic Center, Israel
Federica Rollo	University of Modena and Reggio Emilia, Italy
Yonit Rusho	Shenkar College of Engineering and Design, Israel
Marcin Sikorski	Gdansk University of Technology, Poland
Vijender Kumar Solanki	CMR Institute of Technology, India
Francesco Taglino	IASI-CNR, Italy
Marcus Terra	Universidade Estadual de Londrina, Brazil
Łukasz Tomczyk	Jagiellonian University, Poland
Krzysztof Wencel	Poznań University of Economics, Poland
Paweł Ziemba	University of Szczecin, Poland

ISM 2023

Thematic Track Chairs

Witold Chmielarz	University of Warsaw, Poland
Christian Leyh	Technical University of Central Hesse, Germany
Yanqing Duan	University of Bedfordshire, UK
Zane Bicevska	University of Latvia, Latvia

Program Committee

Mesut Atasever	Usak University, Turkiye
Janis Bicevskis	University of Latvia, Latvia
Bolesław Borkowski	Warsaw University of Life Sciences, Poland
Alberto Cano	Virginia Commonwealth University, USA
Vincenza Carchiolo	Università di Catania, Italy
Beata Czarnacka-Chrobot	Warsaw School of Economics, Poland
Susana De Juana-Espinosa	Universidad de Alicante, Spain
Robertus Damasevicius	Silesian University of Technology, Poland
Monika Eisenbardt	University of Economics in Katowice, Poland
Renata Gabryelczyk	University of Warsaw, Poland
Nitza Geri	Open University of Israel, Israel
Krzysztof Kania	University of Economics in Katowice, Poland
Andrzej Kobyliński	Warsaw School of Economics, Poland
Gloria Miller	maxmetrics, Germany

Karolina Muszyńska	University of Szczecin, Poland
Felix Puime	Universidade de A Coruña, Spain
Uldis Rozevskis	University of Latvia, Latvia
Andrzej Sobczak	Warsaw School of Economics, Poland
Anna Sołtysik-Piorunkiewicz	University of Economics in Katowice, Poland
Jakub Swacha	University of Szczecin, Poland
Symeon Symeonidis	Democritus University of Thrace, Greece
Edward Szczerbicki	University of Newcastle, Australia
Oskar Szumski	University of Warsaw, Poland
Janusz Wielki	Opole University of Technology, Poland
Jin Xuetao	Communication University of China, China
Duan Yanquig	University of Bedfordshire, UK
Marek Zborowski	University of Warsaw, Poland
Dmitry Zaitsev	none

KAM 2023

Chairs

Petr Berka	Prague University of Economics and Business, Czech Republic
Krzysztof Hauke	Wrocław University of Economics and Business, Poland
Mieczysław Owoc	Wrocław University of Economics and Business, Poland
Maciej Pondel	Wrocław University of Economics and Business, Poland

Program Committee

Frederic Andres	National Institute of Informatics, Japan
Yevgeniy Bodyanskiy	Kharkiv National University of Radio Electronics, Ukraine
Iwona Chomiak-Orsa	Wrocław University of Economics and Business, Poland
David Chudán	Prague University of Economics and Business, Czech Republic
Marcin Hermes	Wrocław University of Economics and Business, Poland
Tomáš Kliegr	Prague University of Economics and Business, Czech Republic

Krzysztof Kluza	AGH University of Science and Technology, Poland
Antoni Ligęza	AGH University of Science and Technology, Poland
Eunika Mercier-Laurent	Jean Moulin Lyon 3 University, France
Kazimierz Perechuda	Wrocław University of Economics and Business, Poland
Jeanne Schreurs	Hasselt University, Belgium
Pradeep Singh	KIET Group of Institutions, India
Yashwant Singth	Jaypee University of Information Technology Waknaghat, India
Małgorzata Sobińska	Wrocław University of Economics and Business, Poland
Michael Stankosky	University of Scranton, USA
Sudeep Tanwar	Nirma University, India
Sudhanshu Tyagi	Thapar Institute of Engineering & Technology, India
Julian Vasiliev	University of Economics, Varna, Bulgaria
Yungang Zhu	Jilin University, China

Contents

Methods of Solving Business

IT in Improving of Management Systems

Towards Re-identification of Expert Models: MLP-COMET in the Evaluation of Bitcoin Networks

Bartłomiej Kizielewicz[1]([✉]) [iD], Jakub Więckowski[2] [iD],
and Jarosław Jankowski[1] [iD]

[1] Department of Artificial Intelligence Methods and Applied Mathematics,
West Pomeranian University of Technology in Szczecin, ul. Żołnierska 49,
71-210 Szczecin, Poland
{bartlomiej-kizielewicz,jjankowski}@zut.edu.pl
[2] National Institute of Telecommunications, ul. Szachowa 1, 04-894 Warsaw, Poland
j.wieckowski@il-pib.pl

Abstract. In recent years, the application of complex network techniques has seen substantial progress, driven by enhanced computational capabilities and their efficacy in diverse practical domains. Central to complex network models is the assessment of nodes, often addressed through centrality measures. To face challenges in node evaluation, Multi-Criteria Decision Analysis (MCDA) methods, known for accommodating diverse preferences, are employed. MCDA techniques enable the assessment of decision alternatives against multiple criteria by adjusting criteria weights, reflecting the importance of various decision factors. Despite the advantages of expert knowledge in decision-making models, challenges include inaccessibility, inaccuracy of assessment, and limited reusability. To overcome these issues, this paper focuses on an approach that combines MCDA with a complex network technique, specifically Multi-Layer Perceptron (MLP). The study employs the Characteristic Objects Method (COMET) for evaluation, using MLP as an artificial expert to assess Characteristic Objects in the COMET method. The practical application focuses on assessing the Bitcoin network, showcasing contributions such as re-identifying decision models, an alternative methodology for decision processes without a domain expert, and applying MLP-COMET to analyze the Bitcoin network. Furthermore, the study explores various MLP structures and input parameter values to determine their influence on node evaluation stability within the Bitcoin network problem. By enhancing the stability and reliability of the decision model, this research equips decision-makers with more robust tools, fostering more effective and informed decision-making processes.

Keywords: Decision model re-identification · Complex networks · COMET · MLP

1 Introduction

Complex networks have witnessed significant advancements recently, primarily driven by their substantial practical potential [47]. Particularly, complex net-

© The Author(s), under exclusive license to Springer Nature Switzerland AG 2024
E. Ziemba et al. (Eds.): FedCSIS-ITBS 2023/ISM 2023, LNBIP 504, pp. 3–22, 2024.
https://doi.org/10.1007/978-3-031-61657-0_1

works find applications in diverse areas such as quantum systems [3], information processing [28], decision tree analysis [52], and node relevance assessment problems [40]. The increasing computational capabilities of computer technology have facilitated the development of more intricate and efficient solutions [30], thereby reinforcing the role of complex network techniques in data analysis [53]. These approaches have proven effective across various practical problems, offering more efficient solutions and insights derived from analyzed data.

One notably popular domain for complex network models is the realm of blockchain and cryptocurrencies [50]. As the field of virtual payments expands, there is a growing need for solutions that support informed and rational decision-making. Complex networks are extensively applied to analyze blockchain structures [14], transaction patterns [48], and automation processes [16], among other applications. These techniques extract knowledge crucial for further analysis, facilitating more effective decision-making in blockchain and cryptocurrencies.

Central to complex networks is using nodes in the analysis process [27], often assessing incompatible nodes based on centrality measures. To reduce this issue, various techniques, including Multi-Criteria Decision Analysis (MCDA) methods, are employed [55]. MCDA techniques enable the evaluation of decision alternatives against multiple criteria, accommodating diverse preferences and objectives in the assessment process [36]. This flexibility is achieved by adjusting criteria weights, signifying the importance of different decision factors [33]. Such an approach makes the models highly adaptable and reusable under varying conditions.

Various approaches exist for modeling criteria importance [38], often relying on professional expert knowledge and experience obtained through criteria judgment processes [26]. Subjective weighting methods, like the Analytical Hierarchy Process (AHP) [15], have been traditionally employed for this purpose. However, new methods like Ranking Comparison (RANCOM) [49] demonstrate superior handling of expert judgment inaccuracies. Additional techniques for extracting expert knowledge include Best-Worst Method (BWM) [19], Full Consistency Method (FUCOM) [35], Fixed Point Scoring [33], and Simple Multi-Attribute Rating Technique (SMART) [32], among others.

Despite the advantages of incorporating expert knowledge in decision models, drawbacks exist, including the unavailability of expert knowledge, hesitance, judgment inaccuracies, and the challenge of reproducing defined relationships between criteria relevance [46]. These factors can hinder the reusability of the determined models across different applications. To address this problem, in this paper, we use an approach combining Multi-Criteria Decision Analysis with a complex network technique, specifically Multi-Layer Perceptron (MLP), and verify the performance of the decision model under different MLP structures. The Characteristic Objects Method (COMET) is utilized for evaluation, with MLP serving as the domain expert assessing Characteristic Objects (COs) in the COMET method. The study employs the practical problem of assessing the Bitcoin network to validate the model's performance, presenting contributions such as the ability to re-identify decision models, an alternative methodology for decision processes without a domain expert, and applying MLP-COMET to analyze the Bitcoin network. In addition, this study examines different structures of MLP and compares various input parameter values to indicate how they influence the obtained results. The aim is to indicate which MLP structure provides the most stable results on the node evaluation within the considered problem of the Bitcoin network. The contributions of the study are:

- proposing an approach for defining decision model reflecting domain expert knowledge
- making decision-making models independent of expert knowledge when multiple data are available
- empirical verification of the proposed approach within the Bitcoin network

The rest of the paper is structured as follows. Section 2 reviews the literature on centrality metrics in complex networks, MCDA, and their applications in blockchain-related practical problems. Section 3 provides the preliminaries of complex networks and MCDA. Section 4 describes the proposed approach for re-identifying the multi-criteria decision model. Section 5 illustrates the application of MLP-COMET in re-identifying the decision model in the case of analyzing the Bitcoin network and compares the effectiveness of the defined model within different MLP structures. Finally, Sect. 6 offers conclusions from the research and outlines future directions for the presented approach.

2   Literature Review

To present the current state of the art regarding the complex network problems and approaches based on multi-criteria decision analysis, selected areas addressed in the literature are presented below. The review is focused on describing challenges faced within the selection problems based on centrality metrics, presenting the approaches used for evaluating blockchain and cryptocurrencies with MCDA methods and in complex networks. Moreover, the problems concerning the extraction of expert knowledge in multi-criteria analysis are also presented. The description of related works introduces the currently used approaches for evaluating the multi-criteria problems directed toward complex networks and emphasizes the research gaps that should be filled.

2.1   Selection Problems Based on Centrality Metrics

In the area of complex networks, it is possible to distinguish metrics that define the attractiveness of a node concerning the others available in the analyzed network. Their analysis allows more efficient choices to be made regarding selecting nodes that are key to information propagation. Measures of centrality such as degree, closeness, betweenness, and eigenvector are a group of factors that allow efficient analysis of network nodes and their selection [17]. Alexandrescu et al. used the four mentioned centrality measures to identify the sustainability communicators in urban regeneration [1]. The presented measures were applied as the decision criteria in one of the three dimensions that were determined in the assessment, namely, the informal network influence. Karczmarczyk et al. applied the MCDA techniques to select seeds for targeted influence maximization within social networks, where the centrality, betweenness, closeness, and eigenvector centrality measures were also considered in the evaluation of the node [18]. Muruganantham et al. focused on the problem of discovering and ranking the influential users in social media networks by applying the selected MCDA methods, namely Preference Ranking Organization Method for Enrichment of Evaluations (PROMETHEE) II, ELimination Et Choix Traduisant la REalité (ELECTRE), AHP, Statistical Design Institute Matrix method (SDI), Pugh (also known as Decision Matrix Method), and Technique for the Order of Prioritisation by Similarity to Ideal Solution (TOPSIS) [31]. The authors also used the four above-mentioned measures to assess the social influence in the network. Moreover, the centrality metrics can be grouped based on their scope of operation. The closeness, betweenness, eigenvector, coreness, average clustering coefficient, average shortest path length, and PageRank measures belong to global measures, while degree or semi-local centrality are classified as measures with local scope [44]. The global measures are identified based on the necessity of having access to the whole network to determine the global information for the specific factor. On the other hand, local measures can be calculated using the local information of the node.

2.2   Blockchain and Cryptocurrencies in MCDA

MCDA methods are used in many application areas due to the ability to flexibly select decision criteria based on which decision variants are assessed. This configurability and versatility allow decision-making models to be used in the area related to blockchain and cryptocurrencies. Lai and Liao proposed an approach for MCDM based on Double Normalization-based Multiple Aggregation (DNMA) and Criteria Importance Through Inter-criteria Correlation (CRITIC) for blockchain platform evaluation [24]. The authors considered 8 decision criteria, namely performance efficiency, interactivity, scalability, reliability, security, portability, maintainability, and cost. Erol et al. examined blockchain applicability in sustainable supply chains by the MCDM framework determined with Fuzzy Step-wise Weight Assessment Ratio Analysis (SWARA), Complex Proportional Assessment (COPRAS), Evaluation based on Distance from Average Solution (EDAS) assessment, and COPELAND method [10]. The evaluation considered 6 decision variants and 8 criteria. Öztürk and Yildizbaşi focused on indicating the barriers that keep the implementation of blockchain into supply chain management [34]. Based on the Fuzzy AHP and Fuzzy TOPSIS, the assessment was conducted considering the uncertainties in the problem. The results from the research showed that high investment costs, data security, and utility play the most important role in the evaluation. Çolak et al., on the other hand, directed their research toward an assessment of blockchain technology in supply chain management [7]. Using the Hesitant Fuzzy Sets (HFS) combined with the AHP (HF-AHP) and TOPSIS (HF-TOPSIS), it was possible to examine the decision alternatives and take into account the potential uncertainties. The authors identified 5 main criteria and 17 sub-criteria, which were used to evaluate 5 decision variants. The sensitivity analysis approach was also used to examine if differences in criteria weights could significantly influence the proposed rankings. Based on the obtained results, the authors indicated that the medicine/drug industry seems to be the most suitable sector for introducing blockchain technology.

2.3   Blockchain and Cryptocurrencies in Complex Networks

The problems connected to blockchain analysis are also addressed by researchers using complex network techniques. Since it is important to identify the most significant nodes in the networks that play a crucial role in the information spread, many approaches have been used for this purpose. Moreover, the centrality measures are eagerly used to investigate the network structures allowing for an in-depth analysis. Tao et al. performed a complex network analysis of the Bitcoin blockchain network, using degree distribution, clustering coefficient, shortest path length, assortativity, and rich-club coefficient [48]. Bielinskyi and Soloviev attempted to identify the complex network precursors of crashes and critical events in the cryptocurrency market [4]. The authors used time series of data considering the days in correction, Bitcoin's high price in $, Bitcoin's low price in $, the decline in %, and the decline in $. As the centrality measures, the authors selected eigenvector values and average path length. Lin et al. focused on understanding Ethereum transaction records with a complex network approach [25]. The authors modeled the transaction records using time and amount features and designed several flexible temporal walk strategies. The degree distribution of the Ethereum transaction network was analyzed with an actual feasible path for money flow. Serena et al. represented cryptocurrency activities ad a complex network to analyze the transaction graphs [45]. Four prominent Distributed Ledger Technologies (DLTs), namely Bitcoin, DogeCoin, Ethereum, and Ripple, were considered. The authors considered three selected centrality measures: degree distribution, average clustering coefficient, and average shortest path length of the main component.

2.4   Expert Knowledge in Multi-criteria Problems

Multi-Criteria Decision Analysis models can be personalized with the different preferences of criteria importance. This approach can be used to propose an individual and specific set of results compliant with the expert preferences and expectations. To extract experts' knowledge and use it as the input data in MCDA models, subjective criteria weighting methods are used [2,51]. Since multiple techniques are being developed to assist the expert in identifying the criteria importance, it is important to select methods that are intuitive and reflects the experts' opinion reliably. Various Decision Support Systems (DSSs) were determined to evaluate alternatives using the domain expert knowledge in the specific field. Dweiri et al. proposed a DSS based on the AHP method for supplier selection in the automotive industry, where the AHP method was used to identify the expert preferences regarding the criteria importance [9]. Mahendra used the FUCOM-SAW method to determine the DSS for e-commerce selection in Indonesia [29]. The FUCOM method served as a measure for extracting the expert knowledge based on which the assessment was performed. Sarabi and Darestani applied the Fuzzy Multiple Objective Optimizations on the basis of Ratio Analysis plus full Multiplicative Form (MULTIMOORA) and BWM approach for determining the DSS for logistics service provider selection in mining equipment manufacturing [43]. The BWM method allowed for defining the criteria relevance based on the expert experience in the given field. The RANCOM method was used to identify the decision-maker preferences regarding the laptop selection, and the identified weights were then used in the selected six MCDA methods [49]. Fahlepi proposed a DSS for employee discipline identification, where the SMART method was used for establishing the criteria relevance based on the expert judgment [11]. It can be seen that various approaches are used to define the decision models based on expert knowledge. However, it should be borne in mind that the experts' availability limits these solutions. Moreover, expert knowledge can change over time, translating into assigning different criteria relevance within the same decision problem. The subjectivity of the assessment should also be considered in developing such systems. It should be limited to providing results with high objectivity of the evaluation, increasing the results' reliability. Since it could be challenging to re-identify the experts' preferences over time, it is worth proposing approaches to fill this gap. To this end, the MLP-COMET technique is proposed, which is based on the complex network analysis and aims to identify the decision model that can be applied to assess new decision variants within the same problem.

3   Preliminaries

3.1   Centrality Metrics

Centrality metrics within complex networks serve as analytical instruments to pinpoint nodes with significant importance or influence in a network. The ongoing trend in recent years has been the continuous introduction of new centrality metrics. Among the widely utilized centrality metrics in complex networks are closeness centrality, degree centrality, eigenvector centrality, and betweenness centrality. Other centrality metrics, such as Katz centrality, harmonic centrality, and percolation centrality, contribute to the diverse set of available measures. When evaluating the relevance of nodes within social networks, specific centrality metrics take precedence, as highlighted in [5]. Consequently, this article will delve into the scrutiny of the following social network centrality measures [6,8,54]:

1. **Degree centrality:**

$$D_c(i) = \sum_j^n x_{ij} \qquad (1)$$

where i is the considered node, j is the other nodes present in the network, n is the number of all nodes, and x_{ij} is the connection between node i and node j.

2. **Betweenness centrality:**

$$B_c(i) = \left(\sum_{s \neq i \neq t} \frac{g_{st}(i)}{g_{st}} \right) \frac{n(n-1)}{2} \tag{2}$$

where g_{st} is the count of binary shortest paths from node s to node t, and $g_{st}(i)$ is the count of those paths that pass through node i.

3. **Eigenvector centrality:**

$$E_c(i) = \lambda^{-1} \sum_{j=1}^{n} A_{ij} e_j \tag{3}$$

where e_j is the node score j, A is the adjacency matrix of the network, n is the number of nodes present in the network, and λ is a constant.

4. **Closeness centrality:**

$$C_c(i) = \frac{n-1}{\sum_{j=1}^{n} d_{ij}} \tag{4}$$

where d_{ij} is the distance from node i to node j.

5. **Harmonic centrality:**

$$H_c(i) = \frac{1}{n-1} \sum_{j \neq i} \frac{1}{\text{dist}(x_i, x_j)} \tag{5}$$

where i is the considered node, j is the other nodes present in the network, d_{ij} is the distance from node i to node j.

These centrality metrics are valuable tools for assessing complex networks as they offer distinct perspectives on node importance. For instance, degree centrality highlights nodes with many direct connections, while betweenness centrality identifies nodes that act as critical bridges in facilitating communication between other nodes, providing a nuanced understanding of network dynamics and vulnerability. The continual development and incorporation of new centrality metrics enhance the granularity of network analysis, allowing for a more comprehensive evaluation of node influence and system resilience.

3.2   The Multi-layer Perceptron Regressor

Artificial neural networks emulate the structure and functioning of the human brain through computational models. The Multi-Layer Perceptron (MLP) stands out, extensively employed in solving classification and regression problems. From Frank Rosenblatt's 1957 proposal, an MLP comprises three principal layers: input, hidden, and output. Input data is received by the input layer and transmitted through subsequent layers. The hidden layers between input and output consist of multiple perceptrons. The output layer produces the final network results. Weights, assigned to connections between perceptrons in different layers, govern the impact of one perceptron's output on the input of others.

Supervised learning guides the MLP, necessitating a dataset with input pairs and anticipated output data for training. The objective is to teach the network a function transforming input data into expected output data. The widely employed backward error propagation algorithm drives error from the network's output to the hidden and input layers, adjusting connection weights. The MLP's efficacy hinges on critical hyperparameters, including the number of hidden layers, perceptrons in each layer, learning rate, and activation function. Prudent hyperparameter selection is pivotal for the network's efficiency. Figure 1 illustrates an example of neural network visualization.

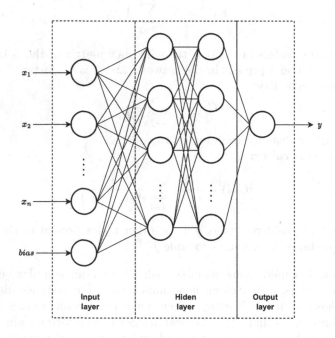

Fig. 1. Example structure of a multilayer perceptron.

3.3 The Characteristic Objects Method

The Characteristic Objects METhod (COMET) is a multi-criteria method proposed by Sałabun in 2015 to eliminate the paradox of Ranking Reversal (RR) [41]. The decision alternatives are evaluated by measuring the distance between them and the Characteristic Objects (COs) that play a crucial role in the model. In addition, this method has been modified with many extensions for uncertain environments such as Normalized Interval-Valued Triangular Fuzzy Numbers (NIVTFN) [13], Intuitionistic Fuzzy Sets (IFS) [12] and Hesitant Fuzzy Sets (HFS) [42]. The main steps of the COMET method can be presented as follows:

Step 1. Identify the problem's dimensionality. Expert selects r number of criteria and their fuzzy values, which is represented by an Eq. (6).

$$C_1 = \{\tilde{C}_{11}, \tilde{C}_{12}, ..., \tilde{C}_{1c_1}\}$$
$$C_2 = \{\tilde{C}_{21}, \tilde{C}_{22}, ..., \tilde{C}_{2c_2}\}$$
$$...$$
$$C_r = \{\tilde{C}_{r1}, \tilde{C}_{r2}, ..., \tilde{C}_{rc_r}\} \tag{6}$$

where $C_1, C_2, \ldots, C_r$ are the criteria represented by the fuzzy numbers.

Step 2. Creating Characteristic Objects (COs) with the Cartesian product from fuzzy number cores. Equation (7) illustrates an example of the construction of characteristic objects.

$$CO = \langle C(C_1) \times C(C_2) \times ...C(C_r)\rangle \tag{7}$$

The result is a set of characteristic objects. This set can be expressed as follows:

$$CO_1 = \langle C(\tilde{C}_{11}), C(\tilde{C}_{21}), ..., C(\tilde{C}_{r1})\rangle$$
$$CO_2 = \langle C(\tilde{C}_{11}), C(\tilde{C}_{21}), ..., C(\tilde{C}_{r2})\rangle$$
$$...$$
$$CO_t = \langle C(\tilde{C}_{1c_1}), C(\tilde{C}_{2c_2}), ..., C(\tilde{C}_{rc_r})\rangle \tag{8}$$

Step 3. Formation of Matrix of Expert Judgments (MEJ) using comparisons of characteristic objects among themselves. The Expert Judgment Matrix (MEJ) is represented by the Eq. (9).

$$MEJ = \begin{pmatrix} \alpha_{11} & \alpha_{12} & \cdots & \alpha_{1t} \\ \alpha_{21} & \alpha_{22} & \cdots & \alpha_{2t} \\ \cdots & \cdots & \cdots & \cdots \\ \alpha_{t1} & \alpha_{t2} & \cdots & \alpha_{tt} \end{pmatrix} \tag{9}$$

where α_{ij} is the degree of preference of comparing one characteristic object to another. If object CO_i is more reflective than object CO_j, assign the value 1. If they are equal, assign the value 0.5. If CO_i is less reflective than CO_j, assign the value 0. It can be shown by the Eq. as follows:

$$\alpha_{ij} = \begin{cases} 0.0, & f_{expert}(CO_i) < f_{expert}(CO_j) \\ 0.5, & f_{expert}(CO_i) = f_{expert}(CO_j) \\ 1.0, & f_{expert}(CO_i) > f_{expert}(CO_j) \end{cases} \tag{10}$$

Once the expert matrix MEJ is determined, the Summed Judgements (SJ) vector must be determined using Eq. (11).

$$SJ_i = \sum_{j=1}^{t} \alpha_{ij} \tag{11}$$

where t is the number of characteristic objects.

After computing the Summed Judgements (SJ) vector, the vector of preferences (P) for the COs should be computed. This is shown as follows [41].

Step 4. Formation of a rule base from characteristic objects and a preference vector. This can be expressed using an Eq. (12).

$$IF \ C\left(\tilde{C}_{1i}\right) \ AND \ C\left(\tilde{C}_{2i}\right) \ AND \ ... \ THEN \ P_i \qquad (12)$$

Step 5. Make an inference to compute the scores of the given alternatives. The alternative A_i comprises the values of every criterion, i.e., $A_i = \{\alpha_{1i}, \alpha_{2i}, \ldots, \alpha_{ri}\}$. By employing Mamdani fuzzy inference, a preference P is computed for every alternative according to [37].

4 Proposed Approach

A novel approach for assessing nodes within a complex network, employing the MultiLayer Perceptron Regressor (MLP Regressor) in conjunction with the Characteristic Objects METhod (COMET) was presented in [21]. The goal is to establish a multi-criteria model for node evaluation. In conventional expert-based multi-criteria models, challenges often arise due to the dynamic nature of knowledge and the limited availability of experts. This approach addresses this by employing the MLP Regressor as an artificial expert trained on existing node evaluations. It enables bypass dependence on human experts and derives node evaluations based on the artificial expert model. Once the artificial expert model is constructed, it assesses Characteristic Objects in the COMET approach. These objects are reference points containing information about the decision maker's preferences. Consequently, a multi-criteria model that incorporates decision-maker preferences, facilitating node evaluations aligned with these preferences, is constructed. This hybrid approach holds potential across various domains where decision-making based on network analysis needs to consider decision-makers preferences.

Figure 2 illustrates the proposed MLP-COMET approach. The initial step involves defining the set of evaluated decision alternatives, hyperparameters for the MLP Regressor model, and decision criteria along with their characteristic values required for the COMET method. Subsequently, the MLP Regressor model-an artificial expert—is trained, providing a stable mapping of decision-maker preferences to the designated set of decision alternatives. Once the decision model is initialized, the structure of the COMET method is modeled based on characteristic values, and the decision model is re-identified using the artificial expert (MLP model). Following determining preferences for characteristic objects, the newly created decision options can be evaluated. For the implementation in this article, the entire algorithm was developed using the `sklearn` library (MLPRegressor class) and the `pymcdm` library (COMET class) [20,39].

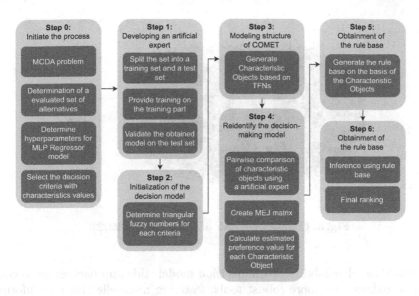

Fig. 2. MLP-COMET approach procedure.

5 Study Case

For this article, a complex network related to cryptocurrencies and, more specifically, Bitcoin was chosen [22, 23]. The selected network is people who trust those using this cryptocurrency. The network presented has 5881 nodes and 35592 edges. In addition, the network is represented as a directed graph, and a weight is assigned to each of its edges. For this article, the weights of each edge were considered in determining centrality measures such as betweenness and eigenvector. In the case of the present network, nodes will play the role of decision variants. A visualization of the Bitcoin user network is shown in Fig. 3.

Centrality metrics were used as criteria to evaluate the nodes of the present complex network. Five centrality metrics were selected, i.e., betweenness centrality (C_1), degree centrality (C_2), eigenvector centrality (C_3), closeness centrality (C_4), and harmonic centrality (C_5). These metrics are described in Sect. 3.1.

For the studies conducted, min-max normalization was applied to the network centrality metrics. This normalization is intended to scale the values of the metrics within a fixed range to allow comparison and interpretation of the results. The model training process can be sensitive to differences in the scale of metrics values. If no normalization is performed, metrics with a more extensive range of values may significantly impact the training process, and metrics with a smaller range may be ignored. Min-max normalization allows the values of metrics to be adjusted to a range of 0 to 1, eliminating scale differences and ensuring that each metric has an equal impact on the learning process. Furthermore, the study focused on a comparative analysis of different MLP structures, evaluating their influence on the multi-criteria assessment results. By enhancing

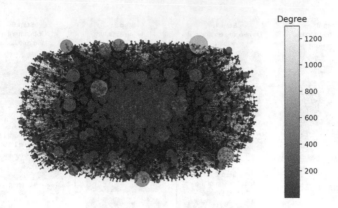

Fig. 3. Complex network of Bitcoin users [22,23].

the stability and reliability of the decision model, this approach aims to equip decision-makers with more robust tools, fostering more effective and informed decision-making processes.

5.1 Artificial Expert Study: MLP Regressor

In the Multi-Layer Perceptron calculations, the model was trained using the *adam* optimizer, a popular optimization algorithm. The activation function chosen for the hidden layers was the *Rectified Linear Unit* (ReLU), known for introducing non-linearity to the network. The loss function employed was *Mean Squared Error* (MSE), indicating the average squared difference between the predicted and actual values. The training process spanned 100 epochs, representing the number of times the entire dataset, partitioned into 67% for training and 33% for testing, was passed forward and backward through the neural network. Additionally, various layer structures were evaluated, including (50,), (100,), (50, 50), and (100, 50, 25), reflecting the number of neurons in each hidden layer. These parameters collectively influenced the training and structure of the MLP model, aiming to optimize its performance for the specific task at hand.

Figure 4 presents the values of the RMSE metric calculated for the MLP model with different layer structures. For the (50,) variant, the loss value curve was characterized by the lowest variations during the performed epochs. On the other hand, results for the (50, 50) layer structure were similar as in the previous case for train and test data. However, the spread of values throughout the training process was significantly more diverse. Furthermore, for variants (100,) and (100, 50, 25), the RMSE values were nearly two times lower for the test data than in the case of using the (50,) layer structure.

Figure 5 depicts a visual comparison between predicted and true values for various MLP layer structures. All data points would align along the diagonal in an optimal scenario, indicating a perfect fit. The visualization reveals that, across the examined structures, the matches closely resemble each other in all

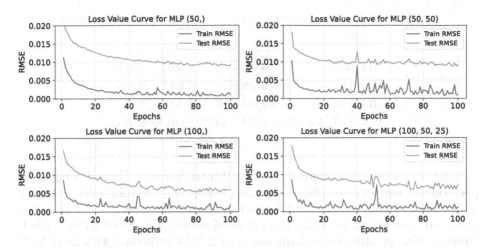

Fig. 4. RMSE values for MLP with different layers structure.

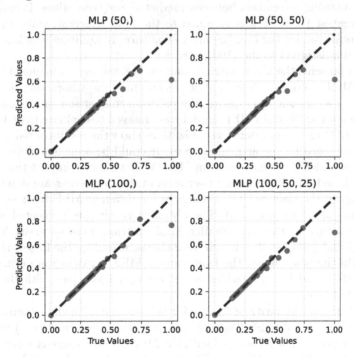

Fig. 5. Predicted values for MLP with different layer structures.

analyzed cases. While minor deviations exist for each scenario, they impact only a small subset of data points within the evaluated dataset, diverging slightly from the ideal match.

Table 1. Results of metrics for different MLP layer structures.

	MSE	MAE	R2
MLP (50,)	8.3839×10^{-5}	0.00124	0.9571
MLP (100,)	3.6138×10^{-5}	0.00201	0.9831
MLP (50, 50)	8.4493×10^{-5}	0.00088	0.9563
MLP (100, 50, 25)	5.1172×10^{-5}	0.00130	0.9744

The diverse layer structures of the MLP models were evaluated using three performance metrics: Mean Squared Error (MSE), Mean Absolute Error (MAE), and R-squared (R2). These metrics provide insights into each model's accuracy, precision, and goodness of fit. The obtained results are presented in Table 1. These results quantify the performance of each MLP structure, with lower MSE and MAE values indicating better predictive accuracy and R2 values approaching 1, showing a strong correlation between predicted and true values. It can be seen that the greatest R2 score was assigned to the (100,) variant, while the lowest MAE was observed for the (50, 50) layer structure. In addition, the lowest MSE value was also assigned to the (100,) structure.

Figure 6 presents the MEJ matrices that are determined as in one of the steps of the COMET method. Those matrices show how the Characteristic Objects are compared with each other during the pairwise comparison. In the case of the proposed research, the train MLP model was engaged to evaluate the COs in the MEJ matrix. Thus, the presented visualizations show the results of pairwise comparisons performed by the artificial expert. It could be seen that different layer structures provided different results in MEJ, which directly impact the obtained fuzzy rule, based on which the multi-criteria evaluation scores are determined.

To compare the obtained MEJ matrices for different MLP layer structures, the Hamming distance was used. The obtained results are presented in Fig. 7. It could be seen that the most similar MEJ matrices were observed for structures (100,) and (100, 50, 25), which were characterized by the lowest Hamming distance. On the other hand, the least similar MEJ matrices were obtained for structures (50,) and (50, 50), which were designated as a pair with the highest Hamming distance.

To analyze the similarity of the rankings obtained with the examined MLP layer structures, the Weighted Spearman correlation coefficient (r_W) was used. The coherence of rankings obtained with the MLP-COMET model was presented in Table 2. It could be seen that for all examined structures, the correlation values were high. Thus, it can be concluded that the analyzed layer variants produced highly similar recommendations regarding the node assessment in the considered Bitcoin complex network. The most correlated results were observed for structures (50,) and (100,) (r_W of 0.9999). Moreover, the reference results obtained in the initial research were compared [21], showing that the examined different MLP layer structures in this study also produce highly correlated rankings.

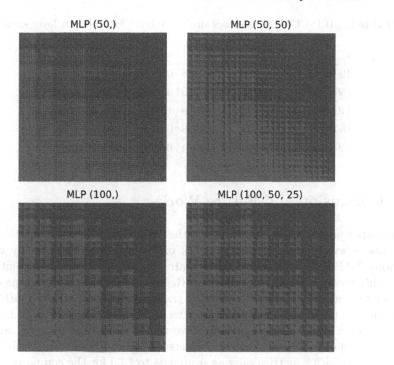

Fig. 6. MEJ matrices in COMET method for different layer structures.

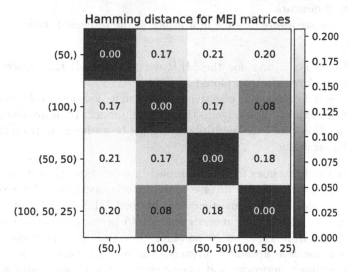

Fig. 7. Hamming distance for MEJ matrices for different layer structures.

Table 2. MLP-COMET rankings similarity (r_W) for different layer structures.

r_w	Reference	(50,)	(100,)	(50, 50)	(100, 50, 25)
Reference	1.0000	0.9878	0.9871	0.9874	0.9905
(50,)	0.9878	1.0000	0.9999	0.9998	0.9994
(100,)	0.9871	0.9999	1.0000	0.9998	0.9995
(50, 50)	0.9874	0.9998	0.9998	1.0000	0.9995
(100, 50, 25)	0.9905	0.9994	0.9995	0.9995	1.0000

6   Conclusion and Future Works

This paper presents the application of the MLP-COMET approach to assessing the nodes within the complex network of Bitcoin users. The study evaluates various MLP layer structures to indicate their impact on assessment quality, revealing the high accuracy of the MLP Regressor model in representing decision-maker preferences across both test and training sets. The MLP-COMET model is then examined, demonstrating its effectiveness in replicating rankings from the reference expert model. Notably, investigations into the training sample size and the number of characteristic objects reveal consistent and stable results, with r_W similarity metrics ranging from 0.98 to 1.00 for the compared rankings. These findings highlight the model's robustness in evaluating nodes within the tested complex network.

However, we are aware of some limitations of the proposed study that should be addressed:

- Only selected structures for the MLP were examined; thus more effective solutions could remain unexplored
- The proposed approach is effective in particular decision problems, aiming to reflect the expert knowledge in the decision model. To apply the proposed solution to other problems, multiple data must be gathered to train the model to keep its accuracy

Future research avenues for this approach involve extending its application to other complex networks or diverse multi-criteria decision-making scenarios. Additionally, exploring the consistency of obtained MEJ matrices in the MLP-COMET method and further investigations into accuracy and considerations for uncertain environments would enhance the method's comprehensiveness. The study's innovative approach advances the understanding of node evaluation within complex networks and opens avenues for broader applications in decision-making processes.

References

1. Alexandrescu, F.M., Pizzol, L., Zabeo, A., Rizzo, E., Giubilato, E., Critto, A.: Identifying sustainability communicators in urban regeneration: integrating individual and relational attributes. J. Clean. Prod. **173**, 278–291 (2018). https://doi.org/10.1016/j.jclepro.2016.09.076
2. Bączkiewicz, A.: Temporal SWARA-SPOTIS for multi-criteria assessment of European countries regarding sustainable RES exploitation. In: Ziemba, E., Chmielarz, W., Wątróbski, J. (eds.) Information Technology for Management: Approaches to Improving Business and Society, vol. 471, pp. 171–191. Springer, Cham (2022). https://doi.org/10.1007/978-3-031-29570-6_9
3. Biamonte, J., Faccin, M., De Domenico, M.: Complex networks from classical to quantum. Commun. Phys. **2**(1), 53 (2019). https://doi.org/10.1038/s42005-019-0152-6
4. Bielinskyi, A.O., Soloviev, V.N.: Complex network precursors of crashes and critical events in the cryptocurrency market. In: CEUR Workshop Proceedings, vol. 2292, pp. 37–45 (2018). https://doi.org/10.31812/123456789/2881
5. Bloch, F., Jackson, M.O., Tebaldi, P.: Centrality measures in networks. Soc. Choice Welf. **61**, 413–453 (2023). https://doi.org/10.1007/s00355-023-01456-4
6. Boldi, P., Vigna, S.: Axioms for centrality. Internet Math. **10**(3–4), 222–262 (2014). https://doi.org/10.1080/15427951.2013.865686
7. Çolak, M., Kaya, İ, Özkan, B., Budak, A., Karaşan, A.: A multi-criteria evaluation model based on hesitant fuzzy sets for blockchain technology in supply chain management. J. Intell. Fuzzy Syst. **38**(1), 935–946 (2020). https://doi.org/10.3233/JIFS-179460
8. Du, Y., Gao, C., Hu, Y., Mahadevan, S., Deng, Y.: A new method of identifying influential nodes in complex networks based on TOPSIS. Phys. A **399**, 57–69 (2014). https://doi.org/10.1016/j.physa.2013.12.031
9. Dweiri, F., Kumar, S., Khan, S.A., Jain, V.: Designing an integrated AHP based decision support system for supplier selection in automotive industry. Expert Syst. Appl. **62**, 273–283 (2016). https://doi.org/10.1016/j.eswa.2016.06.030
10. Erol, I., Ar, I.M., Peker, I.: Scrutinizing blockchain applicability in sustainable supply chains through an integrated fuzzy multi-criteria decision making framework. Appl. Soft Comput. **116**, 108331 (2022). https://doi.org/10.1016/j.asoc.2021.108331
11. Fahlepi, R.: Decision support systems employee discipline identification using the simple multi attribute rating technique (SMART) method. J. Appl. Eng. Technol. Sci. (JAETS) **1**(2), 103–112 (2020). https://doi.org/10.37385/jaets.v1i2.67
12. Faizi, S., Sałabun, W., Rashid, T., Zafar, S., Wątróbski, J.: Intuitionistic fuzzy sets in multi-criteria group decision making problems using the characteristic objects method. Symmetry **12**(9), 1382 (2020). https://doi.org/10.3390/sym12091382
13. Faizi, S., Sałabun, W., Ullah, S., Rashid, T., Więckowski, J.: A new method to support decision-making in an uncertain environment based on normalized interval-valued triangular fuzzy numbers and COMET technique. Symmetry **12**(4), 516 (2020). https://doi.org/10.3390/sym12040516
14. Ferretti, S., D'Angelo, G.: On the ethereum blockchain structure: a complex networks theory perspective. Concurr. Comput. Pract. Exp. **32**(12), e5493 (2020). https://doi.org/10.1002/cpe.5493
15. Ho, W., Ma, X.: The state-of-the-art integrations and applications of the analytic hierarchy process. Eur. J. Oper. Res. **267**(2), 399–414 (2018). https://doi.org/10.1016/j.ejor.2017.09.007

16. Hou Su, V., Sen Gupta, S., Khan, A.: Automating ETL and mining of ethereum blockchain network. In: Proceedings of the Fifteenth ACM International Conference on Web Search and Data Mining, pp. 1581–1584 (2022). https://doi.org/10. 1145/3488560.3502187
17. Karczmarczyk, A., Jankowski, J., Wątróbski, J.: Multi-criteria decision support for planning and evaluation of performance of viral marketing campaigns in social networks. PLoS ONE **13**(12), e0209372 (2018). https://doi.org/10.1371/journal. pone.0209372
18. Karczmarczyk, A., Jankowski, J., Wątrobski, J.: Multi-criteria seed selection for targeted influence maximization within social networks. In: Paszynski, M., Kranzlmüller, D., Krzhizhanovskaya, V.V., Dongarra, J.J., Sloot, P.M.A. (eds.) ICCS 2021. LNCS, vol. 12744, pp. 454–461. Springer, Cham (2021). https://doi.org/10. 1007/978-3-030-77967-2_38
19. Kheybari, S., Kazemi, M., Rezaei, J.: Bioethanol facility location selection using best-worst method. Appl. Energy **242**, 612–623 (2019). https://doi.org/10.1016/j. apenergy.2019.03.054
20. Kizielewicz, B., Shekhovtsov, A., Sałabun, W.: pymcdm-the universal library for solving multi-criteria decision-making problems. SoftwareX **22**, 101368 (2023). https://doi.org/10.1016/j.softx.2023.101368
21. Kizielewicz, B., Wieckowski, J., Jankowski, J.: MLP-COMET-based decision model re-identification for continuous decision-making in the complex network environment. In: 2023 18th Conference on Computer Science and Intelligence Systems (FedCSIS), pp. 591–602. IEEE (2023). https://doi.org/10.15439/2023F5438
22. Kumar, S., Hooi, B., Makhija, D., Kumar, M., Faloutsos, C., Subrahmanian, V.: REV2: fraudulent user prediction in rating platforms. In: Proceedings of the Eleventh ACM International Conference on Web Search and Data Mining, pp. 333–341. ACM (2018). https://doi.org/10.1145/3159652.3159729
23. Kumar, S., Spezzano, F., Subrahmanian, V., Faloutsos, C.: Edge weight prediction in weighted signed networks. In: 2016 IEEE 16th International Conference on Data Mining (ICDM), pp. 221–230. IEEE (2016). https://doi.org/10.1109/ICDM.2016. 0033
24. Lai, H., Liao, H.: A multi-criteria decision making method based on DNMA and CRITIC with linguistic D numbers for blockchain platform evaluation. Eng. Appl. Artif. Intell. **101**, 104200 (2021). https://doi.org/10.1016/j.engappai.2021.104200
25. Lin, D., Wu, J., Yuan, Q., Zheng, Z.: Modeling and understanding ethereum transaction records via a complex network approach. IEEE Trans. Circ. Syst. II Express Briefs **67**(11), 2737–2741 (2020). https://doi.org/10.1109/TCSII.2020.2968376
26. Liu, Y., Eckert, C.M., Earl, C.: A review of fuzzy AHP methods for decision-making with subjective judgements. Expert Syst. Appl. **161**, 113738 (2020). https://doi. org/10.1016/j.eswa.2020.113738
27. Lü, L., Chen, D., Ren, X.L., Zhang, Q.M., Zhang, Y.C., Zhou, T.: Vital nodes identification in complex networks. Phys. Rep. **650**, 1–63 (2016). https://doi.org/ 10.1016/j.physrep.2016.06.007
28. Lynn, C.W., Papadopoulos, L., Kahn, A.E., Bassett, D.S.: Human information processing in complex networks. Nat. Phys. **16**(9), 965–973 (2020). https://doi. org/10.1038/s41567-020-0924-7
29. Mahendra, G.S.: Implementation of the FUCOM-SAW method on E-commerce selection DSS in Indonesia. Tech-E **5**(1), 75–85 (2021). https://doi.org/10.31253/ te.v5i1.662
30. da Mata, A.S.: Complex networks: a mini-review. Braz. J. Phys. **50**, 658–672 (2020). https://doi.org/10.1007/s13538-020-00772-9

31. Muruganantham, A., Gandhi, M.: Discovering and ranking influential users in social media networks using Multi-Criteria Decision Making (MCDM) methods. Indian J. Sci. Technol. **9**(32), 1–11 (2016). https://doi.org/10.17485/ijst/2016/v9i32/95171

32. Németh, B., et al.: Comparison of weighting methods used in multicriteria decision analysis frameworks in healthcare with focus on low-and middle-income countries. J. Comp. Effectiveness Res. **8**(4), 195–204 (2019). https://doi.org/10.2217/cer-2018-0102

33. Odu, G.: Weighting methods for multi-criteria decision making technique. J. Appl. Sci. Environ. Manag. **23**(8), 1449–1457 (2019). https://doi.org/10.4314/jasem.v23i8.7

34. Öztürk, C., Yildizbaşi, A.: Barriers to implementation of blockchain into supply chain management using an integrated multi-criteria decision-making method: a numerical example. Soft. Comput. **24**, 14771–14789 (2020). https://doi.org/10.1007/s00500-020-04831-w

35. Pamučar, D., Stević, Ž, Sremac, S.: A new model for determining weight coefficients of criteria in MCDM models: full consistency method (FUCOM). Symmetry **10**(9), 393 (2018). https://doi.org/10.3390/sym10090393

36. Pamucar, D., Yazdani, M., Montero-Simo, M.J., Araque-Padilla, R.A., Mohammed, A.: Multi-criteria decision analysis towards robust service quality measurement. Expert Syst. Appl. **170**, 114508 (2021). https://doi.org/10.1016/j.eswa.2020.114508

37. Paradowski, B., Drążek, Z.: Identification of the decision-making model for selecting an information system. Procedia Comput. Sci. **176**, 3802–3809 (2020). https://doi.org/10.1016/j.procs.2020.09.007

38. Paramanik, A.R., Sarkar, S., Sarkar, B.: OSWMI: an objective-subjective weighted method for minimizing inconsistency in multi-criteria decision making. Comput. Ind. Eng. **169**, 108138 (2022). https://doi.org/10.1016/j.cie.2022.108138

39. Pedregosa, F., et al.: Scikit-learn: machine learning in Python. J. Mach. Learn. Res. **12**, 2825–2830 (2011). https://doi.org/10.5555/1953048.2078195

40. Qiu, L., Zhang, J., Tian, X.: Ranking influential nodes in complex networks based on local and global structures. Appl. Intell. **51**, 4394–4407 (2021). https://doi.org/10.1007/s10489-020-02132-1

41. Sałabun, W.: The characteristic objects method: a new distance-based approach to multicriteria decision-making problems. J. Multi-Criteria Decis. Anal. **22**(1–2), 37–50 (2015). https://doi.org/10.1002/mcda.1525

42. Sałabun, W., Karczmarczyk, A., Wątróbski, J.: Decision-making using the hesitant fuzzy sets COMET method: an empirical study of the electric city buses selection. In: 2018 IEEE Symposium Series on Computational Intelligence (SSCI), pp. 1485–1492. IEEE (2018). https://doi.org/10.1109/SSCI.2018.8628864

43. Sarabi, E.P., Darestani, S.A.: Developing a decision support system for logistics service provider selection employing fuzzy MULTIMOORA & BWM in mining equipment manufacturing. Appl. Soft Comput. **98**, 106849 (2021). https://doi.org/10.1016/j.asoc.2020.106849

44. Saxena, A., Iyengar, S.: Centrality measures in complex networks: a survey. arXiv preprint arXiv:2011.07190 (2020). https://doi.org/10.48550/arXiv.2011.07190

45. Serena, L., Ferretti, S., D'Angelo, G.: Cryptocurrencies activity as a complex network: analysis of transactions graphs. Peer-to-Peer Netw. Appl. **15**(2), 839–853 (2022). https://doi.org/10.1007/s12083-021-01220-4

46. Shao, M., Han, Z., Sun, J., Xiao, C., Zhang, S., Zhao, Y.: A review of multi-criteria decision making applications for renewable energy site selection. Renew. Energy **157**, 377–403 (2020). https://doi.org/10.1016/j.renene.2020.04.137

47. Silva, T.C., Zhao, L.: Machine Learning in Complex Networks. Springer, Cham (2016). https://doi.org/10.1007/978-3-319-17290-3

48. Tao, B., Ho, I.W.H., Dai, H.N.: Complex network analysis of the bitcoin blockchain network. In: 2021 IEEE International Symposium on Circuits and Systems (ISCAS), pp. 1–5. IEEE (2021). https://doi.org/10.1109/ISCAS51556.2021.9401533

49. Więckowski, J., Kizielewicz, B., Shekhovtsov, A., Sałabun, W.: RANCOM: a novel approach to identifying criteria relevance based on inaccuracy expert judgments. Eng. Appl. Artif. Intell. **122**, 106114 (2023). https://doi.org/10.1016/j.engappai.2023.106114

50. Xiong, H., Chen, M., Wu, C., Zhao, Y., Yi, W.: Research on progress of blockchain consensus algorithm: a review on recent progress of blockchain consensus algorithms. Future Internet **14**(2), 47 (2022). https://doi.org/10.3390/fi14020047

51. Yaman, T.T.: Pythagorean fuzzy Analytical Network Process (ANP) and its application to warehouse location selection problem. In: 2020 15th Conference on Computer Science and Information Systems (FedCSIS), pp. 137–140. IEEE (2020). https://doi.org/10.15439/2020F187

52. Yang, B., Li, J.: Complex network analysis of three-way decision researches. Int. J. Mach. Learn. Cybern. **11**, 973–987 (2020). https://doi.org/10.1007/s13042-020-01082-x

53. Zanin, M., et al.: Combining complex networks and data mining: why and how. Phys. Rep. **635**, 1–44 (2016). https://doi.org/10.1016/j.physrep.2016.04.005

54. Zhang, W., Zhang, Q., Karimi, H.: Seeking the important nodes of complex networks in product R&D team based on fuzzy AHP and TOPSIS. Math. Probl. Eng. **2013** (2013). https://doi.org/10.1155/2013/327592

55. Zhao, H., Li, Z., Zhou, R.: Risk assessment method combining complex networks with MCDA for multi-facility risk chain and coupling in UUS. Tunn. Undergr. Space Technol. **119**, 104242 (2022). https://doi.org/10.1016/j.tust.2021.104242

MBCO: The Materials-Based Business Case Ontology from BPMN-EMMO Integration

Christophe Feltus[1]([✉])(iD), Peter Klein[2](iD), Natalia Konchakova[3](iD),
Damien Nicolas[1](iD), Carlos Kavka[1](iD), Martin T. Horsch[4](iD),
Heinz A. Preisig[5](iD), Djamel Khadraoui[1](iD), and Salim Belouettar[1](iD)

[1] Luxembourg Institute of Science and Technology (LIST),
Avenue des Hauts-Fourneaux, 5, 4362 Esch-sur-Alzette, Luxembourg
{christophe.feltus,damien.nicolas,carlos.kavka,djamel.khadraoui,
salim.belouettar}@list.lu
[2] Fraunhofer Institut für Techno- und Wirtschaftsmathematik, Fraunhoferplatz 1,
67663 Kaiserslautern, Germany
peter.klein@itwm.fraunhofer.de
[3] Institute of Surface Science, Helmholtz-Zentrum Hereon, Max-Planck-Straße 1,
21502 Geesthacht, Germany
natalia.konchakova@hereon.de
[4] Department of Data Science, Norwegian University of Life Sciences,
1432 Ås, Norway
martin.thomas.horsch@nmbu.no
[5] Department of Chemical Engineering, Norwegian University of Science
and Technology (NTNU), 7491 Trondheim, Norway
heinz.a.preisig@ntnu.no

Abstract. Open innovation in materials research involves the collaborative sharing of knowledge, ideas, and resources across organisations. Unfortunately, a lack of mutual understanding between scientific and industrial partners and their respective domain specific digital tools hampers collaboration across the two domains. For this purpose, this work integrates the Business Process Modelling and Notation standard BPMN and the Elementary Multi-perspective Material Ontology (EMMO), yielding a knowledge representation and data documentation standard for research problems, workflows, and results related to the development of new materials and technologies and the underlying challenges in materials science. As a methodology, this work proposes and implements an innovative four-step approach for ontology integration, comprising alignment, mapping, integration, and validation. The result of this integration is pioneering an original Materials-based Business Case Ontology (MBCO), by which BPMN can be deployed an EMMO-compliant way.

Keywords: Applied ontology · BPMN · EMMO · Ontology alignment

E. Ziemba et al. (Eds.): FedCSIS-ITBS 2023/ISM 2023, LNBIP 504, pp. 23–45, 2024.
https://doi.org/10.1007/978-3-031-61657-0_2

1   Introduction

Digitalisation efforts under the European digital transition paradigm in the engineering and materials development domains are today introducing new methods for digital collaboration and open innovation, like the one proposed in VIPCOAT[1]: the EU funded Research and Innovation Action implementing digitalisation approaches offer a multi-sided platform to create a collaborative environment to connect modellers (software owners, academia), and translators [21], manufacturers, governmental bodies and society to initiate and implement innovation projects (Fig. 1). The demonstration focus of VIPCOAT is the development and manufacturing of active protective coatings. However, the approach is applicable to any other industrial case. To assist industrial end-users in making optimal decisions about materials and process design and manufacturing based on predictive modelling, it is increasingly necessary to examine innovation through a quadruple helix approach, which addresses the need for a *Digital Single Market strategy for Open Innovation 2.0* [5]. In parallel, an enormous amount of materials, manufacturing and processing data are currently generated by high throughput experiments and computations (e.g., [35,36], possessing a significant challenge in terms of data integration, sharing and interoperability.

Given that a product or a material system is defined by a combination of its physical, chemical and other technical properties, as well as other business-related aspects, such as cost, environmental footprint, and other information relevant to industry, academia, administration and the society at large, such integration has the advantage of enhancing significantly mutual understanding of human stakeholders and their respective domain-specific digital tools. As an example, considering in VIPCOAT, the physical and chemical properties of a protective coating can have a significant impact on production time, resource utilisation, manufacturing cost, sustainability, and toxicity. Hence, comprehending the properties of materials is critical to streamlining the manufacturing process, identifying appropriate machinery and equipment, and estimating relevant business indicators for informed decision-making [2]. This integration is particularly important in the context of Open Innovation, where companies collaborate to develop new products and services [24].

Although the existing literature (reviewed in Sect. 2) demonstrates a growing recognition of the need for integration between business processes, materials science, and engineering workflows, the integration of BPMN with EMMO does not exist yet and is crucial step forward to support inter-domains mutual understanding. A common ontology is mandatory to lay the foundation for unlocking a huge innovation potential by enabling semantic interoperability of models, experiments, software and data, which is vital for using rational development design principles and testing and manufacturing of materials in general. The aim of this work is consequently to contribute to the current efforts by the European Materials Modelling Council (EMMC)[2] on establishing common standards for

---

[1] https://ms.hereon.de/vipcoat/.
[2] https://emmc.eu/.

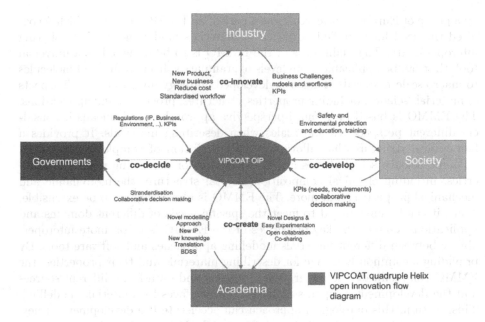

Fig. 1. Quadruple-Helix Virtual Open Innovation Framework: Industry, Society, Academia, and Governments

materials modelling through the Elementary Multi-perspective Material Ontology (EMMO), e.g. [15]. The basic idea is to merge Business Decision Support Systems (BDSS), implemented in terms of the *Business Process Model and Notation* (BPMN) and *Decision Model and Notation* (DMN) standards, with materials modelling workflows by using ontologies as a glue between these hitherto distinct worlds.

BPMN is an efficient tool for Open Innovation processes [34]. BPMN enables organisations to visually depict their business processes and workflows in a standardised format, which fosters more effective communication and collaboration with external stakeholders such as customers, suppliers, and partners. Furthermore, the tool ensure an automatic implementation of some processes between involved in the collaboration (business) players. The standardised representation of business processes using BPMN allows for the identification of inefficiencies, redundancies, and bottlenecks in the workflow, leading to streamlined operations and increased efficiency [19]. Moreover, the use of BPMN provides a common language for discussing business processes, making it easier to share ideas and identify opportunities for improvement [24]. As a result, the ontology facilitates collaboration, accelerates innovation, and promotes the sharing knowledge and best practices between organisations and business partners.

The EMMO, see [14], is a currently very intensive developing comprehensive and versatile ontology for materials science that aims to provide a common language for describing materials and their properties. The EMMO was developed by a group of European researchers as a part of an EMMC activity, which recognised the need for a unified approach to materials modelling and data sharing interoperability. The main ideas of the EMMO is to be designed as a universal tool, that can be applicable to all levels of granularity, from atoms and molecules to macro-scale materials. Thus, the developed ontology aims to cover all aspects of materials science, including properties, structures, processes, and applications. The EMMO is based on a multi-perspective approach, which means it considers different perspectives and scales when describing materials. It provides a hierarchical structure that allows for the description of complex systems and a comprehensive set of classes and relationships for describing materials properties, including chemical composition, crystal structure, thermodynamic and mechanical properties, and more. The EMMO is also designed to be extensible. Thus, it can be customised to meet the specific needs of different domains and applications. One of the key objectives of the EMMO is to promote interoperability between different materials modelling approaches and software tools. By providing a common language for describing materials and their properties, the EMMO can facilitate the integration of models and data from different sources and the development of open standards and interfaces for materials modelling. This, in turn, this ontological approach can accelerate the development of new materials and improve the efficiency of materials design and testing.

The integration of BPMN and EMMO can facilitate communication and collaboration among stakeholders, ultimately leading to the development of new materials and products. The integration of ontologies can lead to faster and more cost-effective research and development and the creation of innovative solutions to address complex material challenges. This paper aims to answer the research question of how BPMN can be connected with EMMO or vice versa, and proposes MBCO: the Materials-based Business Case Ontology. Therefore, we put forward a concrete approach for integrating ontologies, consisting of conceptual alignments, concept mapping, concept integration, and validation.

The proposed schema is applied to a preliminary analysis of integrating BPMN into the EMMO. Section 2 provides an overview of the ontologies, extension mechanisms, and related works, while Sect. 3 describes the process of developing and validating MBCO, the integrated ontology. The paper concludes in Sect. 4 presenting the final conclusions.

2 Background

This section introduces BPMN and EMMO ontologies, reminds the different ontology extension mechanisms at our disposal, and presents the main related works.

2.1 BPMN

BPMN stands for Business Process Model and Notation [27]. It is a graphical representation for specifying business processes in a standardised way. BPMN was created by the Business Process Management Initiative (BPMI) and is now maintained by the Object Management Group (OMG)[3]. The primary purpose of BPMN is to provide a standardised notation that is readily understandable by all business stakeholders, including technical and non-technical users. This notation enables clear communication and collaboration between business and technical teams while modelling and analysing processes and supporting the execution of processes in a technology-agnostic manner. To this end, BPMN provides a set of graphical elements, such as processes, tasks, gateways, and events, that can be used to model various types of business processes. The notation also supports the modelling of more complex process flows, such as parallel and sequential execution, exception handling, and compensation. BPMN is a widely adopted standard that helps organisations to model, to analyse, and to improve their business processes, leading to increased efficiency and effectiveness.

2.2 EMMO

The Elementary Multi-perspective Material Ontology (EMMO) is an ontology that focuses to provide a standardised and structured representation of the domain of materials science and engineering [13]. An ontology is a type of knowledge representation that defines a common vocabulary and formal model for describing concepts and relationships in a specific domain.

The EMMO provides a comprehensive, hierarchical, and interlinked view of the concepts, classes, and relationships that are commonly used in materials science and engineering. It covers a wide range of topics, including material properties, processing techniques, and the relationships between materials and their components. The EMMO aims to support a shared understanding of the concepts and terms used in the field, making it easier for researchers, engineers, and data scientists to collaborate and exchange information.

The EMMO is designed to be used as a resource for a variety of applications, including knowledge management, semantic search, and data integration in materials science and engineering. It can also help to integrate diverse data sources and support interdisciplinary research by providing a common vocabulary and conceptual framework. In this paper, we use EMMO version 1.0.0.beta5 from github.[4]

2.3 Ontology Extension Mechanism

According to [37], the integration of two models (meta-models [6] or ontologies [11]) requires resolving three types of heterogeneity: *syntactic, semantic* and *structural*. For our integration, only the semantic and structural heterogeneity have been addressed. Indeed, the syntactic heterogeneity aims at analysing the difference between the serialisations of meta-model and, as explained by [31], addresses technical heterogeneity like hardware platforms and operating systems,

---

[3] https://www.omg.org/.
[4] https://github.com/emmo-repo/EMMO.

or access methods, or it addresses the interface heterogeneity like the one which exists if different components are accessible through different access languages [9,10]. Hence, it is not relevant in the case of this ontological integration.

Structural heterogeneity exists when the same meta-model concepts are modelled differently by each meta-model primitive. This structural heterogeneity has been addressed together with the analysis of the conceptual mapping and the definition of the integration rules. Finally, the semantic heterogeneity represents differences in the meaning of the considered meta-model's elements and must be addressed through elements mapping and integration rules. Regarding the mappings, three situations are possible: no mapping, a mapping of type 1:1, and a mapping of a type n:m (n concepts from one meta-model are mapped with m concepts from the other).

After analysing the heterogeneities, ontology extension mechanisms are applied. Ontology extension mechanisms refer to the ways in which an existing ontology can be expanded or modified to better suit the needs of a particular application or domain. There are several methods that can be used for ontology extension, including:

- Inheritance (generalisation): This is a common method of ontology extension in which a new class is defined that inherits properties and characteristics from an existing class. This allows new classes to be defined while reusing existing definitions and knowledge (e.g., in [12], inheritance relationships to extend OWL-S).
- Restriction (specialisation): This is a method of ontology extension in which the definition of an existing class is restricted to exclude certain individuals or objects. This can be used to refine a class's definition to better match a particular application's requirements.
- Extension (by adding axioms): This is a method of ontology extension in which new axioms or statements and rules are added to the ontology to provide additional information or, *a priory*, knowledge.
- Modules and Libraries: This is a method of ontology extension in which ontologies can be packaged as modules or libraries and can be imported or reused in other ontologies.

Each of these methods has its own strengths and limitations, and the appropriate method for a particular extension depends on the application's requirements and the design of the ontology being extended on a case-by-case basis.

2.4   Related Work

The integration of business process with industrial ontologies is not new. For instance, research conducted by [20] has explored methods for formalizing product and process requirements using a collaborative ontology, employing semantic reasoning techniques for process formation. Or, in the same vein, [23] used BPMN and ontologies to modeling and to integrating production steps with typical IT functionalities. In [2], another approach consists in integrating material modelling with business data and models to develop a Business Decision Support System (BDSS) [34] that assists in the complex decision-making process of selecting and designing polymer-matrix composites. This system combines materials modelling, business tools, and databases into a single workflow, providing a comprehensive solution supporting decision-making.

In [19], the authors suggest utilising the BPMN and DMN[5] standards [33] to bridge the gap between business processes, materials science, and engineering workflows in the context of composite material modelling, which can potentially open up new horizons for industrial engineering applications. By using these standards ([4,33]), it is possible to establish a connection between the diverse domains and provide a more integrated approach to the modelling process, which could lead to improve efficiency and effectiveness in engineering applications.

In line with the previous approach, [18] extends the analysis by incorporating technical key performance indicators (KPIs) and financial KPIs, such as part costs, calculated using cost modelling applications. By including financial KPIs in the analysis, a more comprehensive understanding of the overall performance can be achieved, which can assist in the decision-making process related to product design and development starting from very early design decisions.

In [17], the authors discuss the development of an ontology called OSMO, which is an extension of the Model Data (MODA)[6] legacy metadata standard for simulation workflows used in some European materials modelling projects [16]. While MODA workflow descriptions are interpretable by human experts in modelling of the target application domains only, OSMO adds rigour to MODA by using an unambiguous ontological language. To this end, [17] explains the purpose, design choices, implementation, and applications of OSMO, including its connections to other domain ontologies in computational engineering. OSMO was created as part of the EU funded VIMMP project[7] and is connected to the larger effort of ontology engineering by the EMMC. A crosswalk from MODA workflows via OSMO to EMMO has been described in previous work [22], making use of a graph transformation system [29] for the required complex structural alignment. In this way, based upon the integration of EMMO and BPMN into a common ontology like the MBCO, as discussed in the next section, a clear conceptual route to integrating the MODA workflows documented in a series of European projects into formal enterprise architectures will be available.

3   MBCO Development by EMMO/BPMN Integration

The development of MBCO involves the integration of EMMO and BPMN into a single ontology that reflects the combined knowledge represented by both initial ontologies [25,26]. The successful integration of ontologies plays a pivotal role in fostering collaborative knowledge representation across domains. Therefore, this

---

[5] https://www.omg.org/dmn/.
[6] https://www.cencenelec.eu/media/CEN-CENELEC/CWAs/RI/cwa17284_2018. pdf.
[7] Virtual Materials Market Place - https://cordis.europa.eu/project/id/760907.

section explores a four-step methodology for ontology integration, illustrated in Fig. 2. Each step is carefully designed to ensure a systematic and coherent synthesis of knowledge from distinct ontologies. The motivation behind this methodology lies in achieving a unified ontology, which amalgamates the strengths of the original ontologies. The method that we propose includes the following four steps:

- **Alignment**: This involves identifying and matching the concepts, classes, and relationships in the two ontologies that correspond to each other. This step requires a careful examination of the structure, content, and meaning of the concepts and relationships in both ontologies. The condition for progressing to the mapping step is a thorough understanding of the structure, content, and meaning of concepts and relationships is essential.
- **Mapping**: This involves creating a mapping between the concepts and relationships in the two ontologies based on the results of the alignment step. This mapping defines how the concepts and relationships in the two ontologies correspond to each other. The condition for progressing to the integration step is a successful completion of the alignment step provides the groundwork for creating an accurate and comprehensive mapping.
- **Integration**: This involves combining the two ontologies into a single ontology (MBCO), using the mapping as a guide. The resulting merged ontology should reflect the combined knowledge represented by both original ontologies. The condition for progressing to the validation step is a well-defined mapping, created in the previous step, acts as a guide for the seamless combination of the ontologies into the integrated MBCO.
- **Validation by Incoherence Solving**: This involves checking the merged ontology to ensure that it is logically consistent and coherent and that it correctly represents the combined knowledge from both original ontologies. The condition for a successful validation is that the integration in the previous steps forms the basis for validating the MBCO, addressing any inconsistencies or incoherence discovered during this critical evaluation.

3.1 Alignment

Conceptual alignment, as explained in [7], is the process of identifying and establishing the syntactic and structural correspondences between concepts or entities from two or more different sources or domains, should it be at the definition or at the association with other concepts level. To achieve this alignment, we listed all BPMN concepts, including their definition and association, and then we looked for correspondence with the EMMO concepts [13].

After a review of all BPMN [4] concepts, we observed that eight concepts from BPMN may be aligned with nine concepts from the EMMO. This alignment is possible based on analysing the concepts' names and definitions (syntactic alignment) and their associations with the other concepts (structural alignment). The alignment result is the following:

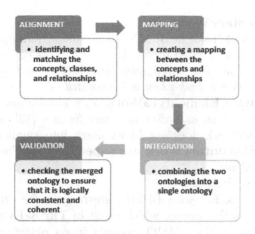

Fig. 2. Four steps of the method used to integrate BPMN into EMMO: Alignment, Mapping, Integration and Validation

- **Process vs. IntentionalProcess.**
  - The definition of **Process** from BPMN is *a Process describes a sequence or flow of Activities in an organisation with the objective of carrying out work* [4].
  - In the EMMO, the **Process** is defined by *A whole that is identified according to criteria based on its temporal evolution that is satisfied throughout its time extension* and the **IntentionalProcess** extends the definition with *occurring with the active participation of an agent that drives the process according to a specific objective (intention)* [13]. Both the **Process** and the **IntentionalProcess** are respectively part of and subClass of Process and are associated with the **Participant**.
- **Participant (BPMN) vs. Participant (EMMO).**
  - In BPMN, a **Participant** *represents a specific PartnerEntity (e.g., a company) and/or a more general PartnerRole (e.g., a buyer, seller, or manufacturer) that are Participants in a Collaboration. A Participant is often responsible for the execution of the Process enclosed in a Pool* [4].
  - In the EMMO, this is *an object which is a holistic spatial part of a process. If plays an active role in the process, this is an Agent* [13]. Both are linked to the concept of BPMN and EMMO's **Process**.
- **Activity vs. Elaboration.**
  - BPMN defines the **Activity** as a *work that is performed within a Business Process* [4]. *An Activity can be atomic or non-atomic (compound).*
  - From the side of the EMMO, an Elaboration is *the process in which an agent works with some entities according to some operative rules* [13]. Elaboration is a subClass of IntentionalProcess, and Activity is a component of Process (although not represented in BPMN meta-model from [4]). Both also have subClasses ElementaryWork, Computation, Workflow for Activity and, similarly, CallActivity, Task, SubProcess for Elaboration.

- **Task vs. ElementaryWork**
  - The definition of **Task** in BPMN is *an atomic Activity within a Process flow. A Task is used when the work in the Process cannot be broken down to a finer level of detail. Generally, an end-user and/or applications are used to perform the Task when it is executed* [4].
  - In the EMMO, a **ElementyraWork** is *an elaboration that has no elaboration proper parts, according to a specific type* [13], which means that an ElementaryWork does not break down into smaller pieces of work. **Task** and **ElementaryWork** are respectively subClasses of **Activity** and **Elaboration**.
- **ThrowEvent vs. Status**
  - *Throwing events*, following BPMN, *are triggers for catching events and are triggered by the process*, which result in **ThrowEvent** [4].
  - **Status**, following the EMMO, consists in *an object which is a holistic temporal part of a process* [13]. Both concepts have no similar association with other modelling concepts.
- **InteractionNode vs. SubProcess and Stage**
  - The alignment between both concepts from both meta-models is more arduous to establish but is real. In BPMN, the **InteractionNode** is *a type of flow object that represents a point in a process where participants interact with each other to exchange information or perform some action* [4].
  - In the EMMO, the **SubProcess** is *a process which is a holistic spatial part of a process*, and the **Stage** is *a process which is a holistic temporal part of a process* [13]. The semantic analysis of these three definitions does not make it possible to establish an indisputable alignment between the concepts. However, the analysis of associations clearly shows the similarities. Indeed, the InteractionNode is a subClass of Activity and FlowElementaryContainer, and is composed of Artifact and similarly, (1) the SubProcess has SubProcess and is SubClass of Process and (2), the stage has Stage and is SubClass of Process.
- **SequenceFlow and WorkFlow**
  - According to BPMN, the **SequenceFlow** *is used to show the order of Flow Elements in a Process or a Choreography. Each Sequence Flow has only one source and only one target* [4].
  - For EMMO, the **Workflow** is *an elaboration that has at least two elaborations as proper parts* [13]. At the association level, the SequenceFlow is a subClass of FlowElement (abstract superclass for all elements that can appear in a Process flow), and the WorkFlow is a SubClass of Elaboration.
- **ItemAwareElement and EncodeData**
  - The **ItemAwareElement** in BPMN refers to *several elements that are subject to store or convey items during process execution* [4].
  - The **EncodedData** are in EMMO *causal object whose properties variation are encoded by an agent and that can be decoded by another agent according to a specific rule* [13]. The ItemAwareElement concept has type

DataObject, DataSTore, DataInput and DataOutput, which are type of information, and the EncodedData is a subClass of Data and has subClass Information.

3.2 Mapping

In order to integrate BPMN concepts and relationships within the EMMO, it is necessary to analyse and select the best ontology extension mechanism (detailed in Sect. 2.3) for each conceptual mapping achieved in Sect. 3.1: Inheritance, Restriction, Extension, or Modules and Libraries – knowing that the last method is inappropriate to the purpose of our work. The result of the mapping is:

- **IntentionalProcess:** The analysis of the definitions provided in Sect. 3.1 demonstrates that both meta-models define the IntentionalProcess/Process based on the same arguments to know: that a process is structured following a sequence of activities and that it aims to reach an objective. BPMN's semantics is richer than the EMMO's semantics in that it associates the process to an organisation. Therefore, the preferred extension mechanism is the restriction (EMMO restricts BPMN conceptual semantics).
- **Participant:** The EMMO's definition of Participant is more generic than the definition from BPMN, which considers that the participant is a human, or an organisation, that is often responsible for the execution of a process [8]. This is more specific than the EMMO's point of view, which considers that an object demonstrating a holistic spatial part of the process is a participant. Accordingly, the extension mechanism that fits this alignment is inheritance. First, the BPMN's participant inherits the characteristics of EMMO's participant, and second, the EMMO's participant is extended with two possible statements: the participant is either a human or an organisation.
- **Elaboration:** The EMMO's definition of Elaboration is semantically a bit different than BPMN's definition of Activity. On one side, BPMN explains that the Activity may be atomic or compound, and on the other side, the EMMO stresses the importance of the Elaboration to work following some operative rules. As a result, the most appropriate extension mechanism is inheritance, and the EMMO Elaboration is extended with a composition link from/to the EMMO Elaboration concept.
- **ElementaryWork:** Task and ElementaryWork have the same semantics, and both refer to the smallest and indivisible piece of work composing a process. The definition of the Task from BPMN (Sect. 3.1) is semantically richer in that it stresses the importance of being within a traffic flow and being performed by an end-user or an application. In this case, the ontology extension mechanism used is the extension (BPMN extends EMMO conceptual semantics).
- **Status:** The definition of Status in the EMMO highlights that this concept stands for an object that reflects a temporal part of a process, whereas BPMN defines ThrowEvent as a trigger for catching events by the process. Although not explicitly embedded in the definition, the Status associated with a process

often triggers other events in practice. Therefore, we consider that this Status may be a type of trigger and, by extension, a ThrowEvent. Therefore, the mapping between both concepts is achieved using the restriction mechanism given that EMMO restricts ThrowEvent to Status.

- **SubProcess and Stage:** Both concepts represent part of the process (spatial or temporal), such as the InteractionNode from BPMN, which is described as a point in a process. The semantic heterogeneity between both BPMN and EMMO meanings is that the first specialises the finality of the concept to a place (or moment) where participants get together to achieve something or to exchange information. The description of the InteractionNode is consequently semantically more expressive, although both SubProcess and Stage refer to a spatial or a temporal dimension. As a result, the extension mechanism is the restriction since both EMMO's concepts restrict BPMN one. This situation is quite similar to the case of the IntentionalProcess, but because two concepts of EMMO are mapped to one concept of BPMN, it is not necessary to extend the concepts with a dedicated extension mechanism.

- **WorkFlow:** Analysing the definitions of the WorkFlow and of the Sequence-Flow, we conclude that the equivalence between both concepts is thin and limited. Both concepts are direct or indirect elements of the process that are associated with at least two flowing elements. The SequenceFlow adds a supplementary characteristic which is the existing sequence between the happening of the flowing elements. The extension mechanism preferred is, by the way, the restriction as WorkFlow restricts the SequenceFlow meaning.

- **EncodedData:** The ItemAwareElement concept in BPMN represents an abstract concept that may be specialised in many types like DataObject, DataStore, DataInput and DataOutput although the EncodedData concept is well defined and refers to properties variation of an object. This definition restricts by the way the definition of the ItemAwareElement and, as a consequence, the restriction extension mechanism is the one naturally designated.

3.3   Integration

In the approach used in this work, all concepts from BPMN without EMMO equivalence have been introduced in the Materials-based Business Case Ontology. The main concepts are: Gateway, Events, Artifact, InteractionNode, FlowElementContainer, FlowElement, MessageFlow, DataAssociation, DataOutputAssociation, DataInputAssociation, DataObject, DataOutput, DataInput, CallableElement. Further explanations of those concepts are available in BPMN 2.0 specifications [27].

The integration of BPMN concepts with EMMO equivalence is achieved based on the mapping performed in Sect. 3.2 and taking in hand the resolution of potential associations-related issues. For each concept, the analysis is the following:

- **IntentionalProcess:** The BPMN process being semantically richer than the IntentionalProcess, we may consider that the IntentionalProcess is a subClass of the BPMN Process concept, which is represented as a **type of** relation in UML. In the Materials-based Business Case Ontology, the IntentionalProcess is preserved. Concerning the relationships, two associations which did not exist for the EMMO concept have been added in MBCO. It consists of (1) the IntentionalProcess that **relates to** Collaboration and (2) the IntentionalProcess **is composed of** Artefact.

- **Participant:** The EMMO's definition of Participant being more generic, we have maintained the EMMO's Participant concept in the integrated ontology, and we have extended it with an attribute inherited from BPMN, to know: *the Participant is an individual or an organisation that is often responsible for the execution of the Process.* Regarding the relationships, two associations which did not exist for the EMMO concept have been added in the integrated version: (1) the Participant **composes** the Collaboration (2) the Participant is a **type of** InteractionNode.

- **Elaboration:** Given the small hetoregenities existing between Elaboration and Activity and the decision to consider the inheritance extension mechanism, we have maintained the EMMO's Participant concept in MBCO, and we have extended it with a composition link, as explained in Sect. 3.2, such as an Elaboration **composes** an Elaboration. In parallel, three additional Activity related associations from BPMN have also been included in EMMO Elaboration: (1) an Elaboration **is composed of** DataInputAssociation, (2) an Elaboration **is composed of** DataOutputAssociation, and (3) an Elaboration is a **type of** FlowNode.

- **ElementaryWork:** Alike the IntentionalProcess, the ElementaryWork is less rich than the Task semantic from BPMN, and for the same reason, the extension mechanism elected during the mapping step was the extension mechanism. Accordingly, we keep the ElementaryWork in EMMO extended ontology. Concerning the associated relationships, we complete the existing ones with (1) the ElementaryWork is a **type of** InteractionNode, and (2) the ElementaryWork **has type** various kinds of tasks (i.e., ScriptTask, ServiceTask, BusinessRuleTask, ManualTask, SendTask, ReceiveTask and UserTask)

- **Status:** The EMMO's definition of Status restricts BPMN's definition of ThrowEvent to a state of a temporal part of a process, and as a result, that a Status is a **type of** ThrowEvent. Accordingly, the Status process is preserved in the EMMO ontology. Concerning the relationships, four associations which previously did not exist in the EMMO have been added in MBCO. It consists of (1) Status is a **type of** Event, (2, 3 and 4) Status **has type** EndEvent, ImplicitThrowEvent and IntermediateThrowEvent.

- **SubProcess and Stage:** SubProcess and Stage's definitions, as reviewed in Sect. 3.2, restrict the definition of InteractionNode. They are both preserved in the EMMO ontology. Moreover, to express that these concepts may correspond to points where participants get together to achieve something or to exchange information, new associations are defined between them and the participants.

- **WorkFlow:** Provided the tight analogy between Workflow from the EMMO ontology and the SequenceFlow from BPMN, our strategy was to use the restriction extension mechanism and, consequently, to preserve the concept of WorkFlow in the Materials-based Business Case Ontology. Two associations are needed to complete the ontology integration with some workflow-related semantics coming from BPMN: (1) the WorkFlow **is the source of** and **targets** FlowNode and (2) the WorkFlow is a **type of** FlowElement.

– **EncodedData:** EncodedData from the EMMO has a precise meaning compared to ItemAwareElement from BPMN, which has more for the purpose of specifying a collection of data. On the opposite, the ItemAwareElement may be of various types described in [4]: DataObject, DataStore, DataOutput and DataInput. Hence, EncodedData will remain in the Materials-based Business Case Ontology. Finally, one additional association must be integrated: EncodedData **is source** and **is target** of DataAssociation.

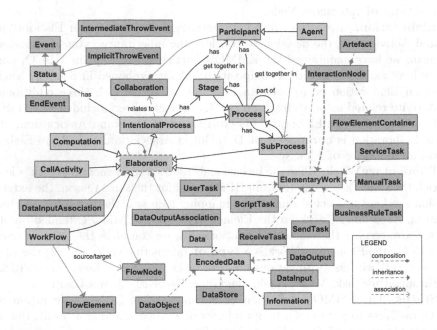

Fig. 3. Materials-based Business Case Ontology (MBCO). The concepts from the EMMO ontology are represented in orange, and the concepts from BPMN in green. (Color figure online)

3.4   Validation by Incoherence Solving

In general, validating a single ontology involves checking whether the ontology adheres to certain principles and standards [3]. Here are the types of validations that can be encountered and applied:

– syntax validation (*Does the ontology follows the correct syntax and format of the ontology language?*),

- consistency validation (*Is the ontology internally consistent?*),
- completeness validation (*Does the ontology cover all the necessary concepts and relationships in the domain?*),
- coherence validation (*Is the ontology coherent with other ontologies and standards in the same domain?*),
- usability validation (*Is the ontology easy to use and understand?*),

but also the validation of specific ontology criteria such as accuracy, coverage, scalability, and maintainability. Concerning the validation of an integrated ontology, such as BMPN with EMMO, we assume that the above validation types have been achieved during the design of each specific ontology and that the item left to be validated is the merging part itself, which involves Checking for inconsistencies between the ontologies.

In paper [7], the integration of BPMN within EMMO (Fig. 3) was validated through a manual incoherence discovery process, which revealed several inconsistencies upon our manual checks. As a reminder, the main type of incoherency discovered through the manual validation of the Materials-based Business Case Ontology was the identification of a cyclic hierarchy introduced between the concepts of **ElementaryWork** from EMMO and **InteractionNode** from BPMN. Solving this incoherency required a deeper analysis of both source ontologies. Therefore, by analysing EMMO and BPMN, we argued that an **Elementary-Work** can be considered a type of **InteractionNode** because an elementary work is a basic process that involves the transformation of materials, energy, or information, often through the application of energy such as heat or mechanical work. This transformation typically involves some kind of interaction between two or more entities, such as a chemical, an electrical or even a nuclear reaction or a physical change in state. Moreover, an **InteractionNode** is a node representing any type of interaction between two or more entities in a business process model. This can include tasks, events, and gateways, which are used to model different types of interactions. Therefore, it can be argued that an elementary work, which represents a basic process that transforms materials, energy, or information, can also be considered an **InteractionNode** because it involves an interaction between two or more entities, even if it is a more fundamental type of interaction compared to other types of nodes. Hence, both **ElementaryWork** and **InteractionNode** represent different types of nodes in a business process model, but an **ElementaryWork** can be seen as a more fundamental type of interaction that involves the transformation of materials, energy, or information, making it a type of **InteractionNode** in a broader sense. As a consequence, the decision was made during the manual Validation by Incoherence Solving step to keep the link "ElementaryWork is a type of InteractionNode" in the integrated model while removing the link "InteractionNode is a type of ElementaryWork".

In this paper, we use the Pellet reasoner [30] to detect and address any inconsistencies within the Materials-based Business Case Ontology. In the context of this automatic validation, a three-step process is undertaken. Initially, we implement the integrated MBCO ontology into Protégé [32]. Following this, a specific scenario is conceptualised, wherein a reasoner is employed to compute inferences. Finally, the results of these inferences are subjected to an analysis. This approach not only streamlines the validation process but also enhances the precision of identifying and resolving any inconsistencies within the ontology.

1. *Implementation in Protégé.*

As a basis for this step, we employed one of the pre-existing ontologisations of BPMN [28]. Upon an examination and comparison with the BPMN notation standard proposed by the Object Management Group (OMG) [27], we identified certain classes that were absent from this particular ontologisation of BPMN, and appended these missing classes. For instance, additions to the ontology included "collaboration" and "elaboration". Finally, the integrated ontology MBCO has been constructed by applying the following steps for each of the following classes:

- **IntentionalProcess**: (1) the process class of the BPMN ontology has been defined as a subclass of IntentionalProcess, (2) the class of collaboration has been created in the integrated ontology, (3) two news Object properties have been created: "IntentionalProcess is composed of Artefact" that has intentionalProcess as domain and Artefact as range, and "IntentionalProcess is linked to Collaboration" that also has intentionalProcess as domain and Collaboration as range.

- **Participant**: (1) A new object property has been created, "Organisation is responsible for the execution of a Process", and this object property has for domain Organisation and for range Process, (2) another object property has also been created "Collaboration is composed of Participant", and this object property has for domain collaboration and for range Participant, (3) the interactionNode class as been imported from the BPMN ontology, with a lowercase i, and (3) Participant has been defined as a subclass of interactionNode.

- **Elaboration**: (1) The class Elaboration is defined as a subClass of itself, (2) three BPMN classes have been created in the integrated ontology: flownode, dataInputAssociation, and dataOutputAssociation, and the flownode class is a subClass of Elaboration, and (3) two news Object properties have been created: "Elaboration is composed of dataInputAssociation" that has Elaboration as domain and dataInputAssociation as range, and "Elaboration is composed of dataOutputAssociation" that has Elaboration as domain and dataOutputAssociation as the range.

- **ElementaryWork**: (1) ElementaryWork has been defined as a subclass of InteractionNode and (2) scriptTask, servcieTask, businessRuleTask, manualTask, sendTask, receiveTask and userTask have been created in the integrated ontology, and they have all been defined as subClasses of ElementaryWork.

- **Status**: (1) event, endEvent, implicitThrowEvent and intermediateThrowEvent have been created in the integrated ontology, (2) Status has been defined as subClasses of events, and (3) endEvent, implicitThrowEvent and intermediateThrowEvent have been defined as subClasses of Status.

- **SubProcess and Stage**: Two news Object properties have been created: "Particiants get together in Stage" that has Participant as domain and Stage as range, and "Particiants get together in SubProcess" that has Participant as domain and SubProcess as range.
- **WorkFlow**: (1) a flowElement class of the BPMN ontology has been integrated, (2) Workflow is defined as a subClass of the flowElement, and (3) two news Object properties have been created: "WorkFlow is source of flowNode" and "WorkFlow targets flowNode" that have both Workflow as domain and flowNode as the range.
- **EncodedData**: (1) a dataAssociation class of the BPMN ontology has been integrated, (2) two news Object properties have been created: "EncodedData is the source of dataAssociation" and "EncodedData is target of dataAssociation" that have both EncodedData as domain and dataAssociation as range.

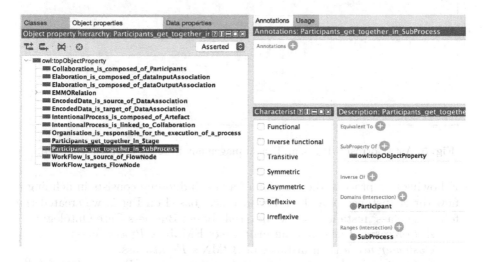

Fig. 4. Example of relation between classes implementation in protégé – *Participants get together in SubProcess*

In the context of implementing specific elements in Protégé, such as a relationship between two classes, it is necessary to address certain requirements or considerations. For instance, the relations between classes must be defined as object properties. As illustrated on Fig. 4, the association name "**Participants get together in SubProcess**" that associates the class "**Participant**" and the class "**SubProcess**" is the property named "**get together in/gather**" and this property has for Domains **Participant** and for Ranges **SubProcess**. Given that all associations with the same name (e.g., "**get together in/gather**") have different Domains and Ranges, we must create as many associations as there exist cases.

2. Application of the ontology to a specific process – Creation of individuals

To validate the ontology and to illustrate how it is possible to use it to infer new knowledge, we have exploited the *anticorrosive pigment test management process*[8] presented on Fig. 5, extracted from [24].

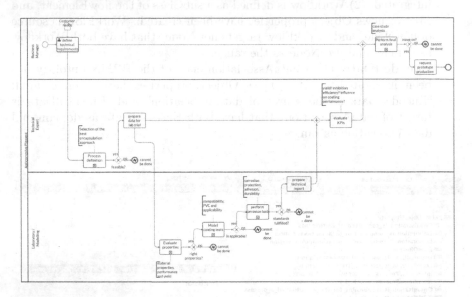

Fig. 5. Anti-Corrosive Pigment Test Management Process, adapted from [24].

Following this process, the creation of a new individual consists in defining a new direct instance of a class. For instance, based on Fig. 5, we created the following class' instances of the Materials-based Business Case Ontology:

- *Anticorrosive Pigment* is an instance of EMMO's *Process* class,
- *Customer needs* is an instance of BPMN's *Event* class,
- *Define technical requirements, Define the process, Prepare data for lab trial, Evaluate properties, Model coating tests, Perform corrosion tests, Prepare technical report, Evaluate KPIs, Perform final analysis, and Request prototype production* are instances of EMMO's instances of *Sub-Process* class,
- *Feasible?, Right properties?, Is applicable?, Standards fulfilled?*, Move on? are instances of BPMN's *InteractionNode* class. They may also be considered as instances of EMMO's *Elementary Works* class, itself being a subClass of the BPMN's *FlowElementContainer* class,
- *Business manager, Technical expert, and Laboratory/Modelling* are instances of EMMO's *Participant* class.
- *StartEvent, EndEvent and Inclusive/exclusive gateways* are instances of respective BPMN's classes.

---

[8] https://www.cardanit.com/resources/coating-materials-development-with-cardanit-bpmn-editor/.

3. *Elaboration of a validation rule.* In the paper [7], a critical inconsistency emerged during the manual validation of the Materials-based Business Case Ontology. This discrepancy specifically involved the creation of a cyclic hierarchy between the concepts of **ElementaryWork** from EMMO and **InteractionNode** from BPMN. Consequently, a validation rule is necessitated to detect cyclic relationships among ontology classes. This rule aims to identify scenarios where Class 1 is defined as a subclass of Class 2 while simultaneously Class 2 is regarded as a subclass of Class 1. The primary objective of this validation rule is to uncover and correct circular dependencies within the structure of the ontology's classes. This rule will, thus, for any class within the ontology, examine its direct connections with other classes and verify that the target class does not have a direct link with the source class.

$$\text{Class(?x)} \ \hat{} \ \text{Class(?y)} \ \hat{} \ \text{hasSubClass(?x, ?y)} \ \hat{}$$
$$\text{hasSubClass(?y, ?x)} \ \text{->} \ \text{CircularIncoherence(?x, ?y)}$$

The validation rule is formulated using the Semantic Web Rule Language[9] (SWRL), an extension of the Web Ontology Language (OWL) that combines predicate logic from OWL with rule capabilities, facilitating the expression of complex knowledge in semantic web applications. This SWRL rule detects and records circular incoherence between classes in an ontology, creating a new class **CircularIncoherence** when two classes (**?x** and **?y**) are found to have bidirectional **hasSubClass** relationships, referencing the ontology classes involved.

4. *Inference of new knowledge by applying the validation rule*
To execute SWRL rules in Protégé, various reasoners are compatible with SWRL, including HermiT and Pellet [1]. HermiT is a high-performance DL (Description Logic) reasoner well-suited for SWRL, commonly used for inference in OWL ontologies. Pellet, another robust reasoner, supports SWRL within Protege. Known for its efficiency in reasoning over large ontologies and its optimised algorithms for processing OWL semantics and SWRL rules, this is the reason we have selected Pellet. Pellet's efficiency in handling complex ontologies, its ability to efficiently process SWRL rules, and its active support for SWRL within Protege made it the optimal choice for our purposes. These factors, along with its compatibility and established performance, prompted our selection of Pellet for our **CircularIncoherence** rule execution within our merged ontology.

5. *Analysis of the results* During the reasoning process, Pellet automatically identifies new inferences and adds new individuals corresponding to the identified inferences to the existing knowledge base. For example, upon analysing the subclass relationship between **?X**, representing **ElementaryWork** from EMMO, and **?Y**, representing **InteractionNode** from BPMN, Pellet detected a **CircularIncoherence**. This inference signifies a cyclic hierarchy introduced between the concepts of **ElementaryWork** and **InteractionNode**. Pellet's reasoning capabilities facilitated the identification and

---

[9] https://www.w3.org/Submission/SWRL/.

subsequent creation of individual instances of **CircularIncoherence**, highlighting the cyclic inconsistency within the ontology's subclass structure. *In fine*, addressing this modelling conflict seeks to prevent cyclic relationships among specific individuals (e.g., *Feasible?* and *Move on?* within the process illustrated in Fig. 5), and improves the process description consistency.

4   Conclusion

The present work integrates a pre-ontologised subset of BPMN with the EMMO into MBCO, the Materials-based Business Case Ontology. Specifically, we utilise the BPMN ontology to support the open innovation process and the EMMO ontology to describe materials and processes. In this way, we construct a more comprehensive framework that can facilitate collaboration and innovation in the materials industry. This integration aims to streamline workflows, improve communication, and enhance the understanding of materials, leading to more effective and innovative solutions. Our approach consists of four key steps: Alignment, Mapping, Integration, and Validation by Incoherence Solving. While alignment and mapping are relatively straightforward, the integration step requires more careful consideration. For instance, when the extension mechanism is an inheritance, the EMMO concept is extended with the attributes inherited from BPMN. Accordingly, for the present work, it was the key objective to enhance the validation of the MBCO through formal reasoning. To accomplish this, we have deployed the MBCO in Protégé. Our objective revolves around the establishment of rules for generating inference when cyclic incoherencies among classes are discovered. This approach, complementing that from our recent previous work [7], allows identifying a cyclic association between **ElementaryWork** and **InteractionNode** in an automatic way. The validation based on inference rules ensures the absence of inconsistencies. Therefore, we are confident that our ongoing efforts to validate the merged ontology will lead to a higher level of coherence and reliability in our knowledge system. The integration of BPMN and EMMO into MBCO in this paper holds significant research implications by offering a standardized framework for collaborative materials research, enhancing communication, and fostering efficiency in materials science. However, limitations may arise in terms of the practical adaptability of MBCO across diverse organizational settings, potentially encountering resistance to adopting a new ontology framework. Future research avenues should focus on the real-world implementation and acceptance of MBCO, addressing identified limitations, and exploring the scalability and adaptability of the proposed ontology in different research contexts to ensure its widespread applicability.

Acknowledgements. This work was supported by the VIPCOAT project: A virtual open Innovation Platform for active protective coatings guided by modelling and optimisation. VIPCOAT project has received funding from the European Union's Horizon 2020 research and innovation programme under grant agreement no. 952903. In addition, co-author M.T.H. acknowledges funding from Horizon Europe under grant agreement no. 101137725 (BatCAT).

References

1. Abburu, S.: A survey on ontology reasoners and comparison. Int. J. Comput. Appl. **57**(17) (2012). https://api.semanticscholar.org/CorpusID:6747274
2. Belouettar, S., et al.: Integration of material and process modelling in a business decision support system: case of COMPOSELECTOR H2020 project. Compos. Struct. **204**, 778–790 (2018). https://doi.org/10.1016/j.compstruct.2018.06.121
3. Cobe, R., Wassermann, R.: Ontology merging and conflict resolution: inconsistency and incoherence solving approaches. BNC@ ECAI 2012 p. 20 (2012). https://www.lirmm.fr/ecai2012/images/stories/ecai_doc/pdf/workshop/W42_BNC-WorkshopNotes.pdf#page=21
4. Correia, A.: Elements of style of BPMN language. arXiv preprint: arXiv:1502.06297 (2015)
5. The Open Innovation Publications. https://digital-strategy.ec.europa.eu/en/library/open-innovation-publications. Accessed 24 Feb 2023
6. Feltus, C., Dubois, E., Petit, M.: Alignment of ReMMo with RBAC to manage access rights in the frame of enterprise architecture. In: 2015 IEEE 9th International Conference on Research Challenges in Information Science (RCIS), pp. 262–273. IEEE (2015). https://doi.org/10.1109/RCIS.2015.7128887
7. Feltus, C., et al.: Towards enhancing open innovation efficiency: A method for ontological integration of BPMN and EMMO. In: Ganzha, M., Maciaszek, L.A., Paprzycki, M., Slezak, D. (eds.) Proceedings of the 18th Conference on Computer Science and Intelligence Systems, FedCSIS 2023, Warsaw, Poland, 17-20 September 2023. Annals of Computer Science and Information Systems, vol. 35, pp. 471–479 (2023). https://doi.org/10.15439/2023F8906
8. Feltus, C., Petit, M.: Building a responsibility model including accountability, capability and commitment. In: 2009 International Conference on Availability, Reliability and Security, pp. 412–419. IEEE (2009). https://doi.org/10.1109/ARES.2009.45
9. Feltus, C., Proper, E.H.: Conceptualization of an abstract language to support value co–creation. In: 2017 Federated Conference on Computer Science and Information Systems (FedCSIS), pp. 971–980. IEEE (2017). https://doi.org/10.15439/2017F9
10. Feltus, C., Proper, E.H., Haki, K.: Towards a language to support value cocreation: an extension to the ArchiMate modeling framework. In: 2018 Federated Conference on Computer Science and Information Systems (FedCSIS), pp. 751–760. IEEE (2018). https://doi.org/10.15439/2018F27
11. Feltus, C., Rifaut, A.: An ontology for requirements analysis of managers' policies in financial institutions. In: Goncalves, R.J., Muller, J.P., Mertins, K., Zelm, M. (eds.) Enterprise Interoperability II, pp. 27–38. Springer, London (2007). https://doi.org/10.1007/978-1-84628-858-6_3
12. Ferndriger, S., Bernstein, A., Dong, J.S., Feng, Y., Li, Y.F., Hunter, J.: Enhancing semantic web services with inheritance. In: Sheth, A., et al. (eds.) The Semantic Web - ISWC 2008. Lecture Notes in Computer Science, vol. 5318, pp. 162–177. Springer, Berlin (2008). https://doi.org/10.1007/978-3-540-88564-1_11
13. Ghedini, E., Hashibon, A., Friis, J., Goldbeck, G., Schmitz, G., De Baas, A.: EMMO the European materials modelling ontology. In: EMMC Workshop on Interoperability in Materials Modelling. St John's Innovation Centre Cambridge (2017)
14. Goldbeck, G., Ghedini, E., Hashibon, A., Schmitz, G., Friis, J.: A reference language and ontology for materials modelling and interoperability. In: National

Agency for Finite Element Methods and Standards (NAFEMS World Congress) – International Conference on Simulation Process and Data Management (SPDM) (2019). https://publica.fraunhofer.de/handle/publica/406693

15. Horsch, M.T., et al.: Ontologies for the virtual materials marketplace. KI-Künstliche Intelligenz **34**, 423–428 (2020). https://doi.org/10.48550/arXiv.1912.01519

16. Horsch, M.T., et al.: Semantic interoperability and characterization of data provenance in computational molecular engineering. J. Chem. Eng. Data **65**(3), 1313–1329 (2019). https://doi.org/10.1021/acs.jced.9b00739

17. Horsch, M.T., Toti, D., Chiacchiera, S., Seaton, M.A., Goldbeck, G., Todorov, I.T.: OSMO: ontology for simulation, modelling, and optimization. In: 2th International Conference on Formal Ontology in Information Systems (FOIS 2021) (2021). http://ceur-ws.org/Vol-2969/

18. Kavka, C., Campagna, D., Koelman, H.: A business decision support system supporting early stage composites part design. In: Knoerzer, D., Periaux, J., Tuovinen, T. (eds.) Advances in Computational Methods and Technologies in Aeronautics and Industry. Computational Methods in Applied Sciences, vol. 57, pp. 263–279. Springer, Cham (2022). https://doi.org/10.1007/978-3-031-12019-0_19

19. Kavka, C., Campagna, D., Milleri, M., Segatto, A., Belouettar, S., Laurini, E.: Business decisions modelling in a multi-scale composite material selection framework. In: 2018 IEEE International Systems Engineering Symposium (ISSE), pp. 1–7. IEEE (2018). https://doi.org/10.1109/SysEng.2018.8544386

20. Kazantsev, N., DeBellis, M., Quboa, Q., Sampaio, P., Mehandjiev, N., Stalker, I.D.: An ontology-guided approach to process formation and coordination of demand-driven collaborations. Int. J. Prod. Res. **62**, 1–17 (2023)

21. Klein, P., et al.: Translation in Materials Modelling: Process and Progress. White paper, OntoTrans – FORCE (2021). https://doi.org/10.5281/zenodo.4729918

22. Klein, P., Preisig, H.A., Horsch, M.T., Konchakova, N.: Application of an ontology based process model construction tool for active protective coatings: Corrosion inhibitor release. In: Proceedings of JOWO 2021, p. 26. CEUR-WS (2021). http://ceur-ws.org/Vol-2969/

23. Köcher, A., Da Silva, L.M.V., Fay, A.: Modeling and executing production processes with capabilities and skills using ontologies and BPMN. In: 2022 IEEE 27th International Conference on Emerging Technologies and Factory Automation (ETFA), pp. 1–8. IEEE (2022)

24. Konchakova, N., Preisig, H.A., Kavka, C., Horsch, M.T., Klein, P., Belouettar, S.: Bringing together materials and business ontologies for protective coatings. In: FOMI 2022: Formal Ontologies Meet Industry (2022). https://hdl.handle.net/11250/3046519

25. Nicolas, D., Feltus, C., Khadraoui, D.: Multidimensional DIH4CPS ontology. In: 21st International Conference on e-Society, p. 20 (2023). https://www.iadisportal.org/digital-library/multidimensional-dih4cps-ontology

26. Nicolas, D., Feltus, C., Khadraoui, D.: Towards a multidimensional ontology model for DIH-based organisations. Int. J. Knowl. Syst. Sci. (IJKSS) **14**(1), 1–19 (2023). https://doi.org/10.4018/IJKSS.326764

27. BPMN Version 2.0. https://www.omg.org/spec/BPMN/2.0. Accessed 14 Dec 2023

28. Rospocher, M., Ghidini, C., Serafini, L.: BPMN-onto – A formalisation of BPMN in Description Logics. Technical Report FBK2008-06-004 (2008). https://dkm.fbk.eu/bpmn-ontology

29. Rozenberg, G.: Handbook of Graph Grammars and Computing by Graph Transformation, vol. 1 (Foundations). World Scientific, River Edge (1997). ISBN: 978-981-02-2884-2

30. Sirin, E., Parsia, B., Grau, B.C., Kalyanpur, A., Katz, Y.: Pellet: a practical OWL-DL reasoner. J. Web Semant. 5(2), 51–53 (2007). https://doi.org/10.1016/j.websem.2007.03.004

31. Spaccapietra, S., Parent, C.: Database integration: the key to data interoperability. Adv. Object-Oriented Data Model., 221–253 (2000). https://doi.org/10.7551/mitpress/1131.001.0001

32. Protégé – The open–source ontology editor and framework. https://protege.stanford.edu/. Accessed 24 Feb 2023

33. Taylor, J., Purchase, J.: Real-World Decision Modeling with DMN. Meghan-Kiffer Press, Tampa (2016)

34. Tomaskova, H., et al.: The business process model and notation of open innovation: the process of developing medical instrument. J. Open Innov.: Technol., Mark., Complex. 5(4), 101 (2019). https://doi.org/10.3390/joitmc5040101

35. Ziemba, E., Chmielarz, W.: Information Technology for Management: Business and Social Issues: 16th Conference, ISM 2021, and FedCSIS-AIST 2021 Track, Held as Part of FedCSIS 2021, Virtual Event, 2–5 September 2021, Extended and Revised Selected Papers, vol. 442. Springer Nature (2022)

36. Ziemba, E., Chmielarz, W., Wątróbski, J.: Information Technology for Management: Approaches to Improving Business and Society: AIST 2022 Track and 17th Conference, ISM 2022, Held as Part of FedCSIS 2022, Sofia, Bulgaria, 4–7 September 2022, Extended and Revised Selected Papers, vol. 471. Springer Nature (2023)

37. Zivkovic, S., Kuhn, H., Karagiannis, D.: Facilitate modelling using method integration: an approach using mappings and integration rules. In: ECIS 2007 Proceedings, pp. 2038–2049 (2007). https://aisel.aisnet.org/ecis2007/122

Digital Technologies in Consulting – Impact of the COVID-19 Pandemic

Christian Leyh[1,2]([envelope]) [iD], Marcel Lange[1], Alisa Lorenz[1] [iD], and Yvonne Engelhardt[3]

[1] Technische Hochschule Mittelhessen (THM), University of Applied Sciences, THM Business School, Gießen, Germany
{christian.leyh,alisa.lorenz}@w.thm.de
[2] Fraunhofer Center for International Management and Knowledge Economy IMW, Leipzig, Germany
[3] Chair of Business Information Systems, Esp. Information Systems in Industry and Trade, Technische Universität Dresden, Dresden, Germany

Abstract. The increasing digitalization of the economy and society has triggered drastic changes in companies and confronted them with enormous challenges. The consulting industry has also been deeply affected by this digital transformation. In order to show the influence of digitalization on business consultancies and which digital technologies are currently being used in those firms, we conducted an exploratory study. To this end, we conducted an online survey with 186 consultants about their assessment of digitalization and the use of digital technologies. Further attention was also paid to the influence of the COVID-19 pandemic on the use of digital technologies and digitalization in business consultancies. Our results revealed that many business consultancies had already relied heavily on digitalization and used a variety of digital technologies in all phases of the consulting process. We were able to show that digitalization increased significantly in business consultancies during the COVID-19 pandemic and that the majority of participants understand digitalization as an opportunity for change. Nevertheless, the business consultancies are currently using digital technologies that primarily support communication and collaboration (like audio/video conferencing tools or mobile computing applications). Although consultants are aware of the growing importance of advanced technologies (such as generative AI), business consultancies are currently reluctant to use these technologies and tend to rely on well-established digital technologies.

Keywords: Digitalization · Digital technology · Consulting · Business consultancy · COVID-19 pandemic

1 Introduction

Today more than ever, society as a whole is undergoing a rapidly evolving digital transformation. Government institutions, households, enterprises, and their interactions are all changing due to the increased prevalence and rapid growth of digital technologies. Especially in enterprises, it has never been more important to be able to rely on a deep

E. Ziemba et al. (Eds.): FedCSIS-ITBS 2023/ISM 2023, LNBIP 504, pp. 46–70, 2024.
https://doi.org/10.1007/978-3-031-61657-0_3

understanding of information technologies (IT) in general and of digital innovation in particular. The persistently high level of dynamism in everyday business today shows that continual changes and adaptations in response, including ones due to digitalization, will be the rule, not the exception, in the future economy. Worldwide digital networking, the automation of individual or even all business processes, and the restructuring of existing business models are just a few of the wide-ranging effects of digitalization. Indeed, the consequences of digitalization are omnipresent, as is the question of whether such changes should be viewed as positive or negative [17, 18, 23, 26]. In either case, nearly all companies will have to pursue increased digital transformation, at least to some extent, in order to remain competitive in the global market [4].

Digitalization has become of unprecedented importance partly owing to the COVID-19 pandemic, which delivered an unparalleled shock of uncertainty across all state borders and industries. Nationwide store closures, contact restrictions, and mandatory home offices forced companies to use contactless distribution channels and to facilitate remote work. Those developments drove a push toward digitalization, as numerous processes in companies had to be digitalized and companies themselves had to prove their resilience. It is often argued that the digitalization driven by the pandemic will continue after the pandemic [11, 19, 22].

One industry especially challenged by uncertainty during the COVID-19 pandemic was the consulting industry. As reported by the German Association of Management Consultancies, the BDU, (https://www.bdu.de/en), the revenue growth of business consultancies collapsed in 2020 for the first time since 2010. The pandemic also dramatically altered the working methods of consultants. Guided by the motto "New Work," the BDU reported massive contact restrictions and significant changes in workplace and working time models [2]. To be sure, business consultancies also had to radically reorient themselves in terms of digitalization aspects to meet the challenges of the COVID-19 pandemic.

Therefore, our main research goal was to gain insight into how relevant digitalization is now and how much more relevant it will become in the consulting industry. We sought to investigate the current and future significance of digitalization in general. We also wanted to investigate the general perception of digitalization among consultants to provide a basic picture of their opinions. Beyond that, to gain comprehensive insight into business consultancies, we aimed to examine the current and future significance of digital technologies and trends for consultants. We also included a specific viewpoint on the impact that the COVID-19 pandemic has had on these areas.

To those ends, we developed a study using an online questionnaire to evaluate the status quo of the use of digital technologies in business consultancies in Germany, which we chose to examine due to our cultural background. The basis of our current study was our own study on the status quo of digitalization in business consultancies conducted in 2019 (before the pandemic), which is hereinafter referred to as *Study 2019*. This will later be used as a comparative basis in the discussion section of this paper. However, the main focus of this research is our survey conducted in 2023 (hereinafter referred to as *Study 2023*).

Therefore, to reach our research goal and to present and discuss our results, the paper (as extended version of [20]) our paper is structured as follows. Following this section addressing our motivation for the study, we provide a short theoretical background with a focus on business consultancies and on the impact of the COVID-19 pandemic from which we derive our research questions. Subsequently, we describe our study's foundation, design, and our method of data collection before presenting and discussing selected results in light of our research questions. The paper closes with a summary of the main results and an outlook for future research in the field.

2 Theoretical Background

2.1 Business Consultancies

Business consultancies can be characterized in light of their consulting focus. In our study, we classified consultancies with reference to the BDU's classification, which divides the market for consulting into four classic fields [2]:

- Strategy consulting,
- IT consulting,
- Organization and process consulting, and
- Human resources consulting.

To begin, **strategy consulting** is considered the most demanding field of consulting. Not only does it occur exclusively within the top management of companies, but the topics also concern the core of all corporate activities—that is, the corporate strategy [27]. The goal of a consultant in strategy consulting is to help the client to define long-term goals and develop a course of action to achieve the corporate strategy. Achieving that goal involves analyzing the current business situation, identifying opportunities and challenges, and developing a tailored strategy [21].

By comparison, **IT consulting** addresses the widest variety of consulting topics of all four of the classic fields of consulting. The topics range from the creation of business-critical individual software and the implementation of standard software and web-based applications to system integration and the optimization of IT architecture and infrastructure [21].

Next, **organization and process consulting** builds on the concepts of strategy consulting. By contrast, however, consultants work at the operational level, and contact between the client company and the consultancy usually occurs not within top management but mostly in middle and lower management [21]. Organization and process consulting deals with the optimization of organizational structures and processes within a company. Its goal is to improve the efficiency, effectiveness, and agility of the company by reviewing and, if necessary, adapting its business processes [6].

Last, **human resources consulting** focuses on both the managers and employees of a company. Among other activities, it involves the promotion of professional and social skills, usually facilitated in training courses [6].

No matter the field, a key factor of success for business consultancies is the consulting approach that they adopt. At its base, successful consulting requires an understanding of the process. In the literature, the consulting process is described in various procedure models, which differ less in their content than in the number of phases conceived as being part of the process. Barchewitz and Armbrüster [1] have described the consulting process in a three-phase model involving planning, realization, and control. Bodenstein and Herget [7], by contrast, have presented a four-phase process model involving conception, contract design, implementation, and conclusion. In our study, we followed the procedure model developed by Seifert [28], which comprises six phases:

- Acquisition,
- Project preparation,
- Problem analysis,
- Problem-solving,
- Implementation, and
- Post-processing.

First, **acquisition** forms the basis of the consulting process, because in that phase a business consultancy seeks to obtain an order from a client [28]. A general exchange of information also occurs, after which the business consultancy submits a bid for the project order. Once the consultancy has received the order, a contract is negotiated between the parties [21]. Second, in **project preparation**, the project team is defined, the team's members are given access to all relevant systems, and further organizational arrangements are made [28]. Third, **problem analysis** focuses on gathering, deepening, and evaluating information. During that phase, the current situation is analyzed, and a formulation to meet the project's objective is finalized [21]. Fourth, **problem-solving** is the core phase of a consulting project [21]. Therein, a strategy for realizing a solution to the problem is presented. To that purpose, different alternative solutions are designed, evaluated, and presented to the client, who subsequently selects one of them to pursue [28]. Fifth, during **implementation**, the selected solution is implemented. The process is carefully planned to ensure successful implementation, and, afterward, the results are reviewed, and, if necessary, the solution is optimized [7]. Sixth and last, **post-processing** considers both the client and the consultancy. On the client's side, the phase involves the conclusion of the project, including the achievement of the project's objectives. On the consultancy's side, it entails the preparation of documentation, assessments, and results for reuse [28].

2.2 Impact of the COVID-19 Pandemic on German Enterprises

The COVID-19 pandemic is sometimes hailed as an accelerator of digital transformation. To clarify, companies should have been, and indeed were, seizing the moment as a launchpad for not only digital transformation but also structural change. In light of this, the KfW (https://www.kfw.de/About-KfW/) conducted special surveys during the COVID-19 pandemic. The evaluation of these surveys is summarized in different digitalization reports (see [13, 14]).

The data from the special surveys show that the level of digitization activity varied during the different periods of the surveys. At the beginning of the COVID-19 pandemic, a surge in digitalization was observed, as home offices had to be set up and expanded within a very short time for many companies in various industry sectors. There was also a significant increase in the use of cashless payment systems, e-health services, virtual communication platforms, and online retail. Digitalization was used not only to react flexibly to bottlenecks in deliveries and declines in demand, but also to remain visible to cooperation partners and customers. Even though digitalization activities increased during the second wave of the pandemic, the proportion of those who did not implement any digitalization measures remained at 33%. In the report for 2020, it was assumed that companies had invested more in digital technologies in order to continue to overcome the crisis [13]. It is possible that digitization activities flattened out as the COVID-19 pandemic progressed due to measures already completed and limited resources. In autumn 2021, there was a renewed increase in digitalization projects due to an economic recovery. It was assumed that companies wanted to better position themselves in terms of digitalization after the COVID-19 period [14]. It was also found that companies that have suffered significant sales losses during the pandemic or those that expected the crisis to last a long time have intensified their digitalization efforts. It is assumed that these were often immediately effective digitalization activities that could be implemented in the short term in order to generate sales or maintain business operations during the crisis. It is possible that long-term projects were postponed more frequently as a result [14]. It can also be assumed that companies that had not dealt with the digital transformation before the pandemic felt significantly more negative effects than those that had already started to digitalize their production and working methods.

In a survey conducted in spring 2020, Krcmar and Wintermann [16] concluded that the three biggest changes in the companies surveyed at the beginning of the pandemic were in the area of internal and external communication and the cooperation and behavior of employees. For example, virtual conferences and other digital applications made working from home immediately possible, and external communication was conducted via new channels. These features could remain in place after the pandemic; furthermore, 66% of the companies surveyed stated that the pandemic would have a long-term impact on increased digital customer contact. In addition, 71% indicated that the scope of digital services would increase, and 63% believed that the company's presence would disappear. Over 80% of respondents stated that working from home and virtual conferencing would continue as a pandemic-induced trend.

Looking at the business consultancies even before the pandemic, consulting companies faced the same challenges associated with digitalization that other companies also faced. New competitors, new demands from customers seeking to professionalize their own digitalization [12], new requirements imposed by digitalization in providing consulting services, and the need for new skills and know-how on the part of consulting companies all confronted the classic people-oriented business of consulting with the need for changes in service provision, just as in other industries [29]. In that light, "business as usual" was not a valid business strategy for many consulting companies even before the COVID-19 pandemic and became especially impractical due to the pandemic. Instead, the consulting industry has had to increasingly implement digital technologies in the various phases of the consulting process and, in turn, deal with emerging opportunities and innovations. In that context, the question thus arises as to what extent business consultancies are already using digital technologies.

Looking at scientific and practice-oriented literature on digitalization, the use of digital technologies and the impact of the COVID-19 pandemic with specific focus on business consultancies, it becomes evident that there is already some research on digitalization and the use of digital technologies in business consultancies (e.g., [8,

9, 25, 30]). However, these studies often predate the start of the pandemic. Since the beginning of the COVID-19 pandemic, many studies have been conducted on the topics of digitalization, digital transformation, and the effects of the pandemic. However, these studies primarily address those aspects from a general viewpoint and are not specifically aimed at business consultancies.

Therefore, we have set up a study addressing the specific characteristics of the current and future use of digital technologies in German business consultancies. With our study we strive to answer the following research questions (RQs):

RQ 1: To what extent do business consultancies in Germany use digital technologies?

RQ 2: What impact has the COVID-19 pandemic had on the use of digital technologies in business consultancies?

In response to these questions (as extended version of [20]), we will present and discuss selected results of our study in the following sections.

3 Research Methodology – Study 2023

Our research questions were designed to afford access to initial insights into how consulting firms view and use digital technologies. To gain such insights, we adopted an exploratory approach, which we conceive as being a starting point for more in-depth research in the future. For that reason, we make no claim regarding the representativeness of participants in the study.

3.1 Foundation of Study 2023

Our initial study (*Study 2019*) was built on the findings of Nissen and Seifert [25]. The authors look at the impact of the digital transformation on the consulting industry and provide insights into the opportunities and challenges it presents. The most relevant finding of [25] is that digitalization is having an enormous impact on the consulting industry. According to the authors, customers are increasingly looking for digital solutions. Due to this market pressure, consultancies have had to adapt. Another finding is that the use of technological innovation, such as artificial intelligence or big data analysis, is opening up new opportunities for consultancies. Overall, the authors show as early as 2015 that digital transformation is fundamentally changing the consulting industry and requires consultants to adapt.

Our *Study 2019* followed-up on the results from [25]. We examined the role of digitalization in two ways. On the one hand, we looked at the company's perspective, and on the other hand, we considered the viewpoint of the consultant. The evaluation showed that consultants perceive the role of digitalization to be more important than the company itself does. In addition, less experienced consultants perceived it as more important than more experienced consultants. Nevertheless, over 95% of study participants expected the importance of digitalization in their role as consultants and in their companies to increase over the next five years.

The use of digital technologies was also examined. We found that the use of digital consulting technologies enabled an increase in efficiency and new consulting markets could be addressed. It was found that from the consultants' perspective, technologies such as audio and video conferencing, mobile computing, and cloud computing were the most important, whereas analytical tools were only used sporadically and were increasingly used in larger consulting firms. The evaluation of *Study 2019* also revealed that trends such as self-service consulting, the virtual marketplace for clients and consultants and crowdsourced consulting were used less frequently. It was clearly evident that the importance of digital technologies would continue to increase over the next five years. After examining the use of digital technologies in the consulting process, it also emerged that the lowest number of different technologies was used in acquisition and follow-up. In contrast, most different technologies were used in the problem-solving phase and the implementation phase. Based on the data, we were able to show that from the consultants' perspective, the use of technologies would increase in all phases of consulting projects in the future. In summary, we found that digitalization played a significant role for consultants. Nevertheless, consulting companies still seemed to be in the early stages of digitalization.

Our *Study 2019* and other research (e.g., [3, 5, 8–10, 25, 30]) showed that digital transformation and the use of digital technologies were unavoidable for business consultancies. However, the impact of the COVID-19 pandemic on business consultancies and their use of digital technologies was often not assessed. This is where *Study 2023* comes in, which is presented in the following sections.

3.2 Questionnaire Design

Our questionnaire in *Study 2023* was based on the original *Study 2019* questionnaire with some additions to capture aspects of the COVID-19 pandemic. Overall, the final questionnaire included 20 questions, divided into seven blocks:

- General information about the participants,
- Importance of digitalization,
- Importance of digital technologies,
- Degree of digitalization,
- Importance of the business model,
- Use of digital technologies, and
- Perception of digitalization and future trends.

General Information About the Participants: In the first block of questions, participants were asked four fact-focused questions as a means to later categorize them in data analysis. Question 1 inquired into the number of employees in the participants' companies, the responses of which were used to classify the companies into micro, small, medium, and large companies. Question 2 asked about the area of consulting in which they were most active. Last, Questions 3 and 4 addressed the participants' professional experience by inquiring into the number of years spent in the profession and the number of clients and consulting projects undertaken.

Importance of Digitalization: The second group, containing Questions 5–8, addressed the current and future importance of digitalization, along with its importance during the COVID-19 pandemic. To that end, participants were asked to indicate digitalization's importance for themselves as consultants in Question 5 and for their company in Question 7. In between, Question 6 asked for an assessment of digitalization's expected importance in the next five years from the participant's perspective. Last, Question 8 inquired into how the pandemic has changed the company's perspective of the importance of digitalization.

Importance of Digital Technologies: In the third block of questions, Questions 9 and 12 sought to determine the importance of digital technologies and trends in business consulting. To that purpose, a list of 14 digital technologies was created with reference to the literature. To ensure consistency in understanding, potentially unfamiliar technologies were briefly explained. Questions 10 and 11 asked participants about the importance of those technologies during the COVID-19 pandemic. Those questions allowed us to determine both the current state of digital technologies in business consultancies and the most significant technologies for consultants during the pandemic.

Degree of Digitalization: In the fourth group of questions, Question 13 asked participants to select one of four statements that best describes the current level of digitalization in their respective companies.

Importance of the Business Model: Question 14 was the only question in the fifth group, and it asked about the COVID-19 pandemic's impact on the company's business model.

Use of Digital Technologies: To gain more granular insight, the first question of the sixth block of questions, Question 15, asked the consultants to rate their current use of digital technologies during the different phases of the consulting process. Subsequently, Question 16 asked the respondents to rate their expected use of digital technologies in the next five years, and Question 17 asked them to select the technologies that they use in each phase of the consulting process.

Perception of Digitalization and Future Trends: The intention of the seventh and final block of questions was to determine how the participants perceived digitalization at present and in the future. To that end, Questions 18 and 19 asked participants to evaluate specific opportunities by responding to different statements. The questions were intended to capture their opinions on digital technologies. Last, Question 20 inquired into the participant's personal attitude toward digitalization.

3.3 Data Collection

As a result of several pretests with various researchers from the Technical University of Central Hesse and different practitioners, the questionnaire was improved. The general aim of the pretests was to assess the questionnaire's instructions as well as the individual questions for comprehensibility and errors.

Next, mostly using email, we invited consultants to participate in our study. For this purpose, we contacted all business consultancies that were members of the BDU at the time of data collection, and their responses were our primary source for contact information. The emails were sent between January 15 and February 15, 2023. We also shared the link to the online questionnaire on business platforms, such as LinkedIn (www. linkedin.com) and XING (www.xing.com), and with personal contacts in our business networks.

When the survey period ended, the online questionnaire had been completed 291 times. Of those questionnaires, 187 had been completed in full. Before data analysis, those 187 questionnaires were checked for plausibility, with special attention to whether any pattern in the answers might suggest that the participant had only clicked through the questionnaire at random. As a result, we had to exclude only one data set, meaning that 186 data sets were analyzed for the results presented in the following section.

4   Selected Results – Study 2023

4.1 Participants' General Characteristics

To differentiate responses along the lines of company size, the business consultancies were grouped according to the number of employees. Table 1 provides an overview of the respective company sizes.

Table 1. Participant Structure by Number of Employees (n = 186)

Number of employees	Absolute frequency	Relative frequency
1–10	47	25.3%
11–49	30	16.1%
50–249	19	10.2%
>250	90	48.4%

Table 1 shows that 47 consultants from micro-enterprises and 30 from small enterprises participated in the survey. The smallest group of participants, totaling 19, was represented by medium-sized companies, whereas the largest proportion of participants, totaling 90, represented large companies.

The distribution of participants across the different fields of consulting (see Sect. 2) was highly heterogeneous. Because Question 2 allowed for multiple answers, the 186 participants provided a total of 245 answers. The most represented field was organization and process consulting, with 78 responses, followed by IT consulting with 70, strategy consulting with 44, and human resources consulting with 36. Added to that, 17 participants selected the answer option "Other."

Concerning the experience of the participants in terms of years spent working as consultants, Table 2 shows that 105 participants had up to 10 years of work experience and that 81 had at least 10 years of work experience. The participants' professional experience with consulting projects was also queried. Whereas only 11 consultants had previously worked on 1–3 projects, 43 had been involved in 4–9 projects, 37 in 10–19 projects, 20 in 20–29 projects, and 17 in 30–39 projects. In the largest group, 58 participants had been involved in more than 40 projects.

Table 2. Participants by Years of Work Experience (n = 186))

Years of work experience	Absolute frequency	Relative frequency
<1	5	2.7%
1–5	66	35.5%
6–10	34	18.3%
11–15	20	10.8%
16–20	20	10.8%
21–25	18	9.7%
26–30	13	7.0%
31–35	4	2.2%
36–40	6	3.2%
>40	0	0%

4.2 Digitalization: General Aspects

The participants were also asked to assess the current role of digitalization in their day-to-day work. For a detailed look at their responses, Fig. 1 shows how participants with up to ten years of professional experience responded versus those with more than ten years of professional experience. On the one hand, those with up to ten years of professional experience attributed "medium significance" and "high significance" to digitalization in their day-to-day work in nearly equal measure, at rates of 44.8% and 48.6%, respectively. By contrast, only 6.7% participants selected "low significance." On the other hand, 63.0% of participants with more than ten years of professional experience characterized digitalization as having "high significance" in their daily work, whereas 30.9% selected "medium significance" and another 6.2% selected "low significance." Remarkably, none of the participants selected "no significance" in response to the question. It is, therefore, clear that digitalization was perceived as playing a greater role in the day-to-day work of consultants with more than ten years of professional experience than for those with up to ten years of such experience.

Regarding digitalization in general, the participants were additionally asked to assess the level of digitalization in their consultancies by choosing one of the following levels:

- **Level 1:** We predominantly rely on consulting processes in which our consultants work together with the customer on-site. Technologies such as chat, video-conferencing, and other digital collaboration tools are rarely used in projects.
- **Level 2:** We carry out projects in which our consultants and customers work together at separate locations. However, most of our projects are based on on-site, face-to-face interactions.
- **Level 3:** Digital technologies are an integral part of our business model. We specifically manage the personal deployment of consultants on-site and no longer include it in every project.

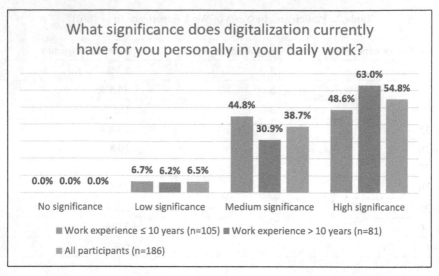

Fig. 1. Significance of Digitalization for Consultants according to Work Experience (n = 186; relative frequency)

- **Level 4:** Our business model is based predominantly on digital technologies. Consultants work on-site with clients only in particularly critical phases and in regard to particularly complex problems.

Given those four descriptive statements, only 22 of the 186 participants selected Level 4 to characterize digitalization at their companies. By contrast, 83 selected Level 3, 68 selected Level 2, and, least frequently, 13 selected Level 1.

To present the level of digitalization in greater detail, Fig. 2 depicts the level of digitalization of the business consultancies by company size. As shown, 18.9% of large companies were characterized as having Level 4 digitalization, followed by 10.5% of medium-sized companies. Micro-enterprises accounted for the largest share of Level 1 digitalization at 12.8%, while small companies had the second-largest share, at 10.0%. These results clearly show that larger companies seem to employ a higher level of digitalization than smaller companies.

Turning to the perception of digitalization, we asked participants whether they perceived digitalization primarily as a threat or an opportunity for their companies. Figure 3 provides a breakdown of their responses based on company size. The top bar of the graph shows the overall results, which indicate that 113 participants perceived digitalization in their companies "clearly as an opportunity" and 61 as "more like an opportunity." The remaining 12 participants perceived digitalization in their companies as both an opportunity and a threat (i.e., "opportunity/threat"). Notably, none of the participants selected the answer options "more like a threat" or "clearly as a threat." The other four bars in the graph show the evaluation by company size. Of the 90 participants from large companies, 56 perceived digitalization at their companies "clearly as an opportunity," 29 as "more like an opportunity," and 5 as "opportunity/threat." The picture sharpens for medium-sized companies; of those 19 consultants, 17 perceived digitalization in their companies

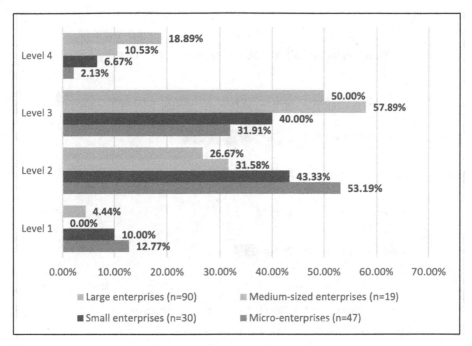

Fig. 2. Level of digitalization by company size (relative frequency)

"clearly as an opportunity" and 2 as "more like an opportunity." Thus, medium-sized companies had the highest proportion of participants who selected "clearly as an opportunity." The 30 participants from small companies also only selected only two answer options; 19 selected "clearly as an opportunity," while 11 selected "more like an opportunity." By contrast, of the 47 participants in micro-enterprises, 21 chose "clearly as an opportunity," 19 chose "more like an opportunity," and 7 chose "opportunity/threat."

4.3 Use of Digital Technologies

This section presents the results of our analysis of the data from questions concerning the use of digital technologies in business consultancies.

To begin, focusing on the current and future significance of digital technologies in business consultancies, participants were asked to assess the current significance of 14 specific technologies. They were next asked to assess the importance of those technologies for their consultancies in the next five years. To evaluate those data, the verbalized answers were coded and recorded as arithmetic mean values. The following coding was chosen:

- 1 = no importance,
- 2 = low importance,
- 3 = medium importance, and
- 4 = great importance.

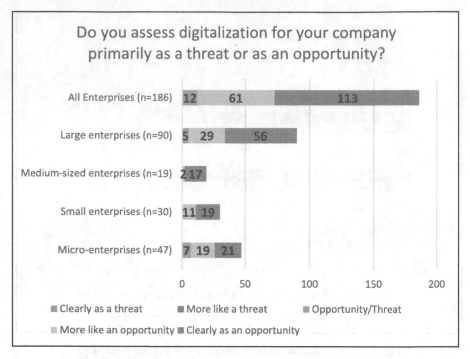

Fig. 3. Perception of Digitalization (n = 186; absolute frequency)

Table 3 provides an overview of the results. Because not every participant assessed every technology, the table also provides the number of participants who assessed the particular technology. As Table 3 shows, audio/video conferencing was viewed as being the most important digital technology, with a mean value of 3.72 out of 4.00. In second place was mobile computing, with a mean of 3.54, followed by cloud computing, with a mean of 3.29. The importance of the mean values becomes particularly clear when looking at the technologies in the lower ranks. Social media ranked in the third lowest position, with a mean value of 2.18, followed by crowdsourced consulting and self-service consulting as lowest in ranking, each with a mean of 2.05.

The difference between the arithmetic means of "current significance" and "future significance" indicates which digital technologies may become the focus of consulting firms in the next five years. The third-largest difference was 0.96 for artificial intelligence technology, closely followed by social media, with a difference of 1.01. The largest difference, 1.03, was with big data analytics.

Next, participants were asked to indicate the current and anticipated future use of digital technologies in their consulting process. Again, the arithmetic mean was used for evaluation. To that end, the verbalized answers were coded as follows:

- 1 = no use,
- 2 = very little use,
- 3 = low use,
- 4 = medium use,

Table 3. Significance of Digital Technologies (n = 186; multiple answers possible)

Digital technology	Current significance (arithmetic mean)	Future significance (arithmetic mean)
Knowledge management systems (n = 180)	2.96	3.38
Virtual marketplace for consultants and customers (n = 180)	2.96	2.99
Social media (n = 180)	2.18	3.29
Self-service consulting (n = 175)	2.05	2.98
Open community and expert platforms (n = 171)	2.32	3.01
Mobile computing (n = 171)	3.54	3.81
Artificial intelligence (n = 182)	2.66	3.62
Document management systems (n = 181)	2.99	3.34
Data/process mining (n = 171)	2.52	3.47
Crowdsourced consulting (n = 170)	2.05	2.96
Cloud computing (n = 180)	3.29	3.69
Chats (n = 183)	3.22	3.31
Big data analytics (n = 176)	2.52	3.55
Audio/video conferencing (n = 186)	3.72	3.75

- 5 = high use, and
- 6 = very high use.

Figure 4 shows the participants' evaluation of the current and anticipated future use of technologies in the consulting process undertaken by their respective business consultancies. The figure readily clarifies that the anticipated future use of digital technologies in all phases was rated higher than the current use.

To gain a comprehensive view of the current use of digital technologies in the consulting process, participants had the opportunity to assign the 14 listed technologies to the individual phases of the process and could select multiple response options. Table 4 provides an overview of the results. When the numbers of the various technologies per phase were totaled, digital technologies emerged as being used most frequently in problem analysis, followed by problem-solving and project preparation. Implementation ranked fourth, followed by acquisition. Last, post-processing was reported to involve the fewest digital technologies. Overall, the results suggest that the diversity of digital technologies used is most often greatest in the middle phases of the consulting process.

Regarding the use of digital technologies in the different fields of consulting, participants in IT consulting selected different digital technologies most frequently in all six phases of the consulting process, closely followed by participants in organization

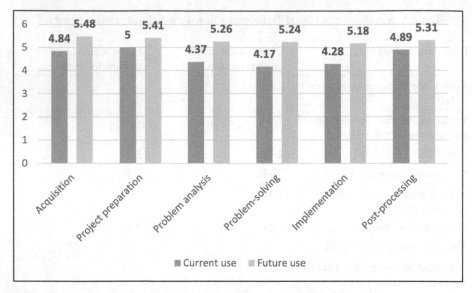

Fig. 4. Use of digital technologies (n = 182; arithmetic mean)

and process consulting. Participants in strategy consulting reported using nearly half as many different digital technologies as in IT consulting or organization and process consulting. Meanwhile, those in human resources consulting reported using the fewest different digital technologies.

Last, Table 5 provides an overview of the participants' opinions on five statements regarding the use of digital technologies. For each statement, the arithmetic mean was again calculated, and the verbalized scale was coded as follows:

- 1 = strongly disagree,
- 2 = somewhat disagree,
- 3 = part/part,
- 4 = somewhat agree, and
- 5 = strongly agree.

Table 5 shows that the statement, "By using digital technologies, the work–life balance in the consulting industry is improved," was only partly agreed with, with a mean value of 3.71. By contrast, the statement, "By using digital technologies, there is an increase in the efficiency of consulting," had the highest level of agreement of the five statements, with a mean of 4.3. The lowest level of agreement, with a mean of 2.82, was achieved by the statement, "By using digital technologies, the quality of the result delivered to the customer is improved." The statement, "By using digital technologies, new customers and markets can be addressed," was agreed to by significantly more participants, with a mean value of 4.25. The rating of the remaining statement, "By using digital technologies, a differentiation from competitors is made possible," had a mean value of 3.82. Based on the five mean scores, it can be concluded that the participants were more likely to agree than disagree with the statements.

Table 4. Digital Technologies per Phase of the Consulting Process (n = 186; absolute frequency, multiple answers possible)

	Acquisition	Project preparation	Problem analysis	Problem-solving	Implementation	Post-processing
Knowledge management systems	66	133	121	125	95	100
Virtual marketplace for consultants and customers	92	36	35	39	27	18
Social media	144	24	21	23	18	20
Self-service consulting	11	29	92	37	23	13
Open community and expert platforms	68	37	41	62	29	16
Mobile computing	123	139	143	140	138	131
Artificial intelligence	19	28	77	78	56	18
Document management systems	92	124	115	117	113	122
Data/process mining	16	32	102	79	35	17
Crowdsourced consulting	17	31	42	62	30	29
Cloud computing	72	118	120	118	116	100
Chats	90	136	126	124	116	112
Big data analytics	20	26	111	67	30	15
Audio/video conferencing	106	166	143	135	128	143

4.4 Impact of the COVID-19 Pandemic

In addition to the results presented thus far, participants were also asked to answer specific questions focusing on the impact of the COVID-19 pandemic.

A first question in this area was aimed at determining whether the topic of digitalization had become more important during the pandemic. Table 6 shows the results of this question. Of the 186 participants questioned, 125 stated that the topic had become significantly more important during the COVID-19 pandemic. In addition, an additional

Table 5. Opinions on the Use of Digital Technologies (n = 186; absolute frequency and arithmetic mean)

By using digital technologies…						
Statement	Strongly agree	Somewhat agree	Part/ part	Somewhat disagree	Strongly disagree	Arithmetic mean
…a differentiation from competitors is made possible. (n = 181)	64	56	31	24	6	3.82
…new customers and markets can be addressed. (n = 182)	89	60	24	8	1	4.25
…the quality of the result delivered to the customer is improved. (n = 186)	48	72	54	10	2	2.82
…there is an increase in the efficiency of consulting. (n = 186)	85	77	19	4	1	4.3
…the work–life balance in the consulting industry is improved. (n = 184)	49	65	42	23	5	3.71

48 participants selected "…has become more important." These two response options, a total of 173 out of 186 participants, i.e. 93%, indicated that the topic of digitalization had gained importance during the COVID-19 pandemic. In addition, 11 companies reported that the topic had not gained in importance, but it had already been very important prior to the pandemic within those companies. Only one participant stated that digitalization did not become more important during the pandemic and it was not very important for their company.

In order to determine the importance of the various digital technologies during the COVID-19 pandemic, the participants were asked to assess the 14 digital technologies previously presented based on their importance during the pandemic. To evaluate this

Table 6. Importance of Digitization during the COVID-19 Pandemic (n = 186)

Has the topic of digitalization become more important for your company during the COVID-19 pandemic?

	Absolute frequency	Relative frequency
Yes, the topic has become significantly more important	125	67.2%
Yes, the topic has become more important	48	25.8%
No, but the topic was already very important in our company before the COVID-19 pandemic	11	5.9%
No, the topic has not gained in importance and is not very important for our company	1	0.5%
No answer	1	0.5%

data, the verbalized response options were recoded and presented using the arithmetic mean. The following coding was selected:

- 1 = no importance,
- 2 = low importance,
- 3 = medium importance, and
- 4 = great importance.

Figure 5 shows the top-seven rated technologies (all technologies with an arithmetic mean above 3). It shows that audio and video conferencing were rated highest with an average score of 3.9 out of a possible 4.0 points. The participants also rated mobile computing with a value of 3.62, chats with a value of 3.41, and cloud computing with a value of 3.33.

A clear difference to the values already considered becomes apparent when looking at the last four technologies. With an average score of 2.35, artificial intelligence was ranked last in fourth place. The third least important technology according to the participants was data/process mining with a value of 2.34. The second least important was crowdsourced consulting with a value of 2.18. The evaluation also shows that self-service consulting was the least important technology for participants during the pandemic with a score of 2.14.

In order to evaluate the potential impact of the COVID-19 pandemic on the business model of business consultancies, participants were asked to state whether their business' model had changed as a result of the pandemic. In relation to this question, 48.1% of participants stated that it had changed "slightly" and a further 28.3% stated that the business model had changed "significantly." This means that over three-quarters of the participants noticed a change in their consulting business model. Only 18.2% had not noticed any changes to their business model as a result of the COVID-19 pandemic. In addition, 5.4% of respondents did not answer this question. When this question is broken down into the four consulting fields, a balanced picture emerges (see Fig. 6). As the consultants could assign themselves to more than one consulting field, the total

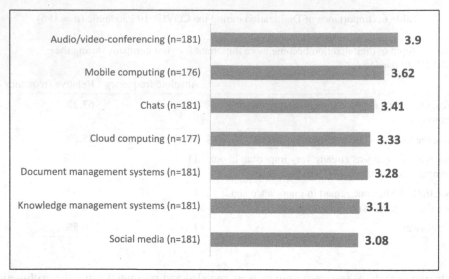

Fig. 5. Topseven of the most important digital technologies during the COVID-19 pandemic (n = 186)

number n in this evaluation is higher than 186 and, therefore, the n is given per consulting field.

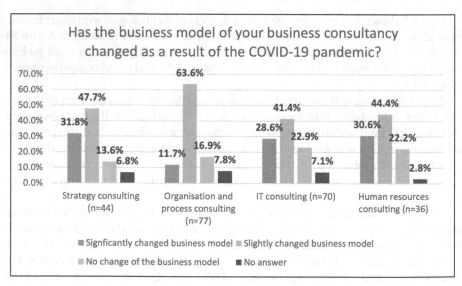

Fig. 6. Change in the business model due to the COVID-19 pandemic per consulting field

None of the four consulting fields showed a significant difference from the others. If the responses "yes, slightly" and "yes, significantly" are added together, a clear picture of the participants emerges, as on average 70% to 80% of participants in the consulting fields selected "yes" and thus identified a change in their company's business model as a result of the COVID-19 pandemic.

5 Discussion

This section will address in greater detail the question of the extent to which the use of digital technologies in business consultancies changed after the COVID-19 pandemic compared to pre-pandemic usage behavior. Pandemic-related questions from both the *Study 2023* and selected results from the *Study 2019* have been used. As *Study 2019* was conducted among 253 consultants between April and June 2019, these results provide a good basis for comparison with a pre-pandemic situation.

As Table 6 shows, 173 out of 186 participants believe that the importance of digitalization increased during the COVID-19 pandemic. In addition, eleven participants believe that the importance in this context has not increased, as the topic of digitalization was already very important in the company prior to the pandemic. These aspects are confirmed by comparing the results from Fig. 1 with the answers to the same question from *Study 2019*. In both studies, participants were asked about the importance of digitalization in their daily work. Before the pandemic, an average of 2.12% of participants answered this question with "no significance," while no one chose this option in the current study. In addition, digitalization only had "low significance" in their daily work for 13.28% of participants on average in *Study 2019*. In contrast, only 6.5% of participants chose this option in the current study. Accordingly, the average number of participants who selected "medium significance" has also changed. While 34.95% answered this question with "medium significance" in *Study 2019*, the current figure has increased to 38.7%. This is also clear with the response option "high significance." While only 49.4% of participants chose this option in *Study 2019*, 54.8% selected it in the current study.

In summary, it can be seen that digitalization in business consultancies has gained in importance due to the COVID-19 pandemic. This is also discussed similarly in the literature. Regardless of the industry sector, the study by Krcmar and Wintermann [16] shows that the Covid-19 pandemic has pushed digitalization forward in companies. The KfW study from 2020 [13] also confirms this. Our study concurs with the KfW study from 2020, that digitalization expanded in many companies during the COVID-19 pandemic and that it has become significantly more important. One reason for this may be that digitalization can be an important tool in acute crisis management.

A further analysis will examine how the use of digital technologies has changed. To this end, the results from Fig. 4 are compared with the corresponding results from *Study 2019*. This comparison is shown in Fig. 7. The intensity with which the consultants currently use digital technologies in the various consulting phases and in *Study 2019* was compared. The graph clearly shows that, with the exception of the problem-solving phase, usage has increased on average in every phase. It is apparent that the use of technology has increased above all in the acquisition, project preparation and post-processing phases. This finding was confirmed by a further comparison of the two studies. By comparing the use of the various digital technologies overall, it becomes clear that use in terms of the number of different digital technologies in each project phase increased significantly in the *Study 2023* compared to the *Study 2019*. The fact that the use of digital technologies in business consultancies in general, as well as in the various consulting phases, must and will increase; this has been called for in previous publications (e.g., [10, 24, 25, 30]). The changes that consulting companies are facing with regard to technological developments and the associated changes in client requirements make the use of a wide range of digital technologies increasingly necessary.

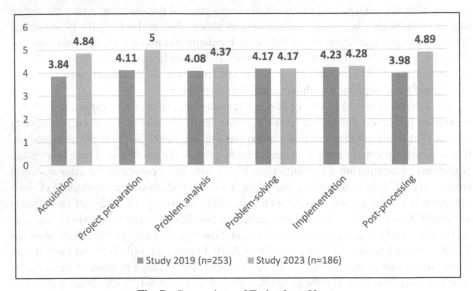

Fig. 7. Comparison of Technology Usage

In terms of specific digital technologies that have gained in importance or were perceived as important during the COVID-19 pandemic, Fig. 5 clearly shows that technologies such as audio/video conferencing, mobile computing, chats, and cloud computing were considered to be particularly important during the pandemic. However, artificial intelligence, data/process mining, crowdsourced consulting, and self-service consulting were found to be less importance. This indicates that digital technologies that enable participants to work more independently from the physical workplace were rated as the most important. Accordingly, digital technologies that are necessary for day-to-day operations were of particularly high importance during the pandemic and technologies that were not necessary for day-to-day operations tended to be classified as less important during the pandemic. However, this classification in the everyday working life of consultants is not so surprising when you consider the impact that the COVID-19 pandemic had on everyday working life in general (with physical contact restrictions, etc.). Therefore, technologies that enable greater flexibility in working, distance communication, and collaboration had to gain importance, and companies were almost forced to implement and use such technologies as quickly as possible.

This is also confirmed by the three KfW studies for 2020, 2021 and 2022 [13–15]. In these cross-industry surveys, it became apparent that digital technologies that enable communication and collaboration with customers, suppliers, and other stakeholders became significantly more important during the COVID-19 pandemic. However, to the best of our knowledge, no publication to date has taken a detailed look at a number of specific digital technologies in the way it has been done in our studies, and therefore, a comparative discussion can only be conducted at a more abstract level and not per technology itself.

To conclude the discussion of the results, we will now turn our attention to the impact of the COVID-19 pandemic on the business model. In this context, the participants were asked whether the pandemic had an impact on the business model of their business consultancy. The results indicate that more than three quarters of the consultants (76.4%) responded "yes." The general discussion that business consultancies need to adapt their business model and can achieve this through the use of digital technologies is also discussed in various publications (e.g., [3, 8, 30]). These suggest that both the consultants and employees as well as the customers of the consulting companies are placing new demands on the consulting companies, and this has been driven by the experiences of the COVID-19 pandemic.

Thus, consulting firms must ask themselves how they want to provide their services in the future so that they can meet the requirements of their customers, while simultaneously enabling their employees to work in a modern and flexible way. Consulting companies must determine how these factors can be achieved through the use of digital technologies.

6 Conclusion

As a result of our study, both research questions could be answered initially. We were able to show that the consultants have attributed a significantly higher importance to digitalization in recent years and also see this development in the future. Digitalization will continue to gain in importance for business consultancies and their respective consultants. It was also seen that the COVID-19 pandemic had an impact on the way consultants do their work and that changes in the use of certain digital technologies were necessary for this and that these changes will continue or even accelerate in the future (depending on further technological innovations).

The results of our analysis suggest that consultants currently consider digitalization to be of medium to high importance in their business consultancies. Considering their work experience, digitalization seems slightly more important for more experienced consultants than for those with less experience. In terms of the four classic fields of consulting that we considered in our study, digitalization currently seems to be most important in strategy consulting and human resources consulting. No matter the field— indeed, overall—digitalization is not perceived as being exclusively a threat (vs. an opportunity). In fact, for 60.1% of consultants, digitalization is clearly perceived as an opportunity, and for 32.8% is perceived as being at least somewhat of an opportunity. Therefore, digitalization is seen in an almost entirely positive light by consultants. In addition, consultants perceive an opportunity to increase efficiency in the consulting process by using digital technologies and believe that the technologies will allow new markets and customers to be reached.

From the consultants' perspective, traditional technologies such as audio/video conferencing, mobile computing, and cloud computing, are currently the most important for their business needs. By contrast, analytical tools are used only sporadically but increasingly more often in larger companies. Beyond that, technologies such as self-service consulting, virtual marketplaces for customers and consultants, and crowdsourced consulting are rarely used. According to the participants, established technologies will continue to play the most important role in their business consultancies in the next five years. Nevertheless, they also expect the use of analytical tools and social media to increase in importance. From their perspective, digital technologies in general will play an important part in developing future business consultancies, and their use stands to have a major impact on the efficient delivery of effective consulting services in the future.

To summarize, business consultancies clearly see the benefits of digitalization and of using digital technologies. Nevertheless, they continue to rely on more established technologies. However, in order to evolve and meet future requirements in an active and non-reactive manner, business consultancies should also turn to other digital technologies that go beyond audio and video conferencing, mobile computing, and cloud computing. This is especially evident considering the potential impact of widely discussed generative AI tools such as ChatGPT.

This is where future research ties in. Future research needs to produce a more detailed, diversified view of the use of different digital technologies. On that count, qualitative studies should be conducted in individual fields of consulting and with more specific consideration of company size, especially the size of the companies using the consulting service, to further pinpoint the importance of digital technologies for the consulting process in general and for its respective phases. Future research should also analyze the use of digital technologies with reference to the different types of consulting projects, including logistics projects, IT/digitalization projects, and human resources projects, in order to identify and highlight differences. Finally, we recommend investigating barriers to and challenges in using digital technologies in business consultancies and how these can be minimized.

As most empirical studies, ours was limited in multiple ways. Due to our approach, our results possess limited statistical generalizability. However, the method applied allowed us to identify important details and obtain initial insights into the experience of business consultants, which was the chief focus of our study. Another limitation was that the participants' origins were limited to German business consultancies. Since German-specific trends could have influenced the results, the results reflect the situation in one country only.

References

1. Barchewitz, C., Armbrüster, T.: Unternehmensberatung - Marktmechanismen, Marketing, Auftragsakquisition. Deutscher Universitätsverlag, Wiesbaden (2004). https://doi.org/10.1007/978-3-322-81779-2
2. BDU e. V.: Facts & Figures zum Beratungsmarkt 2021. BDU - German Association of Management Consultancies, Bonn (2021). https://www.bdu.de/media/355573/facts-figures-vorjahr.pdf
3. Bensberg, F., Buscher, G., Czarnecki, C.: Digital transformation and IT topics in the consulting industry: a labor market perspective. In: Nissen, V. (ed.) Advances in Consulting Research. CMS, pp. 341–357. Springer, Cham (2019). https://doi.org/10.1007/978-3-319-95999-3_16
4. Bley, K., Leyh, C., Schäffer, T.: Digitization of German enterprises in the production sector: do they know how "digitized" they are? In: Proceedings of the 22nd Americas Conference on Information Systems (AMCIS 2016) (2016)

5. Bode, M., Daneva, M., Van Sinderen, M.J.: Characterising the digital transformation of IT consulting services–results from a systematic mapping study. IET Softw. 16(5), 455–477 (2022). https://doi.org/10.1049/sfw2.12068

6. Bodenstein, R.: Unternehmensberatung – Typologie, Felder und Rollen. In: Bodenstein, R., Ennsfellner, I.A., Herget, J. (eds.) Exzellenz in der Unternehmensberatung, pp. 19–39. Springer, Wiesbaden (2022). https://doi.org/10.1007/978-3-658-34589-1_2

7. Bodenstein, R., Herget, J.: Consulting Governance: Strukturen, Prozesse und Regeln für erfolgreiche Beratungsprojekte. Springer, Heidelberg (2022). https://doi.org/10.1007/978-3-662-65299-2

8. Crişan, E.L., Stanca, L.: The digital transformation of management consulting companies: a qualitative comparative analysis of Romanian industry. Inf. Syst. E-Bus Manage. 19(4), 1143–1173 (2021). https://doi.org/10.1007/s10257-021-00536-1

9. Curuksu, J.D.: Analysis of the Management Consulting Industry. In: Curuksu, J.D. (ed.) Data Driven. MP, pp. 1–16. Springer, Cham (2018). https://doi.org/10.1007/978-3-319-70229-2_1

10. Deelmann, T.: Does digitization matter? reflections on a possible transformation of the consulting business. In: Nissen, V. (ed.) Digital Transformation of the Consulting Industry. PI, pp. 75–99. Springer, Cham (2018). https://doi.org/10.1007/978-3-319-70491-3_3

11. Goudz, A., Erdogan, S.: Digitalisierung in der Corona-Krise: Auswahl und Einsatz von innovativen Technologien für die Logistik. Springer Fachmedien, Wiesbaden (2021). https://doi.org/10.1007/978-3-658-33419-2

12. Kawohl, J.M., Waubke, R., Höselbarth: Digitale Transformation von Unternehmensberatungen – wie Consulting sich verändern wird. (2017). http://www.peoplebrand.de/img/studie_transformation-von-unternehmensberatungen.pdf

13. KfW Research: KfW-Digitalisierungsbericht Mittelstand 2020. KfW Bankengruppe, Frankfurt a. M (2021). https://www.kfw.de/PDF/Download-Center/Konzernthemen/Research/PDF-Dokumente-Digitalisierungsbericht-Mittelstand/KfW-Digitalisierungsbericht-2020.pdf

14. KfW Research: KfW-Digitalisierungsbericht Mittelstand 2021. KfW Bankengruppe, Frankfurt a. M. (2022). https://www.kfw.de/PDF/Download-Center/Konzernthemen/Research/PDF-Dokumente-Digitalisierungsbericht-Mittelstand/KfW-Digitalisierungsbericht-2021.pdf

15. KfW Research: KfW-Digitalisierungsbericht Mittelstand 2022. KfW Bankengruppe, Frankfurt a. M. (2023). https://www.kfw.de/PDF/Download-Center/Konzernthemen/Research/PDF-Dokumente Digitalisierungsbericht-Mittelstand/KfW-Digitalisierungsbericht-2022.pdf

16. Krcmar, H., Wintermann, O.: Studie zu den Auswirkungen der Corona-Pandemie in gesellschaftlicher, wirtschaftlicher und technologischer Hinsicht. In: Oswald, G., Saueressig, T., Krcmar, H. (eds.) Digitale Transformation, pp. 59–79. Springer Fachmedien, Wiesbaden (2022). https://doi.org/10.1007/978-3-658-37571-3_5

17. Leyh, C., Schäffer, T., Bley, K., Forstenhäusler, S.: Assessing the IT and software landscapes of industry 4.0-enterprises: the maturity model SIMMI 4.0. In: Ziemba, E. (ed.) AITM/ISM -2016. LNBIP, vol. 277, pp. 103–119. Springer, Cham (2017). https://doi.org/10.1007/978-3-319-53076-5_6

18. Leyh, C., Bley, K., Ott, M.: Chancen und Risiken der Digitalisierung – Befragungen ausgewählter KMU. In: Hofmann, J. (ed.) Arbeit 4.0 – Digitalisierung, IT und Arbeit, pp. 29–51. Springer Fachmedien, Wiesbaden (2018). https://doi.org/10.1007/978-3-658-21359-6_3

19. Leyh, C., Köppel, K., Neuschl, S., Pentrack, M.: Critical success factors for digitalization projects. In: Proceedings of the 16th Conference on Computer Science and Intelligence Systems (FedCSIS 2021), pp. 427–436 (2021). https://doi.org/10.15439/2021F122

20. Leyh, C., Lange, M., Lorenz, A.: The use of digital technologies in German business consultancies. In: Proceedings of the 18th Conference on Computer Science and Intelligence Systems (FedCSIS 2023), pp. 151–160 (2023). https://doi.org/10.15439/2023F7831
21. Lippold, D.: Grundlagen der Unternehmensberatung. Springer Fachmedien, Wiesbaden (2016). https://doi.org/10.1007/978-3-658-12882-1
22. Luban, K., Hänggi, R., Bernard, G.: Einleitung. In: Luban, K., Hänggi, R. (eds.) Erfolgreiche Unternehmensführung durch Resilienzmanagement, pp. 1–14. Springer, Heidelberg (2022). https://doi.org/10.1007/978-3-662-64023-4_1
23. Mathrani, S., Mathrani, A., Viehland, D.: Using enterprise systems to realize digital business strategies. J. Enterp. Inf. Manag. 26(4), 363–386 (2013). https://doi.org/10.1108/JEIM-01-2012-0003
24. Nissen, V., Füßl, A., Werth, D., Gugler, K., Neu, C.: On the current state of digital transformation in the German market for business consulting. In: Nissen, V. (ed.) Advances in Consulting Research. CMS, pp. 317–339. Springer, Cham (2019). https://doi.org/10.1007/978-3-319-95999-3_15
25. Nissen, V., Seifert, H.: Digital transformation in business consulting—status quo in Germany. In: Nissen, V. (ed.) Digital Transformation of the Consulting Industry. PI, pp. 153–190. Springer, Cham (2018). https://doi.org/10.1007/978-3-319-70491-3_7
26. Pagani, M.: Digital business strategy and value creation: framing the dynamic cycle of control points. MIS Q. 37 (2), 617–632 (2013). https://doi.org/10.25300/MISQ/2013/37.2.13
27. Scheer, A.-W., Köppen, A.: Entwicklungen nachvollziehen und antizipieren: Der Wandel als ständige Herausforderung für die Beratung. In: Scheer, A.-W., Köppen, A. (eds). Consulting: Wissen für die Strategie-, Prozess- und IT-Beratung, pp. 5–14. Springer, Berlin, Heidelberg (2000). https://doi.org/10.1007/978-3-642-98079-4_2
28. Seifert, H.: Virtualisierung von Beratungsleistungen: Grundlagen der digitalen Transformation in der Unternehmensberatung. Dissertation. Technische Universität Ilmenau, Ilmenau (2017)
29. Strack, R., Carrasco, M., Kolo, P., Nouri, N., Priddis, M., George, R.: The Future of Jobs in the Era of AI (2021). https://www.bcg.com/publications/2021/impact-of-new-technologies-on-jobs
30. Treichler, C.: Consulting industry and market trends: a two-sided view. In: Nissen, V. (ed.) Advances in Consulting Research. CMS, pp. 253–272. Springer, Cham (2019). https://doi.org/10.1007/978-3-319-95999-3_12

Integrating Non-financial Data into a Creative Accounting Detection Model: A Study in the Saudi Arabian Context

Maysoon Bineid[1,3](✉) ⓘ, Anastasia Khanina[2] ⓘ, Natalia Beloff[3] ⓘ,
and Martin White[3] ⓘ

[1] University of Jeddah, Jeddah 23218, Saudi Arabia
m.bineid@sussex.ac.uk
[2] University of Brighton, Brighton BN2 4NU, UK
[3] University of Sussex, Brighton, Falmer BN1 9RH, UK

Abstract. Global financial scandals have demonstrated the harmful impact of creative accounting, a practice in which managers creatively manipulate financial reports to conceal a company's performance and influence stakeholders' decision-making. Studies showed that Saudi-listed companies engage in creative accounting when preparing financial statements. However, big data analytics has found practical applications in auditing, and recently, the use of Deep Learning in financial statement fraud detection has yielded remarkably accurate results. Therefore, our research aims to train a hybrid learning Creative Accounting Detecting Model (CADM) proposed by [18]. This study seeks validation for non-financial data to be used in CADM training. Among the chosen factors that represent non-financial data, the reputation of the external auditor is the most influential factor in the credibility of information extracted from financial statements. The analysis also revealed that the accounting subject showing the most variability in interpretation within the Saudi business environment is the disclosure of management compensations. Additionally, many innovative accounting systems are still awaiting adoption in Saudi Arabia despite the government's implementation of advanced interconnected systems. Lastly, a consensus was reached on most of the recommended data sources, particularly those obtained from Saudi authorities. Despite providing the foundation for the non-financial data integration phase, the results will provide insights into the reliability and transparency of financial statements of Saudi-listed companies. It can enhance multiple stakeholders' decisions and inform Saudi regulators about areas requiring their attention in financial reporting. However, this study is limited by the sample size and the methods employed in analysing the results.

Keywords: Creative Accounting · Big Data · Deep Learning

1 Introduction

Creative accounting (CA) practices have negatively affected the quality of financial reporting and disturbed trust in the information extracted from financial statements (FS). While several attempts have been made in the literature to detect and predict financial

E. Ziemba et al. (Eds.): FedCSIS-ITBS 2023/ISM 2023, LNBIP 504, pp. 71–92, 2024.
https://doi.org/10.1007/978-3-031-61657-0_4

statement fraud (FSF), CA practices that operate within the boundaries of International Financial Reporting Standards (IFRS) are still challenging to detect. This is due to the enigmatic nature of the practice, which makes it almost impossible to detect using traditional auditing techniques, although it has the same severe consequences as FSF [41].

Despite the positive impression of the name, CA has been considered the primary cause behind many financial scandals, such as Enron and WorldCom in the U.S. and Parmalat, Royal Ahold, and Vivendi Universal in Europe [14, 16, 24, 31, 48, 55]. These incidents confirm that account manipulation is designed to gain a temporary benefit, eventually leading to financial scandals and substantial losses. CA can exceed the regulations and become fraudulent, yet it is easier to detect in this case. The practice we investigate is considered legal within IFRS but deviates from its goal and spirit as it operates in the grey area between legitimacy (in the context of IFRS) and fraud. In other words, fraudulent creative accounting is not included in the scope of our research.

In Saudi Arabia (SA), cases of CA exist, and according to the literature, the same accounting techniques are employed for similar reasons. Considering the proposition that less efficient markets tend to have greater tolerance to manipulations, the weak-form efficiency of the Saudi stock market Tadawul, as proved by [15], indicates the high possibility of manipulations. Many studies have investigated the practice in the region, but none include real-time case studies [4, 9, 13, 17]. The results of these studies agreed that financial statements in SA do not represent the true and fair position of a company, although being approved by auditing procedures. Other studies outside the region contributed statistical models (e.g., accrual-based detection models); however, these models lack accuracy and require non-public, inaccessible, and time-consuming financial data to reach [1].

On the other hand, big data analytics and AI models are currently employed in different business sectors, providing high-accuracy results. Many models and techniques have been developed and validated to replace or supplement traditional accounting and auditing procedures [58]. In our context, the literature is rich with significant contributions in FSF detection using data mining and machine learning (ML) [50, 53]. The availability of data types like financial data (FIN) and non-financial data (N-FIN) and the possibility of including these data types in advanced intelligent models motivated researchers to develop many applications that meet business needs. One successful example is the employment of Deep Learning (DL) in training models that can learn from time-series datasets to predict future insights [30, 49, 50] or to detect specific patterns in data.

However, the capabilities of ML models in big data motivate us to add a new approach to overcome information misrepresentation in financial reports and enhance financial reporting quality. As we have previously proposed a framework for our big data model CADM [18], our current focus is defining inputs for the model and assessing their feasibility in the Saudi context. In particular, this paper constitutes a phase of our ongoing research to detect CA in Saudi-listed companies by developing a deep-learning model. In this phase, we aim to address N-FIN data that can be utilised in training our model by surveying business professionals and academics in SA. The insights gathered through this survey are crucial for informing the training process of our model and advancing our understanding of the state of financial reporting practices in SA.

The rest of this paper will provide a theoretical background on CA in a general context and with a specific focus on the Saudi context. It also discusses the employment of Big Data in accounting manipulation research. The third section will outline this study's objectives, research questions, and the methodology to address them effectively. The survey analysis follows, followed by the discussion of the findings and answers to the research question. Finally, the concluding section will demonstrate the significant contributions of this research and its limitations.

2   Research Background

CA is a term to describe the accounting procedures employed to present an enhanced image of a company that may mislead users [7]. 'creative' means using new and innovative ways of preparing accounts [31] to make the company more attractive to stakeholders without necessarily engaging in fraud. The literature has no particular definition for the practice [39]. Yet the most recent definition by [31] described these practices as follows:" *They are the methods which deviate from the rules and regulations, it is an excessive complication and use of innovative ways to visualise income, assets, and liabilities, it is an innovative and aggressive way of reporting financial statements, it is a systematic misrepresentation of the true and fair financial statements.*" However, investigations in the literature often focus on Earnings Management (EM), which describes managing reported earnings to make them higher or more consistent than they might be under specific accounting standards. In our perspective, EM is a common form of CA, and findings from EM research are considered in this study. Any accounting procedure meant to present non-realistic financial information and affect financial reporting quality is considered CA.

Nevertheless, there is often ambiguity regarding the classification of CA as fraudulent or non-fraudulent. Some studies consider CA as FSF, while others identify the thin line between them [41]. Since we consider the probability of CA in FSs as our prime dependent variable, it is logical to represent our perspective regarding the categorisation of it. As shown in Fig. 1, IFRS-compliant has two levels of quality; the white area represents fair financial reporting, where FRs have sustainable returns and high-quality earnings, and it occupies a relatively limited space in the IFRS-compliant context. The following quality level in the IFRS complaint area, often denoted as the "grey area", constitutes the scope of our research, where FSs involve biased choices and unsustainable low-quality earnings (i.e., EM). The lowest and most concerning level of quality describes non-compliant accounting, including occasional fictitious transactions, and is illustrated here in red. In particular, we argue that CA practices vary between the two areas, yet they deviate from the goals of IFRS even if they are still within its boundaries.

2.1   The Case of Saudi Arabia

Based on the 2022 ACEF Occupational Fraud Report [3], SA was ranked second in the Middle East for the highest number of occupational fraud cases, as shown in Table 1. A comparison between SA, the UAE, and other countries on the list reveals a notable variance, suggesting either substantially higher levels of fraud activity in UAE and

SA relative to other countries or the fact that these countries probably employ more advanced detection procedures, leading to a relatively higher number of reported cases. Consequently, we aim to enhance our ability to identify similar cases at early stages. The successful implementation of our detection model could contribute to early detection practices and potentially be adopted by a broader range of countries.

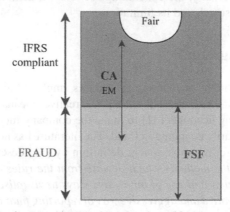

Fig. 1. CA and FSF, adopted and modified from [18]

Table 1. Financial Statement Fraud cases in the Middle East, as in the ACEF 2022 report

Variable	No. of cases	%	Variable	No. of cases	%
Algeria	1	0.76%	Oman	4	3.03%
Bahrain	3	2.27%	Qatar	7	5.30%
Egypt	8	6.06%	Saudi Arabia	29	21.97%
Iraq	1	0.76%	Tunisia	2	1.52%
Jordan	4	3.03%	United Arab Emirates	60	45.45%
Kuwait	8	6.06%	Yaman	2	1.52%
Lebanon	3	2.27%			

In fact, many studies investigated the problem in Saudi-listed companies. Although most of these studies were quantitative [16], some were empirical papers focused on the business type [4, 8] or the business size [9], applying a linear detection model with successful results. Moreover, accounting professionals have been using ML models, especially in some audit procedures employed in accounting firms.

Recently, SA has gone through several steps of economic transformation that have influenced the governing materials of accounting. An instance of these steps is joining the World Trade Organization (WTO) and adopting the International Financial Reporting Standards (IFRS) [45]. In addition, during the last 20 years, the Kingdom has established new institutions to regulate businesses and control the Saudi stock market. Some of these institutions were specifically designed to fulfil an essential Saudi vision for the future: Vision 2030[1] [42]. An instance of these institutions is the Saudi Data and Artificial Intelligence Authority (SADAIA), which has provided many valuable services and facilities for market and academic research. It is a helpful attempt to support the effort to improve financial reporting and leverage the Saudi business environment with innovative technologies through adequate investment in the country's prospects.

2.2 Big Data to Limit Creative Accounting

Recognising CA practices as a crime is an extensively debated argument [12, 29, 31, 55]. Therefore, big data analytics studies were limited to FSF detection [20, 34, 35, 37, 40, 51, 54, 57] and FSF prediction models [47, 49]. Earlier FSF detection models, like the M-score model [29], were mainly quantitative based on numerical FIN data. In contrast, recent models are qualitative intelligent models (i.e., ML models) that have proved to outperform the earlier models [5, 25, 36, 38]. As revealed by [24], fraud detection has the highest percentage (39.4%) of published studies in the Journal of Emerging Technologies in Accounting JETA.

Since the speed of uncovering FSF can limit its consequences [24], the need to find faster and more accurate models is becoming essential. Unfortunately, the literature has no research on detecting CA as an IFSR practice using big data analytics as far as this study. Due to the ambiguous nature of the practice and the sophisticated historical actions involved, no specific financial ratios or traditional mathematical model can accurately detect it. However, FSF prediction scenarios can be considered in our proposal for many reasons. First, FSF prediction models use historical FSs (i.e., time-series dataset) labelled as fraudulent to learn from and reflect which variables can be used to classify the case. This can help predict future fraud or financial distress. Presuming that CA practices eventually lead to FSF (e.g., Enron started using SPEs legally, then it became 'increasingly doubtful' over time [41]), CA detection has similar domain characteristics of predicting FSF. It can be adapted to detect further activities that do not exceed IFRS limits. Another reason is that both procedures aim to prevent future fraud and provide alerting flags that do not usually appear to stakeholders in their usual financial information reviews.

The accounting literature is rich with innovative analytical models that have the potential to enrich the accounting environment, develop accounting regulations and reduce the profession's defects [19]. The JETA has 51.5% of its publications between 2005 and 2015 on data analytics [43]. Moreover, 13% of published research on emerging technologies in the accounting domain was about big data analytics [21]. Although studies address the limitation in the literature regarding the use of big data in accounting [23, 32], there is a consensus that ML algorithms in big data used in accounting research are growing remarkably [10], providing new services to the business environment that were never possible before. Further, standardising accounting data through new unified formats like XBRL and secure data structures like Blockchain added promising opportunities for efficient research and improved accounting outcomes.

By professional means, accounting and auditing embrace big data analytics in different procedures. The Big 4 are investing heavily in data analytics and artificial intelligence [11] and promoting embracing big data technologies. For instance, the recent

---

[1] https://www.vision2030.gov.sa/.

adaptation of the *Halo* online platform by *PwC* implemented the inclusion of whole population analysis, which outperforms the sampling techniques that are usually used in auditing procedures along with many recalculations and risk assessment tools (e.g., journal entry testing and general ledger analysis) that become possible by its enhanced connectivity and high server-based processing capabilities. Moreover, regulatory agencies' results have been enhanced by incorporating non-financial data as a supplement to the traditional financial data in their systems (e.g., the UK government's tax authority uses different sources of data from the internet, social media, land registry records, international tax authorities, and banks [33]).

The research on applying big data in accounting, summarised in Table 2, is more focused on auditing. The analytical nature of auditing procedures made it more likely to benefit from these applications. For instance, DL models were used in auditing research, giving insightful results because they could learn from massive amounts of data. However, DL models can be used parallelly with other ML models to build a model with improved capabilities, such as in hybrid learning (HL). They can also be combined, and the output of one model is the input for the second, called Ensembled Learning (EL), as in [5, 49].

CADM is not intended to definitively ascertain whether a particular FS was prepared using CA, as no single model can. Detecting CA typically entails a combination of models and expert judgment. Auditors, analysts, and researchers employ these models as integral components of a comprehensive evaluation of a company's financial statements. Therefore, the results we expect from CADM are probabilities and red flags regarding areas necessitating further investigation. However, CADM training will involve learning patterns and structures that reside in data in our dataset and finding relations in data. It requires an Artificial Neural Network (ANN) model that can handle sequential interconnected data, which justifies our proposed use of the Long Short-Term Memory (LSTM).

LSTM is a type of ANN that can handle time-series datasets and include previous states in the calculation. It is commonly used in DL application research in finance, like stock price predictions and portfolio management [44]. It can remember short-term and long-term values, which makes it helpful in learning from historical patterns [46]. Since CA techniques evolve, the probability of detecting them increases significantly when considering changes over time.

3   Research Methodology

Previous studies have investigated internal and external attributes that may have incentivised managers to engage in CA. These incentives can be categorised into incentives related to internal affairs, incentives related to the stock market, and incentives related to third-party decisions [18]. While some of these incentives have been empirically tested in the literature, these studies were limited and more focused on FSF [2]. Therefore, we contribute to the literature by examining the correlation between these incentives and the legal forms of CA. For that, hypothesis development and research questions were built on the assumption that the probability of a legal form of CA in a company's FSs is correlated to a defined set of internal and external attributes associated with that company. This section demonstrates the tool used to test our hypothesis and outlines the research questions we seek to answer.

Table 2. Big Data in FSF Research

Method	Model	Dataset/sources	Objective	Study	Year
Data Mining	LR, DT NN (BP)	Data related to the fraud triangle (incentive, opportunity, attitude)	Detecting FSF	37	2015
	DT, SVM, K-NN, RS	FSs	Predict audit opinion	50	2021
ML	BERT	TXT	Analysis of AD	51	2021
	GLRT	Audio data (Conference calls)	Detecting FSF	57	2015
Hybrid ML	MLP, PNN	ARs, FRs, RRs, FRs,	Predict audit opinion	27	2016
	MLogit, SVM, BN, CSL	FS, Market Variables, and Governance measures	Detect FSF	35	2016
	Meta-Learning (SG + AL)	FS + context-based data	Detect FSF	1	2012
	BOW + SVM	FS + TXT	Detect FSF	30	2010
	BOW + HAN	FIN + TXT	Detect FSF	25	2020
Ensemble ML	XGBoost	FS	Detect FSF	5	2023
	ADABoost, XGBoost, CUSBoosr, RUSBoost	FS	Predict FSF	49	2023
Hybrid DL	RNN, CNN, LSTM, GRU	Selected financial features	Detecting FSF	20	2023
	RNN	FIN + non-FIN features	Detecting FSF	34	2021
	NN	FS	Detection of accrued EM	36	2023

LR: Logistic Regression, **DT**: Decision Trees, **BOW**: Bag Of Words, **EM**: Earning Management, **FR**: Financial Reports, **AR**: Auditor's Report, **RR**: Regulatory Report, **FS**: Financial Statement, **NN**: Neural Networks, **RNN**: Recurrent Neural Network, **CNN**: Convolutional Neural Network, **GRU**: Gate Recurrent Unit, **LSTM**: Long Short-Term Memory, **HAN**: Hierarchical Attention Network, **SG**: Stack Generalization, **AL**: Adaptive Learning, **BERT**: Bidirectional Encoder Representation from Transformation, **AD**: Accounting Disclosure, **SVM**: Support Vector Machine, **K-NN**: K-Nearest Neighbor, **RS**: Rough Sets, **MLogit**: Multinomial Logistic Regression, **BN**: Bayesian Network, **CSL**: Cost-Sensitive Learning.

3.1 Hypothesis Development

This paper explores the primary factors that significantly influence the probability of CA in FSs and the possible data sources to consider in the dataset integration phase. The probability of CA is presented in our context by the level of credibility of information extracted from FSs and the variability of interpretations of the accounting subjects presented in FSs. In addition, the data sources are determined by exploring the level of technology in the business environment and the effectiveness of some suggested data sources. The study is designed to determine which variables and data sources to include in building the proposed CADM. To achieve these objectives, we build on the findings in the literature to hypothesise that a set of internal and external attributes influence the credibility of information extracted from FSs (i.e., probability of CA). Accordingly, we seek answers to the research questions in the following section.

3.2 Research Questions

In the Saudi context, findings from [2] indicate that entities with higher measures of board attributes, corporate governance attributes, external auditor reputation, government ownership, and institutional ownership tend to disclose substantially more than those with lower measures. Other studies presented that the frequency of board meetings improves the quality of accruals [26]. In addition, influential variables, such as regulations, market attributes, technological advancements, and environmental circumstances, are also consequential [15]. Therefore, we aim to collect professional perspectives regarding these factors, leading to answer the following research question:

Q1: Which of the suggested factors influences the credibility of information extracted from FSs in SA?

Another issue addressed in our model building is variability between market participants in interpreting accounting-related items. It has been proved that disclosures of Saudi-listed companies are based on inconsistent interpretations of accounting subjects [17, 22]. Considering the effects of this variability on the credibility of information extracted from FSs, we aim to assess the level of variabilities according to business professionals and academics in SA, and we ask the following question:

Q2: How variable are the interpretations of our set of accounting subjects in the disclosures of Saudi-listed companies?

A further concern that we should examine is the technological level adopted by companies in SA. Business practitioners' views on utilising useful technologies in the business context can improve our understanding of the technological status in SA. In addition, we consider the importance of adopting advanced technologies to enhance the quality of financial reporting [56] and recognise the need to assess these technologies in Saudi companies to evaluate the data integration process; this paper poses the following question:

Q3: How practical is adopting new technologies that enable advanced analytical services in the Saudi business environment?

Finally, although the FSs and reports of Saudi-listed companies are accessible through various portals in standardised formats, integrating them with the proposed N-FIN data can be challenging. The suggested N-FIN dataset varies in formats, accessibility, and presentation methods. Therefore, we aim to identify the most useful sources of data by asking the following:

Q4: What are the most critical data sources to consider in our model building?

3.3 Population and Survey Instrument

To explore the viewpoints of Saudi professionals, we decided to participate broadly in exploring different perspectives and aligning them with our research objectives. Invitations were sent randomly to CEOs, managers, accountants, auditors, consultants, and researchers actively engaged in the Saudi market. The background diversity of our sample has added to the confidence level, although the sample size was relatively small. However, the survey instrument was a web-based questionnaire implemented in Arabic and English, as some business professionals in SA were non-Arabic speakers. The questionnaire comprised four main parts, as shown in Fig. 2. Part 1 was designed to collect demographic information such as professional achievements, years of experience, and qualifications. Parts 2, 3, 4, and 5 are explained in the findings section.

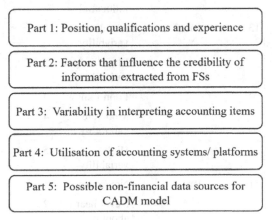

Part 1: Position, qualifications and experience

Part 2: Factors that influence the credibility of information extracted from FSs

Part 3: Variability in interpreting accounting items

Part 4: Utilisation of accounting systems/ platforms

Part 5: Possible non-financial data sources for CADM model

Fig. 2. Survey structure

3.4 Variables

We selected variables from prior FSF studies to investigate their inclusion in our model. Researchers have tested many FIN features, such as indices and financial ratios, and N-FIN features, such as board attributes, market attributes, governance measures, economic changes, and regulation changes. As shown in Table 3 Study variables, quantitative interpretation, and FIN and N-FIN features are stored in three groups: internal attributes, external attributes, and accounting items. Each variable group is assigned to a specific question in the survey for its value. We aim to examine the correlation between these independent variables and three dependent variables that represent the probability of CA, as explained in Fig. 3. Since a limited number of values is essential for any AI model to be accurate [27], this study attempts to limit the range of variables by excluding the variables with insignificant correlations. The survey also yielded two additional issues: accounting software/platform and data sources. The accounting software is derived from questions in part 4 and will be analysed to address Q3 in this paper. Similarly, adopted technologies are obtained from questions in part 5 and will be examined to answer Q4.

Table 3. Study variables and quantitative interpretation

Variable group	No. of Variables	Questions	Likert-scale description	Likert-scale	Likert-scale intervals
Internal attributes	5	Part 2 Qs: 2.3,2.5, 2.7, 2.8, 2.9	Definitely no influence	1	1–1.79
			Possibly no influence	2	1.80–2.59
			I don't know	3	2.60–3.39
External attributes	6	Qs: 2.1, 2.2, 2.4, 2.6, 2.10, 2.11	Probably influential	4	3.40–4.19
			Definitely influential	5	4.20–5
Accounting items	13	Part 3	Absolutely no variability	1	1–1.79
			Most likely no variability	2	1.80–2.59
			I don't know	3	2.60–3.39
			Moderate variability	4	3.40–4.19
			High variability	5	4.20–5
Accounting software/platforms	21	Part 4	Not in use	1	1–1.66
			Never heard about it	2	1.67–2.33
			In use	3	2.34–3
Data sources	18	Part 5	Totally not useful	1	1–1.79
			Not useful	2	1.80–2.59
			I don't know	3	2.60–3.39
			Useful	4	3.40–4.19
			Extremely useful	5	4.20–5

4   Findings

Parts 2, 3, 4, and 5 constitute the dimensions of this survey; each has 11, 13, 21, and 18 statements, respectively. The survey was conducted in December 2023, and responses were received promptly. A total of 48 responses were obtained from the 60 invitations sent to professionals and academics in Riyadh, Jeddah, and Dammam. We also received responses from Saudi researchers in the UK. However, the participant pool comprised individuals with professional roles as Accountants, Bankers, External Auditors, Consultants, and Researchers Fig. 4. Nonetheless, 12 responses were excluded due to a comparatively low completion rate.

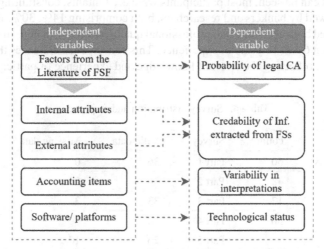

Fig. 3. Independent and dependent variables

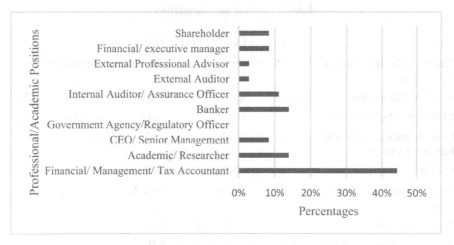

Fig. 4. Positions in the sample

The approach adopted to handle the missing values was part-related, as shown in Table 4. Recognizing the potential impact of missing data on the reliability of our analysis, we chose to analyse each survey question separately. This strategy allowed us to maximise the available responses for each question while mitigating the potential bias introduced by missing values.

4.1 Results and Analysis

The response values were characterised by descriptive statistics (mean, standard deviation, variance and frequencies), interpreted according to the stated intervals and presented in Table 5. As can be seen, most participants were accountants, constituting 44% of the sample, followed by bankers and researchers, both comprising 14%. 30% of the participants possessed both academic and professional qualifications, with 36% of respondents having between 6 and 10 years of experience. This convergence enhances the reliability of the findings, reflecting the relevant knowledge and experience of participants.

Table 4. Survey distribution and responses

Distribution	count	Survey	Valid data	Missing data	Total
Total invitations	60	Part 1	36	0	36
Responses	48	Part 2	36	0	36
Excluded	12	Part 3	33	3	36
Included	36	Part 4	28	8	36
		Part 5	26	10	36

Table 5. Population characteristics

Factor	Freq.	Exp.	Freq.	Qualification	Freq.
Financial/Management/Tax Accountant	16	None	3	Secondary or equivalent	16
Academic/Researcher	5	<1	7	Bachelor or equivalent	15
CEO/Senior Management	3	1–5	7	Master's or equivalent	4
Government Agency/Regulatory Institution Officer	0	6–10	12	PhD or equivalent	1
Banker	5	11–20	6	SOCPA	5
Internal Auditor/Assurance Officer	4	21–30	0	ACCA	1
External Auditor	1	>30	1	CIA	1
External Professional Advisor	1			CIPA	2
Financial/executive manager	3			CPFP	1
				CMA	1

Part 2 of the survey addressed two sets of variables: internal and external factors influencing the credibility of information extracted from FSs and reports. Findings revealed that the reputation of the external auditor exerted the most substantial influence, followed by the historical financial performance of the company and the adopted accounting standards, as shown in Table 6. Furthermore, the standard deviation for these three factors was minimal, suggesting a narrow dispersion of responses.

Conversely, participants perceived the company's classification in the business sector as having the least significant influence on the credibility of information extracted from its FSs. The remaining proposed factors exhibit comparable means, confirming their influence as well. However, participants maintained a neutral position regarding the impact of a company's presence on social media.

The second category of variables under consideration, represented in Part 3, involves a collection of accounting items that could vary in interpretation. As seen in Table 7, participants were offered to assess the variability in interpreting eight accounting items from FSs and five additional accounting items recognised in the literature as subjects in CA practices.

The analysis revealed that management compensation is the only item with varied interpretations from the participants' perspectives. Other elements on the list share similar means but possess a high standard deviation, indicating significant differences in the opinions gathered. Moreover, the "Other" free text response option yielded disclosures of future risk, future liabilities, sector performance, and investments as items with variability in interpretation.

Part 4 of the survey investigates the prevalent technologies employed in the Saudi business environment. To achieve this, we compiled a list of the most widely used accounting software, selecting examples that have demonstrated widespread utility. Participants were then queried regarding using the specified software or platforms, as presented in Table 8. As anticipated, Microsoft, SAS, and Oracle software were reported to be used alongside AuditBoard, AuditDesktop, and Workiva. However, notable findings emerged in the responses related to Tableau, IDEA, and ACL Analytics, where participants indicated a lack of familiarity. Additionally, three participants included SAP as commonly used software in the free text field "other", highlighting its extensive functionalities beyond those outlined in the list, positioning it more as a management system than conventional accounting software.

The last area of our survey investigates the potential data sources for obtaining evidence during the audit of FSs. Identifying suitable data sources is crucial to train our model. We proposed various data sources, drawing on those previously mentioned in the literature on FSF and those recommended by the Saudi Organization for Certified Public Accountants (SOCPA) [52]. The usability of these sources, as perceived by various business professionals, is presented in Table 9. The calculated means highlight variations in perspectives, as indicated by the substantial standard deviation. This discrepancy is understandable given the significance of professional experience, especially considering that most participants were accountants.

Nonetheless, the findings indicate a high level of usability for the majority of the suggested sources. There is robust support for incorporating data from various regulatory bodies such as ZATCA and the reports and figures published by these authorities. Additionally, participants strongly believe in the utility of security monitoring data (e.g., log files) and inventory management data (e.g., RFID) for acquiring additional information to assess audit procedures. However, the suggestion of using social media posts as

Table 6. Factors that influence the credibility of information extracted from FSs in SA

Factor	Mean	Std. deviation	Variance	Level
The business sector/industry	3.53	1.404	1.971	Probably influential
The business type (e.g., a private company, public company, non-profit)	4.28	0.974	0.949	Definitely influential
The reputation of the external auditor	4.81	0.467	0.218	Definitely influential
Track record of compliance with ZATCA	4.31	1.117	1.247	Definitely influential
Track record of compliance with other regulations (e.g., CMA, SAMA)	4.28	1.031	1.063	Definitely influential
Historical financial performance	4.56	0.558	0.311	Definitely influential
Adoption of advanced technologies /software packages (i.e., for accounting, business analysis, tax reporting, auditing)	4.25	0.906	0.821	Definitely influential
Accounting standards adopted by the company (e.g., IFRS, IFRS and SOCPA combined)	4.47	0.810	0.656	Definitely influential
Changes in organisational structure/management (e.g., new managers, merges, new strategies)	3.97	1.276	1.628	Probably influential
Changes in business /market environment (e.g., financial crisis, pandemics)	3.89	1.304	1.702	Probably influential
Social media presence of the company	3.36	1.291	1.666	I do not know
Other, please specify:	–	–	–	None

ZATCA: Zakat, TAX, and Custom Authority, **CMA**: Capital Market Authority, **SAMA**, Saudi Central Bank, **MOJ**: Ministry of Justice, **MC**: Ministry of Commerce., **IFRS**: International Financial Reporting Standards, **SOCPA**: Saudi Organization for Chartered and Professional Accountants.

a data source did not receive explicit approval or disapproval from participants. Despite that, all other proposed data sources were considered valuable inputs for constructing our model. Finally, it is essential to consider the data sources, such as Central Bank transaction data, information about competitors, and the company's long-term vision, as suggested by participants using the free text option.

Table 7. Variability in interpreting accounting elements in Saudi-listed companies

Item	Mean	Std. deviation	Variance	Level
Assets and liabilities	3.09	1.128	1.273	I do not know
Intangible assets	3.12	1.111	1.235	I do not know
Earnings	3.15	1.278	1.633	I do not know
Expenses	3.21	1.244	1.547	I do not know
Revenues	3.21	1.341	1.797	I do not know
Cashflow	3.09	1.182	1.398	I do not know
Financing	3.18	1.211	1.466	I do not know
SPEs (Special Purpose Entities)/Subsidiaries	3.21	1.193	1.422	I do not know
Management compensations	3.64	1.141	1.301	Moderate variability
Accruals	3.24	0.969	0.939	I do not know
Currency	2.79	1.139	1.297	I do not know
Extraordinary Items	3.45	1.003	1.006	Moderate variability
Accounting choices	3.39	1.029	1.059	I do not know
Other, please specify:	–	–	–	Disclosures of future risk Future liabilities Sector performance Investments

5   Discussion

The survey aimed to collect opinions from professionals and academics in SA regarding the factors that impact the quality of financial reporting and the data sources available to obtain information on these factors. The survey analysis has validated existing literature and confirmed our tuition regarding some of the N-FIN data we intend to use in training CADM. This section discusses these findings and answers each research question we raised.

5.1   CA Enablers

Q1: What factors influence the credibility of information extracted from FSs in SA?

As indicated in the results of part 2 of the survey, professionals in the SA business sector expressed significant confidence in the influence of the external auditor's reputation on the quality of information extracted from FSs. This finding aligns with existing literature, which suggests that engaging one of the Big Four auditing firms contributes substantially to the quality of financial reports [6, 28] and corporate governance disclosures [6]. However, it is crucial to emphasise that this result does not inherently criticise

Table 8. The potential of common accounting systems/software/platforms in SA

Software	Mean	Std. deviation	Variance	Level
Halo	2.00	0.471	0.222	Never heard about it
Aura	2.14	0.525	0.275	Never heard about it
ACL GRC	2.04	0.508	0.258	Never heard about it
TeamMate+	2.29	0.600	0.360	Never heard about it
AuditBoard	2.37	0.629	0.396	In use
AuditDesktop	2.32	0.612	0.375	In use
Oracle NetSuite	2.52	0.829	0.687	In use
FirstAudit	2.11	0.577	0.333	Never heard about it
SaftyCulture	2.04	0.576	0.332	Never heard about it
Workiva	2.54	2.487	6.184	In use
Onspring	2.07	0.466	0.217	Never heard about it
Intellect	2.14	0.591	0.349	Never heard about it
MetricStream	2.00	0.471	0.222	Never heard about it
DataSnipper	2.00	0.544	0.296	Never heard about it
1Audit	2.79	2.485	6.175	In use
Tableau	2.18	0.548	0.300	Never heard about it
IDEA	2.18	0.548	0.300	Never heard about it
ACL Analytics	2.21	0.568	0.323	Never heard about it
MS Excel	2.68	0.548	0.300	In use
MS Power BI	2.96	2.426	5.888	In use
SAS Analytics	2.61	0.685	0.470	In use
Other:	–	–	–	SAP

the performance of smaller offices; instead, it warrants further exploration in our model development.

Our findings also identify two additional internal factors of influence: a company's historical financial performance and the adoption of accounting standards. Both factors align with the primary input of CADM training, which relies on a time-series dataset of financial statements. Furthermore, we recognise the significance of other perceived influential external and internal factors, such as business type and the integration of advanced technologies. However, certain factors may pose challenges for inclusion, such as compliance with Saudi business regulations, as the required data is still inaccessible.

Q2: How variable are the interpretations of accounting subjects in the disclosures of Saudi-listed companies?

The attempt to investigate the perspectives of business professionals in SA regarding potential differences in the preparation of FSs yielded limited success, as the mean

Table 9. Possible data sources to use in building the model.

Data Source	Mean	Std. Deviation	Variance	Level
Custom Data (imports/exports)	4.46	0.859	0.738	Extremely useful
Tax Data	4.54	0.647	0.418	Extremely useful
Reports/Statistics published by authorities. (ZATCA, MOI, SAMA, SMA,SFDA, MC)	4.23	1.070	1.145	Extremely useful
Press/News	3.42	1.391	1.934	Useful
Management correspondence	3.77	1.142	1.305	Useful
Information about the board of directors	4.15	1.008	1.015	Useful
Recordings of board meetings (video/audio)	4.00	1.059	1.200	Useful
Financial analysts' forecasts	3.85	1.008	1.015	Useful
Employees information	3.69	0.884	0.782	Useful
Social media posts (e.g., LinkedIn, X)	3.31	1.158	1.342	I do not know
Textual contents in annual reports (management comments)	4.38	0.804	0.646	Extremely Useful
Changes in business environment	4.00	1.095	1.200	Useful
National/International financial circumstances	4.19	0.849	0.722	Useful
Security monitoring data (e.g., log files)	4.54	0.761	0.578	Extremely Useful
Inventory management data (e.g., RFID)	4.42	0.758	0.574	Extremely Useful
Tracking data (e.g., GPS)	3.50	1.304	1.700	Useful
Access control data (e.g., CCTV)	4.04	1.076	1.158	Useful
Company's profile record with regulators:	3.42	0.758	0.574	Useful
Other, please specify:	–	–	–	long-term vision Central bank transaction data

responses tended to be broadly neutral. However, there was a notable moderate variability in the interpretations of management compensation disclosures among different companies. Considering that financial statement fraud is predominantly associated with CEOs and upper management rather than employees [3], we deduce that the observed variability may be attributed to CA practices.

Furthermore, the accounting treatment of extraordinary items was perceived to exhibit diverse methodologies among market participants. It is noteworthy that managers have employed this accounting item to reclassify various accounting items into it. Hence, incorporating this factor as a primary variable in constructing the CADM is subject to the accounting standards adopted, as the IFRS (recently adopted in SA) does not recognise the concept of extraordinary items.

5.2 The Feasibility of CADM in SA

Q3: How practical is adopting new technologies that enable advanced analytical services in the Saudi business environment?

The findings indicate a relatively limited usage of accounting software in SA. Adopting new technologies is likely more prevalent among larger firms like the Big Four. Nevertheless, responses suggest that Microsoft, SAS, and Oracle software packages are popular in Saudi businesses, which is reasonable considering their long-standing presence in the industry. Regarding our model building, FIN data (FSs) are digitally accessible in various file types, including XBRL, Excel, CSV, and PDF. In contrast, N-FIN data differs according to the data sources discussed in the next section.

5.3 New Data Sources for CADM Training

Q4: What are the most critical data sources to consider in our model building?

Commonly referenced data sources in the literature primarily involve FIN data sources. N-FIN data sources have been applied to utilise big data for detecting FSF, such as corporate governance disclosures [3] and audio recordings of board conferences [49]. However, it's important to note that these N-FIN data were sourced from FRs, and the objective is to rely on external or independent data sources for data analysis. As anticipated, the findings indicate that most of the suggested data sources were viewed as extremely useful. Notably, the most valuable sources, according to Saudi business professionals and academics, are export/import data and Zakat/tax data from the ZATCA, along with reports published by other governmental authorities like the MC and the MOJ. While these sources are available for external auditors, accessing them for research is still being determined.

Furthermore, internal monitoring and inventory management data are helpful when accessible. Again, while these data sources may be available to external auditors as audit evidence, they are not publicly accessible for academic research. All other suggested data sources were considered valid, except data collected from social media.

6 Conclusion

The Saudi literature has drawn attention to the presence of Creative Accounting (CA) in the financial reports of Saudi-listed companies. Our results consistently confirm the existing literature showing significant insights about financial reporting in Saudi Arabia

(SA) from the perspectives of business professionals and academics. Notably, the integration of financial and non-financial data (FIN and N-FIN) for detecting CA has yet to be explored in the Saudi survey studies, making our study a valuable contribution to the literature.

The findings highlighted variabilities in interpreting some accounting items in financial statements (FS) and evaluated the credibility of information extracted from FSs. As CA is proven to have detrimental effects, identifying these variabilities in interpretation holds critical insights that will mitigate the negative impacts of CA in SA and offer stakeholders an opportunity to depend on enhanced sources of financial information for better decision-making. Considering our aim to develop a Creative Accounting Detection model (CADM) [18], the findings of this study will also serve as a foundation for integrating non-financial data into the dataset.

However, our survey revealed the significance of including information about the external auditor in training the model. This finding is consistent with the literature's documented relationship between financial reporting and audit quality. Previous FSF detection attempts have overlooked this factor as a significant influencer on account manipulations. We also noticed the importance of considering compliance with Saudi Arabian authorities and regulations, the level of technology used, the adoption of accounting standards, and management compensations in the dataset used in training CADM.

Finally, we recognised the importance of reports and data results published by Saudi Arabian authorities such as the Zakat, Tax, and Customs Authority (ZATCA). Nevertheless, some influential factors hold significance but remain beyond our reach, such as security information and inventory datasets within a company's database. Still, auditors and monitoring bodies have access to these sources of information, and they can enhance their investigations by incorporating such sources.

While results have validated existing literature and contributed critical additional insights regarding N-FIN (independent variables), it is essential to acknowledge some limitations that may affect interpreting these results. The sample size was relatively small due to the limited study time frame. However, the diversity within our sample will mitigate its impact. On the other hand, a substantial amount of unexplored information could be valuable to train our model if it was included in the analysis. For example, the study did not investigate the correlation between participants' responses and their position, years of experience, or the relationship between the qualifications and perspective of each participant. In the next stage, we will start integrating datasets of the variables considered in our findings from the data sources we identify and prepare them to be used in training CADM.

References

1. Abbasi, A., Albrecht, C., Vance, A., Hansen, J.: Metafraud: a meta-learning framework for detecting financial fraud. MIS Q. **36**(4), 1293–1327 (2012). https://doi.org/10.2307/41703508
2. Abdou, H.A., Ellelly, N.N., Elamer, A.A., Hussainey, K., Yazdifar, H.: Corporate governance and earnings management nexus: evidence from the UK and Egypt using neural networks. Int. J. Financ. Econ. **26**(4), 6281–6311 (2021). https://doi.org/10.1002/ijfe.2120
3. ACEF: Occupational Fraud 2022: A Report to The Nations (2022). https://legacy.acfe.com/report-to-the-nations/2022/

4. Al Shetwi, M.: Earnings management in Saudi non-financial listed companies. Int. J. Bus. Soc. Sci. **11**(1), 18–26 (2020). https://doi.org/10.30845/ijbss.v11n1a3
5. Alali, A., Khedr, A.M., El-Bannany, M., Kanakkayil, S.: A powerful predicting model for financial statement fraud based on optimized XGBoost ensemble learning technique. Appl. Sci. **13**(4), 1–16 (2023). https://doi.org/10.3390/app13042272
6. Al-Bassam, W.M., Ntim, C.G., Opong, K.K., Downs, Y.: Corporate boards and ownership structure as antecedents of corporate governance disclosure in Saudi Arabian publicly listed corporations. Bus. Soc. **57**(2), 335–377 (2018). https://doi.org/10.1177/0007650315610611
7. Al-bayati, H.R.: Creative accounting and its role in misleading decision makers. University Iraq J. **50**, 423–431 (2021). https://www.iasj.net/iasj/download/ed9cf54e908fdb20
8. Al-Hasan, A.F.: Earnings management using accruals: empirical study on Saudi companies. Arabic J. Adm. **38**(4), 55–72 (2018). https://doi.org/10.21608/aja.2018.22437
9. Alhebri, A.A., Al-Duais, S.D.: Family businesses restrict accrual and real earnings management: case study in Saudi Arabia. Cogent Bus. Manag. **7**(1), 1–15 (2020). https://doi.org/10.1080/23311975.2020.1806669
10. Alles, M.G.: Drivers of the use and facilitators and obstacles of the evolution of big data by the audit profession. Account. Horiz. **29**(2), 439–449 (2015). https://doi.org/10.2308/acch-51067
11. Alles, M., Gray, G.L.: Incorporating big data in audits: identifying inhibitors and a research agenda to address those inhibitors. Int. J. Account. Inf. Syst. **22**, 44–59 (2016). https://doi.org/10.1016/j.accinf.2016.07.004
12. Almustawfiy, H.: Creative accounting applications, opportunistic behavior, and integrity of accounting information system: the case of Iraq. J. Legal Ethical Regulatory Issues **24**(6), 1–11 (2021)
13. Alsehli, M.S.: Earnings management in Saudi Arabia. Inst. Public Adm. **46**(3), 511–546 (2006). https://search.mandumah.com/Record/497080
14. Al-Shabeeb, R.S., Al-Adeem, K.R.: The ethics of earnings management: a survey study. Glob. J. Econ. Bus. **6**(1), 62–80 (2019). https://academia-arabia.com/en/reader/2/142921
15. Asiri, B., Alzeera, H.: Is the Saudi stock market efficient? A case of weak-form efficiency. Res. J. Financ. Account. **4**(6), 35–48 (2013). https://ssrn.com/abstract=2276520
16. Baajajah, S.M.B., Khalifah, M.: The effect of creative accounting practices on investments decision makers in Saudi stock market. King Abdulaziz Univ. J. Econ. Adm. **29**(1), 3–64 (2015). https://doi.org/10.4197/eco.29-1.1
17. Bineid, M., Assiri, A.: Creative accounting incentives and techniques in Saudi public companies: a survey study. King Abdulaziz Univ. J. Econ. Adm. **27**(2), 107–168 (2013). https://doi.org/10.4197/Eco.27-2.2
18. Bineid, M., Beloff, N., White, M., Khanina, A.: CADM: big data to limit creative accounting in Saudi-listed companies. In: Proceedings of the 18th Conference on Computer Science and Intelligence Systems, vol. 35, pp. 102–110 (2023). https://doi.org/10.15439/2023F3888
19. Cainas, J.M., Tietz, W.M., Miller-Nobles, T.: Kat insurance: data analytics cases for introductory accounting using Excel, Power BI, and/or Tableau. J. Emerg. Technol. Account. **18**(1), 77–85 (2021). https://doi.org/10.2308/JETA-2020-039
20. Chen, Z.Y., Han, D.: Detecting corporate financial fraud via two-stage mapping in joint temporal and financial feature domain. Expert Syst. Appl. **217**, 1–12 (2023). https://doi.org/10.1016/j.eswa.2023.119559
21. Chiu, V., Liu, Q., Muehlmann, B., Baldwin, A.A.: A bibliometric analysis of accounting information systems journals and their emerging technologies contributions. Int. J. Account. Inf. Syst. **32**, 24–43 (2019). https://doi.org/10.1016/j.accinf.2018.11.003
22. CMA. Capital Market Authority Annual Report 2021 (2021). https://cma.org.sa
23. Cockcroft, S., Russell, M.: Big data opportunities for accounting and finance practice and research. Aust. Account. Rev. **28**(3), 323–333 (2018). https://doi.org/10.1111/auar.12218

24. Cole, R., Johan, S., Schweizer, D.: Corporate failures: declines, collapses, and scandals. J. Corp. Finan. **67**, 1–11 (2021). https://doi.org/10.1016/j.jcorpfin.2020.101872
25. Craja, P., Kim, A., Lessmann, S.: Deep learning for detecting financial statement fraud. Decis. Support. Syst. **139**, 1–13 (2020). https://doi.org/10.1016/j.dss.2020.113421
26. Dokas, I.: Earnings management and status of corporate governance under different levels of corruption—an empirical analysis in European countries. J. Risk Financ. Manag. **16**(10), 1–23 (2023). https://doi.org/10.3390/jrfm16100458
27. Fernández-Gámez, M.A., García-Lagos, F., Sánchez-Serrano, J.R.: Integrating corporate governance and financial variables for the identification of qualified audit opinions with neural networks. Neural Comput. Appl. **27**(5), 1427–1444 (2016). https://doi.org/10.1007/s00521-015-1944-6
28. Francis, J.R., Yu, M.D.: Big 4 office size and audit quality. Account. Rev. **84**(5), 1521–1552 (2009). https://doi.org/10.2308/accr.2009.84.5.1521
29. Gherai, D.S., Balaciu, D.E.: From creative accounting practices and Enron phenomenon to the current financial crisis. Annales Universitatis Apulensis: Series Oeconomica **13**(1), 34–41(2011). https://api.semanticscholar.org/CorpusID:55798141
30. Goel, S., Gangolly, J., Faerman, S.R., Uzuner, O.: Can linguistic predictors detect fraudulent financial filings? J. Emerg. Technol. Account. **7**(1), 25–46 (2010). https://doi.org/10.2308/jeta.2010.7.1.25
31. Gupta, C.M., Kumar, D.: Creative accounting a tool for financial crime: a review of the techniques and its effects. J. Financ. Crime **27**(2), 397–411 (2020). https://doi.org/10.1108/JFC-06-2019-0075
32. Ibrahim, A.E.A., Elamer, A.A., Ezat, A.N.: The convergence of big data and accounting: innovative research opportunities. Technol. Forecast. Soc. Chang. **173**, 121–171 (2021). https://doi.org/10.1016/j.techfore.2021.121171
33. ICAEW: Big data and analytics: the impact on the accountancy profession. Institute of Chartered Accountants, England and Wales (ICAEW), London, UK, pp. 1–20 (2019)
34. Jan, C.L.: Detection of financial statement fraud using deep learning for sustainable development of capital markets under information asymmetry. Sustainability **13**(17), 1–20 (2021). https://doi.org/10.3390/su13179879
35. Kim, Y.J., Baik, B., Cho, S.: Detecting financial misstatements with fraud intention using multi-class cost-sensitive learning. Expert Syst. Appl. **62**, 32–43 (2016). https://doi.org/10.1016/j.eswa.2016.06.016
36. Li, J., Sun, Z.: Application of deep learning in recognition of accrued earnings management. Heliyon **9**(3), 1–11 (2023). https://doi.org/10.1016/j.heliyon.2023.e13664
37. Lin, C.C., Chiu, A.A., Huang, S.Y., Yen, D.C.: Detecting the financial statement fraud: the analysis of the differences between data mining techniques and experts' judgments. Knowl. Based Syst. **89**, 459–470 (2015). https://doi.org/10.1016/j.knosys.2015.08.011
38. Liu, R., Mai, F., Shan, Z., Wu, Y.: Predicting shareholder litigation on insider trading from financial text: an interpretable deep learning approach. Inf. Manag. **57**(8), 1–17 (2020). https://doi.org/10.1016/j.im.2020.103387
39. Malik, A., Abumustafa, N.I., Shah, H.: Revisiting creative accounting in the context of Islamic economic and finance system. Asian Soc. Sci. **15**(2), 80–89 (2019). https://doi.org/10.5539/ass.v15n2p80
40. Maniatis, A.: Detecting the probability of financial fraud due to earnings manipulation in companies listed in Athens Stock Exchange Market. J. Financ. Crime **29**(2), 603–619 (2022). https://doi.org/10.1108/JFC-04-2021-0083
41. Michael, J.: Creative Accounting, Fraud, and International Accounting Scandals. Wiley, Hoboken (2011)

42. Moshashai, D., Leber, A.M., Savage, J.D.: Saudi Arabia plans for its economic future: vision 2030, the National Transformation Plan and Saudi fiscal reform. Br. J. Middle Eastern Stud. **47**(3), 381–401 (2020). https://doi.org/10.1080/13530194.2018.1500269
43. Muehlmann, B.W., Chiu, V., Liu, Q.: Emerging technologies research in accounting: JETA's first decade. J. Emerg. Technol. Account. **12**(1), 17–50 (2015). https://doi.org/10.2308/jeta-51245
44. Nosratabadi, S.: Data science in economics: comprehensive review of advanced machine learning and deep learning methods. Mathematics **8**(10), 1–25 (2020). https://doi.org/10.3390/math8101799
45. Nurunnabi, M., Jermakowicz, E.K., Donker, H.: Implementing IFRS in Saudi Arabia: evidence from publicly traded companies. Int. J. Account. Inf. Manag. **28**(2), 243–273 (2020). https://doi.org/10.1108/IJAIM-04-2019-0049
46. Ozbayoglu, A.M., Gudelek, M.U., Sezer, O.B.: Deep learning for financial applications: a survey. Appl. Soft Comput. **93**, 1–29 (2020). https://doi.org/10.1016/j.asoc.2020.106384
47. Perols, J.L., Bowen, R.M., Zimmermann, C., Samba, B.: Finding needles in a haystack: using data analytics to improve fraud prediction. Account. Rev. **92**(2), 221–245 (2017). https://doi.org/10.2308/accr-51562
48. Rabin, C.E.: Determinants of auditors' attitudes towards creative accounting. Meditari Accountancy Res. **13**(2), 67–88 (2005). https://doi.org/10.1108/10222529200500013
49. Rahman, M.J., Zhu, H.: Predicting accounting fraud using imbalanced ensemble learning classifiers – evidence from China. Account. Financ. **63**(3), 3455–3486 (2023). https://doi.org/10.1111/acfi.13044
50. Saeedi, A.: Audit opinion prediction: a comparison of data mining techniques. J. Emerg. Technol. Account. **18**(2), 125–147 (2021). https://doi.org/10.2308/JETA-19-10-02-40
51. Siano, F., Wysocki, P.: Transfer learning and textual analysis of accounting disclosures: applying big data methods to small(er) datasets. Acc. Horiz. **35**(3), 217–244 (2021).https://doi.org/10.2308/HORIZONS-19-161
52. SOCPA. Live Auditing Evidence (2022). https://socpa.org.sa/Home.aspx
53. Sun, J., Li, H.: Data mining method for listed companies' financial distress prediction. Knowl. Based Syst. **21**(1), 1–5 (2008). https://doi.org/10.1016/j.knosys.2006.11.003
54. Tang, J., Karim, K.E.: Financial fraud detection and big data analytics – implications on auditors' use of fraud brainstorming session. Manag. Audit. J. **34**(3), 324–337 (2019). https://doi.org/10.1108/MAJ-01-2018-1767
55. Tassadaq, F., Malik, Q.A.: Creative accounting and financial reporting: model development and empirical testing. Int. J. Econ. Financ. Issues **5**(2), 544–551 (2015). https://www.econjournals.com/index.php/ijefi/article/view/1047
56. Tawiah, V., Borgi, H.: Impact of XBRL adoption on financial reporting quality: a global evidence. Account. Res. J. **35**(6), 815–833 (2022). https://doi.org/10.1108/ARJ-01-2022-0002
57. Throckmorton, C.S., Mayew, W.J., Venkatachalam, M., Collins, L.M.: Financial fraud detection using vocal, linguistic and financial cues. Decis. Support. Syst. **74**, 78–87 (2015). https://doi.org/10.1016/j.dss.2015.04.006
58. Warren, J.D., Moffitt, K.C., Byrnes, P.: How big data will change accounting. Account. Horiz. **29**(2), 397–407 (2015). https://doi.org/10.2308/acch-51069

Effective Communication of IT Costs and IT Business Value

Constanze Riedinger[1]([✉]) [iD], Melanie Huber[2] [iD], Niculin Prinz[1] [iD],
and Robin Kaufmann[3] [iD]

[1] kips, Konstanz University of Applied Sciences, 78462 Konstanz, Germany
{constanze.riedinger,niculin.prinz}@htwg-konstanz.de
[2] BITCO3 GmbH, 78467 Konstanz, Germany
melanie.huber@bitco3.com
[3] VOICE - Bundesverband der IT-Anwender e.V., 10115 Berlin, Germany
robin.kaufmann@voice-ev.org

Abstract. Digital transformation urges organizations to strategically invest in information technology (IT) to keep up with the competition. The responsible strive to choose the right digital initiatives that can maximize the benefit. Thereby, they still struggle to communicate IT costs and demonstrate the business value of IT. The goal of this paper is to get a deeper understanding of the perception of IT costs and business value and support their effective communication. Applying the focus group method, we analyzed in four interview sessions that stakeholders perceive IT costs and business value differently and that a common perception serves as the basis of communication. We then identified and evaluated 20 success factors to establish effective communication of IT costs and IT business value. Hence, this paper enables a better understanding of the perception and the operationalization of effective communication mainly between business and IT executives regarding IT costs and IT business value.

Keywords: Effective Communication · Success Factors · IS/IT Costs · IS/IT Business Value · Business-IT Alignment · COBIT

1 Introduction

Over time, organizations have dealt with the ongoing challenge of operating efficiently and managing resources strategically pushed in the last years by the COVID-19 pandemic and currently exacerbated by external factors such as inflation and war [48]. To stay competitive and address security risks, they are increasing their information technology (IT) spending [11] and striving to choose the right digital initiatives [10]. As a result, they need strategic cost management [42] and effective communication about IT costs and the benefit they derive from their IT investments [28]. However, for 63% of the 166 Chief Information Officers (CIOs) surveyed, communicating this business value of IT [12] is still a challenge, as confirmed by other studies [19, 40]. Similarly, decision-makers struggle to foster transparent cost discussions [40]. Therefore, the purpose of this paper is to understand how IT costs and the business value of IT are perceived and effectively communicated.

E. Ziemba et al. (Eds.): FedCSIS-ITBS 2023/ISM 2023, LNBIP 504, pp. 93–115, 2024.
https://doi.org/10.1007/978-3-031-61657-0_5

Effective communication describes the "bidirectional exchange" [49] of information that leads to common ground [38]. The foundation of effective communication and the prerequisite for achieving business value from IT is alignment [18]. Researchers extensively investigate the success factors for business-IT alignment (BITA) and the resulting impact of better communication on the relationship between business and IT [8, 26, 31]. This relationship also influences the effective communication of IT cost and the business value of IT itself [9, 16, 33]. Besides BITA, studies highlight other aspects of business value communication, such as a common language [16] or appropriate methodologies and metrics [33]. Furthermore, convergence [1] and the stakeholder perception [51] play critical roles in communication. However, the perception of IT costs and business value in the context of their successful communication has not been investigated in detail. Furthermore, there is a lack of a comprehensive overview of the success factors for communication that follows an established framework [16] that supports the operationalization of conceptual models [15]. Our study aims to fill these research gaps: we conduct focus group interviews to gain practical insights and generate an overview using the established governance framework the *Control OBjectives for Information and Related Technology* (COBIT) [20]. In doing so, we contribute to the scientific research by shedding light on the current perception of IT costs and business value of IT and their communication. Furthermore, we present the success factors and support the operationalization of effective communication. In addition, this study has practical implications: practitioners can use the results to recognize symptoms of non-constructive communication in their organizations and to gain awareness of how to develop an effective communication of IT costs and business value.

This paper (as extended version of [41]) is structured as follows: First, we present our theoretical foundations related to communication. We thereby focus on communication between business and IT executives, enterprise governance of IT, business-IT alignment, and aspects of cost and value communication. We then show our research method, which comprises focus groups followed by a qualitative analysis. Finally, we present our findings, discuss them, and draw conclusions.

2   Theoretical Background for Communication

Collaboration between business and IT departments and especially the communication between their executives is the basis for the strategic alignment and contribution of IT to the business [22, 44]. The basic elements for this collaboration are structures, processes, and relational mechanisms defined and implemented as Enterprise Governance of IT (EGIT) [14]. Business-IT Alignment (BITA) thereby acts as a "mediating mechanism" between EGIT and IT business value [14]. It builds the base for effective communication between the business and IT departments [23]. In the following, we describe communication between business and IT executives as well as the three elements of effective communication represented in the conceptual model in Fig. 1.

Fig. 1. EGIT-Alignment-Value Concept following [14]

2.1 Communication Between Business and IT Executives

Former research on communication between business and IT executives emphasizes that communication is only effective when the interlocutors strive for a "state of convergence" [1, 22]. A convergence model by [43] describes this communication as a dynamic process of information exchange to achieve mutual understanding: unlike the Shannon and Weaver's linear model (sender-receiver-model), the convergence model represents a cyclical model that focuses on the continuous sharing, interpreting and effectively perceiving of information. In the process of communication, this leads to collective action, mutual agreement, and then mutual understanding. The communication partners, therefore, need conversational skills such as attentive listening and productive explanations [44]. A study identifies 26 criteria for a mutual understanding between business and IT executives grouped into four determining factors: semantics (language) and mental model, environment, shared IT and business domain knowledge, and relationship management [1]. Furthermore, a study proves that frequent communication positively influences the convergence between the Chief Executive Officer (CEO) and the CIO regarding the role of IT for the business [22].

In this context, we define effective communication as a bidirectional exchange in which interlocutors aim to develop a similar representation of the content of the conversation. Enhancements in effective communication have a significant impact on commitments and strategic conversations between business and IT executives [44]: the effective communication of the defined commitments can narrow the gap between business and IT. Strategic conversations, enabled by effective communication and commitment, then shape BITA and the joint development of the organizations. Better agreement between the interlocutors on the current role of IT also leads to a higher financial contribution from IT to the organization [22]. Therefore, effective communication between business and IT executives, previously also researched in the context of IT projects [35], serves as basis for strategic alignment and bridges the gap between business and IT [44]. However, in order to implement effective communication, organizations require "an excellent example to follow" [35], such as patterns, best practices, or success factors.

2.2 Enterprise Governance of IT

A successful EGIT leads to a better IT controllability and thus to a higher business impact [36]. To achieve this successful governance, research investigates determinants that lead to an "integrated model of IT governance success and its impact" [5]: success factors analyzed in this context are e.g., the understanding of the IT value chain, top management commitment, IT's business orientation, and the persuasiveness of communication. To establish successful governance and management of IT, COBIT as a "good-practice framework" gives guidelines for organizations [15]. Thereafter, organizations should establish a governance system consisting of several components [14]: (1)

Organizational Structures, (2) Processes, (3) People, Skills, and Competencies, (4) Information, (5) Culture, Ethics, and Behavior, (6) Services, Infrastructure, Applications, (7) Principles, Policies, and Frameworks. These components lead to a comprehensive and functioning governance system and influence effective IT management [20]. Therefore, earlier studies apply the components to ensure comprehensiveness [40] or to transfer the practical functioning to a conceptual framework [15]. COBIT highlights that open and transparent communication about performance enables "a good relationship between IT and enterprise" [20]. It thereby recommends organizations to involve and align all relevant stakeholders to overcome communication gaps [20].

2.3 Business-IT Alignment

The alignment between business and IT has been extensively studied for several decades [6, 37]. The Strategic Alignment Model (SAM) [18] is an established model used to describe this relationship between business and IT. Thereafter, alignment is based on the strategic fit between external and internal domains, as well as the functional integration between business and IT domains. This results in multivariate relationships between business and IT, always considering the linkage of three out of the four domains (compare Fig. 3). The most common alignment perspective is the first perspective *Strategy Execution* (1). In this case, the business strategy serves as a driver for organizational decisions and subsequently influences the design of the IT infrastructure. Alignment through *Technology Transformation* (2) also originates from the business strategy followed by an appropriate IT strategy. This leads to the required IT infrastructure and processes. The *Competitive Potential* (3) perspective is driven by emerging IT capabilities that generate new strategic orientations of the business, such as new products and services. Their implementation follows the adaption of the operational business processes. The *Service Level* (4) perspective describes how IT infrastructure and processes are built to better support business operations driven by the IT strategy.

The alignment between business and IT is a continuous process that requires communication and understanding [8, 18]. It is described as "dynamic and evolutionary" [30]. To improve BITA, organizations should consider six criteria: governance, partnership, scope and architecture, skills, value measurement and communication [30]. The communication between business units and IT departments can be optimized and lead to informal and pervasive communication, depending on the maturity level of the alignment [30]. Various enablers and inhibitors influence the maturity level of BITA and thereby also the effectiveness of communication [31]. A literature review on critical success factors of BITA presents those factors in three dimensions [26]: the human, social, and intellectual dimension. Success factors, such as IT or technical skills and knowledge of business and IT executives, indirectly influence effective communication regarding the costs and value of IT. Earlier studies highlight BITA itself as an important factor for their effective communication [16].

2.4 IT Costs and Business Value of IT

In organizational communication regarding IT costs and business value, there is often a shared perception that "IT costs too much" [46]. To measure the impact of IT, research proposes key performance indicators (KPIs) to support executives [16]. For several of these KPIs, such as return on investment (ROI) [24], IT costs form the foundation [33]. Conceptual frameworks enable executives to measure IT performance and consider all IT-related costs as a valid calculation basis [27]. Researchers emphasize that IT costs include not only the direct expenditures for development and implementation, but also various indirect costs related to human and organizational factors [34]. However, organizations often lack a clear understanding of the term "IT costs". Therefore, CIOs face the challenge of transforming non-constructive discussions about IT costs into discussions about the business value contributed by IT investments [40]. The concept of "IT business value"[1] has been discussed in literature since the rise of IT [3]. Consistent with prior research, we adhere to the notion that IT business value is "measured by performance metrics on dimensions that stakeholders find important" [33] and while "performance can be measured, value can be communicated" [33]. Effective communication requires stakeholders to have a shared understanding of cost and value [33], as stakeholder perception plays a crucial role in communication [51]. We address this current perception of the stakeholders in our first research question (RQ): *(1) What is the perception of business and IT stakeholders of "IT costs" and "IT business value"?*

In addition to BITA and the common perception and understanding of the terms [33], further aspects affect the communication of IT costs and business value [16]. Transparency in IT cost information and the awareness of IT costs and cost drivers are essential for communicating and demonstrating the value of IT [40]. KPIs formulated in business language from this cost information are also crucial for effectively communicating IT business value [33]. Furthermore, [30] mentions the use of metric portfolios and dashboards to visualize value in communication. Success factors also include Business-IT structures that evaluate IT investments together [47]. Effective value communication throughout the organization should then be audience-oriented and employ different channels [23]. To summarize the relevant aspects of value communication, [16] conduct a literature review and investigate how to conceptualize it. The article presents various categories, such as transparency, understanding, collaboration, methods, and transparent communication. However, research indicates that especially establishing a common language and implementing collaboration on an equal footing are challenging [40]. Therefore, CIOs continue to face the challenges of successfully implementing communication [28] and demonstrating the business value of IT investments in their organizations [40]. They miss practicable success factors that operationalize the successful communication between business and IT on IT costs and IT business value. This gap leads to our second RQ: *(2) What factors do organizations need to consider for implementing an effective communication of IT costs and business value?*

3 Research Method

The focus group (FG) research method is utilized in academic studies to examine specific topics in groups through focused interviews with a predetermined direction [4]. Previous research in the field of Information Systems (IS) has employed FGs to evaluate design

---

[1] The term "IS business value" could be used in place of "IT business value". We follow the interpretation of [24].

science artifacts [13] or to identify factors influencing students' decisions to study IT [32]. Small groups, with an optimal size of 5 to 8 participants, allow for in-depth exploration of specific topics [25]. Direct feedback and group interaction can challenge interviewees' views and inspire new ways of thinking [4]. This approach enables researchers to gain an in-depth understanding and a wide range of opinions or perceptions regarding an issue, behavior, or practice, thereby uncovering factors that influence those opinions [25]. This is why, the qualitative method of FGs support our study's aim to understand in depth the perception of IT costs and IT business value and identify success factors to optimize effective communication. We divide our FG study into two phases [50]: first, the planning phase, including the participant selection [25], and second, the sessions and the analysis.

3.1 Planning and Participant Selection

In order to achieve our research goal, we chose a single-category design for our FGs and developed questions to guide the discussion and in a next step answer our research questions outlined in Sect. 2. The guiding questions were open-ended to motivate participants to answer according to their specific situation [25]:

- What are we talking about when we talk about IT costs or IT value? Which costs belong to the total IT costs? What is IT value for you?
- How do you communicate IT costs and business value within your organization?
- What are the challenges in those discussions? What is required to effectively communicate IT costs and IT business value in organizations?

To discuss these questions and through that answer our RQs, we included a broad spectrum of people coming from different industries to cover a variety of perspectives. As a decisive criterion for the selection of the FG participants, we specified that each of them must have a relevant responsibility and expertise in the communication of IT costs and IT business value. All participants were already part of the network of the research team. Table 1 provides an overview of the participants in the four FGs.

Table 1. Participants of the focus group sessions.

ID	Function (Industry | #Employees (EMP))	ID	Function (Industry | #Employees (EMP))
FG1-1	Head of IT Governance (Transportation | 30.000 EMP)	FG2-1	Head of IT Governance (Transportation | 2.700 EMP)
FG1-2	CIO (Service Industry | 600 EMP)	FG2-2	IT Controlling (Insurance | 3.000 EMP)
FG1-3	CIO (Electronics | 1.000 EMP)	FG2-3	IT Controlling (Retail | 35.000 EMP)

(*continued*)

Table 1. (*continued*)

ID	Function (Industry | #Employees (EMP))	ID	Function (Industry | #Employees (EMP))
FG1-4	CIO (Pharmaceuticals| 78.500 EMP)	FG2-4	Controlling (Electronics | 1.000 EMP)
FG1-5	CIO Office Insurance (3.000 EMP)	FG2-5	Controlling (Banking (2.500 EMP)
FG1-6	Head of Value Mgmt. (Energy | 91.000 EMP)	FG2-6	Controlling (Electronics | 1.000 EMP)
FG1-7	CIO (Infrastructure | 1.000 EMP)	FG2-7	IT Portfolio Mgmt. (Energy | 91.000 EMP)
FG1-8	IT Controller (Agriculture | 22.300 EMP)	FG2-8	IT Controlling (Transportation | 30.000 EMP)
FG3-1	Director Audit and Inspection (Oil and Gas | 15.000 EMP)	FG4-1	CIO (Insurance | 2.500 EMP)
FG3-2	Director Technical Control (Oil and Gas | 15.000 EMP)	FG4-2	IT Portfolio Management Transportation (338.000 EMP)
FG3-3	Project Lead Tunisian IT Society (Society for Economic Development |170 companies)	FG4-3	IT Business Administration (Workwear & Service Industry | 11.000 EMP)
FG3-4	Director IT Society Exchange (German Society for IT | 2600 companies)	FG4-4	Professor for Information Technology University of Applied Sciences

3.2 Focus Group Sessions and Data Analysis

The FG sessions with the first and the second group were executed in September and October 2022. We then conducted a French-speaking session with a third FG in June 2023 with practitioners from Tunisia to enrich the results with insights from another cultural setting. To verify the results and achieve saturation, we performed another session with a fourth FG in October 2023. We facilitated the FGs following the leading questions. We audio-recorded the sessions and took field notes. We then conducted qualitative coding [7] across the group results to answer our research questions. The results for RQ1 were rediscussed in a second session with FG1 and FG2 and verified with FG3 and FG4. To respond to RQ2, we deducted success factors for effective communication: Sessions of FG1 and FG2 led to 16 success factors. FG3 and FG4 verified and extended them to 20 success factors. They were reviewed and adjusted in two further iterations by the research team, consisting of three researchers. We further applied selective coding to assign the identified success factors to the COBIT components as displayed in earlier research [40]. Through the alignment of the factors to the categories, we ensure a holistic approach and the link to an existing framework [40, 45]. Following earlier research on success factors [2, 29], we chose the Ishikawa diagram to visualize the relationship between the identified factors. It further allows structuring the problem and the determining factors [29].

4 Findings

In the following, we outline our findings from the FG sessions and thereby answer our research questions. To do so, we present the perception of IT costs and value and describe the factors for effective communication of IT costs and IT business value.

4.1 The Perception of IT Costs and IT Business Value

In this subsection, we describe the results of our first research question: *What is the perception of business and IT stakeholders of "IT costs" and "IT business value"?* We start with the perception of IT costs followed by IT business value.

IT Cost Perception. The interpretation of IT costs varies among the participants of the FGs. Some consider *only the costs allocated to the IT department,* while others include *all input factors related to information technology, regardless of their place of origin.* However, even if all input factors related to IT are perceived as IT costs, identifying, and capturing cost for shadow IT and new technologies such as Low-Code Development Platforms, which are largely based in the business, can be challenging. The perception of IT costs often differs between IT and business employees: while the IT department distinguishes between service development and operations, or project implementation and management, business departments mainly focus on total project or service costs. One participant states that his organization achieves a consensus on how to proceed with cost management, despite differing personal perceptions, due to regular exchange and a corporate guideline for the definition of IT costs (FG1-2).

In collaboration with the participants from FG1 and FG2, we develop a layer model to compare different perceptions of IT costs (see [41]). The participants of FG3 and FG4 evaluate the model and express their experience regarding the actual perception of IT costs and the desired understanding needed for effective IT cost management in their organization. Figure 2 illustrates these distinctions and levels of detail: *Direct IT costs* (A) related to activities assigned to the IT department are displayed in the first layer. The FG participants follow definitions of direct costs propagated by [27] and consider costs for the development and operation of hardware and software, personnel costs, external services, and shared services as general IT costs. The next layer comprises *management costs in the IT department* (B). They include the planning functions of IT, such as governance or enterprise architecture management (EAM), which indirectly contribute to value creation. According to the most participants, these overhead costs are part of the overall IT costs that are "charged to the business units as an overhead fee" (FG2-1). The layers A and B are perceived and captured in the experts' organizations as IT costs and are considered a must for an effective IT cost management (ITCM). Equally the third layer (C) is regarded essentially by both FG3 and FG4. However, *IT project costs* (C) that arise within *business departments* are often not fully attributed to IT costs within their organizations. These costs are related to activities such as process definition or testing within the business departments. The fourth layer comprises *IT-related coordination costs in business departments* (D). The costs primarily consist of the time spent by business departments on IT tasks, such as training, key user activities, or committees for process and project portfolio coordination. Most FG participants perceive these costs as IT costs and believe they should be captured for effective ITCM – particularly due to the rising complexity that leads to more coordination activities and related costs. Yet, organizations do only partially or not at all capture these costs in layer D. The consideration of *overall process costs* (E) is related to the capturing of all (IT) costs throughout a whole process. However, the "effort of a holistic end-to-end consideration of all IT costs in a process does often not pay off" (FG1-3). Therefore, the interviews show that organizations rarely apply an integral approach such as activity-based costing, even though it could lead to a more effective management.

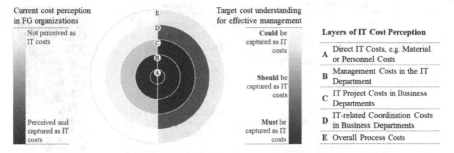

Fig. 2. Layers of IT cost perception

IT Business Value Perception. The participants in the focus groups acknowledge that measuring and presenting the business value of IT is a significant challenge. For most of them, the term "business value of IT" refers to the contribution of IT activities to the overall value of a company as perceived by the business. However, this perception varies among the stakeholders in the companies: top management often perceives value only in terms of the financial benefits of IT. Therefore, IT business value perception is initially categorized into two dimensions: monetary and non-monetary. The monetary value contribution of IT is typically measured through revenue, while the non-monetary value contribution is reflected by other features such as enhancing business capabilities. Similarly, added value can be found in the optimization of existing processes or capabilities. The external perception of customers or partners can also determine the non-monetary value of IT, particularly in relation to new business fields or security risks.

The collaboration between business and IT can lead to different perceptions of the business value of IT. The dimensions discussed in the FG sessions relate to the SAM model and its alignment perspectives [18], as displayed in Fig. 3: In terms of strategy execution (1), IT's added value lies in maintaining operational capability and sustaining the business. IT is an integral part of the business. It provides basic services and meets technical requirements to keep operations running. The perspective of technology transformation (2) ensures that IT supports strategic differentiation and through that provides business value. Here, IT enables the development and implementation of the business strategy, builds strategic competencies, and supports the strategic differentiation of the organization. Participants mention IT's value through the provision of data, which enables better decision-making, such as for predictive maintenance or risk modeling. In addition, IT can provide value by facilitating the growth of new business areas or the repositioning of the strategic product market combination through innovation. This can be accomplished by aligning on the competitive potential perspective (3). Lastly, alignment on a service level perspective (4) leads to IT value through continuous improvement. The FGs perceive this perspective of the business value of IT in the development of tools and processes that enable automation and process optimization. The new IT capabilities offer opportunities to reduce costs, increase efficiency and effectiveness, and support business capabilities.

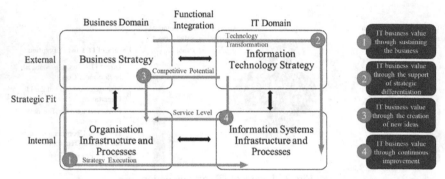

Fig. 3. Differing perceptions of business value of IT related to SAM

4.2 Success Factors of Effective Communication

Next, we answer our second research question: *(2) What factors do organizations need to consider for implementing an effective communication of IT costs and business value?* Our findings show that organizations need to consider various factors to operationalize an effective communication of IT costs and business value of IT. The Ishikawa diagram in Fig. 4 illustrates those factors. In the following, we outline the identified success factors based on the seven components of the COBIT framework.

Organizational Structures. COBIT 2019 presents organizational structures as "key decision-making entities in organizations" [20]. For the effective communication of IT costs and business value, organizations require interface functions and cooperative governance as structural elements:

- **Interface functions:** establish key functions or roles for the dialogue to discuss business and IT strategies and IT costs and value.
- **Cooperative governance:** ensure responsibility and decision competencies of both business and IT communication part.

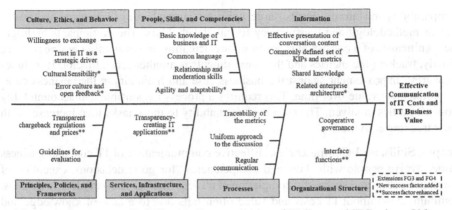

Fig. 4. Success Factors for Effective Communication of IT Costs and IT Business Value

For the FGs, an important success factor are interface functions that communicate information on IT cost and business value. For example, a "business analyst with competencies of strategy knowledge, business and technology understanding and communication skills could be situated within the IT department" (FG3-2). However, a collaboration also requires a determined counterpart to become the "voice of IT within the business" (FG1-1). Those interface functions request responsibilities for decision-making. Decisions should made cooperatively to foster involvement and commitment on both sides. This also requires "clearly defined roles and transparent reporting lines" (FG4-1), regardless of the organizational structure. Such a cooperative governance enables a strategic discussion on IT investments and metrics and leads to effective communication of the IT business value. Also, top management should be involved in discussions through boards and commit to decisions.

Processes. The component processes describes "activities to achieve certain objectives and [...] overall IT-related goals" [20]. Effective communication requires activities such as regular dialogues and a uniform approach to the discussion. Furthermore, the activity of tracking metrics and committed tasks accounts for a success factor.

- **Regular communication:** establish a dialogue format between business and IT counterparts for regular communication.
- **Uniform approach to the discussion:** foster a defined approach to the evaluation and discussion of value.
- **Traceability of the metrics:** track the defined metrics and ensure commitments and consistency.

The participants emphasize the importance of regular communication and propose a dialogue format to discuss the strategic use of IT and associated costs. This dialogue should be integrated into the planning and steering processes to ensure that the topics are incorporated into the budget plan, as well as the demand and project portfolio discussions. The frequency of these dialogues may vary depending on the business requirements. Secondly, it is important to have a uniform approach to this discussion as it enables comparability and fairness. Furthermore, uniformity in evaluating IT investments ensures a clear methodology and transparency for all stakeholders. The participants highlight the significance of a consistent procedure for calculating and evaluating business cases. Finally, tracking the metrics and the commitments is another crucial factor. It includes measuring improvement against the business case and maintaining the business cases to demonstrate value over time. This requires a process responsible and accountability from all parties involved. The stakeholders' liability to those tasks then increases with clear tracking activities.

People, Skills, and Competencies. Effective communication of IT cost and business value involve people with skills and competencies "for good decisions, execution of corrective action and successful completion of all activities" [20]. According to the FGs, communication about IT costs and value often fails due to a lack of knowledge and know-how, both in the business and in the IT department, as well as a lack of efficiency in implementation. The involved stakeholders, therefore, require a basic knowledge of the business and IT domain, the competency to communicate about the costs and value associated with IT, agility, and adaptability in times of rapid change, as well as agile skills that enable effective communication and problem-solving.

- **Basic knowledge of business and IT:** build knowledge in business and IT departments to understand the specialization of the conversation partner.
- **Common language:** establish the competency to develop a common language to communicate IT costs and IT business value.
- **Relationship and moderation skills:** ensure effective communication tailored to the target group through relationship and moderation skills.
- **Agility and Adaptability:** develop skills for flexible and open-minded conversation as well as quick decision-making and navigate conversations according to context and required timeliness.

The acquisition of knowledge is important for all parties involved. Employees in the business sector need to possess technical knowledge and be aware of the challenges they may face. It is essential that they understand the processes and operations of the IT department. Additionally, they must have the ability to articulate their IT requirements, as well as any problems or deficiencies they encounter. Thereby "a basic knowledge about digital business models would also be helpful" (FG4-1). In contrast, IT employees require business knowledge about the capabilities and processes as well as methodical know-how on cost accounting. Furthermore, both conversation partners should establish a common language. This competency not only involves the common definition of IT costs and value but particularly understanding where the value of IT can be realized in the respective business units and for the whole organization. Business and IT counterparts should understand how to generate value and what drives the thereby occurring IT costs. For this conversation, soft skills are essential to build trust and communicate audience-oriented. The IT counterpart should "take a pragmatic approach and build a relationship through honesty" (FG1-3). Thereby, a "structured way of moderation" (FG2-8) strengthens the credibility and leads to an efficient conversation. In addition, effective communication requires an agile mindset and adaptability due to the fast pace of change and the blurring of organizational boundaries between business and IT. An agile way of working enables "greater flexibility within the conversation and when making quick decisions" (FG3-2). Thereby, they should act as "change managers for a continuous improvement of communication" (FG4-3).

Information. The COBIT 2019 framework states that information is omnipresent throughout any organization [20]. The effective communication of IT costs and business value requires information to build a shared knowledge base. Additional success factors are a commonly defined set of KPIs and metrics, transparency about the related IT landscape and the effective presentation of the conversation content.

- **Shared knowledge base:** report basic information necessary to understand counterparts and find common ground.
- **Commonly defined set of KPIs and metrics:** agree on a set of metrics to measure IT performance quantitatively and qualitatively.
- **Related enterprise architecture information:** share information on applications, services and business capabilities to connect IT cost and business value.
- **Effective presentation of conversation content:** visualize the information on IT cost and business value of IT appropriately for the respective stakeholders.

For the FG participants, a shared knowledge base enables effective communication. It relates to a structured approach beginning with the alignment of the IT strategy with business objectives and financial constraints. Thereby the business strategy and planned strategic fields of action should be openly communicated. This information promotes a common understanding among all parties of how IT can contribute to business objectives and the potential complexity that may impede its contribution. The focus of communication should be on the impact of IT use instead of purely cost-based discussions. This involves asking questions such as where IT can deliver value, what the costs and "cost drivers" (FG4-1) are, and how they can be optimized, highlighting the strategic significance of IT. To communicate this business value, the stakeholders should come up with an agreed set of KPIs and metrics to measure IT performance. However, defining and implementing these KPIs is often a challenge. The participants, therefore, see an important factor in defining the KPIs in cooperation between business and IT. Moreover, they propose to use business capabilities as a baseline and to develop metrics that capture IT's contribution, both in terms of monetary value and soft factors. Those business capabilities are, together with e.g. services and applications, part of an EAM. By transparently sharing information on those and their contribution to the business, IT costs are more tangible and the value for the business is relatable. An active co-design of the IT landscape enables its business-oriented and cost-efficient management. However, it requires a high data quality to achieve real transparency and value-add (FG4-2). Lastly, successful communication of IT cost and value requires a well-crafted presentation. This entails the creation of a management-ready consolidation of the outcomes that adheres to the organization's standards. Additionally, a participant mentions a "portfolio visualization that enables better understanding in the business and that allows stakeholders to measure progress through the agreed targets" (FG1-6).

Culture, Ethics, and Behavior. The factors concerning culture, ethics, and behavior "are often underestimated" [20], however, for the FGs, corporate culture plays an essential role in the effective communication. They highlight the willingness to exchange information, the trust in IT to deliver value drive the business strategically as well as a culture that is open for error and a general cultural sensibility:

- **Willingness to exchange:** foster acceptance of IT as a discussion partner and the commitment to exchange information.
- **Trust in IT as a strategic driver:** foster awareness of the qualitative value proposition of IT instead of rather number-driven management.
- **Error culture and feedback:** establish a culture of constructive criticism and appreciation of feedback to foster continuous improvement and build trust.
- **Cultural Sensibility:** foster awareness of cultural differences and understanding, and respect for the cultural nuances, values, beliefs, and norms to adapt verbal and nonverbal communication in multicultural contexts.

The participants report encountering a "transparent wall" (FG2-5) between business and IT that obstructs effective communication and the recognition of the business value of IT. The commitment to exchange at all levels and the acceptance of the IT department as a "discussion partner at eye level" (FG1-1) counts as a success factor. Business and IT should commit together to savings and their consequences because a "successful exchange is also about putting the same intentions – the overall success of the company – in the center of attention" (FG2-7). Thereby, especially business employees should trust that IT may drive business development strategically. A shared worldview on the strategic importance of IT then enables effective communication and acceptance of potential value contribution of IT. The interlocutors should acknowledge that in addition to quantitative performance measures, IT's contribution may also be qualitative. Therefore, the success of communication requires a cultural shift from number-driven management to the acceptance of qualitative arguments, even on the business side. A culture of learning from mistakes and the opportunity for open feedback are also essential for successful communication: Through a culture of error, "communication is not characterized by accusations about lacking value delivery and non-transparent cost chargeback but by a common striving for improvement" (FG4-1). Constructive feedback enables this continuous improvement concerning the value delivery as well as the collaboration between business and IT in general. During this effective cooperation, the cultural backgrounds of those involved also play a decisive role, especially in an international context or in multinational corporations as discussed in FG3. For example, there were differences in the understanding of hierarchies and individual terms such as IT/IS business value. To achieve a common understanding, "cultural differences must be appreciated and openly communicated" (FG3-2).

Services, Infrastructure, and Applications. For the support of processing and management in organizations with information technology, COBIT 2019 mentions services, infrastructure, and applications [20]. Also, effective communication necessitates technology support to create transparency.

- **Transparency-creating IT application:** provide technical support for illustration of IT costs, IT landscape and metrics as well as tracking mechanisms for communicated targets.

For the participants, transparency of IT costs is crucial for honest communication. Therefore, IT applications must integrate cost information from different databases and present relevant numbers. Applications should support the communication of business value by comparing actual and target figures, as well as the budget plan and the actual project portfolio. This enables comparability and traceability of IT investments and their generated impact. Furthermore, EAM tools improve transparency regarding the IT landscape, providing a better understanding of "which applications are being delivered and where money is being spent on" (F4-3).

Principles, Policies, and Frameworks. For "practical guidance for day-to-day management" [20], organizations apply principles, policies, and frameworks. The participants mention tense discussions in day-to-day management about cost allocation and service delivery. They, therefore, highlight practical guidance through transparent chargeback regulations and guidelines for IT investment evaluation as success factors.

- **Transparent chargeback regulations and prices:** set up agreed rules for the allocation of IT costs and transparent prices for the supply with IT services.
- **Guidelines for evaluation:** set up transparent guidelines for decision-making and if required business case calculation for IT investments.

A prerequisite for the setup of cost allocation rules is a comprehensible service offer of IT and the related prices. Then business requires transparency on what they will be charged for. Preselected chargeback regulations foster the acceptance of IT costs in the business. Thereby, the participants mention that e.g. in the case of cost allocation with planned prices, the decision on how these allocated costs are compared with the actual amounts at the end of the fiscal year should be announced transparently (true up or true down). For the participants mechanisms to support this transparency are clearly defined service catalogues of IT and a catalogue management aligned to business needs (FG4-1/2/3). Furthermore, organizations need clear guidelines on how to decide on IT investments and if business case calculation is valuable. If a business case is required there should be clear calculation specifications and evaluation mechanisms. However, the participants stress that not every decision requires a business case, particularly if the "projects are business critical or legally necessary" (FG1-6). In general, IT management mechanisms and decision processes should be based on established "standardized frameworks such as ITIL or COBIT to ensure continuous service improvement, cost control, optimized communication" (FG4-4).

5 Discussion

The findings give answers to our research questions. In the following, we discuss and interpret those results in relation to the research questions. We thereby debate the significance of the differing perceptions of IT costs and business value among the stakeholders and their relevance to communication. Furthermore, we examine the identified success factors, compare them to previous research, and outline how they can contribute to the operationalization of effective communication in organizations.

5.1 Differing Perceptions of IT Costs and Business Value of IT

The costs of IT "appear more tangible in nature" [27] than the value and therefore are "often perceived to be easier to estimate" [27]. The findings stress that business and IT departments, however, rely on different understandings of IT costs. This lack of a clear definition and a common understanding hampers transparency and leads to difficulties in cost management [40]. The developed layer model visualizes the complexity and multidimensional nature of IT costs for the participants. It emphasizes that the stakeholders generally agree on the core IT costs, referred to as *direct IT costs* [27], and the *management cost in the IT department*. However, indirect costs, i.e., the outer layers, are often not treated or perceived as IT costs within organizations. We identified those "human and organizational factors" [27], especially outside the IT department. In their detailed study, [34] present various characteristics of indirect costs and emphasize the importance of recognizing these costs as IT costs to enable a holistic evaluation. Therefore, the perception of what IT costs are and to what extent they should be included in metric calculations must follow a clear process and be "determined by a clear cost structure" (FG2-3). Besides, a lack of standardization also leads to challenges in comparing IT costs externally [40]. One FG participant also mentions that "benchmarks, therefore, create false expectations" (FG1-3) because comparison with other companies is often difficult. The layer model displays those different possibilities of perception and creates awareness of the multifaceted complexity of IT costs. Therefore, it provides a basis for a common understanding of how to define IT costs within the organization, as well as a basis for performance metrics and how to compare them beyond.

The inconsistent perception of IT costs and resulting difficulties in IT evaluation hinder the communication of value. This is especially true when the "business value of IT is equated with revenue and the non-monetary contribution of IT is not acknowledged" (FG2-2). One common contrast, also highlighted by the participants, is the differentiation between monetary and non-monetary contribution: business cases are calculated to express the monetary contribution in comparison to IT costs. The non-monetary contribution of IT, however, is challenging to communicate and "misunderstandings about the definition of value can lead to feelings that value was not delivered" [47]. Therefore, it is essential to have alignment between business and IT to ensure their mutual understanding and the perception of value [30]. To illustrate this point, we align the various perceptions of value in Fig. 3 with the SAM. We show that the value contribution of IT and its perception differ depending on the alignment perspective. The participants emphasize that IT is primarily perceived as a facilitator that sustains the business, which is in line with the most common alignment perspective [18], Strategy Execution (1). However, if business and IT foster alignment on different perspectives, it can also improve the perceived value contribution of IT [14]. The study suggests that IT executives, who mainly manage IT strategy, should take the initiative, and empower the other perspectives to amplify value contribution and its perception in the business.

5.2 Communication as the Basis of Perception and Vice Versa

The findings indicate that organizations with regular exchange and clear definitions struggle less to adopt a shared perception of IT costs and business value. An earlier study investigates how executives achieve consensus on the perception of business value and identifies communication as one supportive factor for this consensus [49]. The FGs highlight that a lack of constructive communication between business and IT departments leads to "accusations that the IT department is too expensive" (FG1-1). This statement confirms a previous study's findings that communication shortfall provoke varying perceptions and limited understanding of business expectations [3]. Also, non-constructive discussions about the costs and value contribution of IT can provoke cultural differences [3, 21]. The participants describe this as a lack of trust in the IT department and in IT to be a strategic driver for the business. For this, the ability to develop a "common language is indispensable" (FG1-6). This common language should ideally be expressed in business terms to ensure consistent perception across stakeholders [33]. Thus, our findings stress that for a shared perception of IT costs and business value, it requires effective communication.

Effective communication of IT costs and business value, however, also necessitates a shared understanding of the relevant topics. The stakeholders' perception, therefore, is decisive so that both communication partners feel satisfied and consider the communication effective [51]. Several identified success factors foster the development of this "similar representation in the interlocutors" [38]: Besides the ability to develop a **common language**, the skill to have a **basic knowledge** about the domain of the interlocutor supports a common ground in the conversation. For this, the given information should serve as a **shared knowledge basis**. The **effective presentation of the conversation content** then assists communication through visualization. In conclusion, shared perception and understanding are necessary for effective communication, and establishing these requires active efforts from all participants. The interdependence of perception and communication reinforces that besides the common language, a shared knowledge base, and effective presentation, regularity is decisive for effective communication of IT costs and business value. The success factor of **regular communication** supports this required continuous communication process. This dynamic process aligns with the convergence model theory [43] and research on mutual understanding between business and IT executives for effective communication [1].

5.3 Success Factors for Communication

The effective communication of IT costs and business value is based on successful governance and alignment [14]. Our findings support this interrelation by addressing the success factors mentioned in the EGIT and BITA literature: Specifically, the factors identified in the categories of *people, skills, and competencies,* as well as *culture, ethics, and behavior,* incorporate the success factors of EGIT and BITA mentioned in the theoretical background section. The cultural aspects outlined in the text include factors such as mutual trust and respect [31], business-IT partnership [31], and IT's business orientation [5]. Success factors identified in the category of *people, skills, and competencies* comprise BITA prerequisites such as various skills and knowledge of both business and IT executives [26] as well as the understanding of the IT value chain and persuasiveness of communication [5] required for EGIT success. Even in the evaluation of the success factors presented in [41] conducted by FG3 and FG4, the comprehensive view was extended by factors in those categories such as **agility and adaptability, cultural sensibility** as well as **error culture and feedback**. This illustrates once again that the people involved, and the prevailing corporate culture are crucial for effective communication. However, our study indicates that the effective communication of IT costs and business value requires additional consideration, such as the inclusion of **related enterprise architecture information**. This information can be obtained through better data collection and preparation. Nonetheless, people then need to understand how to interpret the information and thus generate knowledge for effective communication. Therefore, organizations necessitate successful EGIT as a basis and need to drive BITA as a continuous process [8] but additionally, they should consider specific factors when communicating IT costs and business value.

Previous studies in the business value context have already identified shortcomings in communicating IT costs and business value and highlighted relevant aspects for effective communication [16]. The developed factors in our study are in line with these factors of those previous studies: e.g. the required **interface function** represents "business-IT structures to recognize and evaluate opportunities" [47]. The processual factor of **regular communication** mentions regular collaboration [16] and a **uniform approach to the discussion** includes "a clearly defined portfolio value management process" [47]. Earlier studies further establish metric portfolios [16, 33] as a prerequisite for effective measurement and communication of business value or balanced dashboards to "demonstrate the value" [30]. In this study, factors related to information such as a **commonly defined set of KPIs and metrics** and the **effective presentation of conversation content** include those aspects. This close connection with individual aspects investigated in other studies validates our findings. In contrast to these isolated mentions of success factors in previous research, our study develops a comprehensive overview. It thereby includes not only existing aspects but expands them including factors in the category of *principles, policies, and frameworks* neglected in previous studies. The developed overview of success factors, therefore, provides an extension of existing literature aligned with the factors for business value communication identified in earlier studies.

5.4   From Success Factors to Successful Communication

The mapping of relevant success factors onto the COBIT 2019 framework provides an overview from different perspectives. With the seven components, referred to as "enablers" [14] in earlier COBIT versions, our categorization enables the implementation leading to successful IT management [15]. However, as organizations face difficulties in the implementation of effective communication [12, 28, 40], they require further practical guidance for the operationalization of effective communication beyond the aforementioned success factors. Research could, therefore, propose a detailed design of **regular communication** based on the other identified factors. As outlined, the focus thereby needs to lie on the unified understanding and perception. Earlier studies emphasize the importance of a common language [16] based on "terms that the business understands"

[30]. In addition, proven approaches to communication plans [16, 33] should be considered. With the success factors presented, we provide a basis for future research on the operationalization of effective communication regarding IT costs and the business value of IT.

This operationalization is a challenge for organizations and requires a holistic approach that considers the various components (FG 4-4). For the convergence between business and IT executives [1] and to increase knowledge on both sides, organizations incorporate various options: they set up roles such as IT business partner [17] or establish decentral IT functions or IT functions as product IT [39]. However, this does not automatically lead to strategic alignment between business and IT and the maximization of value. Regardless of the organizational structure, relevant information, communication skills and a constructive corporate culture are required. Only then organizations achieve effective communication and through that align business goals and IT opportunities. This enables them to effectively discuss the rising costs of IT and increase the added value for the entire company through IT. Nevertheless, constructive culture cannot be developed on demand but must evolve through relationships that rely on efficient processes and structures [39]. A dialogue format between business and IT would be a format to establish the processes and structures for communication of IT costs and business value. Aligned with organizational principles and existing applications, they can then discuss relevant information, bring people together, and shape culture into a constructive and value-oriented corporate culture.

6 Conclusion

Increasing inflation and security risks urge organizations to manage IT costs effectively and efficiently. Thereby, the communication of IT costs and the impact generated through IT is crucial to remain competitive and to strategically plan investments. However, CIOs face challenges to create a common understanding of IT costs and the business value of IT and furthermore, effectively communicate them. Even if earlier studies also highlight communication as essential for business and IT, a current view on the perception of IT costs and business value as well as a holistic and updated overview of success factors to operationalize effective communication is missing. Therefore, the goal of this publication as extended version of [41] is to identify and evaluate how business and IT stakeholders perceive IT costs and IT business value. With this understanding, we further aim support their effective communication by giving an overview of the success factors that organizations need to consider. To reach this goal, we conduct a FG study and discuss the findings. In summary, the investigation of the perception shows that it differs between the stakeholders for IT costs as well as for the business value of IT. We conclude that to create a common understanding in organizations, they require communication about the perception and a common ground to discuss IT costs and IT business value. The result of the mapping to the seven COBIT components ensures a holistic perspective and enables transparency on the 20 identified factors for effective communication. It thereby offers a structured representation as a basis for the operationalization of effective communication about IT costs and IT business value. Furthermore, the paper highlights that communication is a cyclical process and the interchange is based on the stakeholder's competency to communicate in a common language. This common language then should enable the transparent demonstration of the value of IT for the organization and lead to a constructive and value-oriented corporate culture.

This paper makes a theoretical contribution by providing an insight into the current perception and communication of IT costs and business value of IT, and thus by identifying the relevant factors to operationalize an effective communication. Moreover, practice gains awareness about possible reasons for non-constructive IT cost communication and guidelines on how to turn it into effective communication with a focus on the business value of IT.

However, the study itself has limitations: first, the FGs were conducted mainly with stakeholders close to IT or a good understanding for IT within their organization. Although we mitigated this limitation by including participants with diverse backgrounds and roles, further FGs with a strong business focus could enrich our research findings and add even more validity. Additionally, a quantitative research based on the companies accounting standards would enable a comparison between perception and defined cost types or business cases and therefore be subject of further research. Second, the study does not distinguish the perceptions and success factors by company size or industry which could provide a more differentiated view. We applied the traditional single category design in order to reach a saturation point and to be able to respond to the availability of the study participant. An adapted multiple category design would enable comparison and stakeholder-specific success factor analysis. Third, the study lacks proof that the identified success factors facilitate the operationalization of IT cost and value communication. To overcome this limitation, researchers could in a next step develop and implement a dialogue format to evaluate in a practical case study whether considering these success factors leads to more positive perception and effective communication between business and IT on IT costs and business value.

References

1. Adnan, N.I.M., Jambari, D.I.: Mutual understanding determinants for effective communication in business and IT strategic alignment planning. IJASEIT 6(6), 914–921 (2016)
2. Ahmad, F., Abd Ghani, W.A., Arshad, N.H.: Ishikawa diagram of critical factors for information technology investment success: a conceptual model. In: Proceedings of the 4th ICIME 2013, p. 27 (2013)
3. Bartsch, S.: Ein Referenzmodell zum Wertbeitrag der IT. Zugl.: Marburg, Univ., Diss., (2014). Research. Springer Vieweg, Wiesbaden (2015)
4. Bryman, A., Bell, E.: Business Research Methods, 3rd edn. Oxford University Press, Oxford (2011)
5. Buchwald, A., Urbach, N., Ahlemann, F.: Business value through controlled IT: toward an integrated model of IT governance success and its impact. J. Inf. Technol. 29(2), 128–147 (2014). https://doi.org/10.1057/jit.2014.3
6. Chan, Y.E., Reich, B.H.: IT alignment: what have we learned? J. Inf. Technol. 22(4), 297–315 (2007). https://doi.org/10.1057/palgrave.jit.2000109
7. Corbin, J.M., Strauss, A.L.: Basics of Qualitative Research: Techniques and Procedures for Developing Grounded Theory, 4th edn. Sage Publications, Thousand Oaks (2015). https://doi.org/10.4135/9781452230153

8. Cybulski, J., Lukaitis, S.: The impact of communications and understanding on the success of business/IT alignment (2005)
9. De Haes, S., Gemke, D., Thorp, J., Van Grembergen, W.: KLM's enterprise governance of IT journey: from managing IT costs to managing business value. MIS Q. Executive 10(3), 109 (2011)
10. Gartner Inc.: 2023 CIO Agenda. 4 Actions to Ensure Your Tech Investments Pay Digital Dividends (2022). https://www.gartner.co.uk/en/information-technology/insights/cio-agenda/cio-agenda-ebook
11. Gartner Inc.: Gartner Forecasts Worldwide IT Spending to Grow 5.1% in 2023. Gartner IT Symposium/Xpo™ 2022, Orlando (2022)
12. Gartner Inc.: Communicate IT's Business Value (2023). https://www.gartner.com/en/inform ation-technology/insights/business-value-of-it. Accessed 28 Mar 2023
13. Gibson, M., Arnott, D.: The use of focus groups in design science research. In: ACIS 2007 Proceedings (2007)
14. de Haes, S. (ed.): Enterprise Governance of Information Technology, 3rd edn. Springer, Cham (2020)
15. de Haes, S., Huygh, T., Joshi, A., Van Grembergen, W.: Adoption and impact of IT governance and management practices. Int. J. IT/Bus. Alignment Gov. 7(1), 50–72 (2016). https://doi.org/10.4018/IJITBAG.2016010104
16. Held, T., Westner, M.: IT business value measurement and communication among German CIOs: a conceptual framework. In: Proceedings of 24th CBI, pp. 146–155. IEEE (2022). https://doi.org/10.1109/CBI54897.2022.00023
17. Helouani, W.B.: Business-it alignment: the emerging role of it business partner, EAESP FGV (2022). https://hdl.handle.net/10438/31794. Accessed 21 Dec 2023
18. Henderson, J.C., Venkatraman, H.: Strategic alignment: leveraging information technology for transforming organizations. IBM Syst. J. 32(1), 472–484 (1993). https://doi.org/10.1147/sj.382.0472
19. Hillebrand, P., Westner, M.: Success factors of long-term CIOs. Inf. Syst. E-Bus. Manag. 20(1), 79–122 (2022). https://doi.org/10.1007/s10257-021-00546-z
20. ISACA: COBIT 2019®. Framework: Introduction and Methodology. ISACA, Schaumburg (2018)
21. Peppard, J., Ward, J.: 'Mind the Gap': diagnosing the relationship between the IT organisation and the rest of the business. J. Strat. Inf. Syst. 8(1), 29–60 (1999). https://doi.org/10.1016/S0963-8687(99)00013-X
22. Johnson, A.M., Lederer, A.L.: The effect of communication frequency and channel richness on the convergence between chief executive and chief information officers. JMIS 22(2), 227–252 (2005). https://doi.org/10.1080/07421222.2005.11045842
23. Kohli, R., Devaraj, S.: Realizing the business value of information technology investments: an organizational process. MIS Q. Executive 3(1), 6 (2004)
24. Kohli, R., Grover, V.: Business value of IT: an essay on expanding research directions to keep up with the times. J. Assoc. Inf. Syst. 9, 1 (2008)
25. Krueger, R.A., Casey, M.A.: Focus Groups. A Practical Guide for Applied Research, 5th edn. SAGE, Los Angeles, London, New Delhi, Singapore, Washington DC (2015)
26. Kurti, I., Barolli, E., Sevrani, K.: Critical success factors for business-IT alignment: a review of current research. Rom. Econ. Bus. Rev. 8(3), 79 (2013)
27. Love, P., Irani, Z., Fulford, R.: Understanding IT costs: an exploratory study using the structured case method. In: PACIS 2003 Proceedings, Adelaide, Australia, p. 45 (2003)
28. Lozada, C., Naegle, R.: Effective communication is critical to successful cost optimization efforts (2020). https://www.gartner.com/en/documents/3990229. Accessed 13 Apr 2023
29. Luca, L.: Success factors for R & D projects. In: MATEC Web of Conferences (2018)

30. Luftman, J.: Assessing business-IT alignment maturity. CAIS **4** (2000). https://doi.org/10. 17705/1CAIS.00414
31. Luftman, J., Papp, R., Brier, T.: Enablers and inhibitors of business-IT alignment. CAIS **1** (1999). https://doi.org/10.17705/1CAIS.00111
32. Merhout, J., Havelka, D., Rajkumar, T.: Determining factors that lead students to study information systems using an alumni focus group. In: ACIS 2016 Proceedings (2016)
33. Mitra, S., Sambamurthy, V., Westerman, G.: Measuring IT performance and communicating value. MIS Q. Executive **10**(1), 47 (2011)
34. Mohamed, S., Irani, Z.: Developing taxonomy of information system's indirect human costs. In: Proceedings of 2nd ICSTM 2002 (2002)
35. Muszyńska, K.: Patterns of communication management in project teams. In: Ziemba, E. (ed.) ISM AITM 2016. LINIB, vol. 277, pp. 202–221. Springer, Cham (2017). https://doi. org/10.1007/978-3-319-53076-5_11
36. Urbach, N., Buchwald, A., Ahlemann, F.: Understanding IT governance success and its impact. In: ECIS 2013 Proceedings, Utrecht, The Netherlands, p. 55 (2013)
37. Njanka, S.Q., Sandula, G., Colomo-Palacios, R.: IT-business alignment: a systematic literature review. Procedia Comput. Sci. **181**, 333–340 (2021). https://doi.org/10.1016/j.procs.2021. 01.154
38. Pickering, M.J., Garrod, S.: Alignment as the basis for successful communication. Res. Lang. Comput.Comput. **4**(2–3), 203–228 (2006). https://doi.org/10.1007/s11168-006-9004-0
39. Rentrop, C.: IT-Governance - Erfolgsfaktor der digitalen Transformation. Erich Schmidt Verlag GmbH & Co. KG, Berlin (2023)
40. Riedinger, C., Huber, M.: An expert view on challenges in managing IT costs in the digital age. In: IADIS IS 2023 Proceedings, Lisbon, Portugal (2023)
41. Riedinger, C., Huber, M., Prinz, N.: Factors for effective communication of IT costs and IT business value. In: Proceedings of the 18th FedCSIS, pp. 677–687. IEEE (2023). https://doi. org/10.15439/2023F7224
42. Riedinger, C., Huber, M., Prinz, N., Rentrop, C.: Towards a taxonomy of strategic drivers of IT costs. In: Papadaki, M., Rupino, P., da Cunha, M., Themistocleous, K.C. (eds.) EMCIS 2022, vol. 464, pp. 555–569. Springer, Cham (2023). https://doi.org/10.1007/978-3-031-30694- 5_39
43. Rogers, E.M., Kincaid, D.L.: Communication Networks: Toward a New Paradigm for Research. Free Press; Collier Macmillan, New York, London (1981)
44. Roses, L.K., Brito, J.C.B., de Lucena Filho, G.J.: Conversational competences model for information technology and business strategic alignment. JISTEM **12**, 125–144 (2015)
45. Saunders, M.: Research Methods for Business Students, 8th edn. Pearson, Harlow (2019)
46. Smith, H.A., McKeen, J.D.: From technology to value: the perennial IT challenge. Queen's University Canada (2020). https://smith.queensu.ca/_templates/documents/it-forum/techno logy-to-value.pdf. Accessed 20 Sept 2022
47. Smith, H.A., McKeen, J.D.: Developments in practice VII: developing and delivering the IT value proposition. CAIS **11** (2003). https://doi.org/10.17705/1CAIS.01125
48. Solanki, S., Bant, A.: 9 winning actions to take as recession threatens (2022). https://www. gartner.com/en/articles/9-winning-actions-to-take-as-recession-threatens. Accessed 28 Mar 2023
49. Tallon, P.P.: Do you see what I see? The search for consensus among executives' perceptions of IT business value. Eur. J. Inf. Syst. **23**(3), 306–325 (2014). https://doi.org/10.1057/ejis. 2013.2

50. Toppenberg, G.: Expanded understanding of IS/IT related challenges in mergers and acquisitions: methods & research context. In: ECIS 2015 Proceedings 2015, p. 182 (2015)
51. van Ruler, B.: Communication theory: an underrated pillar on which strategic communication rests. Int. J. Strateg. Commun.Strateg. Commun. **12**(4), 367–381 (2018). https://doi.org/10. 1080/1553118X.2018.1452240

Approaches to Improving of Social Problems

A Quantitative and Qualitative Exploration of Critical Factors in the IAI-CGM Framework: The Perspective of Saudi Patients with Type 1 Diabetes Mellitus

Hamad Almansour[1,2]([⊠]), Natalia Beloff[1] [iD], and Martin White[1] [iD]

[1] Department of Informatics, University of Sussex, Brighton, UK
{ha432,n.beloff,m.white}@sussex.ac.uk
[2] The Applied College, Najran University, Najran, Saudi Arabia

Abstract. An internet of things-enabled continuous glucose monitor (IoT-CGM) is a medical device designed for continuous monitoring of patients' glucose levels without the need for frequent fingerstick blood samples. This study aims to measure the adoption intention of individuals with type-1 diabetes in Saudi Arabia, with a specific focus on identifying the critical factors influencing their intention to adopt IoT-CGMs. The surge in the number of type-1 diabetes patients in Saudi Arabia demands prompt and effective measures. This medical condition is becoming significantly more prevalent, with reports indicating that a quarter of Saudi adults are expected to develop diabetes by 2030. This study employed both quantitative and qualitative approaches to investigate the significance of practical, technological, and user behaviour factors in the intention to adopt internet of things-enabled continuous glucose monitors (IAI-CGM) among patients with type-1 diabetes mellitus (T1DM) in Saudi Arabia. Quantitative data were collected from 873 T1DM patients in Saudi Arabia. Simultaneously, semi-structured interviews were conducted with 15 T1DM patients from King Khaled Najran Hospital (KKNH) and the Najran region in Saudi Arabia. The framework predicts a significant impact of all factors on the adoption intention except for technology-related self-efficacy (TRSE), allowing for the assessment of Saudi T1DM patients' readiness for IoT-CGM. Conversely, accuracy and accessibility emerge as the primary driving themes, with accurate results significantly influencing individuals towards adopting IoT-CGMs, as revealed in the qualitative results. The complexity of new technologies and the lengthy process involved in acquiring the device hindered the adoption of IoT-CGMs. However, the user-friendly interfaces of such devices contributed to the adoption intention. Patients' attitudes significantly influenced the tendency to adopt the technology, although concerns about appearance were also evident. The results of this study provide recommendations to enhance the overall quality of the user experience with IoT-CGMs. It is recommended that CGM makers explore ways to reduce the cost of these devices through mass production, particularly for individuals residing in countries with lower standards of living. Furthermore, the novelty of the framework may inspire the development of comparable frameworks for wearable or attached health-monitoring devices catering to patients with various medical conditions and in different geographical locations.

E. Ziemba et al. (Eds.): FedCSIS-ITBS 2023/ISM 2023, LNBIP 504, pp. 119–140, 2024.
https://doi.org/10.1007/978-3-031-61657-0_6

Keywords: IAI-CGM · TIDM · IoT · CGM · AI · TAM · SA

1 Introduction

Type 1 diabetes is on the rise, especially in developing countries and expected to increase rapidly in coming years, with the majority of prevalent cases are seen in adults [21]. Given that diabetes is a life-long condition, it is very important for patient's empowerment and general quality of life to be able to achieve high degree of autonomy in self-care for diabetes and its corresponding effects [6]. Patient empowerment, a concept, involves actively involving patients in the diagnosis and monitoring of their health condition within the healthcare process facilitated by the use of IoT healthcare systems [13]. The realization of an IoT healthcare system not only holds the promise of enabling remote treatment for patient monitoring and disease detection, representing a current trend [26] but also signifies a transformative shift in healthcare dynamics.

The rising prevalence of diabetes in Saudi Arabia is attributed to Westernized food and sedentary lifestyles. By 2030, it is expected that a quarter of Saudi adults will develop diabetes, with over half of Saudis over the age of 30 having diabetes or being at risk [2]. To address this, empowering patients to manage their blood glucose levels is crucial [16]. However, patients often struggle to follow physicians' advice on self-care management, thus necessitating the use of complex technology. Innovative wearable technology has led to the creation of wireless body area networks that can monitor healthcare delivery, including diabetes self-management [37]. To standardize internet of things (IoT)-enabled continuous glucose monitoring (CGM) devices in Saudi Arabian primary care institutions, an in-depth analysis of the IoT within the healthcare system is necessary.

This study aims to measure patients' preparedness and willingness to use CGM devices in Saudi primary diabetes care settings to promote patient autonomy. A literature review was conducted to establish the extent to which intelligent technologies have become incorporated within the Saudi healthcare system. The technology acceptance model (TAM) was employed to measure patients' autonomy and preparedness to adopt IoT-CGMs, which was surveyed among people with T1DM. The study utilized a mixed-methods approach, encompassing both quantitative and qualitative analysis of diabetic patients in Saudi Arabia regarding their preparedness for autonomy.

Given the resource constraints and significant health management risks faced by emerging nations, research in this field is crucial. Additionally, the study aims to fill a gap in knowledge by examining Saudi Arabia's efforts in digital transformation and its readiness for the incorporation of the IoT into healthcare [4]. The results of this study will contribute to an improved understanding of how advancing IoT-CGM adoption and primary diabetes self-management in Saudi Arabia can help the country to achieve its digital transformation goals [36] by 2030.

2 Theoretical Background

The theoretical background provides the role of CGM in type-1 diabetic patients in primary care and addresses their concerns regarding the adoption of IoT-CGMs.

2.1 Role of CGM in T1DM Primary Care

CGM is crucial in the management of T1DM in primary care. It enables patients to respond to their readings and maintain safe levels of blood glucose, leading to improved self-management of their diabetes [33]. CGMs provide continual feedback on blood sugar levels, encouraging patients to take their prescribed medication as required, thus improving glucose levels. However, poor drug compliance is a serious issue in Saudi Arabia [27]; it is attributed mainly to inadequate education and urban lifestyles.

To improve technology tolerance among low-income and urban patients, the deployment of IoT-CGMs requires improvements to patients' health literacy [31]. The provision of instructions for self-management and follow-up by primary care institutions can help to reduce patients' blood glucose levels. Self-management increases patients' health-related autonomy, competence, and motivation, but if it is to be effective, patients must be educated about their responsibilities in controlling T1DM. Encouraging patients' autonomy facilitates doctors' regulation of blood glucose levels. This implies that the provision of health education to patients could improve their sense of responsibility for controlling their own T1DM via personal empowerment [24]. The study concludes that IoT-CGMs might improve patient autonomy, but their adoption is uncertain [41], and issues affecting this adoption need to be addressed.

2.2 IoT-CGM: Adoption Concerns

The use of IoT-CGM devices has been demonstrated to provide a range of benefits for diabetic patients, including improved management of long-term complications [32]. However, despite advancements in their dependability and accuracy, these devices have not yet been widely adopted, with most diabetic patients still relying on the traditional method of drawing a sample of blood from a fingertip to measure their blood sugar. Various factors contribute to the slow uptake of IoT-CGMs, such as initial concerns about the devices' lack of accuracy [1], patients' ignorance of the advantages they can bring, and economic and sociopsychological barriers to their adoption.

Studies have shown that appropriate use of CGM devices, advice from medical professionals, and prompt responses to CGM alarms can significantly reduce long-term complications in diabetic patients [12, 28]. Gia et al. [18] provided evidence that proper medical guidance can help to reduce the rate of long-term complications from 75% to 40%.

However, without a study using the TAM, it is difficult to determine the likelihood that patients nationwide will adhere to medical recommendations and sustain benefits from the management of long-term complications. Furthermore, wearable smart gadgets, including IoT-CGMs, are still at an emergent stage, and work is needed to persuade developing nations to adopt them.

According to Rodbard [34], only 8% to 17% of T1DM patients are using CGM devices. However, researchers [30] have provided evidence that the IoT healthcare sector is expected to become a 2 trillion US dollar industry by 2025. Despite this ambitious prediction, the adoption rate remains very low.

Another study, conducted by Ayanlande et al. [8], elaborated that the acceptability of CGM devices is also determined by patients' socio-psychological characteristics, and by the affordability of these devices, both for patients and for the healthcare system of the region in which they reside. Meanwhile, another study indicated that the availability of such devices depends on the scope of the service to fulfil minimum requirements [15]. Furthermore, Gray and Gilbert [20] discussed the development of health information technology (HIT)-enabled patient care that empowers patients and provides them with the capability to engage in self-management, with the ultimate goal of ensuring that health matters such as diabetes care are not poorly managed.

While Saudi Arabia is a prosperous nation, it has an unequal distribution of incomes, and has only recently started using IoT-CGMs. It has a diverse patient population, including those who have already adopted IoT-CGMs, those who are aware of them but are reluctant to use them, and those who have not yet heard of them. Therefore, research on the adoption of IoT-CGMs in Saudi Arabia includes a range of complex factors.

To assess the slow uptake of IoT-CGMs in Saudi Arabia, the present study proposes a new paradigm for adoption with its theoretical foundations in the TAM. The TAM considers a range of factors, including economic, sociopsychological, and healthcare infrastructure determinants of acceptance, accessibility, affordability, and satisfaction across the breadth of the service [29]. However, there is a dearth of knowledge on the usage of healthcare technology designed specifically for T1DM, which is a health issue that must be handled very carefully.

Increasing the use of IoT-CGMs in Saudi Arabia and other nations is a significant issue, and the first stage in achieving the criteria set for improving healthcare quality in Saudi Arabia is to understand the viability of such adoption. The literature on CGMs for diabetes using the IoT is extensive, but most of the studies conducted to date have focused on the benefits and effectiveness of self-management and on identifying the variables that influence the slow uptake of medical technology.

Therefore, the initial stages of such research involve determining the adoption characteristics of T1DM patients and providing an adoption framework that is specific to these patients. Wearable smart devices offer the most appropriate solutions, but patients are not required to use them, and health factors and technological adoption scales are not always considered. Thus, it is crucial to develop a framework for IoT-CGM adoption that is tailored to T1DM patients. The structure proposed in the present study provides the theoretical underpinnings for this framework and a clear overview of the nation's present adaptability.

2.2.1 Introduction of the Framework

The authors proposed the Intention to Adopt IoT-enabled Continuous Glucose Monitors (IAI-CGM) framework in [4]. Based on this framework, the present study seeks to identify the factors that influence adoption in order to analyse the preparedness and willingness of primary patients with T1DM, particularly in Saudi Arabia, to use IoT-CGM technology.

2.2.2 Predictive Capabilities and Constituting Factors

The framework (see Fig. 1) has strong predictive capabilities for assessing the adoption of IoT-CGM to monitor blood glucose levels. The factors that constitute the proposed framework, as designed by Borges and Kubiak [10], include perceived reliability (PR), perceived usefulness (PU), ease of use (EU), information overload (IO), technology-related self-efficacy (TRSE), attitude (AT), intention to use (IT), and visibility of body change (VBC).

The theoretical framework is based on the TAM and is categorized into three main factors: practical factors, technological factors, and user behaviour factors. This framework is used to investigate the spread of cutting-edge technologies with the aim of enhancing patients' adoption of IoT-CGMs. This represents a significant step towards patients' self-empowerment through the widespread adoption of IoT-CGMs.

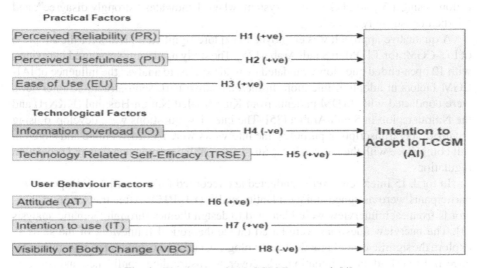

Fig. 1. The proposed IAI-CGM Framework [4]

3   Research Methodology

This study aims to investigate the factors that influence the adoption of IoT-CGM devices by T1DM patients in Saudi Arabia. The study used a mixed-methods approach to collect quantitative and qualitative data from participants. In the quantitative part, Qualtrics was used for survey creation and administration, while Microsoft OneDrive was utilized for data storage. In addition, IBM SPSS was used for data analysis. The survey questions were grounded in the theoretical framework of the study, which identified usability, technology, and user behaviour as the primary drivers of adoption intention. The study sample size was calculated based on a confidence level of 95% and a confidence interval of 5%; the total population is 11,662 of T1DM, and based on the statistics provided by [16], at least 372 responses were required. Therefore, an accurate total sample of 873 was collected from the T1DM patients from King Khalid Hospital Saudi Arabia and the Najran region.

There are three categories of human factors that influence patients' decision to embrace IoT-CGM devices: those that are purely theoretical, those that pertain to technology, and those that pertain to user behaviour. Perceived reliability, perceived utility, and simplicity of use are three of the metrics used to assess the practical factors of a product's performance. The technological factors are measured by the innovation orientation and the technology-related self-efficacy measures, while the user behaviour factors are measured by the attitude, the intention to use, and the visibility of body change factors.

The survey questionnaire was developed based on the findings of a previous study [10]. The theoretical framework of this study provides the foundation for the survey. The survey consists of questions that allow for assigning values to each variable. This is done using a 5-point Likert scale system, where 1 indicates "strongly disagree", and 5 indicates "strongly agree".

A qualitative approach was employed to explore significant factors for the adoption of IoT-CGMs for T1DM in Saudi Arabia [25]. The study used semi-structured interviews with 12 open-ended questions, validated by field experts, to analyse the influence of IAI-CGM factors in adoption intention. In the qualitative part, semi-structured interviews were conducted with T1DM patients from King Khaled Najran Hospital (KKNH) and the Najran region in Saudi Arabia [35]. The interview questions were developed using Qualtrics. For transcription purposes, the interviews were recorded online and stored in full compliance with the University of Sussex research data management and protection regulations.

In total, 15 interviews were conducted and recorded for transcription purposes. All participants were assigned unique identity codes **(P1–P15).** After transcription, keywords from each interview were identified to design themes through thematic analysis [3]. The interview questions were based on the theoretical framework of the study to explore the significance of practical, technological, and user behaviour factors that influence IAI-CGM adoption intention. Moreover, to ensure their confidence and trust, no personal information was collected from any T1DM patients. The interview questions were designed based on the findings of [5].

The study took ethical measures to protect the interests of all those involved, making sure participants knew that taking the survey was completely optional and that they could stop at any time without consequences or explanations. Participants were also made aware that their data would not be sold or otherwise distributed to outside parties and were assured of complete privacy. The study did not seek individual information in the questionnaires, and participants were instructed not to provide any identifying information in the survey. In the case of a participant's comment warranting a quotation, a unique numeric identity would be issued instead. Data collection methods and research instruments were approved by the University of Sussex Science and Technology Research Ethics Committee (ER/HA432/2) and by the Institutional Review Board (IRB) in Saudi Arabia, the Ministry of Health, and King Khaled Najran Hospital (KKNH) by assigning IRB registration number with KACST, KSA: H-11-N-081; IRB Log Number 2022-01E.

4 Results

In a quantitative part of study, selecting an appropriate sample size is critical to ensure reliable and transferable results while eliminating bias. The sampling strategy employed in this study followed scientific principles and focused on patients with type 1 diabetes at King Khaled Najran Hospital and the Najran region in Saudi Arabia. The survey was administered online using Qualtrics, with data immediately entered into a database. Outliers are exceptional data points that fall outside of the norm and can result from typos, the poor wording of questionnaires, or data input errors. Univariate outliers stand out in only one way, while multivariate outliers have multiple scores that deviate from the norm [17]. The frequency distribution test and other normality tests can help detect outliers [11]. The research variables in this study had z-scores of less than 3.29 and a standard deviation range of 0.708 to 1.302, indicating no extreme values among the outliers.

In the qualitative part, thematic analysis was performed in which themes were identified based on factors that affected the patients' intentions to adopt IoT-enabled CGM devices. This study was approved by the University of Sussex Science and Technology Research Ethics Committee (ER/HA432 /1).

4.1 Data Analysis and Confirmatory Factor Analysis (CFA)

Confirming the theoretical structure of variables is a crucial part of CFA analysis. It involves conducting one-dimensionality, reliability, and divergent and convergent validity tests. Researchers can determine whether to adopt a theory based on these results. To establish relationships in SEM, researchers should perform CFA on all latent variables, with a minimum latent concept loading of 0.60 for the assessment items measured by one-dimensionality [7]. CFA findings are founded on nine different latent constructs. A few examples of these constructs are technology-related self-efficacy (TRSE), information overload (IO), perceived reliability (PR), perceived usefulness (PU), ease of use (EU), attitude (AT), intention to use (IT), visibility of body change (VBC), and adoption intention (AI).

Table 1. Reliability and Construct Validity

Constructs	Cronbach (above 0.7)	CR	AVE	MSV
TRSE	.756	0.763	0.521	0.274
IO	.772	0.776	0.537	0.383
PR	.842	0.844	0.643	0.127
PU	.821	0.848	0.652	0.475
EU	.821	0.835	0.629	0.241
AT	.773	0.785	0.553	0.441

(continued)

Table 1. (*continued*)

Constructs	Cronbach (above 0.7)	CR	AVE	MSV
IT	.786	0.790	0.557	0.475
VBC	.856	.0.868	0.623	0.397

4.2 Measures of the Model Validity

To ensure construct validity and composite reliability, Cronbach's alpha and composite reliability (C.R.) values were used before hypothesis testing. The present study used Cronbach's alpha with a cut-off value of 0.70, and another study suggests cut-off values of 0.60 for C.R. and 0.70 for Cronbach's alpha [19]. The reliability scores in Table 1 are greater than 0.70. Both Cronbach's alpha and C.R. were used to examine internal consistency, showing the convergent and discriminant validity and reliability of the findings and comparing them with the cut-off-points [22]. The results indicate that all variables are free from measurement error. Assessment for consistency refers to measurements on the same point on two different scales, assuming that an instrument can assess a similar context over time. Cronbach's alpha is considered the initial step to ensure reliability. The present study used Cronbach's alpha and C.R. to test instrument reliability. The study also used average variance extracted (AVE) to identify any variation in the latent variables caused by random measurement errors, with a cut-off value of 0.50 or greater. AVE values were between 0.537 and 0.644. Discriminant validity was achieved through the maximum shared squared variance (MSV), the Fornell-Larcker test, and the average shared squared variance (ASV), with AVE for each construct higher than MSV [23]. The CFA assessment of the model showed that both the convergent and discriminant validity met the fitness criteria.

Table 2. Descriptive Analysis and Factors Loadings for Items

Measure	Chi-square (CMIN)/Degrees of freedom (D.F.)	Comparative fit index (CFI)	Standardized root mean square residual (SRMR)	Root mean square error of approximation (RMSEA)	Normed Fit index (NFI)
Estimate	4.380	0.913	0.054	0.062	0.901
Threshold	Between 1 and 5	>0.90	<0.08	<0.08	>0.90
Interpretation	Good fit	Good fit	Good fit	Good fit	Good fit

4.3 Model Good FitS

The study involved 873 participants, and the observed results for the fitness of the model indicated that all observed statistical values were under the cut-off threshold as given

(CMIN/DF = 4.380, CFI = 0.913, SRMR = 0.054, RMSEA = 0.062, NFI = 0.901). Therefore, no issue was observed regarding the good fit of the model. The results are shown in Table 2.

4.4 Discriminant Validity

Table 3 illustrates that there were no problems regarding discriminant validity, as the square roots of the AVEs' "diagonal line" showed values greater than the values below the diagonal, as demonstrated below. The findings suggest that the CFA model's evaluation was valid with respect to both convergent and discriminant validity criteria.

Table 3. Discriminant Validity

	TRSE	IO	PR	PU	EU	AT	IT	VBC	AI
TRSE	**0.722**								
IO	−0.249	**0.733**							
PR	−0.066	0.356	**0.802**						
PU	0.523	−0.294	−0.034	**0.807**					
EU	0.270	−0.400	−0.230	0.375	**0.793**				
AT	0.430	−0.274	0.023	0.664	0.377	**0.744**			
IT	0.429	−0.431	−0.062	0.689	0.458	0.617	**0.747**		
VBC	−0.350	0.619	0.313	−0.494	−0.491	−0.428	−0.610	**0.789**	
AI	0.421	−0.584	0.059	0.713	0.484	0.669	0.725	−0.630	**0.725**

4.5 Structural Equation Model

In order to test the hypotheses designed for quantitative analysis, structural equation modelling (SEM) was used to investigate the interrelationship between the latent and observed variables via the software AMOS version 28. The SEM approach is widely used in various research fields, such as psychology, behaviour studies, and education in order to perform hypothesis testing. Meanwhile, CFA was conducted to ensure the accuracy and assess the validity of the collected data. The SEM includes both structural and measurement models. Therefore, the AVE score in the convergent validity test should be greater than 0.5, indicating a good model fit [22].

All factors caused a significant change in the dependent factors except hypothesis 5, where TRSE does not have a significant effect on the intention to adopt IoT-CGM. The present study discusses critical factors related to the intention to adopt IoT-CGM.

The results clearly indicate significant differences from previous findings, which may be attributable to regional or cultural differences in the corporate climate or at the individual level. After obtaining empirical evidence from the quantitative part based on SEM, it was observed in Table 4 that perceived reliability (**PR**) has a significant positive influence on the intention to adopt IoT-CGM ($\beta = 0.154$ along with p-value < 0.001). Similarly, perceived usefulness (**PU**) has a significant positive influence on the intention to adopt IoT-CGM ($\beta = 0.251$ along with p-value < 0.001). Next, it was observed that ease of use (**EU**) has a significant positive influence on the intention to adopt IoT-CGM ($\beta = 0.077$ along with p-value < 0.001). Similarly, information overload (**IO**) has a significant negative influence on the intention to adopt IoT-CGM ($\beta = -0.128$, along with $p < 0.001$). On the one hand, technology-related self-efficacy (**TRSE**) does not have a significant influence on the intention to adopt IoT-CGM ($\beta = -0.017$ along with p-value > 0.05). Furthermore, attitude (**AT**) positively influences adoption intention (AI), β value $= .194$ along with $p < 0.05$). Next, the results show that intention to use (**IT**) positively influences the intention to adopt IoT-CGM, with β value $= 0.171$ along with $p < 0.05$). Results further indicate that visibility of body change (**VBC**) has a significant negative impact on intention to adopt IoT-CGM along with $\beta = -0.153$ and p-value < 0.05. Based on overall results, it is observed that all independent variables cause a significant change in intention to adopt IoT-CGM except TRSE, as it did not cause a significant change in the intention to adopt IoT-CGM. One reason could be the mistrust that makes people reject IoT-CGMs. So, the intention to not use an IoT-CGM is correlated with a lack of knowledge, little desire to learn, and doubt related to the technology or its adoption.

Table 4. Regression Weights for Path Coefficients and its Significance

Structural Relation			Regression Weight	Standard Error (S.E.)	Critical ratio (C.R.)	P-value	Results
AI	<---	TRSE	−0.017	0.035	−0.484	> 0.629	Rejected
AI	<---	IO	−0.128	0.032	−3.986	<.001***	Supported
AI	<---	PR	0.154	0.024	6.433	<.001***	Supported
AI	<---	PU	0.251	0.050	5.045	<.001***	Supported
AI	<---	EU	0.077	0.028	2.737	<0.006**	Supported
AI	<---	AT	0.194	0.049	3.929	<.001***	Supported
AI	<---	VBC	−0.153	0.036	−4.209	<.001***	Supported
AI	<---	IT	0.171	0.058	2.928	<0.003**	Supported

4.6 Descriptive Statistics

The descriptive results in Table 5 show that in the survey, there were 440 males (50.4%), and 433 females (49.6%). Furthermore, 36.7% of participants were in the age group of 18–25, 37.1% were in the age group of 26–35, 22.0% of participants were in the age group of 36 to 45 and only 3.9% of participants were in the age group of 46 to 60 and only 3 participants (0.30%) were older than 60. The majority, 43.5%, were reported to have a bachelor's degree, 29.1% had a secondary school education, and Ph.D. degree holders only accounted for 0.5%. Furthermore, only 2.1% had only completed primary school, while 18.3% had diplomas, 2.7% had master's degrees, and 3.8% had only completed elementary school education.

Table 5. Sample Characteristics (N = 873)

		Frequency	Percentage			Frequency	Percentage
Gender	Male	440	50.4%	Education Level	Primary School	18	2.1%
	Female	433	49.6%		Elementary School	33	3.8%
Age	18–25	320	36.7%		Secondary school or less	254	29.1%
	26–35	324	37.1%		Diploma	160	18.3%
	36–45	192	22.0%		Bachelor's degree	380	43.5%
	46–60	34	3.9%		Master's degree	24	2.7%
	60 +	3	0.3%		Doctoral degree	4	0.5%

4.7 Thematic Analysis

In the thematic analysis part, all the themes driven from interviews are grouped into three types as shown in Fig. 2 namely practical factors, technological factors, and user behaviour factors. The themes used to measure the practical factors were perceived reliability **(PR)**, perceived usefulness **(PU)**, and ease of use **(EU)**. The themes used to measure technological factors were information overload **(IO)** and technology-related self-efficacy **(TRSE)**, and those used to measure user behaviour factors were attitude **(AT)**, intention to use **(IT)**, and visibility of body change **(VBC)**.

Theme 1. Perceived Reliability
Based on the outcomes of this survey, **(PR)** has a strong link with the adoption of IoT-CGM and can hinder or delay the adoption process. As one of the participants mentioned:
"I think that it's concerning, as so many people are already dependent on technology. It brings up concerns of 'how far will it go?' as most people feel that they cannot even go for a walk without some device on them, including myself. If technology becomes more involved, although, it does make life easier and makes things less time-consuming, so that is positive." **[P7]**

The accuracy of the devices is essential for their use as treatment aids. It is essential to provide patients with a system that they can rely on when managing a chronic illness. Another participant said:

"Smart tech devices help you have better blood glucose control. This, in turn, helps users have better A1cs and overall health. Type 1 diabetes is a life-long disease, so for many, it is a tool to live a healthier and possibly longer life." **[P5]**

As a result, users of such devices are free to concentrate on other matters without being preoccupied with their blood sugar levels at all times. Thus, it appears that perceived reliability **(PR)** positively influences adoption intention towards IoT-CGM for T1DM patients in Saudi Arabia.

Theme 2. Perceived Usefulness

Results suggest that perceived usefulness **(PU)** has a strong impact on the intention to adopt IoT-CGM. The more benefits patients expect to enjoy from using this technology, the more inclined they will be to use a CGM. As one participant mentioned:

"My opinion is that it can be a good thing – as mentioned before, it can make monitoring health a lot easier and make other daily tasks quicker to carry out." **[P5]**

Patients prefer technologies that are easy to use and hassle free, providing quick and accurate readings. Another participant mentioned that IoT-CGM can bring *"Convenience – not having to stop and check blood sugars during work, exercising, or sleeping"* **[P4]**

With the help of technology, patients, particularly those who have diabetes, can make an effort to lead a normal life (to some extent). One participant mentioned that *"such devices could make a huge difference, as insulin pumps and CGMs have been revolutionized in the past 10 years, as technology has become smarter and more flexible, with better results and less stress while managing a patient's health condition."* **[P7]**

These findings clearly show the positive influence of **(PU)** on adoption intentions towards IoT-CGM for T1DM patients in Saudi Arabia.

Theme 3. Ease of Use

The outcomes within this theme **(EU)** show that some participants feel that the devices should be simple to use and have flawless information-sharing capabilities, because even a momentary loss of packets could be life-threatening. Accordingly, one participant said that such devices should be:

"Smaller, cheaper, and more accessible, without requiring much expertise, and possibly more accurate, with information that is easily sharable." **[P3]**

Some respondents cited the complexity of new technologies as a potential barrier to their widespread usage. For example, one participant emphasised that:

"…it must be taken into account that such technologies must also be barrier-free for people with visual impairments, for example." **[P10]**

Users are able to monitor their blood sugar levels and get a clear picture of where they are, where they have been, and where they are going. On participant mentioned that this had made:

"A huge difference. Insulin pumps and CGMs have been revolutionized in the past 10 years, as technology has become smarter and more flexible, with better results, as well as reducing stress while managing a patient's health condition." **[P1]**

Patients receive valuable information from these devices without experiencing any discomfort, and they are simple to operate once the proper procedures have been learned. These findings clearly show the positive influence of (**EU**) on adoption intention IoT-CGM for T1DM patients in Saudi Arabia.

Theme 4. Information Overload

The abundance of data may seem overwhelming to the general public. A large quantity of information can be helpful, but it can also be difficult to process. As mentioned by one respondent:

"For some people, the information can be overwhelming and contribute to anxiety." **[P11]**

The information is useful when analysed by expert health professionals. However, one participant mentioned that:

"It's sometimes overwhelming, and some of the information is not useful. Expertise is needed to evaluate the data. Otherwise, it might cause patients to worry when we don't need to." **[P3]**

Many of the participants expressed the opinion that the additional information that is generated by such devices is not helpful to them in any way, as they are not specialists in the field. One participant said:

"It is overwhelming and does not give people the opportunity to ever turn completely off." **[P4]**

Therefore, (**IO**) has a negative influence on adoption intention towards IoT-CGM for T1DM patients in Saudi Arabia.

Theme 5. Technology-Related Self-efficacy

The interfaces of the various devices have their own unique appearance; while they are easy to use, mastering them takes some practice. Therefore, one participant said that:

"The difficult part could be learning how the device works and how to apply it." **[P13]**

People who used the CGMs admitted that they had experienced difficulties when they first started using them. One participant said:

"I do trust the device, but I am still being vigilant to check my glucose levels by taking a blood reading if needed." **[P10]**

It can be hard to rely fully on technology due to the lack of trust. Confidence in using systems, fears of privacy invasion, device and software complexity, cost, and the feeling of being left out if using a different system than one's peers are all factors that impede the development of a person's ability to learn how to use technological devices. Another participant cited several difficulties:

"Accessibility, as it's expensive, the devices are not the latest ones available in the market, and patients are not involved in the decision-making process taken by the healthcare system." **[P6]**

Even though the devices come with all of the features required to provide accurate results, the adoption of CGMs is still hindered by a lack of technical know-how, proper education and training, and trust in the new technology. The following comment illustrates this:

"If I had been given proper education and training with these devices, I'm sure it would be easier for me to use them." **[P3].**

These are among the main reasons why technology related self-efficacy (**TRSE**) had no significant impact on adoption intention towards IoT-CGM among T1DM patients in Saudi Arabia.

Theme 6. Attitude

A positive attitude (**AT**) will increase patients' adoption of IoT-CGM. Some participants believed that they had become inherently dependent on the CGM, and if it was unavailable for any reason, they struggled to adjust. As one participant said:

"Technology has incredible capabilities to improve the quality of life for many people with type 1 diabetes." **[P15]**

CGM is vastly superior to the old method, which required patient to prick their fingers multiple times a day, and provides users with more up-to-date information. Another participant said:

"I think the usage of technology in health and lifestyle can be really beneficial for people, especially because technology is so widely used these days." **[P9]**

Many of the participants expressed the opinion that the new technology is a significant improvement over the painful method that was previously used to check their health condition, enabling them to monitor their blood sugar levels during different activities. As one participant mentioned:

"I think it's helpful to be able to see blood sugar numbers around-the-clock: during exercise, sleep, and other activities." **[P12]**

The use of CGMs is an essential component of diabetes management in T1DM patients. The patients in the present study reported that the information and security provided by these devices' around-the-clock monitoring have been of great assistance to them. One participant said:

"Having integrated technology as part of the management of chronic health conditions such as type 1 diabetes is incredible. It gives security, as the technology is reliable, so you can depend on it and go through the day knowing you'll be alerted if there is an issue. It also relieves a lot of the mental pressure to manually measure blood sugars, for example." **[P14]**

The implementation of an IoT-CGM can thus have a positive impact on patients' lives. It is beneficial for them to receive continuous notifications about their condition because it reduces the stress associated with their health. Therefore, one participant said:

"My opinion on the usage of technology in regard to health and lifestyle is that it is a very positive thing! With advances in technology, the quality of life for people suffering from physical illness has definitely improved." **[P8]**

Thus, it appears that there is a clear positive association between (**AT**) and adoption intention towards IoT-CGM for T1DM patients in Saudi Arabia.

Theme 7. Intention to Use

Patients appreciated the fact that they no longer needed to draw blood to test their blood glucose levels. They perceived benefits in being able to view their blood glucose history in real time and to react more quickly and effectively to changes in levels. The simple fact that they could control their diabetes however they pleased was a significant step forward for them. One participant said:

"What motivated me to use a smart device to monitor my glucose levels was quite simple – not having to prick my fingers anymore." **[P8]**

The ability to share data and trends with loved ones and medical professionals, allowing patients' insulin doses to be managed or discussed openly and at any time, will attract a large number of users to develop positive intentions to adopt IoT-CGM. As mentioned by one participant:

"I would expect it to help to identify and record my blood sugar levels and appreciate that it is quick and convenient." **[P4]**

Patients are better able to monitor their own internal functions and control their blood sugar levels when they experience fluctuations. The ability to share patient data in real time with medical professionals is a game-changer because it enables these professionals to guide patients through the next steps in their treatment.

A number of individuals expressed their happiness at not being required to prick their fingers in order to check their blood sugar levels, and their responses provide evidence of positive intentions to use IoT-CGM.

Theme 8. Visibility of Body Change

Apart from participants' attitudes towards and intention to adopt CGMs, another behaviour aspect remains. The size of the device was a primary cause for concern, as it has the potential to become caught on various objects while walking, which would result in it being removed too soon, depending on where it needed to be placed on the body. One participant also expressed concern that the device would be an irritant:

"One of the biggest problems I have experienced is that my body will start to "attack" my sensors as a foreign object – the same way it would with any foreign body such as a splinter." **[P2]**

The participants displayed these opinions when they had invested significant time in managing their diabetes and lacked concern for appearance. In the words of one participant:

"I think the concern would probably be malfunction, and maybe the inconvenience of having something stuck to me all of the time." **[P9]**

Whenever foreign objects are placed inside the body, there is a risk that components will become detached, causing illness or injury. Moreover, there is always a risk of infection or blood loss during the process. Sometimes problems can arise as a result of device placement that is inconvenient and unpleasant. Thus, visibility of body change **(VBC)** had a negative impact on intention to adopt IoT-CGM among T1DM patients in Saudi Arabia.

The thematic analysis diagram gives details of the connectivity and flow of themes under each factor, i.e., practical factors, technological factors and user behaviour factors. This diagram clearly demonstrates that all the factors are equal in the qualitative results as was observed in quantitative findings previously.

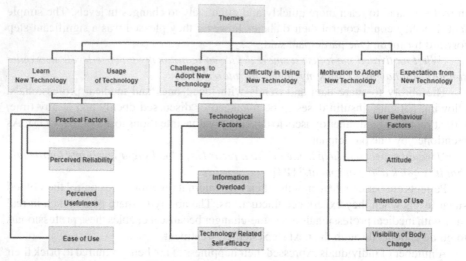

Fig. 2. Thematic Analysis Diagram

5 Discussion

5.1 Intention to Adopt IoT-CGM

The study provided an updated framework based on the empirical findings on the use of IoT-CGMs, which empowers type 1 diabetics as seen in the results from Table 4. The approach illustrated how several factors affect patients' inclinations to use internet-enabled continuous glucose monitoring. The dimensions of human factors that affect the patients' intentions to adopt IoT-CGM devices are grouped into three factors.

Practical Factors: This is the first set of factors that influence the adoption of IoT-CGMs.

The study found that perceived reliability (**PR**) was a significant factor that affected the adoption of IoT-CGMs [42]. Similarly, empirical results from the present study show that PR has a significant positive influence on intention to adopt IoT-CGM along with $\beta = 0.154$ and a p-value < 0.001. Therefore, there are 0.154 units of positive change in IAI-CGM when PR changes by 1 unit. Another study revealed that customers' feelings regarding new technology were positively correlated with their faith in the gadget's accuracy [40]. Trust was found to be the most crucial attribute while communicating with doctors.

The perceived usefulness (**PU**) of IoT-CGMs improves behaviour intention. User satisfaction with CGMs may be affected by various aspects, including the availability of trend and graph glucose readings and the ability of CGMs to compensate automatically for glucose level swings in real-time [38]. The present study also observed that **PU** is a significant factor that positively influences intention to adopt IoT-CGM with $\beta = 0.251$ and a $p < 0.001$. Furthermore, it shows 0.251 units change in IAI-CGM due to PU.

Ease of use (**EU**) is an essential practical factor when adopting a product. Furthermore, the simplicity of use is a critical factor that influences early computer adopters' behaviour intentions [38]. Similarly, the present study also observes EU has a significant positive influence on IoT-CGM with $\beta = 0.077$ and a $p < 0.001$. However, there is a positive influence of EU on IAI-CGM.

Technological Factors: This is the second set of factors that affect the adoption of IoT-CGM.

Information overload **(IO)** is one of the critical technological factors. Tansey et al. [38] suggested that an excessive number of features in CGMs can lead to information overload for users. Although real-time glucose readings in IoT-CGMs may be an attractive feature, a constant influx of information can also be burdensome for users, potentially resulting in a negative response to the technology. Similarly, it was observed in the empirical results that IO has a significant negative influence on intention to adopt IoT-CGM with $\beta = -0.128$ and $p < 0.001$. However, the presence of an overload feature in IAI-CGM can have a negative impact on user adoption, as users may become overwhelmed by the excess information provided.

Technology-related self-efficacy **(TRSE)** [4] is characterized as type 1 diabetes patients' perception of their capability to utilize IoT-CGMs and their ability to trust new technology. Apart from expectations and the ability to trust, there could also be the issue of technology and the lack of knowledge and know-how to use the technology, which might be the reason for the low adoption rate causing the insignificant relationship of TRSE with the intention to adopt [9] Similarly, results show that TRSE does not have a significant influence on the intention to adopt IoT-CGM $\beta = -0.017$ and $p > 0.05$.

User Behaviour Factors: This is the third set of factors that affect the adoption of IoT-CGM.

Users' views on technology are measured in this factor. Technology perception is also reflected in consumers' mental processes, which shows intention to use **(IT)** [14]. Empirical results also show that IT positively influences IAI-CGM, with $\beta = .171$ and $p < 0.05$. Patients' perspectives of how others view them also influence their technology choices. The patients' scheduled activities were based on their attitudes and personal values [39]. A person's behaviour intention also depends on how much they value their own attitudes and the societal norms around them. Similarly, the empirical results show that attitude **(AT)** positively influences adoption intention (AI), β value $= .194$ and $p < 0.05$. Furthermore, visibility of body change **(VBC)** is found to have a negative influence on AI, β value $= -.153$ with $p < 0.05$.

The qualitative findings showed that the main driving factors in terms of practicality were accuracy and accessibility. Providing instant, accurate results will significantly push people towards using IoT-CGMs. The ability to share information from such devices is also viewed as significant. Both the complexity of new technologies and the long process involved in their acquisition hinder the adoption of IoT-CGMs. In terms of technological factors, the results show that the provision of extensive information is valuable for users, but that too much information is overwhelming. Furthermore, the user-friendly interface of such devices contributes to their adoption. The results show that, with regard to user behaviour factors, patients' attitude significantly affects the tendency to adopt the technology. There are, however, concerns regarding invasion of privacy. A positive attitude seems to contribute significantly towards the adoption of IoT-CGMs. Furthermore, patients are conscious about their appearance, which is negatively related to the adoption of IoT-CGMs.

The updated framework (IAI-CGM) that is presented below in Fig. 3 can be used to determine the adoption intention of IoT-CGMs and has been termed the Intention to Adopt IoT-enabled CGM (IAI-CGM) framework. This framework has been proposed to determine the adoption intention based on the practical factors of using IoT-CGMs, the technological factors of using IoT-CGMs, and factors regarding user behaviour. PR, PU, and EU are all practical factors that increase the adoption intention among users. IO and TRSE are technological factors; IO decreases adoption intention, and TRSE has an insignificant effect on adoption intention. User behaviour factors are AT, IT, and VBC. AT and IT factors increase adoption intention, while VBC decreases adoption intention.

The present study discusses critical factors related to the intention to adopt IoT-CGMs. Some differences in the empirical findings may be attributable to regional or cultural perspectives while there may be cultural and individual differences that need to be addressed before adopting the IAI-CGM framework.

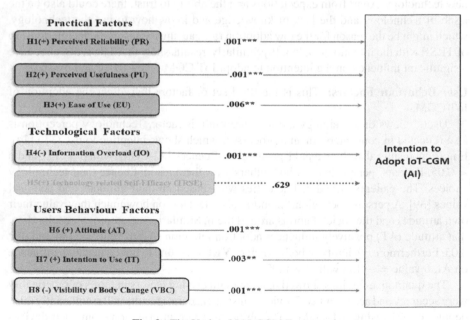

Fig. 3. The Updated IAI-CGM Framework

5.2 Implications

This study makes a significant contribution to our understanding of the topic by providing a novel theoretical framework (IAI-CGM) for analysing the aspects that affect Saudi consumers' decision to adopt IoT-CGMs. A framework to evaluate adoption intention was developed through the application of qualitative and quantitative research methods. Practical factors, technological factors, and user behaviour factors are the three key components included in the framework. This offers a novel theoretical perspective on the reasons for and the means by which CGMs are being embraced. Each of the criteria in the framework evaluates the pervasiveness of the usage of IoT-CGMs.

This information may advise all parties involved on how to improve the overall quality of the user experience. It is recommended that the device manufacturers try to make such devices cheaper for those living in countries with a lower standard of living.

The study was conducted on Saudi Arabian citizens with type 1 diabetes, and the findings revealed new avenues for future research. The study recommends that future research focus on specific areas, such as software development models and process structure models, to better understand the factors that contribute to acceptance and the hurdles that must be overcome. This research emphasizes the importance of addressing adoption challenges to improve healthcare delivery. Furthermore, it is recommended that comparative study be conducted, preferably with a larger number of T1DM patients from different regions with diverse socio-economic status, to investigate what are the most important socio-economic factors in the IAI-CGM framework based on comparative study results to come up with different solutions after considering cultural and socio-economic diversity.

6 Conclusion

In this study, we constructed the updated IAI-CGM framework to identify the critical factors that influence the adoption of IoT-CGM. We present the theoretical background by way of a literature review that outlines previous empirical findings related to type 1 diabetic patients using IoT-CGM from King Khalid hospital Saudi Arabia and the Najran region. Then, our updated IAI-CGM framework is based on investigating three main categories of factors, namely, practical factors, technological factors, and user behaviour factors.

This study analysed the factors affecting the adoption of IoT-CGMs among Saudi users. The authors used an integrated research methodology that incorporated the TAM and other factors to examine the perceived reliability and utility of the monitors, as well as technological factors and user behaviour factors (see Fig. 3). The study found that an individual's perceived reliability and ease of use of continuous glucose monitoring and its utility were the most important factors affecting adoption. People are more likely to embrace the use of a CGM the more benefits they derive from employing this technology in their daily lives [40]. Additionally, technology related self-efficacy came out insignificant with the fact that citizens of Saudi Arabia have developed a mistrust for the medical services provided by their government is one probable cause. Physical changes in the body negatively impacted adoption, and technology-related self-efficacy did not affect adoption intention. Next, it is observed that overwhelmed brains are unable to make sound judgments and forget things, both of which have negative effects on daily life. The mental health of humans may be negatively impacted by an excess of information with IoT devices [38].

The study also revealed that Saudi Arabians were sceptical of government hospitals and their ability to train them in wearable technologies. The number of persons who responded to the survey were Saudis as all data was collected from Saudis only. It is important to conduct further empirical studies in other regions to come up with cultural disparities to updated or validate the proposed IAI-CGM framework. This study provides valuable insights into the adoption of IoT-CGM and can aid in future research in this area. In conclusion, future research may focus on a specific aspect of IAI-CGM, such as IoT-CGM software development models and process structure models. This approach will help to identify crucial factors contributing to acceptance that can be generalized.

Acknowledgement. The authors extend their appreciation to the Directorate General of Health Affairs in Najran. We would like to express our gratitude to Najran Research Department, King Khalid Hospital Najran and Diabetes and Endocrine Centre. Finally, we would like to express our heartfelt appreciation to all participants for their time and effort.

References

1. Ajjan, R., et al.: Continuous glucose monitoring: a brief review for primary care practitioners. Adv. Ther. **36**(3), 579–596 (2019). https://doi.org/10.1007/s12325-019-0870-x
2. Al-Rubeaan, K., et al.: Epidemiology of abnormal glucose metabolism in a country facing its epidemic: SAUDI-DM study. J. Diabetes **7**(5), 622–632 (2015). https://doi.org/10.1111/1753-0407.12224
3. Ali, M., et al.: University social responsibility: a review of conceptual evolution and its thematic analysis. J. Clean. Prod. **286**, 124931 (2021). https://doi.org/10.1016/j.jclepro.2020.124931
4. Almansour, H., et al.: IAI-CGM: a framework for intention to adopt IoT-enabled continuous glucose monitors. Presented at the (2022). https://doi.org/10.1007/978-3-031-16072-1_46
5. Almansour, H., et al.: Type 1 diabetes mellitus Saudi patients' perspective on the adopting IoT-enabled CGM: validation of critical factors in the IAI-CGM a framework. Presented at the September 26 (2023). https://doi.org/10.15439/2023F4851
6. Alsayed, A.O., et al.: A comprehensive review of modern methods to improve diabetes self-care management systems. Int. J. Adv. Comput. Sci. Appl. **14**(9) (2023). https://doi.org/10.14569/IJACSA.2023.0140920
7. Awang, Z., et al.: Parametric and non parametric approach in structural equation modeling (SEM): The application of bootstrapping. Mod. Appl. Sci. **9**(9), 58 (2015)
8. Ayanlade, O.S., et al.: Health information technology acceptance framework for diabetes management. Heliyon. **5**(5) (2019). https://doi.org/10.1016/j.heliyon.2019.e01735
9. Barnard, K.D., et al.: Psychosocial assessment of artificial pancreas (AP): commentary and review of existing measures and their applicability in AP research. Mary Ann Liebert Inc. (2015). https://doi.org/10.1089/dia.2014.0305
10. Borges, U., Kubiak, T.: Continuous glucose monitoring in type 1 diabetes: human factors and usage. J. Diabetes Sci. Technol. **10**(3), 633–639 (2016). https://doi.org/10.1177/1932296816634736
11. Brown, T.A.: Confirmatory Factor Analysis for Applied Research. Guilford publications (2015)
12. Chang, H.S., et al.: Wearable device adoption model with TAM and TTF. Int. J. Mob. Commun. **14**(5), 518 (2016). https://doi.org/10.1504/IJMC.2016.078726
13. Cleveland, S.M., Haddara, M.: Internet of Things for diabetics: Identifying adoption issues. Internet of Things. **22**, 100798 (2023). https://doi.org/10.1016/j.iot.2023.100798

14. Davis, F.D., et al.: User acceptance of computer technology: a comparison of two theoretical models. Manage. Sci. **35**, 928–1003 (1989)
15. Davoody, N., et al.: Post-discharge stroke patients' information needs as input to proposing patient-centred eHealth services. BMC Med. Inform. Decis. Mak. **16**(1), 1–13 (2016). https://doi.org/10.1186/s12911-016-0307-2
16. Al Dawish, M.A., Robert, A.A.: Diabetes mellitus in Saudi Arabia: challenges and possible solutions. In: Laher, I. (ed.) Handbook of Healthcare in the Arab World, pp. 1–18. Springer, Cham (2019). https://doi.org/10.1007/978-3-030-36811-1_45
17. Domino, G., Domino, M.L.: Psychological Testing: An Introduction. Cambridge University Press, Cambridge (2006)
18. Gia, T.N., et al.: IoT-based continuous glucose monitoring system: a feasibility study. Procedia Comput. Sci. **109**, 327–334 (2017). https://doi.org/10.1016/j.procs.2017.05.359
19. Gliem, J.A., Gliem, R.R.: Calculating, interpreting, and reporting Cronbach's alpha reliability coefficient for Likert-type scales. Presented at the (2003)
20. Gray, K., Gilbert, C.: Digital health research methods and tools: Suggestions and selected resources for researchers. In: Holmes, D., Jain, L. (eds.) Advances in Biomedical Informatics. Intelligent Systems Reference Library, vol. 137, pp. 5–34. Springer, Cham (2017). https://doi.org/10.1007/978-3-319-67513-8_2
21. Gregory, G.A., et al.: Global incidence, prevalence, and mortality of type 1 diabetes in 2021 with projection to 2040: a modelling study. Lancet Diabetes Endocrinol. **10**(10), 741–760 (2022). https://doi.org/10.1016/S2213-8587(22)00218-2
22. Hair, J.F., et al.: Multivariate Data Analysis: A Global Perspective. Prentice Hall, Upper Saddle River (2009)
23. Hair, J.F., Jr., et al.: PLS-SEM or CB-SEM: updated guidelines on which method to use. Int. J. Multivar. Data Anal. **1**(2), 107–123 (2017)
24. Heisler, M., et al.: How well do patients' assessments of their diabetes self-management correlate with actual glycemic control and receipt of recommended diabetes services? Diabetes Care **26**(3), 738–743 (2003). https://doi.org/10.2337/diacare.26.3.738
25. Holden, M.T., Lynch, P.: Choosing the appropriate methodology: understanding research philosophy. Mark. Rev. **4**(4), 397–409 (2004)
26. Hossain, M.I., et al.: Factors influencing adoption model of continuous glucose monitoring devices for internet of things healthcare. Internet Things. **15**, 100353 (2021). https://doi.org/10.1016/j.iot.2020.100353
27. Khan, A., et al.: Factors contributing to non-compliance among diabetics attending primary health centers in the Al Hasa district of Saudi Arabia. J. Fam. Community Med. **19**(1), 26 (2012). https://doi.org/10.4103/2230-8229.94008
28. Kim, Y.J., et al.: Continuous glucose monitoring with a flexible biosensor and wireless data acquisition system. Sens. Actuat. B Chem. **275**, 237–243 (2018). https://doi.org/10.1016/j.snb.2018.08.028
29. Krist, A.H., et al.: Engaging patients in primary and specialty care. In: Oncology Informatics, pp. 55–79. Elsevier (2016). https://doi.org/10.1016/b978-0-12-802115-6.00004-5
30. Mahdavinejad, M.S., et al.: Machine learning for internet of things data analysis: a survey (2018). https://doi.org/10.1016/j.dcan.2017.10.002
31. Norris, S.L., et al.: Self-management education for adults with type 2 diabetes. A meta-analysis of the effect on glycemic control. Diabetes Care. **25**(7), 1159–1171 (2002). https://doi.org/10.2337/diacare.25.7.1159
32. Olczuk, D., Priefer, R.: A history of continuous glucose monitors (CGMs) in self-monitoring of diabetes mellitus (2018). https://pubmed.ncbi.nlm.nih.gov/28967612/, https://doi.org/10.1016/j.dsx.2017.09.005
33. Rhee, M.K., et al.: Patient adherence improves glycemic control. Diabetes Educ. **31**(2), 240–250 (2005). https://doi.org/10.1177/0145721705274927

34. Rodbard, D.: Continuous glucose monitoring: a review of successes, challenges, and opportunities (2016). https://pubmed.ncbi.nlm.nih.gov/26784127/, https://doi.org/10.1089/dia.2015.0417

35. Saghafian, M., et al.: Organizational challenges of development and implementation of virtual reality solution for industrial operation. Front. Psychol. **12** (2021). https://doi.org/10.3389/fpsyg.2021.704723

36. SaudiVision2030: National Transformation Program Delivery Plan 2018–2020, https://vision2030.gov.sa/sites/default/files/attachments/NTPEnglishPublicDocument_2810.pdf. Accessed 12 May 2021

37. Solanas, A., et al.: Smart health: a context-aware health paradigm within smart cities. IEEE Commun. Mag. **52**(8) (2014). https://doi.org/10.1109/MCOM.2014.6871673

38. Tansey, M., et al.: Satisfaction with continuous glucose monitoring in adults and youths with type1 diabetes. Diabet. Med. **28**(9), 1118–1122 (2011). https://doi.org/10.1111/j.1464-5491.2011.03368.x

39. Taylor, M., Taylor, A.: The technology life cycle: conceptualization and managerial implications. Int. J. Prod. Econ. **140**(1), 541–553 (2012). https://doi.org/10.1016/j.ijpe.2012.07.006

40. Wang, N. et al.: Analysis of public acceptance of electric vehicle charging scheduling based on the technology acceptance model. Energy. **258** (2022). https://doi.org/10.1016/j.energy.2022.124804

41. Williams, G.C., et al.: Testing a self-determination theory process model for promoting glycemic control through diabetes self-management. Heal. Psychol. **23**(1), 58–66 (2004). https://doi.org/10.1037/0278-6133.23.1.58

42. Yildirim, H., Ali-Eldin, A.M.T.: A model for predicting user intention to use wearable IoT devices at the workplace. J. King Saud Univ. - Comput. Inf. Sci. **31**(4), 497–505 (2019). https://doi.org/10.1016/j.jksuci.2018.03.001

Technostress Experiences Under Hybrid Work Conditions in South Africa: Causes and Coping Mechanisms

Shelley Dowrie[1] , Marita Turpin[2]([✉]) , and Jean-Paul Van Belle[1]

[1] Department of Information Systems, University of Cape Town, Rondebosch 7701, South Africa
dwrshe001@myuct.ac.za, jean-paul.vanbelle@uct.ac.za
[2] Department of Informatics, University of Pretoria, Lynnwood Road, Pretoria 0001, South Africa
marita.turpin@up.ac.za

Abstract. During the COVID-19 pandemic, South African organisations required their employees to work from home, which caused technostress. The stress while working from home was believed to be partly influenced by feelings of COVID-19-related anxiety. Since the hybrid model was adopted in some South African organisations, it was possible that there were new and different experiences of technostress within the hybrid workplaces. The purpose of this study was to understand how employee technostress experiences changed during the adoption of hybrid work models in South African organisations. Furthermore, the research intends to explain the underlying causes of these new experiences and how employees were coping with these new instances of technostress. A qualitative study was conducted under respondents working under a hybrid model and who use ICTs for work purposes. The findings reveal several hybrid working specific causes of technostress, including instances of stressful workstation setups, office disruptions and power outage issues as a result of loadshedding (rolling power blackouts). Loadshedding related stress appears to be a specific South African issue. To deal with technostress, employees adopted reactive and proactive coping behaviours driven by problem-focused and emotion-focused coping strategies respectively. This paper contributes by highlighting the stressors and coping mechanisms used in the relatively under-researched hybrid working scenario. The study was limited with regard to its sample size, representation and time frame. Future research is suggested to compare the different modes of working over a longer time period and within a larger diversity of organisations, including SMEs.

Keywords: Technostress · Hybrid Workplaces · South African Organisations

1 Introduction

The adoption and use of Information and Communications Technology (ICTs) in organisations have created space for increased productivity, efficiency, and effectiveness [20]. It was found that integrating ICTs with work-related tasks increases remote access to

E. Ziemba et al. (Eds.): FedCSIS-ITBS 2023/ISM 2023, LNBIP 504, pp. 141–163, 2024.
https://doi.org/10.1007/978-3-031-61657-0_7

these tasks, while improving employee job performance and satisfaction [40]. Business processes and organisational decision making have also been improved by the integration of ICTs [20].

However, the relationship between the user/employee and ICTs needs to healthily coexist with one another for ICTs to fully integrate into organisational settings. This isn't always the case since the phenomenon technostress emerged as a by-product of an unhealthy relationship between the ICT user and the ICT [32]. Technostress, in an organisational environment, is defined as the stress that ICT users/employees experience when engaging with Information Systems in the workplace [37]. This must not be mistaken with the momentary frustration and irritation with the use of technology that most ICT users experience at some point in their lives [32]. It is rather more concerned with the increased cognitive demands triggered by ICT use that enforces that unhealthy relationship.

Technostress escalated once the COVID-19 pandemic unexpectedly disturbed the way many things operated [12]. Organisations were forced to impose response plans to resume work as smoothly as possible [6]. Many resorted to work-from-home (WFH) styles where employees had to adapt their current work dynamic with the incorporation of ICTs. This caused an obligated reliance on technology by the employees and the organisations [17]. An increased demand of the use of ICTs leads to high workload demands on employees [7]. This induces the inability to manage these demands therefore stifling the capability to process further information often leading to burnout and technostress [7, 11]. In other words, technostress occurs when there are changes in working conditions that stem from the adoption and use of ICTs. This evidently forces employees to adapt and adjust almost instantaneously [7].

Since the COVID-19 pandemic environment remains unpredictable, workplaces during the existence of the pandemic have constantly been reconstructed to adapt to what the new norm is beginning to look like. It is possible that there are now new experiences of technostress which exist due to the new way of working through a hybrid approach. Employees have grown accustomed to working with ICTs during purely remote working environments that involved, amongst other things, an increased usage of online conferencing tools to conduct meetings. This also forced organisations to provide employees with appropriate software for cloud services, network equipment, hardware infrastructure and bandwidth expansion [10]. In hybrid working environments, employees are required to find a working dynamic that compliments varying reliance on ICTs between the alternating working locations i.e., at home and at the office. This unanticipated shift in working modes could either cause more technostress amongst employees or alleviate some of the technostress experienced during pure remote working. Due to the adoption of a hybrid working being relatively new for most organisations, there remains a gap in literature pertaining to the experiences of technostress within this new working environment.

The purpose of this study is to explain the shift of employee technostress experiences along with the underlying causes and coping mechanisms. With this research purpose in mind, the research aims to address the following research questions:

Primary Research Question:

- How have the experiences of employee technostress changed when hybrid workplaces were implemented in South Africa?

  Secondary Questions:

- Why are South African employees experiencing technostress in these hybrid workplaces?
- How are South African employees currently coping with such instances of technostress?

The research objectives for this study are therefore to 1) explain how the experiences of employee technostress changed when hybrid workplaces were implemented in South Africa; 2) understand why South African employees are experiencing technostress in these hybrid workplaces; and 3) explain how South African employees are currently coping with such instances of technostress.

The rest of the paper is organized as follows. The background section contains the literature review that considers technostress in workplaces, causes and impacts and coping mechanisms. The research methodology section outlines the research approach, strategy, data collection and analysis and ethics. Thereafter, the research findings and analysis are presented, followed by the discussion of the research findings and study limitations, and lastly the conclusion and research recommendations.

2 Background

This section provides background on the notion of technostress within organisational settings along with its causes and impacts. This is followed by a look into technostress experiences within different work models and considers what employees usually use as coping mechanisms to combat instances of technostress.

2.1 Technostress Under Different Models of Work

ICTs within the workplace are evolving to become much more ubiquitous and relatively more complex [13]. This evidently creates challenges for end users to keep up with the demands especially in changing work environments such as remote working and the relatively new working model, namely hybrid working.

Remote/Work-from-Home Model. Remote workers often experience the pressure of longer workdays and higher workloads which all lead to feelings of technostress [30]. This comes in various forms, one being in the form of consecutive online meetings where workers must alternate between different technological tools while trying to maintain concentration levels which are referred to as a state of being "hyper focused" [10]. This was regarded to have led to "virtual meeting fatigue and lower wellbeing of workers" [30]. In addition, technostress is amplified by a state of loneliness in such a way that the lonelier a worker feels in a remote workplace, the higher the levels of technostress will be [39].

Hybrid Working Model. Hybrid working involves a combination of remote and on-site work [24]. Ideally employees within this working model can enjoy the benefits of autonomy where they could determine where and when they work [15, 22]. This also contributes to an improved work-life balance. Work-life balance reflects how people evaluate the way they combine work roles and life roles [19]. This was previously seen to be distorted by the usage of IT which constantly blurs work and life boundaries. However, once job boundaries become blurred, as is the case under a hybrid working model, stress tends to surface due to these once well-defined jobs starting to become ambiguous and flexible in nature [43]. This is believed to lead to work overload.

Companies may decide to opt for implementing a hybrid workplace as some activities can be conducive in corporate offices while others are more suitable for home-based offices [44]. However, it is suggested that it is the very nature of the work that determines whether remote work is suitable as a whole [41]. Work that demands extensive collaboration as well as creative work or new work streams may be slightly more difficult to realise through remote work alone [9, 41].

However, with a hybrid working approach employees may struggle to find complete ease with the constant synchronisation and reconfiguration of devices which comes with the alternation between home and office [41]. This is because of the need to constantly setup hardware such as monitors and laptops which enable the smooth transition between the two setups [41]. In addition, teleconferencing within the office space was deemed challenging as workers found it difficult to find a sufficiently equipped space with technology [44]. It must be also noted that the pandemic has shaped the perceptions employees have towards working remotely or through a hybrid model [44]. It was found that technostress had a positive correlation with COVID-19 anxiety [30]. This therefore means that this perception may change "post pandemic".

Employees in office can still communicate and collaborate with other employees at home through various collaborative technologies therefore interacting with both physical and virtual spaces [44]. Since working from home was introduced employees are now expected to take on the costs of space and utilities. Since employers are saving on traditional office costs, it is expected of them to provide employees support with regards to technology and ergonomic furniture [44]. It was found that the future of hybrid working models should concentrate on utilising office space for collaboration and socialising with appropriate space design. This type of work-place design is referred to as unassigned workstations used for varying activities aligned with collaboration and concentration [23]. These non-designated desks require employees to remove personal belongings and equipment once they have finished the workday [23].

2.2 Causes of Technostress

The following section will discuss the causes or determinants of technostress. It looks at the standard technostressors: system performance issues, technology demands, lack of digital literacy and differing personalities in the workplace.

The Big Five Technostressors. Technostress literature has established the five standard technostressors - techno-overload, techno-invasion, techno-complexity, techno-insecurity, and techno-uncertainty. These all tend to cause technostress. Techno-overload is triggered when ICT users are required to work for longer and at a faster pace when using ICTs [21]. This also deals with the handling of excess features and information when using ICTs for work [37]. Techno-invasion requires the employee to be constantly connected and available to respond timeously even outside work hours [37]. Techno-complexity refers to feelings of incompetency amongst employee when using the ICTs [34]. This is because of the inherent quality of Information Technology (IT) and ICTs [16]. Due to these feelings of appearing inadequate with IT skills, ICT users invest in spending more time and effort to fully understand the particulars of the technology [21]. Techno-insecurity refers to ICT users fearing the loss of their jobs in terms of having some sort of technology eventually take over their role or that their fellow colleagues possess a better understanding of the usage of the ICT. Finally, techno-uncertainty refers to the constant ICT upgrades that unsettle ICT users forcing them to continually learn and familiarise themselves with the new technology [21].

System Performance Issues. Technostressors can also extend to system performance issues such as problems with security, usability, and system breakdown [21]. Security issues originate from insecure system infrastructure that allow threats which compromise the information involved in that system. Technostress emerges when users are forced to comply with security policies implemented by the organisation which require them to remember passwords and multiple usernames [21]. Usability issues stem from poorly designed systems and can fall in the realms of flawed interfaces, challenges in intuitively navigating around the application/system and in general lack of effectiveness, efficiency and learnability [32]. This causes the users of these system to experience higher cognitive overloads. Finally, system breakdown refers to the malfunctioning of ICTs such as an error message [21].

ICT Use in the Workplace. The "technology demands" predictor signifies the costs employees incur as a result of the effort needed for ICT use. These costs are of psychological and physiological natures [1]. These types of demands involve role ambiguity, ergonomic stress, monotonous ICT activities and general work overload [1]. Role ambiguity occurs when ICT tasks are ill defined [1] which is further claimed to restrain the user's abilities and development [45]. Demands can also originate from a societal sense whereby employees experience social isolation, role conflict and emotional overload when trying to form human relationships around the usage of ICTs [1]. Role conflict refers to the instance of differing work dynamics that arise when new and old systems function concurrently [1]. This also arises when there is a perception of incompatibility with regards to the requirements of the role a user has with that particular ICT [16]. It was found that technostress has a positive relationship with how often ICTs are used for work purposes. Technostress can also be instantiated by the usage of multiple ICTs at once. This is derived from higher demands or greater pressure on workers to learn and embrace multiple ICTs [7]. This can also allude to the constant interruptions of this frequent use of technology for work purposes which has found to heighten exhaustion as a result from work demands triggering this frequent use [7].

The extent of ICT use for work indicates the type of ICT end user that is engaging with the ICT. Some end users make little to no use of ICTs and others heavily rely on ICTs to conduct their work [33]. Nisafani et al. [21] further defend this by stating that technostress can be induced by having a high dependency on an evolving ICT/Information System in the workplace. Studies show that the higher an individual's computer/IT skills are, the less technostress he/she will suffer [3]. Therefore, if a user possesses high skill levels of digital literacy/skills, he/she will find it relatively easier to learn and adapt to new technologies [3].

Personality traits can also explain users' relationships with technostress. In literature, these traits are commonly known as the Big Five personality traits and include openness, neuroticism, agreeableness, conscientiousness, and extraversion [42]. These personality differences are claimed to influence the extent and nature of technostress experienced [35]. This also dictates how the user responds and copes with the technostress as technostressors affect individuals in different ways due to the differing personality traits [12].

2.3 Impacts of Technostress

The following impacts of technostress will be discussed in the context of impacts on the individual and then will look at how technostress effects the organisation as a whole.

Individual Impacts. The following direct impacts of technostress refer to the impacts experienced at an individual level and are regarded as symptoms related to technostress [34]. Once the technostress starts manifesting within the individual, it can lead to emotional and physical strains known as techno-strain. Techno-strain embodies 4 main constructs including scepticism, inefficiency, anxiety, and fatigue [1]. Scepticism refers to attitudes of detachment and indifference often stemming from feeling discouraged or exhausted when using ICTs [3]. Fatigue and anxiety results from low psychological and high physiological levels respectively [3].

Organisational Impacts. Indirect impacts of technostress refer to the group effects of technostress on the organisation and people that surround the employee. These implications of technostress involve less job commitment and less job engagement which in turn increases user resistance to any new technology introduced [21]. As technology is welcomed for its potential to encourage productivity, it can also adversely impact on productivity by mimicking the law of diminishing theory when there are extreme usages of technology.

Technostress also holds significant adverse effects on employee absenteeism [12]. This also includes instances of employee burnout and a decrease in professional work satisfaction [12]. Work satisfaction is crucial to maintain has it can influence the functioning of the employee which impacts organisational costs. This satisfaction can be directly linked to the intentions to expand the use of new ICTs [18]. Technostress can enforce higher work-related conflict and isolation which is not great for company culture [28]. In addition, technostress can enforce higher employee turnover which can become a cost to the organisation [28].

2.4   Coping with Technostress

The following section considers the coping mechanisms that can be used to combat instances of technostress. It will commence with coping theory, followed by the various coping behaviours and corresponding strategies.

Coping Theory. By using the lens of coping theory, responses to technostress can be understood and recommended. Coping theory suggests that end users undergo cognitive appraisals and coping efforts [8]. Primary appraisal is the process where a user experiences a perceived threat [14]. However primary appraisals can also be induced by irrelevant or benign-positive encounters, not just an encounter that is perceived to be threatening [8]. Secondary appraisals involve the response strategies to overcome the encounter [8]. More specifically, coping strategies are implemented to counter disruptive/threatening situations. This, however, depends on the available coping resources at hand to execute effectively which is often related to the competency with regards to coping as well as the given circumstances [8].

Coping Behaviours. Proactive coping involves the employee handling continuous stressful scenarios through constant preparation via accumulating enough resources and through personal growth [25]. This builds up the employee's resilience against anticipated stressful ICT situations. Proactive behaviour often involves planning in hopes of implementing actions and efforts to improve the stressful situation [26]. On the other hand, reactive coping refers to instinctively responding to a stressful situation. This encompasses the venting of frustrations and negative emotions [25]. This type of coping is found to be ineffective when utilised in isolation to proactive coping [25]. The main purpose of this type of coping is to reinstate emotional stability after the stressful situation occurred.

Coping Strategies. Problem-focused coping makes use of proactive coping behaviour. It involves having a belief that the stressful situation can be solved by a corrective approach [8]. This happens in the forms of gaining control of the stressful situation and seeking instrumental support from fellow colleagues [14]. These techniques also include considering separating personal and work life by using different devices for the different ICT related tasks therefore limiting the exposure to work-related ICT tasks outside of work settings [26]. Employees could also develop building habits of integrating calendar reminders to save tasks for later therefore coping with constant input [36]. The more ambitious coping strategy that takes much more resilience and dedication involves trying to develop IT capacity. This takes on the form of building IT use skills through "learning by doing" that requires the user to practice using multiple IT applications and ICT devices at the same time to gain the skill to manage ICT related interruptions [38]. It was also found that users can specifically allocate time for ICT use to help avoid interruptions related to ICT [38]. This also includes taking breaks between ICT use and demarcating areas/boundaries at home which is designated for ICT use and those areas which are of limits [38]. This ideally helps to establish how and when to make use of ICT to avoid instances of technostress.

Emotion-focused coping rather tries to manipulate the emotional stimulation which is in response to a stressful reaction to a situation [31]. Distancing allows the employee to temporarily separate themselves from the IT-related task and focus on something different [38]. This creates brief relief from a technostress related situation whereby the employee can come back at later stage which can diminish the overall effects of technostress on themselves much like the problem-focused coping strategy mentioned above with regards to time allocation for ICT use. Venting allows the employee to let go of any negative emotions which in turn aids them to connect with other employees who might feel the same way. In contrast, this can contribute to the employee feeling emotionally exhausted to have to continuously vent and it can negatively impact on productivity [26].

Technology self-efficacy is the belief that one can achieve a computer-related task [33]. The idea here is that the higher an employee's self-efficacy, the more eager they are to overcome IT-related issues. This helps them embrace a positive coping attitude therefore decreasing the extent of technostress [21]. It attempts to enhance an employee's motivation to work with ICTs which ultimately benefits the organisation as it contributes to more organisational commitment and better performance from employees [27].

2.5 Propositions

Table 1 below indicates the research propositions adapted from literature that drove the data collection process:

Table 1. Research Propositions

Research Area	Relationship/Themes	Reference
ICT use in the Workplace	Technostress can be induced by having a high dependency on an evolving ICT/Information System in the workplace	[21]
	If a user possesses high skill levels of digital literacy/skills, he/she will find it relatively easier to learn and adapt to new technologies	[3]
Technostressors	Techno-complexity, techno-overload, techno-invasion, techno-insecurity and techno-uncertainty instantiate experiences of technostress	[37]
	Unreliability of ICTs cause technostress	[21]
Coping Behaviours	Reduce ICT related distress: Distancing and venting	[38]
	Establish ICT use demarcations: Time-related use, Separation of use, autonomy	[38]

3 Research Methodology

3.1 Research Philosophy, Approach and Strategy

An interpretive philosophy was adopted for this research. Interpretive research assumes that human experiences shape the social realities and invites subjective interpretations of the respondents in the social context, in this case the virtual and physical workplaces in organisations [4].

The research approach was abductive as it merged characteristics of inductive and deductive approaches. The phenomenon at hand was explored by identifying themes and patterns that were guided by a conceptual framework [29]. While there existed extensive literature on technostress in organisational settings, there was not much literature on technostress within hybrid working models in South Africa specifically, therefore an inductive approach was used to explore this relatively untouched area. Overall, an abductive approach seemed the most fitting to guide the research.

As this study adopted an interpretivist paradigm, the most suitable strategy to be adopted was a qualitative one. Qualitative research intends to derive meaning-based forms of data analysis. It enforces the notion of contextual understanding through providing in-depth descriptions of insights that cannot be shown through quantitative measures [2]. A qualitative strategy also makes it possible to detect body language, voice tone and other general social cues in contrast to a quantitative approach. This is crucial in identifying the underlying causes and coping mechanisms of the new experiences of Technostress which can help isolate the true depictions of frustrations through giving the respondent room to elaborate on their first-hand experiences.

This research was conducted within a cross-sectional time frame which ran over eight months in 2022.

3.2 Data Collection

The primary data collection instrument was semi-structured interviews [2]. The aim of the semi-structured interviews was to investigate the underlying assumptions and beliefs which could be helpful in understanding why participants had certain perceptions about how technostress was experienced in the hybrid workplace. Due to the unpredictability of the COVID-19 pandemic at the time of data collection, as a contingency, an option of face-to-face or virtual interviews was given to participants. As there were varying locations of participants in terms of office-based and remote-based work, these factors were considered to inform the mode of the interviews conducted.

In addition to the semi-structured interviews, secondary data sources deemed relevant to the study were obtained from one of the respondents during the interviews and therefore was included during data analysis.

The target audience for this study consisted of employees within organisations who have had to drastically adapt working styles with the incorporation of ICTs once the pandemic hit. These employees needed to be using some sort of ICTs for work purposes while they have worked/are working remotely. The target audience also needed to be in positions of returning to work at the office in combination with working from home on some days hence working under a hybrid working model. All participants were sampled from an insurance company and a Higher Education Institution (HEI). Both organisations were making use of a hybrid working model and respondents could be conveniently accessed.

The sample size for the study incorporated twelve participants for the semi-structured interviews. This was with the belief that it was sufficient for a homogenous population under investigation to involve such a sample size [5]. Since the study focused on large organisations to explore the causes and coping mechanisms of technostress, convenience sampling was chosen as the sampling technique. This technique restricted the data to two large organisations as it involves accessing a homogenous population readily available. The plan was to sample ten participants from the insurance company and five participants from the HEI however, only two HEI respondents could be found within the time frame. Snowball sampling was used in addition to convenience sampling during the data collection process. This meant that some respondents referred contacts within in their organisation who they knew to display the criteria as mentioned before.

3.3 Data Analysis

Since the research adopted an abductive approach, the data analysis combined analysis techniques from both deductive and inductive approaches. The deductive analysis made use of a coding process that established themes from literature in hopes of spotting these themes within the collected data [2]. Inductive data analysis involved systematically reviewing interview transcripts and any relevant observation notes. This is what drove the analysis through exclusively using the participant's experiences [2]. The analysis took on the form of categorizing themes and patterns that derived at a set of concepts (codes), constructs (categories) and relationships [4]. This was done through coding and labelling techniques. NVivo was used as the electronic analysis tool to perform the thematic analysis of the qualitative text gathered during the data collection phase.

Ethical clearance for the study was obtained from the ethics committee of the university under whose auspices the study was undertaken.

A total of twelve respondents were interviewed with ten respondents obtained from the insurance company and two respondents from the HEI. Each respondent was assigned a pseudo name to represent the organisation code and the order in which they were interviewed. This code served to organise the respondents as well as to maintain confidentiality thereby attaching an alias name to each of them. Table 2 shows each respondent in terms of their age, work role, industry, IT skill level, dependency on using ICTs and their estimate technostress level. As can be seen in Table 2, there is a high level of similarity among the respondents' profiles, with all having specialist or middle management roles with similar profiles in terms of their knowledge and usage of ICT. Data saturation was achieved after 9 of the 12 interviews.

Table 2. Descriptive Summary of Respondents

Pseudo name	Age Group	Role	Industry	Skill level	Depen-dency	Techno stress level
OM01	50–65	Specialist: Client Relationship Manager, Complaints and Escalations	Insurance	Intermediate	High	Medium
OM02	35–50	Manager: Finance Team Leader	Insurance	Intermediate	High	Medium
OM03	50–65	Manager: Section 14 Technical Team Leader	Insurance	Intermediate	High	Low
OM04	35–50	Manager: Business Specialist, MIS	Insurance	High	High	Low-Medium
OM05	35–50	Specialist: Client Relationship Manager, Corporate Client Services	Insurance	Intermediate	High	Dependent
OM06	50–65	Manager: Corporate Client Services Team Leader	Insurance	Intermediate	High	Medium
OM07	35–50	Manager: Servicing Team Leader	Insurance	High	High	Low- Medium

(continued)

Table 2. (*continued*)

Pseudo name	Age Group	Role	Industry	Skill level	Depen-dency	Techno stress level
OM08	50–65	Specialist: Client Relationship Manager, Corporate Client Services	Insurance	Intermediate	High	Medium
OM09	35–50	Specialist: Social Media Complaints	Insurance	Intermediate	High	Medium-Intense
OM010	50–65	Specialist: Complaints Handler	Insurance	Intermediate	High	Medium-Intense
UCT01	50–65	ICTs: Senior Business Analyst	HEI	High	High	Low-Medium
UCT02	25–35	Specialist: HR Analytics	HEI	High	High	Medium

4 Research Findings and Analysis

The emergent themes from the data analysis are discussed below.

4.1 Hybrid Working Specific Causes of Technostress

Non-assigned Desk Setup (Hot Desks) Creates Unnecessary Technostress. On the days designated to go work at the office, three respondents indicated device configuration issues between the provided monitors and their own laptops. These experiences were also discovered in China by [41]. Five respondents complained about insufficient technical support at the office should they encounter tech-related difficulties. Two respondents alluded to occurrences of missing equipment at the office which meant search for appropriate equipment to set up their workstation. One respondent mentioned being forced to hide a cable or keyboard in a cupboard to ensure that the next time they're in office, there would be equipment available. Having to source sufficient equipment was found to delay the start of their working day.

Other, more subtle stresses stemmed from the effort of unplugging and packing up at home to go into the office on the designated days. Having to factor in all these things triggered varying levels of stress. This was more prominent at the start of being under the hybrid model and didn't occur to the same extent when the respondents were interviewed. Six respondents mentioned that this they didn't experience such struggles at home because their organisations provided adequate equipment such as a dongle and laptop (should they had previously only worked on a desktop at the office) to enable them to work from home.

"I've gotta rush to the office to make it in time. Then I've got to go and connect all these things and then switch on, log on and heaven help me if like at the one instance...the second monitor is not compatible. Now it's shut down, disconnect everything move to another desk, do the whole process over. This one doesn't work either."- OM09.

OM09 specifically referred to the differences in ergonomic levels of her work chair between the office and home. This is because at home, she has her customised chair with her correct ergonomics but at the office she must use any chair available which is not tailored to her ergonomics. This not only created stress but also negatively impacts on her physical being. This can also be seen in literature where technology demands enable ergonomic stress to be a stressor of technostress [1].

Office Distractions Related to ICT Use Causes Stress. Eight respondents expressed that being in office meant having to endure office-based interruptions where otherwise they wouldn't have experienced while working from home. Three out of the eight claimed that there are challenges with having partial teams present at the office on designated days. Those in-office would have to dial in the rest of the team who are working from home. This meant holding vir-tual meetings via MS Teams which would create echoes in the office, often distracting other teams and employees who are also in that day. This claimed to add to stress as it would disturb concentration levels and productivity.

Power Issues Creating Stress. Seven respondents from the interviews and three instances from the secondary data referred to the disturbances that loadshedding has had on their workstation setup at home and in office resulting in downtime. While most of them confirmed that their organisation provided adequate support for power outages at home such as an UPS or a dongle, some referred to the stress of worrying whether there would be enough stored power to last the loadshedding slots, especially under the higher levels of loadshedding. Several respondents indicated that this meant they would need to contribute more hours of work on those affected days as to catch up on time lost during the power outage. This added to stress which otherwise wouldn't have been there.

"My blood pressure almost went up one day 'cause I was panicking. I thought, where am I gonna work?" - OM05.

4.2   The Change in Traditional Technostressors Under Hybrid Working

Techno-Uncertainty Was Introduced with the Adoption of a New ICT/Technology when Remote Working. Six respondents expressed that they have experienced initial stress with familiarising themselves with new systems implemented by their organi-sation. OM02 mentioned experiencing communication inconsistencies when trying to liase with her IT department about the introduction of a new system. She expressed how stressful it was to interpret the technical jargon therefore this created misunderstandings in the requirements for the new system.

Five respondents alluded to the minimal/insufficient technical support and training for new system rollouts. This created stress in a sense that employees were now forced to learn the new systems by themselves. This resulted in them having to factor in time to learn the new systems which meant neglecting work duties for a time period, hence creating more stress.

"There's no training on it. It's like we just learning on the job, like on top of each other, on multiple applications besides all our existing applications."- OM10.

Techno-Overload Creating Technostress While WFH. Nine respondents indicated feelings of hyperconnectivity while working from home on the designated days which made it easier to be interrupted thorough application notifications and alerts. This also stems from organisational expectations on employees to be able to respond quickly and often outside of work hours.

"So, what I found is when you're working from home, then the Teams buzzes and you're like, OK [oh no] I gotta answer my Teams and your cell phone's buzzing because someone couldn't get you on your Teams. Then your e-mail is coming in at the same time. Your Skype's ringing. In this environment it's almost an expectation that you're always ready, always available, always online." - UCT02.

Three respondents mentioned how incorporating and using multiple applications at the same time can become overwhelming and stressful especially since sometimes the systems don't easily speak to each other. This is consistent with the belief that using multiple ICTs can instantiate technostress [7].

Techno-insecurity Creating Technostress. Experiences of techno insecurity weren't that significant amongst the sample, with only two respondents referring to feeling insecure about their IT skills. OM10 mentioned the impact of the imbalance of IT skills within the team that creates stress. This was to do with new employees in the team possessing IT skills that they have gained from experience in other teams/departments which instantiated feelings of insecurity within the old employees who don't possess such experience. This also made them feel as if it was burdensome when bothering these new employees for IT-related help.

Techno-Invasion Distorting Work/Life Balance When WFH. This theme relates to the distortion of work life balance as a result of ICT use for work. Six instances within the secondary data referred to challenges with work life balance under the hybrid working model. In line with [30], nine respondents from the interviews recalled feelings of techno invasion where they often found themselves logging in after work hours, on weekends and late in the evenings. This was mainly due to having a convenient setup at home which enabled them with the ability to connect or simply the use of laptops which made it easy to resume working when coming back from the office. This meant naturally putting in additional work hours without even realising it. OM10 referred to many of her employees having work-related applications such as Outlook and MS Teams on their phones which enabled them to remain connected outside of work hours. She expressed how, for her, this would increase her stress levels should she do the same. One respondent mentioned the negative impact techno invasion had on her personal relationships at home.

"Technology has invaded our private space and the lines between your work day and your domestic day have become blurred. I believe, that has led to stress in my life."- UCT01.

Techno-Complexity Causing Technostress. Ten respondents indicated that some of the systems are quite complex to understand at first, sometimes even after the system/application has been used for a while. One respondent mentioned feeling as if she had to become fluent in multiple applications to be able to tackle error messages which created stress and pressure. Four of these respondents referred to instances of system upgrade inconsistencies. Some expressed that the new systems that were introduced were often counterintuitive, and some systems were not familiar to the employees when a new version was released.

"These programs have to be complex. And as much as they're trying to be user intuitive, they don't often succeed there because they're trying to be different from their competitors."- OM04.

4.3 Coping Mechanisms Reduce Technostress

Proactive Coping Behaviour. According to [26], separating personal and work life by using different devices for the different ICT related tasks limits the exposure to work-related ICT tasks outside of work settings. This is consistent with some of the respondents when asked how they cope with technostress. However, there was a contradiction where one respondent had work-related applications on one device and personal apps on another for the purposes to reduce stress. Yet, another respondent felt that having no separation of ICT use doesn't reduce stress at all and would prefer having all applications on one device to moderate information and communication that would be work-related.

Other forms of ICT use demarcation found in the responses was related to structuring ICT use according to time periods. UCT01 mentioned blocking out a period of time to sort out an IT-related issue or to limit usage of technology by blocking out time in his calendar to avoid using technology.

Four respondents alluded to sticking to a routine therefore proactively coping with the technostress. This was described as attempts to come in early to the office as to factor in as much time to deal with a stressful incident should it arise. OM10 stated that: *"You tend to go early so you can get that desk cause other person's gonna take it."* This also linked with trying to find a suitable, adequately equipped desk with the correct devices and cables.

Six respondents mentioned preferring to work longer hours in hopes of reducing future instances of stress, therefore displaying proactive coping behaviours. This shows that by leveraging what once were technostressors (techno-overload and techno-invasion), additional stress can actually be reduced, therefore decreasing the overall techno stress level of the ICT user.

Reactive Coping Behaviour. Three responses pertained to reactive coping behaviours such as walking away from the stressful situation, regrouping, and closing all applications. Therefore, this demonstrates the distancing coping mechanism where employees can temporarily separate themselves from the IT-related task and focus on something else [38].

Five respondents expressed that they would usually resort to venting tactics, a reactive coping behaviour, should they encounter a stressful incident related to using an ICT/ICTs.

This was believed to help employees not feel isolated and to see if others are going through similar situations.

5 Discussion of Findings

The descriptive findings uncovered relationships between different characteristics of employees and their corresponding technostress levels. The data showed that the older the employee is, the higher the levels of technostress will most likely be, where most employees between the ages of 50–65 experienced moderate-intense techno stress levels. Some didn't express that they experience high levels of technostress, and this can be because of the nature of their job (ICTS) that require them to possess high IT skills. Employees in fast-paced, client-facing roles would experience higher levels of technostress as their reliance on technology increases. However, exclusively looking at the relationship with dependency on ICTs and the levels of technostress, no significant positive relationship can be drawn as literature suggests. The higher the IT skills the employee possesses, the lower the levels of technostress experienced will be. This is consistent with literature where it was found that the higher an individual's computer/IT skills are, the less technostress he/she will suffer [3].

5.1 Discussion of Findings Around the Standard Technostressors

It was evident from the findings that there has been a shift in employee technostress experiences under the working model. This change pointed to the decrease in technostress the more employees got accustomed to this new way of working. This could also point to the alternation of working environments where stressors occurring while working from home are eliminated once the employee returns to the office on their designated days in the week. This also indicates that there now exist different experiences of technostress unique to the hybrid working model.

The data showed how technostress remained heightened at the beginning of the implementation of the WFH model. As suggested by most of the respondents, most of the stressful incidents that they could recall happened at the start of the introduction of remote working and have reduced to an extent once the hybrid model was adopted. This pertained to the experiences of the five standard technostressors. While respondents could resonate with the five technostressors, it was evident that they had more encounters with it during purely remote working and not under the hybrid model.

Techno-Uncertainty as a Technostressor. There was reference to techno-uncertainty triggers that occurred when new systems were introduced when remote working was initially adopted where the reliance on ICTs spiked. This caused stress related to the initial familiarisation of the new system and the minimal technical support to accompany the new system rollout. This meant employees had to dedicate additional time to learn the new system, potentially outside of work hours therefore increasing stress levels. This wasn't a stressor that was unique to the hybrid model implementation.

Techno-Overload as a Technostressor. Respondents mentioned experiencing techno overload with regards to technology-related interruptions while working from home which triggered stress levels. Some also referred to feeling overwhelmed with the use of multiple applications that they deal with daily. This feeling of overwhelm can extend to experiences at the office as respondents confirmed that they use the same number of devices and applications at the office as they do at home. Therefore, this stressor can be seen as a constant between the alternation between office and home during the work week.

Techno-Insecurity as a Technostressor. This particular technostressor wasn't that suggestive as a trigger of technostress. There were only two respondents expressing feeling stressed that fellow employees may cope better with technological demands than themselves. These responses were more concerned with the imbalance of skills between new and old employees within the team. This extended to departmental differences in IT skills that equipped some with skills in systems across departments while others lacked these skills. This indicates that IT skill training needs to be made priority to counteract potential stressful encounters triggered by techno insecurity which can also extend to techno uncertainty.

Techno-Invasion as a Technostressor. The data showed instances of techno-invasion in the form of extending work hours into an employee's personal time therefore distorting boundaries between work and personal spaces when working from home specifically. This was seen to also diminish work life balance. Some respondents expressed instances of lack of separation of work-related ICTs on different devices which generated stress while one respondent relies on the lack of separation to re-duce stressful encounters. While some respondents confirmed that there are no explicit obligations imposed by the organisation to log in after hours, employees still naturally do so in order to keep up with work demands. This stressor is not unique to the hybrid model and relates more to WFH.

Techno-Complexity as a Technostressor. The data suggested employee challenges with system complexity that instantiated feelings of stress. This pointed to IT skills levels struggling to match with systems' expectations which mainly stemmed from the perceived system complexity that existed, especially in new versions of systems. This can be seen to be a result of the counter intuitiveness expressed by some of the respondents which made the systems seem unfamiliar therefore triggering feelings of stress. Either employees need to be upskilled through training programmes to have their skills match with system expectations or system's need to be more simply designed.

5.2 Discussion of Findings Around the Hybrid-Specific Technostressors

Since the hybrid working model presented a disturbance to employee's working styles, it was anticipated that there are unique experiences of technostress under such a model. The data analysed for this research suggested that there are distinctive causes of technostress where one specific cause was seen to align with the findings of a study based in China, related to struggles with setting up workstations at the office [41]. It was interesting to see some similarities in the South African hybrid workplace context.

Undesignated Desk Setup (Hot Desks) Creates Unnecessary Technostress. Since some respondents (which was found to exclude most managers) had to secure a desk each time they came into the office on their designated days, the desks often varied in equipment availability. As a result, they had to ensure coming into the office early enough to secure an appropriate desk or to hide some equipment in cupboards to ensure they would be sorted the next time coming into the office. This was mainly due to the instances of missing equipment such as monitors, adapters, keyboards, cables etc. which meant that the equipment floated around from desk to desk.

All employees originally transferred all equipment to their homes when lockdown began to ensure that they could set-up their workstations at home and resume work as quickly as possible. This meant that there were hardly any duplicates of equipment at the office. This could indicate the possibility of the organisation attempting to cut costs but as expressed by several respondents, organisations rather invested in providing them with abilities to work from home. This implies that should organisations opt to keep hybrid working models, adequate resources in terms of equipment and amenities should be provided for employees on their days in-office so as to mirror their home working stations. In addition, some respondents mentioned how stressful it was to configure and synchronise various devices when coming into the office. There was reference to compatibility issues which can be seen as a direct cause of the lack of equipment availability mentioned already.

Office Distractions Related to ICT Use Causes Stress. The comparison between working at home and at the office surfaced consistencies across some respondents regarding the disruptive atmosphere of the office. In addition to the usual office disruptions that existed before the COVID-19 lockdown, some respondents found having partial teams present at the office raised some unusual disruptions. This broke their concentration and added to their stress levels. The reason for only having partial teams present was initially to adhere to social distancing standards that organisations had to uphold. This meant that members of teams in-office had to conduct meetings with members at home using online conferencing tools. This created noise and echoes in office which disrupted other teams also in-office on that day as teams would sit at their desk and not in boardrooms. In addition, employees on-site had to sit at their own individual portable computers (PCs) and couldn't congregate around one PC due to the upholding of social distancing standards. This meant that sound from the virtual meeting was duplicated and echoed throughout the office. Now that the COVID-19 pandemic environment is adapting yet again, organisations can now consider allowing all employees in office therefore mitigating partial teams.

Power Issues Impacting Access to ICTs Creates Stress. Loadshedding and power issues presented challenges for employees to conduct their work using ICTs that demanded sufficient power. While the organisations provided infrastructure support, often the loadshedding schedules were unpredictable and left employees in crisis situations. This meant employees experienced anxiety and stress as they were now unable to complete any work and had to make drastic arrangements to resume work. This is a macro issue specific to South Africa that can't be solved by the organisation itself but remains crucial to implement as much support as possible to counter the unpredictable instances of loadshedding.

5.3 Discussion of Findings Around Coping Mechanisms

Proactive Coping Behaviours. Amongst the sample, it can be gathered that the main coping behaviour was of a proactive nature utilising a problem-focused coping strategy. Most respondents expressed that they resorted to proactive tactics like demarcating ICT use according to time and separation of use. Others expressed enforcing a routine to maintain a structure that could mitigate the impacts of a stressful encounter should it occur. Most respondents confirmed that working longer hours actually helped them reduce further anticipated stress. This meant logging onto systems to perform work activities on the weekend in order to reduce work backlog and hence further stress. This was only made possible by the capabilities of having a laptop and WIFI.

Reactive Coping Behaviours. The data showed how the standard reactive coping behaviours remain prominent when dealing with stress. This referred to emotion-focused coping strategies such as distancing oneself from the stressful situation and venting to others in hopes of reducing feelings of isolation and anxiety.

6 Conclusion

Technostress is claimed to emerge when there is a change in working environments [7]. This stems from the unexpected reliance on ICTs to conduct work which can trigger feelings of stress. Employees within these spaces are constantly adapting their perceptions about the workplace which initially was believed to be partly influenced by feelings of COVID-19-related anxiety. Therefore, since the hybrid model was adopted in some South African organisations, it is possible that there are new experiences of technostress within hybrid workplaces because of this shift in perceptions. Given this, the purpose of this research was to understand how employee technostress experiences have changed since hybrid models were adopted in South African organisations. Furthermore, the research intends to explain the underlying causes of these new experiences and how employees are currently coping with these new instances of technostress.

Firstly, the data suggested positive relationships between fast-paced and client-facing work roles and older age groups with levels of technostress. Therefore, the higher these factors are, the higher the levels of technostress will be. IT skills levels and system performance supported negative relationships with the levels of technostress in that higher IT skills levels and stronger system performance expose lower levels of technostress. Finally, the relationship between the level of dependence on ICTs and the level of technostress was shown to be insignificant and therefore no direct influence of higher levels of dependence.

To answer the first research question, the research suggested that the standard technostressors weren't as prevalent in the hybrid working model. These seemed to be more heightened at the start of implemented the purely WFH approach and decreased to some extent under hybrid. This concludes that technostress experiences amongst South African employees have adapted under hybrid, pointing to new emerging experiences driven by causes that will be discussed next.

From the responses gathered, it can be concluded that hybrid-working-specific causes of technostress triggered feelings of technostress. These include stressful workstation setups upon return to the office on designated days which involved configuration, compatibility, and synchronisation issues along with the lack of equipment on hand. On the days at the office, it was shown that office distractions caused unwarranted stress within employees in-office. This specifically pertained to virtual meeting noise and echoes which caused an unproductive working environment. Lastly, the issue of power shortages as a result of loadshedding became a hinderance and contributed to feelings of stress. The stresses related to loadshedding and power outages appeared to be a distinctive South African issue.

To deal with these instances of technostress, employees adopted reactive and proactive coping behaviours driven by problem-focused and emotion-focused coping strategies respectively. Reactive behaviours involved distancing from the stressful situation and venting to others. Proactive behaviours involved demarcating ICT use through structured time use and separation of use. This behaviour also included implementing a structured routine and working longer hours to reduce future stressful encounters.

Research Contribution. This paper contributes to the academic body of knowledge by highlighting the different types of stressors and coping mechanisms used in the hybrid working scenario – which is relatively under-researched due to its newness. The rich findings can form the basis for future elaboration, theoretical model building and more quantitative research. From a practical perspective, managers and decision-makers in organisations transitioning to a hybrid working model will be better informed about the differences with the prior remote working model. Hopefully this will enable them to create a better, more humane and more productive working environment that benefits both the organisation and the employees. The latter should benefit indirectly from better mental and physical health, as well as a better understanding of the range of coping mechanisms available to them.

Research Limitations. This research was limited in scope with regard to the sample size and representation. As the target audience involved a focus on two South African organisations (one with a more concentrated focus than the other), the results can't be used as generalisations. Since both organisations are large in nature, the technostress experiences could have been depicted at a lower intensity as these organisations provide substantial access to technology, enabling its employees to deal with stressful encounters. Therefore, a more even distribution of respondents in a bigger sample size will allow a better representation of the findings. Since the research made use of a cross-sectional study, time constraints were a big limitation especially since qualitative analysis is time consuming. This also meant that technostress experiences under the hybrid model could only be recorded within the early stages of its inception where otherwise if the research was conducted over a longer period of time, a more holistic understanding could have been extracted.

Suggestions for Future Research. The first recommendation is to compare the three modes of working (purely remote, hybrid and purely onsite) over a longer period of time to uncover more accurate understandings of the differences in the experiences of technostress. The second recommendation is to expand on the sample size, by including a bigger variety of South African organisations with a more even distribution of respondents from each and a diversity in organisation size such as including Small and

Medium Enterprises (SMEs). The last recommendation is to research the impacts of technostress experiences within South African hybrid workplaces in order to build on the implications of the causes of hybrid working specific experiences of technostress found in this study.

Disclosure of Interests. The authors have no competing interests to declare that are relevant to the content of this article.

References

1. Atanasoff, L., Venable, M.A.: Technostress: implications for adults in the workforce. Career Dev. Q. **65**, 326–338 (2017). https://doi.org/10.1002/cdq.12111
2. Azungah, T.: Qualitative research: deductive and inductive approaches to data analysis. Qual. Res. J. **18**, 383–400 (2018). https://doi.org/10.1108/QRJ-D-18-00035
3. Berger, R., Romeo, M., Gidion, G., Poyato, L.: Media use and technostress. In: INTED 2016 Proceedings, pp. 390–400. IATED (2016). https://doi.org/10.21125/inted.2016.1092
4. Bhattacherjee, A.: Social Science Research: Principles, Methods, and Practices (2012)
5. Boddy, C.R.: Sample size for qualitative research. J. Cetacean Res. Manag. **19**, 426–432 (2016). https://doi.org/10.1108/QMR-06-2016-0053
6. Bussin, M.H.R., Swart-Opperman, C.: COVID-19: considering impacts to employees and the workplace **19** (2021). https://doi.org/10.4102/sajhrm.v19i0.1384
7. Camarena, L., Fusi, F.: Always connected: technology use increases technostress among public managers. Am. Rev. Public Adm. **52**, 154–168 (2021). https://doi.org/10.1177/027507 40211050387
8. Chen, J.V., Tran, A., Nguyen, T.: Understanding the discontinuance behavior of mobile shoppers as a consequence of technostress: an application of the stress-coping theory. Comput. Hum. Behav. **95**, 83–93 (2019). https://doi.org/10.1016/j.chb.2019.01.022
9. Chujfi, S., Meinel, C.: Design thinking and cognitive science: an exploratory approach to create intellectual capital with decentralised organisations. In: FedCSIS (Communication Papers), pp. 303–310 (2017). https://doi.org/10.15439/2017F232
10. De', R., Pandey, N., Pal, A.: Impact of digital surge during Covid-19 pandemic: a viewpoint on research and practice. Int. J. Inf. Manag. **55**, 102171 (2020). https://doi.org/10.1016/j.iji nfomgt.2020.102171
11. Dowrie, S., Van Belle, J.-P., Turpin, M.: Employee technostress in South Africa's hybrid workplaces: causes and coping mechanisms. In: 2023 18th Conference on Computer Science and Intelligence Systems (FedCSIS), pp. 943–947. IEEE (2023). https://doi.org/10.15439/ 978-83-967447-8-4
12. González-López, Ó.R., Buenadicha-Mateos, M., Sánchez-Hernández, M.I.: Overwhelmed by technostress? Sensitive archetypes and effects in times of forced digitalization. Int. J. Environ. Res. Public Health **18**, 4216 (2021). https://doi.org/10.3390/ijerph18084216
13. Harris, K.J., et al.: Technostress and the entitled employee: impacts on work and family. Inf. Technol. People **35**, 1073–1095 (2022). https://doi.org/10.1108/ITP-07-2019-0348
14. Hauk, N., Göritz, A.S., Krumm, S.: The mediating role of coping behavior on the age-technostress relationship: a longitudinal multilevel mediation model. PLoS ONE **14**, e0213349 (2019). https://doi.org/10.1371/journal.pone.0213349
15. https://www.wework.com/ideas/workspace-solutions/flexible-products/what-is-the-hybrid-workplace-model#:~:text=The%20hybrid%20workplace%20model%20is,working%20f rom%20a%20central%20office

16. Hwang, I., Cha, O.: Examining technostress creators and role stress as potential threats to employees' information security compliance. Comput. Hum. Behav. **81**, 282–293 (2018). https://doi.org/10.1016/j.chb.2017.12.022

17. Khuzaini, K., Zamrudi, Z.: Technostress among marketing employee during the COVID-19 pandemic: exploring the role of technology usability and presenteeism. JEMA: Jurnal Ilmiah Bidang Akuntansi dan Manajemen **18**, 36–60 (2021). https://doi.org/10.31106/jema.v18i1.10050

18. La Torre, G., Esposito, A., Sciarra, I., Chiappetta, M.: Definition, symptoms and risk of techno-stress: a systematic review. Int. Arch. Occup. Environ. Health **92**(1), 13–35 (2018). https://doi.org/10.1007/s00420-018-1352-1

19. Ma, J., Ollier-Malaterre, A., Lu, C.-Q.: The impact of techno-stressors on work–life balance: the moderation of job self-efficacy and the mediation of emotional exhaustion. Comput. Hum. Behav. **122**, 106811 (2021). https://doi.org/10.1016/j.chb.2021.106811

20. Mahapatra, M., Pati, S.P.: Technostress creators and burnout: a job demands-resources perspective. In: Proceedings of the 2018 ACM SIGMIS Conference on Computers and People Research, pp. 70–77. Association for Computing Machinery, Buffalo-Niagara Falls (2018). https://doi.org/10.1145/3209626.3209711

21. Nisafani, A.S., Kiely, G., Mahony, C.: Workers' technostress: a review of its causes, strains, inhibitors, and impacts. J. Decis. Syst. **29**, 243–258 (2020). https://doi.org/10.1080/12460125.2020.1796286

22. Nowacka, A., Jelonek, D.: The impact of the multi-variant remote work model on knowledge management in enterprises. Applied tools. In: 2022 17th Conference on Computer Science and Intelligence Systems (FedCSIS), pp. 827–835 (2022). https://doi.org/10.15439/2022F26

23. Oygür, I., Göçer, Ö., Karahan, E.E.: Hybrid workplace: activity-based office design in a post-pandemic era. J. Interior Des. **47**, 3–10 (2022). https://doi.org/10.1111/joid.12218

24. Pataki-Bittó, F., Kapusy, K.: Work environment transformation in the post COVID-19 based on work values of the future workforce. J. Corp. Real Estate **23**, 151–169 (2021). https://doi.org/10.1108/JCRE-08-2020-0031

25. Pirkkalainen, H., Salo, M., Tarafdar, M., Makkonen, M.: Deliberate or instinctive? Proactive and reactive coping for technostress. J. Manag. Inf. Syst. **36**, 1179–1212 (2019). https://doi.org/10.1080/07421222.2019.1661092

26. Rohwer, E., Flöther, J.-C., Harth, V., Mache, S.: Overcoming the "Dark Side" of Technology—a scoping review on preventing and coping with work-related technostress. Int. J. Environ. Res. Public Health **19**, 3625 (2022). https://doi.org/10.3390/ijerph19063625

27. Saleem, F., Malik, M.I., Qureshi, S.S., Farid, M.F., Qamar, S.: Technostress and employee performance nexus during COVID-19: training and creative self-efficacy as moderators. Front. Psychol. **12**, 595119 (2021). https://doi.org/10.3389/fpsyg.2021.595119

28. Satpathy, S., Patel, G., Kumar, K.: Identifying and ranking techno-stressors among IT employees due to work from home arrangement during Covid-19 pandemic. Decision **48**, 391–402 (2021). https://doi.org/10.1007/s40622-021-00295-5

29. Saunders, M., Lewis, P., Thornhill, A.: Research Methods for Business Students, vol. 4. Pearson Publishing Limited (2019)

30. Savolainen, I., Oksa, R., Savela, N., Celuch, M., Oksanen, A.: COVID-19 anxiety—a longitudinal survey study of psychological and situational risks among Finnish workers. Int. J. Environ. Res. Public Health **18**, 794 (2021). https://doi.org/10.3390/ijerph18020794

31. Schmidt, M., Frank, L., Gimpel, H.: How adolescents cope with technostress: a mixed-methods approach. Int. J. Electron. Commer. **25**, 154–180 (2021). https://doi.org/10.1080/10864415.2021.1887696

32. Sellberg, C., Susi, T.: Technostress in the office: a distributed cognition perspective on human–technology interaction. Cogn. Technol. Work **16**, 187–201 (2014). https://doi.org/10.1007/s10111-013-0256-9

33. Shu, Q., Tu, Q., Wang, K.: The impact of computer self-efficacy and technology dependence on computer-related technostress: a social cognitive theory perspective. Int. J. Hum.-Comput. Interact. **27**, 923–939 (2011). https://doi.org/10.1080/10447318.2011.555313

34. Spagnoli, P., Molino, M., Molinaro, D., Giancaspro, M.L., Manuti, A., Ghislieri, C.: Workaholism and technostress during the COVID-19 emergency: the crucial role of the leaders on remote working. Front. Psychol. **11**, 620310 (2020). https://doi.org/10.3389/fpsyg.2020.620310

35. Srivastava, S.C., Chandra, S., Shirish, A.: Technostress creators and job outcomes: theorising the moderating influence of personality traits. Inf. Syst. J. **25**, 355–401 (2015). https://doi.org/10.1111/isj.12067

36. Stana, R.A., Nicolajsen, H.W.: A cautionary tale: how co-constructed work obligations lead to ICT-related technostress. In: 54th Hawaii International Conference on System Sciences, pp. 6631–6640. HICSS (2021). http://hdl.handle.net/10125/71417

37. Tarafdar, M., Cooper, C.L., Stich, J.-F.: The technostress trifecta - techno eustress, techno distress and design: theoretical directions and an agenda for research. Inf. Syst. J. **29**, 6–42 (2019). https://doi.org/10.1111/isj.12169

38. Tarafdar, M., Pirkkalainen, H., Salo, M., Makkonen, M.: Taking on the "dark side"—coping with technostress. IT Prof. **22**, 82–89 (2020). https://doi.org/10.1109/MITP.2020.2977343

39. Taser, D., Aydin, E., Torgaloz, A.O., Rofcanin, Y.: An examination of remote e-working and flow experience: the role of technostress and loneliness. Comput. Hum. Behav. **127**, 107020 (2022). https://doi.org/10.1016/j.chb.2021.107020

40. Upadhyaya, P., Vrinda: Impact of technostress on academic productivity of university students. Educ. Inf. Technol. **26**, 1647–1664 (2021). https://doi.org/10.1007/s10639-020-10319-9

41. Wang, Y., et al.: Returning to the office during the COVID-19 pandemic recovery: early indicators from China. In: Extended Abstracts of the 2021 CHI Conference on Human Factors in Computing Systems. Association for Computing Machinery, Yokohama (2021). Article 417. https://doi.org/10.1145/3411763.3451685

42. Weinert, C., Maier, C., Laumer, S., Weitzel, T.: How do users respond to technostress? An empirical analysis of proactive and reactive coping. In: 52nd Hawaii International Conference on System Sciences (2019). https://hdl.handle.net/10125/59947

43. Xie, J.L., Elangovan, A.R., Hu, J., Hrabluik, C.: Charting new terrain in work design: a study of hybrid work characteristics. Appl. Psychol. **68**, 479–512 (2019). https://doi.org/10.1111/apps.12169

44. Yang, E., Kim, Y., Hong, S.: Does working from home work? Experience of working from home and the value of hybrid workplace post-COVID-19. J. Corp. Real Estate **25**, 50–76 (2023). https://doi.org/10.1108/JCRE-04-2021-0015

45. Zhao, X., Xia, Q., Huang, W.: Impact of technostress on productivity from the theoretical perspective of appraisal and coping processes. Inf. Manag. **57**, 103265 (2020). https://doi.org/10.1016/j.im.2020.103265

Experimenting Emotion-Based Book Recommender Systems with Social Data

Elena-Ruxandra Luțan[(✉)] [iD] and Costin Bădică[iD]

Department of Computers and Information Technology, University of Craiova,
200585 Craiova, Romania
elena.ruxandra.lutan@gmail.com, costin.badica@edu.ucv.ro

Abstract. In this contribution, we present two methods for book recommendations incorporating emotions extracted from online reviews, using two distinct recommender systems techniques: Content-based filtering and Collaborative filtering. This paper is based on a previous conference publication [14] and extends the system description and experimental setup. The recommender systems are experimentally validated using three datasets of different sizes, collected from *Goodreads* website - a popular book social network, using our customized web scraper. Lastly, we propose and use two evaluation metrics: Coverage and Average Recommendations Similarity, and discuss our results.

Keywords: Recommender System · Emotion Analysis · Book Recommendations

1 Introduction

Due to lack of personal experience, people tend to seek the experience of peers in order to choose products or services. Peers experience comes as recommendations in various forms, such as word of mouth, surveys, articles [24]. Today, social media plays an increasingly important role in peoples' decisions, as it allows people to interact and share their opinion [7,20], which results in various user-generated products' features, including sentiments and emotions [22].

Recommender systems are powerful tools which filter information in order to offer users personalized content [25]. The aim of a recommender system is to provide meaningful recommendations to the users based on the products which might interest them, the recommendations trustworthiness being a mandatory characteristic.

The design of a recommender system varies depending on the nature of products for which recommendations will be issued [16]. Three main recommender system techniques can be identified: Content-based filtering, Collaborative filtering and a combination of both [2]. Depending on the principle that is used, data sources are differently interpreted, analyzed and processed for building the recommendations [10,16].

Content-based filtering refers to recommending products which are similar to the product that is being watched [2], while Collaborative filtering aims to mine the most similar users with the user of interest and to observe their preferences, such that these preferences can be used to make predictions about what the user of interest might enjoy [4].

This paper is an extended version of our preliminary conference paper [14]. We focus on a specific category of products - literature books, and propose two recommender systems using the two different recommendation techniques: Content-based filtering and Collaborative filtering.

The recommender systems incorporate emotion information extracted from social media data to identify similarities between the books, in addition to other publisher details available for a given book.

In this contribution, we introduce three new experimental datasets of different sizes, that we collected using our customized web scraper from a popular book-oriented website and social network - *Goodreads*. Each dataset consists in a set of books and associated reviews. The reviews are split into two categories: training and testing. Training reviews are used for defining the emotional characteristics of the books, while testing reviews are given as input to the recommender systems in order to obtain recommendations. Afterwards, we define two evaluation metrics and discuss the performance of our recommender systems.

Compared to the preliminary version of our paper, this extended version includes: (i) new experimental datasets, enlarging both number of books and number of reviews per book, (ii) new attributes collected for each entity, (iii) additional preprocessing step of reviews for excluding reviews not written in English language, (iv) detailed description of application interface used for experimental datasets, (v) comparison of performance measures on datasets of different dimensions.

The paper is structured as follows. In Sect. 2, we present related works. Section 3 describes our proposed book recommendation algorithms, using Content-based filtering and Collaborative filtering. In Sect. 4, we provide an overview of the dataset and the application used for experiments, and then we discuss the experimental results. The last section presents our conclusions.

2   Literature Review

Chhavi Rana and Sanjay Kumar Jain [23] propose a system which makes Content-based book recommendations based on the user navigation pattern. The system analyzes user's behaviour and then it predicts the category of books that would interest the user using Content-based filtering. The authors observe the lack of accuracy of Content-based recommendations, as after a certain amount of time, the users will be recommended the same similar items. Therefore they introduce a temporal dimension, which means that user navigation and most visited links are periodically analyzed and revised when using the Content-based approach to make recommendations.

In [28], Jessie Caridad Martin Sujo and Elisabet Golobardes i Ribe present a system which recommends the book that best suits the reader based on the semantics of his or her writing style. They use posts from Twitter social network in order to determine the psychological profile of the user. The authors use a database consisting in characters text, associated personality type and corresponding book. Their proposed method computes the similarity between the Twitter post text and the cases database in order to recommend the most suitable book to the user.

An Enhanced Personalized Book Recommender System (EPBRS) is described in [29]. The proposed system uses the a similarity function based on Euclidean distance in order to identify users with similar interests. The recommendations are done using Collaborative filtering by considering the books preferred by similar users. A dataset of reviews, users and associated ratings from Amazon bookstore was used for experiments. The book ratings are considered as features when making the predictions.

In [30], authors propose a system which is able to provide replies to queries regarding products details. The answer that is returned to the query is actually a review available for the product, which contains the relevant details. For experiments, they use two neural models, a simple model (NNQA) and a Transformer-based model (BERTQA). These models are evaluated regarding their ability to find the relevant reviews.

Anil Kumar and Sonal Chawla [12] make an analysis of the recommendation techniques which are most frequently used for book recommender systems. They also propose a new book recommender system based on Hybrid recommendation technique. The Hybrid recommender system works as follows: when the user searches for a book, the system computes the list of book recommendations using Collaborative filtering on book ratings. Then the positive and negative user reviews for each book are identified such that the recommendation list will be sorted based on the number of positive reviews. The user is displayed the book recommendation list together with the details of the searched book.

Harsh Dubey and Suma Kamalesh Gandhimathi [5] propose a recommender system which uses Deep Learning GPT3 (Generative Pre-trained Transformer). The project refers to building an application which finds books that are similar to a certain book provided as input. On a web interface, the user must describe a book that he or she has enjoyed reading. OpenAI API module is used for generating the recommendations of books that are similar with the input book description, and the top 3 recommendations are displayed together with details about the books availability obtained using Google Books API.

In [15], authors attempt to overcome the limitation of basic filtering techniques (Content-based filtering and Collaborative filtering) introducing a hybrid recommender system that combines the basic filtering techniques with sentiment extraction and analysis of book tweets.

Mala Saraswat et al. [26] present a model for providing top N movie recommendations using emotional aspects extracted from online reviews. The authors use Parrott's emotions model and *WordNet* [17] to extract the basic emotions from reviews. Each movie is seen as defining an emotional profile of the six basic emotions (joy, sadness, fear, anger, surprise and love), and similarity between the movies is computed using cosine metric.

Yiu-Kai Ng [19] focuses on a specific category of users - teenagers and proposes a book recommender system called TBRec. Recommendations are provided using a set of book features which impact the teenagers preference and satisfaction: topic relevance, emotional traits, reader's advisory, readability levels and predicted ratings. The system works as follows: the teenager has to provide the title of an enjoyed book, named target book. Afterwards, TBRec analyses the similarity between the target book and all books from the corpus and retrieves the candidate books to be recommended. Yiu-Kai Ng uses the eight basic emotion model proposed by [21] for determining the emotion traits. Each word from the book content is associated with a combination of the eight fundamental emotions – anger, anticipation, disgust, fear, joy, sadness, surprise, and trust.

Amarajyothi Aramanda et al. [3] propose an Enhanced Emotion Specific Prediction (*enemos-p*) model to refine the user rating data using the emotional words extracted from user reviews. Each word is assigned an emotional state set considering the basic emotion list (anger, anticipation, disgust, fear, joy, sadness, surprise, trust), and a word is considered "emotional word" if it expresses at least one emotion. The emotional words are extracted from each sentence of the user review, thus identifying the sentence-level emotions.

Takumi Fujimoto and Harumi Murakami [6] propose a model for book recommendations considering the similarity of the vectors of contents and emotions extracted from tweets. Each book is represented as 10-dimensional vector considering following dimensions: joy, anger, sadness, fear, shame, fondness, dislike, excitement, relief and surprise. The similarity between user interest and the corpus books is calculated using cosine metric.

3   Research Methodology

3.1   Methodology Overview

We propose two recommender system algorithms for literature book recommendation, corresponding to the two distinct techniques: Content-based filtering and Collaborative filtering. Both algorithms incorporate the emotion categorization of each book as an important feature for determining similarities between books.

The emotions are extracted from online book reviews and then used for creating an emotion-based categorization of books using the system we previously proposed in [13]. In total, there are 35 emotions considered: 'cheated', 'singled out', 'loved', 'attracted', 'sad', 'fearful', 'happy', 'angry', 'bored', 'esteemed', 'lustful', 'attached', 'independent', 'embarrassed', 'powerless', 'surprise', 'fearless', 'safe', 'adequate', 'belittled', 'hated', 'codependent', 'average', 'apathetic', 'obsessed', 'entitled', 'alone', 'focused', 'demoralized', 'derailed', 'anxious', 'ecstatic', 'free', 'lost', 'burdened'. The emotion extraction workflow takes as input the review, performs standard NLP text preprocessing techniques (tokenization, lower casing, removal of stop words) and determines the emotions present in the text by making word-matching with a list of adjectives and their corresponding emotion.

Our proposed recommendation algorithms are validated on three experimental datasets, representing 1000 books categorized by users as best books and their associated reviews. The datasets were collected by us from *Goodreads* website using our own customized web scraper.

We set as target to collect 180 reviews for each book. The default sorting order for reviews available on *Goodreads* was used - reviews sorted by popularity. The set of collected reviews is preprocessed using *Langdetect* Python package to define the language used when writing the review. *Langdetect* package [18] can detect 49 languages with a very good precision of 99.8% and performs slightly better than other language detection packages in terms of accuracy [8,11].

The target is to keep only English language reviews for performing Emotion extraction, since our emotion model uses a list of English adjectives and associated emotions.

The datasets contains tabular data describing two entities, Book and Review, which are interrelated by a one-to-many relationship. For both entities, several parameters available on *Goodreads* website were extracted and captured as separate columns. They are described in Tables 1 and 2.

Table 1. Book Entity Description

Field Name	Field Description
Book Id	Id which uniquely identifies the book
Book Title	Title of the book
Book Series	Book series name if applicable, for standalone books it is filled with "no"
Book Author	Author(s) of the book
Book Overall Rating	The book rating, a number in interval [1, 5]
Book Ratings Number	The number of ratings available on Goodreads for the book
Book Reviews Number	The number of reviews available on Goodreads for the book
Book Description	Description of the book
Book Genres	Top 7 genres available for the book on Goodreads website
Book Pages	The number of pages of the book
Book Year	The year in which the book was published
Publication Info	The date when the book was first published
Ratings Histogram	Histogram which shows the distribution of Book Reviews Number per Rating Class - integer number in interval [1, 5]
Emotions	The book emotions computed using [13]

Table 2. Review Entity Description

Field Name	Field Description
Review Id	Id which uniquely identifies the review
Book Id	Id of the book for which the review is given
Author Id	Id of the user who wrote the review
Review Stars	The rating given by the review author, as integer in interval [1, 5]
Review Date	The date when the review was written
Review Tags	Review tags or keywords given by the review author
Review Content	The review (text) provided by the review author
Review Likes	Number of Likes given by other users
Review Comments	Number of Comments given by other users
Language	Review Language detected using langdetect Python package
Emotions	The book emotions computed using [13]

3.2 Content-Based Filtering

Content-based filtering approach recommends items considering user preferences. The hypothesis of Content-based filtering is that users are usually more interested in those items that are similar to items they liked in the past [4].

We analyzed which fields of each book item can be used to better define its characteristics. We decided to use the Book Title, Book Series, Book Author, as well as the main emotions triggered by the book reading, which are computed during the extraction of sentiments from the book reviews.

The recommendation algorithm takes as input a review of a given user for a given book which is available in the database. The review consists of two components: a number in range [1, 5] which represents a scaled value capturing how much the user liked the book (which will be referred as Review Stars) and the opinion of the user expressed in natural language text (which will be called Review Content).

The general idea of the algorithm is to use the input review in order to decide how much the user enjoyed the current book and to recommend other relevant books to the user.

The Review Stars is used to classify the level of satisfaction that the book provided to the user, as follows:

- The user did not like the book (Review Stars = 1 or 2).
- The user liked the book, but was not over-joyed (Review Stars = 3 or 4).
- The user loved the book (Review Stars = 5).

We detail each case of the algorithm used for Content-based filtering (Algorithm 1). The algorithm contains 3 main IF clauses that deal with each one of the possible three satisfaction levels extracted from the input review.

The first IF clause (line 1) refers to the case when the user did not like the book (Review Stars = 1 or 2). In this case, we need to know what caused this

Algorithm 1. Content-Based Filtering Algorithm

1: **if** Review Stars < 3 **then**
2:     Extract the emotions from the Review Content
3:     **if** Review Content Emotions match Book Emotions > *threshold* **then**
4:         Recommend a book which differs from the rated book
5:     **else**
6:         Recommend a book similar with the rated one
7:     **end if**
8: **end if**
9: **if** Review Stars ≥ 3 and Review Stars <5 **then**
10:     Recommend a better book similar with the rated one
11: **end if**
12: **if** Review Stars = 5 **then**
13:     Recommend a book similar with the rated one
14: **end if**

---

dissatisfaction. We will take into consideration the Review Content and extract the emotions. In order to decide what kind of books to recommend, we decided to compare the Review Content Emotions with the Book Emotions. In case they match with high value, we considers this indicates that the user did not like the overall idea of the book, the kind of emotions that the book made him or her feel. In this case, we will recommend a completely different book emotions-wise, because it is most likely that the user will prefer something different. If the Review Content Emotions and the Book Emotions do not match, we interpret this as indicating that the user did not perceive the book as expected; maybe he or she did not actually understand the meaning of the book. In this case, we will recommend a book that is similar with the current one, as we guess that the user is likely to enjoy a new book which provides emotions rather close with the ones present in current book.

The second IF clause (line 9) refers to the case when user liked the book, but was not over-joyed by it. The aim of the recommender system is to provide recommendations for products which are likely to offer the greatest experience. For this reason, we will recommend books which provide similar sentiments, but are higher in ratings than the current book.

The last IF clause (line 12) refers to the case when the user loved the book. In this case, we recommend to the user a book which is very similar to the current one, because he or she is likely to enjoy it as much.

When recommending new books, we include only books that the user has not seen, i.e. books to which the user has not yet given reviews.

By applying the Content-based filtering algorithm (Algorithm 1) we obtain a list of books which are considered the user might enjoy, and the top 5 books are displayed to the user as recommendations.

3.3   Collaborative Filtering

Collaborative filtering method aims to find similarities between users based on the user-item interaction [1]. The system divides the users into clusters by considering their past interactions and makes recommendations according to the preference of the cluster the user belongs [4].

Similarly to the Content-based filtering method, the Collaborative filtering algorithm takes as input a review of a user for a given book which is available in the database, with its two components, Review Stars and Review Content. Its pseudocode is presented as Algorithm 2.

Algorithm 2. Collaborative Filtering Algorithm

1: Compare the user of interest with all the users who provided reviews for the given book
2: **if** A similar user which matches > *threshold* is found **then**
3:    The users are similar, recommend a book that the similar user liked
4: **end if**

So, we are interested in evaluating the similarity of the user of interest with other users from the database. In our model, the similarities between the user of interest and each of the users in database are computed based on the emotions that exist in their reviews given for the given book. Then we determine the 5 topmost users similar with the user of interest and we analyze their preferences. This means that we analyze their reviews to determine which other books these top 5 users rated.

We consider that a user liked a book if he or she provided 4 or 5 stars. Therefore, from all the books rated by the top 5 users, we will select only those which got 4 or 5 stars in the reviews. This will lead to a set of books which we consider the user of interest might enjoy.

In order to offer the greatest experience, we decided to filter the set of books according to the Book Overall Rating, assuming that higher rating means better book. Book Overall Rating is an attribute present for each book in our dataset and it represents the book rating as it is recorded on the *Goodreads*.

When a new review is given, the first step is to compute the emotions present in the review. The content of the review is pre-processed by removing unnecessary text from the review, tokenizing the review text into words and removing the stop words. Then we extract the emotions from the pre-processed text, using our own Emotions Extraction Algorithm introduced in [13]. Our emotion model is based on a list of maximum 35 emotions and their weights.

Following, we extract from the reviews dataset the set of reviews available for the rated book. This subset will be used with the purpose of finding similar users with the user who provided the review. Two users are considered similar if they provided review for the same book and the emotions which are available in their reviews match at least 50%.

The next step of the Collaborative filtering algorithm is to identify the books that similar users liked in order to recommend them to the user of interest. In order to make recommendations, for each of the matching users we identify the rated books which received more than 3 stars (as we assume that the similar users liked these books) and were not yet rated by the user of interest, and we add them to the list of recommendations.

At this stage, we have obtained a list of recommendations which can be provided to the user of interest. Initially, we considered the default ordering of this list according to how were the books appended to the list. According to this ordering, the books preferred by the most similar users are located as topmost entries of this list. However, after a deeper analysis, we realized that this might not be the best possible ordering, because we would rely only on the most similar users in order to make recommendations, and this would restrict too much the space of possible recommendations. Therefore, we decided to define a better way to order the recommendations such that to not rely only on the preferences of the single topmost similar user. Consequently, we considered that a possibility is to order the recommendations list by the Book Overall Rating value, before providing the top recommendations to the user.

If the recommendation list does not contain the minimum number of 5 recommendations, the list is completed by adding the books with the highest rating available in the dataset.

4   Research Findings and Discussion

4.1   Application Interface

In order to simplify the use of the proposed system, we developed a convenient application interface using *Tkinter* Python Library, which can be seen in Fig. 1.

The button "Process input dataset" from Step 1 refers to processing the reviews and books dataset by extracting the emotions from reviews and categorizing the books emotions based using our approach previously introduced in [13].

Step 2 refers to applying one of the recommendation algorithms. For both recommendation algorithms, we have created two approaches: the first that takes into consideration only one review manually inserted by the user, and the second that takes as input a list of reviews provided in a *CSV* file. From the main console of the application, the user can choose which function to execute, by using the corresponding button on Step 2.

Using the first approach (a manually inserted review), another panel will appear on the screen (Fig. 2). The user has to insert using the keyboard the following information: the user id, the book id, the number of stars and the review content. If the Recommender System would be used in a real setting, the information about the user id and book id would be automatically collected from the context (current book selection and authentication information), but since our project is focused on the experimental evaluation of our algorithms

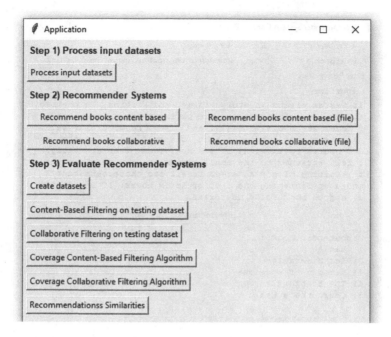

Fig. 1. Application Main Panel

(not on the actual graphical user interface of a Web-based deployed system), this information needs to be manually inserted by the user.

After filling in all the required fields, the user must press the button "Recommend" thus triggering the recommendation process. The Recommender System processes the input fields, applies the selected recommendation algorithm and displays the top 5 recommendations in the lower part of the panel.

The second implementation approach uses a list of reviews given in an input CSV file and applies the selected recommendation algorithm to each given review, rather than using a single review which was provided by the user as input.

Since using the second approach the results cannot be displayed in the same way as for the first approach, we had to find a meaningful way to display the output recommendations. We decided to store the results as a list inside an output text file. For readability, we also added to this file the information about the processed review, respectively Author Id, Book Id, Review Stars, Review Content and Emotions, together with the recommendations themselves.

The Step 3 section (Fig. 1) contains buttons that trigger the methods for system experimental evaluation.

Create datasets splits the reviews dataset into training and testing datasets. The training reviews dataset is used for defining the book emotions feature, which means that the emotions are extracted from the review content and are attached to the book using our procedure previously introduced in [13].

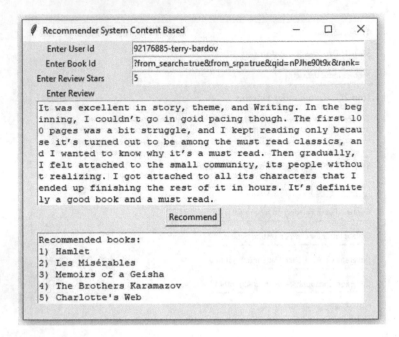

Fig. 2. Application Panel for insertion of review details and results obtained using Content-Based Filtering Recommendations Algorithm

The testing reviews dataset contains those reviews based on which the system provides recommendations in order to perform the experimental evaluation of our proposed recommendation algorithms. Each entry in the testing dataset can be seen as a new review that is currently added by a user who expects to receive book recommendations.

Content-Based Filtering on testing dataset starts the method for generating Content-based filtering recommendations introduced in Sect. 3.2. The system goes through the testing reviews sequentially and for each review it generates the top 5 recommendations. Afterwards the recommendations are stored inside the output text file.

Collaborative Filtering on testing dataset is similar to *Content-Based Filtering on testing dataset*, but for generating recommendations it uses Collaborative filtering recommendation algorithm described in Sect. 3.2.

Coverage Content-Based Filtering Algorithm, *Coverage Collaborative Filtering Algorithm* and *Recommendations Similarities* are used for calculating our proposed performance measures detailed in Sect. 4.4.

4.2 Dataset Preparation

The data set was pre-processed before the application of the recommendation algorithm. The aim of the pre-processing is to compute the books similarity matrix that contains the similarity value for each pair of books in the dataset.

We did not use all the fields of a book entity (see Table 1) for our recommendation algorithms. Therefore we selected only those book features which are relevant and we combined them into a single text field.

We consider to be relevant the following fields: Book Title, Book Series, Book Author and Emotions. The resulting string is stored into the books dataset as an additional column named "Combined Features".

Then we converted each "Combined features" field of a book into a vector of token counts. We applied this processing for each book of the dataset, thus obtaining a matrix T of token counters with elements natural numbers. The total number of tokens is equal to the size of the vocabulary that is found by analyzing the "Combined Features" field of each book. So, if there are n books and the size of the vocabulary is m the resulting matrix of token counts will have size $n \times m$. The count matrix was created using *CountVectorizer* class of *Scikit-learn* library available in Python [27].

Each row i of matrix T is a vector of counters describing book i. The similarity of two books i and j can be determined by applying a similarity measure to the vectors represented by rows i and j of T. In our implementation we have used the cosine similarity measure. If there are n books then the similarity matrix is a squared and symmetric matrix S of size n with real values in interval $[0, 1]$. We determined the books similarity matrix and we saved it into variable *cosine_similarity_matrix* [9].

For each input book $1 \leq i \leq n$, the books that are most similar with it can be determined by examining the row i of matrix S consisting of elements $S_{i,j}$ for all $1 \leq j \leq n$ of higher value.

4.3   Dataset Overview

We used three datasets collected from *Goodreads* shelf "Best Books Ever": top 100 books (Dataset 1), top 500 books (Dataset 2), and respectively top 1000 books (Dataset 3) for conducting our experiments. The aim of our experiments is to investigate the performance of our algorithms considering datasets of different dimensions.

Dataset 1 contains 100 books and 17999 collected reviews. 99 books contain maximum number of reviews (180) and one of them contains 179 reviews. 13957 reviews were classified using *Langdetect* as written in English language, while 4042 were classified as either not defined (46) or written in other languages (3996), like Spanish, Arabic, Italian to Macedonian, Albanian or Swahili.

After removing language-undefined reviews and non-English ones, the 13957 reviews are distributed as numbers in range [87, 170] for the set of 100 books. These reviews were written by a total of 5052 users. 3190 users have written only 1 review, 1631 users have written between 2 and 10 reviews, while 231 users have written more than 10 reviews (between 11 and 63 reviews).

Dataset 2 contains 500 books and 89707 collected reviews. 479 books contain 180 reviews, and 21 contain less than 180 reviews: 14 contain 179 reviews, 1 contains 178 reviews, 5 contain 150 reviews and 1 only 53 reviews. 70401 reviews are classified as written in English language, while 19306 are classified as wither not defined (311) or written in other languages (18995). We observe that the top languages are similar as the ones identified in Dataset 1: Spanish is the first, followed by Arabic, Italian, Greek and Polish.

Considering only the reviews of interest - 70401 English reviews - the books contain number of reviews in range [43, 179], written by a total of 21898 users. 14576 users have written only one review, 6064 users have written between 2 and 10 reviews and 1259 users have written more than 10 reviews (between 11 and 190).

Dataset 3 contains 1000 books and 163574 collected reviews. 479 books contain maximum number of 180 reviews, 511 contain between 100 and 179 reviews, while 10 contain less than 100 reviews (between 10 and 78). 129713 reviews are classified as written in English language, 614 are not defined and 33247 are written in other languages. We observe that again the top languages are similar to Dataset 1 and Dataset 2.

The 129713 English language reviews are distributed as numbers in range [10, 179] for the 1000 books available in the dataset and were written by a total of 38048 users. 25842 users have written only 1 review, 9987 users have written between 2 and 10 reviews, and 2219 users have written more than 10 reviews (between 11 and 263).

The characteristics of the experimental datasets are summarized in Table 3.

Table 3. Experimental Datasets Statistics

Statistic	Dataset 1	Dataset 2	Dataset 3
Number of Books	100	500	1000
Number of Collected Reviews	17999	89707	163574
Collected Reviews Number per Book	[179, 180]	[53, 180]	[10,180]
Number of English Reviews	13957	70401	129713
Number of non-English Reviews	4042	19306	33861
Reviews Number per Book	[87, 170]	[43, 179]	[10, 179]
Number of Users	5052	21898	38048
Number of Users 1 review	3190	14576	25842
Number of Users [2, 10] reviews	1631	6064	9987
Number of Users > 11 reviews	231	1259	2219
Maximum Number of Reviews written by 1 User	63	190	263
Training Reviews	11151	56235	103758
Testing Reviews	2806	14166	25955

4.4   Experimental Results

We have split the *Goodreads* datasets of reviews as 80% for training and 20% for testing using stochastic sampling. As different number of reviews are contained in the datasets for each separate book, training - testing split was done for each book reviews.

In the experiments we have taken into consideration the fact that Dataset 2 is an extension of Dataset 1, and Dataset 3 is an extension of Dataset 2, and in all experiments a certain review r_i is always placed in the same experimental dataset, either training or testing. This means that a book b_j is defined by the same set of "Combined features" in all experiments.

Observing the range number of collected reviews per book, for Dataset 1 almost all books have 180 reviews, while for Dataset 2 and Dataset 3 the number of books with less than 180 reviews is slightly higher. The reason why there are less than 180 reviews collected is that on *Goodreads* website there were no further reviews available. This result is expected, because Dataset 1 is the one which contains top 100 "Best Books Ever" as rated by user, which means higher amount of users appreciated these books and it is expected that they have more reviews compared to lower ranked books, available in Dataset 2 or Dataset 3.

When it comes to the amount of English reviews available in the collected datasets, we observe an interesting result. Dataset 1 has 77.54% English reviews, while Dataset 2 has 78.48% and Dataset 3 has 79.29%. This shows that higher "Best Books Ever" ranked books are reviewed by different nationalities users who tend to write reviews in their country language rather than in English language.

The average number of reviews per book is relatively consistent for the three experimental datasets: 139 reviews per book for Dataset 1, 141 reviews per book for Dataset 2 and 130 reviews per book for Dataset 3, although the review ranges are quite different - [87, 170] for Dataset 1, [43, 179] for Dataset 2, [10, 179] for Dataset 3.

The percentage of users who wrote only one review increases with the dimension of the dataset, from 63.14% in Dataset 1, to 66.71% in Dataset 2 and 67.92% in Dataset 3. The number of users who wrote between [2, 10] reviews decreases (32.28% for Dataset 1, 27.69% for Dataset 2 and 26.25% for Dataset 3), as the users are reassigned from this category to the category of users with more than 11 reviews (4.58% for Dataset 1, 5.76% for Dataset 2 and 5.83% for Dataset 3).

Expected results are obtained for statistic "Maximum Number of Reviews written by 1 User", it is normal that the higher the dimension of the reviews dataset, the more reviews are written by a single user.

Let us define the following parameters that are used for the rigorous definition of our proposed evaluation metrics:

– *Recommendation space R* refers to the total number of possible recommendations, i.e. the total number of books available in the books dataset (in our case 78).

- *User input space* U refers to the total number of user inputs u. A user input is a new review added for a certain book from the dataset.

$$u = (book, review), \text{where } book \in R$$

- *Test space* T refers to the subset of the input space $T \subset R$ used for experimental evaluation.
- A *recommendation* $f_i(u)$ refers to the output recommendation obtained when applying recommendation algorithm i. The output is a set of 5 books $r_i \in R$. $i = 1$ denotes the Content-based filtering Algorithm, while $i = 2$ denotes the Collaborative filtering Algorithm.

$$f_i : U \to R^5$$

$$f_i(u) = (r_1, r_2, r_3, r_4, r_5)$$

- *Total number of unique recommendations* $TNUR_i$ refers to the amount of unique books from the dataset which are returned as recommendations by algorithm i. In our case, $TNUR_1$ refers to the books returned as recommendations by Content-based filtering algorithm and $TNUR_2$ refers to the books returned as recommendations by Collaborative filtering algorithm.

$$TNUR_i = \bigcup_{u \in U} \{f_i(u)\}$$

- *Recommendations similarity* s refers to the similarity between recommendations $f_1(u)$ and $f_2(u)$ provided for the same user input u using the Content-based filtering algorithm, respectively Collaborative filtering algorithm.

$$s : R^5 \times R^5 \to [0, 1]$$

s is determined using Jaccard index.

$$s(f_1(u), f_2(u)) = \frac{|f_1(u) \cap f_2(u)|}{|f_1(u) \cup f_2(u)|}$$

Considering that each of the two algorithms provides a list of 5 recommendations, it follows:

$$s(f_1(u), f_2(u)) = \frac{|f_1(u) \cap f_2(u)|}{10 - |f_1(u) \cap f_2(u)|}$$

We propose two performance measures for evaluating our recommendation algorithms, as follows:

- *Coverage* C_i determines the proportion of books from R that the system was able to recommend using recommendation algorithm i.

$$C_i = \frac{|TNUR_i|}{|R|}$$

– *Average Recommendations Similarity ARS* is the average of the similarity between recommendations provided using Content-based filtering and Collaborative filtering algorithms.

$$ARS = \frac{1}{|T|} \sum_{u \in T} s(f_1(u), f_2(u))$$

Table 4. Coverage Performance Measure Results

Performance Measure	Dataset 1	Dataset 2	Dataset 3
Coverage Content-Based Filtering	95%	87.4%	86.5%
Coverage Collaborative Filtering	100%	97.8%	96.1%

The values obtained for Coverage metric are summarized in Table 4.

For Content-based filtering Recommendations Algorithm, we obtained a coverage of 95% for Dataset 1, which means that 95 out of 100 books available in the dataset were given as recommendations for the testing reviews, 87.4% for Dataset 2 (413 out of 500 books were given as recommendations) and 86.5% for Dataset 3 (865 out of 1000 books were given as recommendations).

For Collaborative filtering Recommendations Algorithm, we obtained maximum coverage on Dataset 1. Coverage 97.8% is obtained for Dataset 2 (489 out of 500 books were given as recommendations) and 96.1% for Dataset 3 (961 out of 1000 books were given as recommendations).

We appreciate that, in general, we obtained a better recommendations coverage using the Collaborative filtering Recommendation Algorithm than using the Content-based filtering Recommendations Algorithm.

For both recommendations algorithms, we remark a decrease in the coverage when the dimension of the dataset increases. This is an expected behavior because our algorithms consider certain book features when doing the recommendations, and the datasets contain several books with different features. When the dataset increases, it increases of course the number of books with different features.

For Dataset 1, we obtained an *Average Recommendation Similarity* of 8.19%. Although this seems a rather low value, it was expected as it shows that applying both recommendations algorithms on the same user input review generates rather different recommendations. In total, for the 2806 input reviews, 14030 recommendations were obtained using Content-based filtering and 14030 were obtained using Collaborative filtering, as both recommendations algorithms provide to the user the top 5 recommendations. Out of the 14030, only 1150 were identical.

We observe a decrease of *Average Recommendation Similarity* to 3.14% for Dataset 2, respectively 2.43% for Dataset 3 (Table 5), which shows that in case of bigger books datasets, there are more options of books that can be recommended,

Table 5. Average Recommendations Similarity Performance Measure Results

Performance Measure	Dataset 1	Dataset 2	Dataset 3
Average Recommendations Similarity (ARS)	8.19%	3.14%	2.43%
Number Input reviews	2806	14166	25955
Number Recomm. received per recomm. algorithm	14030	70830	129775
Number Similar recommendations	1150	2225	3154

and by using two different recommendations techniques, the recommendations that are received for the same user input prove to be unalike.

5 Conclusions

In this contribution, we proposed two recommender system algorithms which extend the basic recommender system techniques of Content-based filtering and Collaborative filtering with emotion information extracted from online reviews in order to improve the quality of recommendations.

We introduced three new experimental datasets of different sizes with books descriptions and reviews extracted from *Goodreads* website and we used them for evaluating our proposed algorithms. We used stochastic sampling to partition each dataset into training set and testing set.

Evaluation was done using two performance measures that we proposed in this paper: *Coverage* and *Average Recommendations Similarity*.

Coverage refers to the percentage of books which are received as recommendations and it was evaluated on the testing dataset. Our experiments show a good books dataset coverage, as almost all books from the dataset are given as recommendations for all the possible user inputs. We observe that the *Coverage* decreases with the increase of dataset size, and this is justified by the fact that the books in our datasets are ordered by the popularity, meaning that more popular books tend to be recommended more often than less popular books.

Average Recommendations Similarity quantifies the similarity between recommendations provided using the proposed methods. We obtained low values for *Average Recommendations Similarity*, which is somehow anticipated considering that the recommendations methods involved different techniques – Content-based filtering, and respectively Collaborative filtering. Similarly to *Coverage* metric, we observe a decrease of *Average Recommendations Similarity* with the increase of the dataset size, which is expected since the recommendations algorithms have a larger candidate recommendation space to choose from, and different recommendations techniques will identify different recommendations candidates.

In extension to our previous research, we investigated if the size of the dataset influences the performance results of our recommendation algorithms, by using datasets of different sizes. We noticed only a slight decrease of the performance measures with the increase of dataset size. However, a limitation is identified because the books existing in our datasets are ordered according to *Goodreads* users' opinions. We assume this can be avoided by: (1) rearranging books in a random order to have a uniform distribution of books quality across the datasets, (2) using another mechanism of choosing the top 5 recommendations from the recommendations candidates list, such as roulette wheel.

As future directions, we aim to (1) study how much the emotions influence the process of books recommendations, by using different "Combined Features" which characterize the book when seeking for similarities between the books in order to provide recommendations, (2) create new emotional categorizations of books using reviews extracted from other social networks and observe in which degree this influences the recommendations suggested by our algorithms.

References

1. Aggarwal, C.: Recommender Systems: The Textbook. Springer, Cham (2016). https://doi.org/10.1007/978-3-319-29659-3
2. Agrawal, R.: How to build a book recommendation system (2021). https://www.analyticsvidhya.com/blog/2021/06/build-book-recommendation-system-unsupervised-learning-project/
3. Aramanda, A., Abdul, S.M., Vedala, R.: enemos-p: An enhanced emotion specific prediction for recommender systems. Expert Syst. Appl. **227**, 120190 (2023). https://doi.org/10.1016/j.eswa.2023.120190
4. Dey, V.: Collaborative filtering vs content-based filtering for recommender systems (2021). https://analyticsindiamag.com/collaborative-filtering-vs-content-based-filtering-for-recommender-systems/
5. Dubey, H., Gandhimathi, S.K.: Book recommendation system using deep learning (GPT3). Int. Res. J. Eng. Technol. (IRJET) **9**(5), 347–353 (2022). https://www.irjet.net/archives/V9/i5/IRJET-V9I572.pdf
6. Fujimoto, T., Murakami, H.: A book recommendation system considering contents and emotions of user interests. In: Proceedings of 12th International Congress on Advanced Applied Informatics, IIAI-AAI, pp. 154–157 (2022). https://doi.org/10.1109/IIAIAAI55812.2022.00039
7. Gogula, S.D., Rahouti, M., Gogula, S.K., Jalamuri, A., Jagatheesaperumal, S.K.: An emotion-based rating system for books using sentiment analysis and machine learning in the cloud. Appl. Sci. **13**, 773 (2023). https://doi.org/10.3390/app13020773
8. Grancharov, S.: Text language detection with Python (2023). https://medium.com/@monigrancharov/text-language-detection-with-python-beb49d9667b3
9. Karbhari, V.: What is a cosine similarity matrix? (2020). https://medium.com/acing-ai/what-is-cosine-similarity-matrix-f0819e674ad1
10. Kharwal, A.: Content based filtering and collaborative filtering: difference (2023). https://thecleverprogrammer.com/2023/04/20/content-based-filtering-and-collaborative-filtering-difference/
11. Kostelac, M.: Comparison of language identification models (2021). https://modelpredict.com/language-identification-survey
12. Kumar, A., Chawla, S.: Framework for hybrid book recommender system based on opinion mining. Int. J. Recent Technol. Eng. (IJRTE) **8**(4), 914–919 (2019). https://doi.org/10.35940/ijrte.D7518.118419

13. Luţan, E.-R., Bădică, C.: Emotion-based literature book classification using online reviews. Electronics **11**, 3412 (2022). https://doi.org/10.3390/electronics11203412
14. Luţan, E.-R., Bădică, C.: Emotion-based literature books recommender systems. In: Proceedings of the 18th Conference on Computer Science and Intelligence Systems, vol. 35, pp. 275–280 (2023). https://doi.org/10.15439/2023F8647
15. Malik, S., Rana, A., Awasthi, M., Sajwan, V.: Book recommendation considering emotions and sentiments for good health. In: 5th International Conference on Contemporary Computing and Informatics (IC3I), pp. 1746–1750 (2022). https://doi.org/10.1109/IC3I56241.2022.10073217
16. Melville, P., Sindhwani, V.: Recommender systems. In: Sammut, C., Webb, G.I. (eds.) Encyclopedia of Machine Learning and Data Mining, pp. 1056–1066. Springer, Boston (2017). https://doi.org/10.1007/978-1-4899-7687-1_964
17. Miller, G.A.: WordNet: a lexical database for English. Commun. ACM **38**(11), 39–41 (1995). https://doi.org/10.1145/219717.219748
18. Nakatani, S.: Language detection library – 99% over precision for 49 languages (2010). https://www.slideshare.net/shuyo/language-detection-library-for-java
19. Ng, Y.-K.: Read to grow: exploring metadata of books to make intriguing book recommendations for teenage readers. Knowl. Inf. Syst. **65**, 4537–4562 (2023). https://doi.org/10.1007/s10115-023-01907-5
20. Nowak, K.L., McGloin, R.: The influence of peer reviews on source credibility and purchase intention. Societies **4**, 689–705 (2014). https://doi.org/10.3390/soc4040689
21. Plutchik, R.: Circumplex models of personality and emotions. In: The Circumplex as a General Model of the Structure of Emotions and Personality. American Psychological Association (1997). https://doi.org/10.1037/10261-000
22. Polignano, M., de Narducci, F., Gemmis, M., Semeraro, G.: Towards emotion-aware recommender systems: an affective coherence model based on emotion-driven behaviors. Expert Syst. Appl. **170**, 114382 (2021). https://doi.org/10.1016/j.eswa.2020.114382
23. Rana, C., Jain, S.K.: Building a book recommender system using time based content filtering. WSEAS Trans. Comput. **11**(2), 27–33 (2012). https://wseas.com/journals/computers/2012/54-571.pdf
24. Resnick, P., Hal R.V.: Recommender systems. Commun. ACM **40**(3), 56–58 (1997). https://wseas.com/journals/computers/2012/54-571.pdf
25. Roy, D., Dutta, M.: A systematic review and research perspective on recommender systems. J. Big Data **9**, 59 (2022). https://doi.org/10.1186/s40537-022-00592-5
26. Saraswat, M., Chakraverty, S., Kala, A.: Analyzing emotion based movie recommender system using fuzzy emotion features. Int. J. Inf. Technol. (Singap.) **12**(2), 467–472 (2020). https://doi.org/10.1007/s41870-020-00431-x
27. Sucky, R.: Movie recommendation model using cosine_similarity and CountVectorizer: Scikit-Learn (2019). https://regenerativetoday.com/movie-recommendation-model-using-cosine_similarity-and-countvectorizer-scikit-learn/
28. Sujo, J.C.M., Golobardes i Ribé, E.: BRAIN L: a book recommender system. arXiv:2302.00653 (2023). https://doi.org/10.48550/arXiv.2302.00653
29. Usman, A., Roko, A., Muhammad, A.B. Almu, A.: Enhancing personalized book recommender system. Int. J. Adv. Netw. Appl. **14**(3), 5486–5492 (2022). https://www.proquest.com/docview/2758392858?pq-origsite=gscholar&fromopenview=true&sourcetype=Scholarly%20Journals
30. Zhang, S., Lau, J.H., Zhang, X.J., Chan, J., Paris, C.: Discovering relevant reviews for answering product-related queries. In: IEEE International Conference on Data Mining (ICDM) (2019). https://doi.org/10.1109/ICDM.2019.00192

Sign Language Interpreting - Assessment of the Efficiency of the Translation Model

Barbara Probierz[1,2](✉)(iD), Maciej Kuchcik[1](iD), Grzegorz Adamiec[1](iD),
Adam Piasecki[1](iD), and Jan Kozak[1,2](iD)

[1] Łukasiewicz Research Network – Institute of Innovative Technologies EMAG,
Leopolda 31, 40-189 Katowice, Poland
`{maciej.kuchcik,grzegorz.adamiec,adam.piasecki}@emag.lukasiewicz.gov.pl,`
`jan.kozak@ue.katowice.pl`
[2] Department of Machine Learning, University of Economics in Katowice, 1 Maja 50,
40-287 Katowice, Poland
`barbara.probierz@ue.katowice.pl`

Abstract. The article assessed the effectiveness of a model translating text written in Polish into Polish Sign Language using animation identifiers (animation identifiers) based on verbal data. Collaboration with sign language experts aims to identify and address performance issues, emphasizing irregularities in generated sentences. The study focuses on offering recommendations for improving translation quality by analyzing problems in the training data and incorporating expert insights. Initially considering dissimilarity algorithms proved unsuitable due to the model's non-autoregressive architecture. Instead, a graphical user interface web application facilitated expert input, fostering an open dialogue on model effectiveness. Results revealed incorrect model operation, illogical outputs, and issues with translations beyond the training set. Low data volume and quality, along with nonrepresentative examples, contributed to subpar performance. This research offers valuable insights for future Polish Sign Language translation model enhancements within a concise framework.

Keywords: Polish Sign Language · Translation model · Machine learning

1 Introduction

Sign language holds a crucial role in the lives of individuals with hearing impairments, serving as a means for communication, emotional expression, and societal engagement. The presence of sign language interpreters is vital to ensure equitable access to information and services for the deaf community. These interpreters play a pivotal role in facilitating the exchange of information between deaf and hearing individuals, enabling comprehensive involvement in various social and professional domains [20].

© The Author(s), under exclusive license to Springer Nature Switzerland AG 2024
E. Ziemba et al. (Eds.): FedCSIS-ITBS 2023/ISM 2023, LNBIP 504, pp. 183–202, 2024.
https://doi.org/10.1007/978-3-031-61657-0_9

Being a natural language, sign language possesses its own grammar, vocabulary, and sentence structure, akin to other languages [24]. Various sign languages worldwide exhibit unique characteristics, making translation from a national language into sign language a complex process. This complexity demands interpreters to possess not only linguistic proficiency but also an understanding of the cultural and social contexts of the users. Successful translation requires consideration of not just the literal meanings but also the connotations and cultural nuances of the words. Additionally, proficient use of gestures, facial expressions, and body movements is crucial for conveying the speaker's emotions and intentions effectively [32].

Addressing the social exclusion of deaf individuals is imperative for promoting equal opportunities and societal participation. The obligation to ensure equal access to services and information for all citizens has led to increased awareness and legal mandates. Consequently, there is a pressing need for research and development in solutions for the automatic translation of natural language into sign language. Such advancements have the potential to eliminate communication barriers, fostering complete participation of deaf individuals in diverse social and professional spheres.

Exploring automatic translation of natural language into sign language necessitates the incorporation of advanced technologies such as artificial intelligence, machine learning, and natural language processing. The development of these solutions not only contributes to technological progress but also finds applications in fields like machine translation and speech recognition. Crucially, scientific research and the creation of automatic translation solutions directly enhance the quality of life for the deaf community by dismantling communication barriers and promoting greater equality and social inclusion.

The aim of the research in this article is to conduct a comprehensive assessment of the efficiency of the model translating text written in Polish into Polish sign language. By analyzing the results obtained in cooperation with experts, the goal is to identify specific problems in the performance of the model. Focusing on detecting irregularities, illogicalities and inconsistencies in the generated sentences allows for an accurate assessment of translation efficiency. Through our research, we want to develop recommendations to improve the quality of model translations. Therefore, based on the results of the analysis of problems in the training data and suggestions obtained from experts, it is planned to introduce modifications to the model, which will allow its further development and improvement of the translation process between Polish and sign language, as well as the development of recommendations aimed at improving the quality model translations.

Our primary objective is to execute a project dedicated to creating a virtual human representation delivering public administration content in Polish Sign Language. In our other paper [25], we reviewed research related to sign language interpreting, focusing on various aspects such as interpreting effectiveness, quality of interpreting services, technological support, and social and cultural contexts The aim of the project is to enhance accessibility for the deaf community, especially for those proficient in Polish Sign Language but not fluent in spoken Polish. This entails developing a comprehensive solution that encompasses both a language translation module and a corresponding avatar responsible for signing the translated texts. Achieving this goal requires a thorough understanding of research, scientific, and theoretical advancements in sign language translation and their practical implications.

While many of the scrutinized studies span various disciplines, discernible trends exist in researchers' pursuits within specific domains. Consequently, we aim to present an overview of the work within the proposed research areas and encourage scholars to delve deeper into research and development in the realm of sign language interpretation. By highlighting areas warranting further investigation and outlining existing challenges, this article seeks to instigate discussions and innovations that will contribute to the ongoing enhancement of sign language services and the complete integration of individuals with hearing impairments into society.

This article is organized as follows. Section 1 is an introduction to the topic of the article, introducing the reader to the research context. Then, in Sect. 2 a thorough overview of work related to sign language interpretation methods is presented, presenting a significant reference framework. In Sect. 3, a project is discussed, the aim of which is to develop a solution for translating speech from Polish into Polish sign language, using an avatar and artificial intelligence. Section 4 presents the model architecture, while Sect. 5 details the data used to train and evaluate the translation model. The experimental analysis and assessment of model variance are performed in Sect. 6, while the validation of the model translation data is presented in Sect. 7. Finally, in Sect. 8, general comments on the work are presented, emphasizing its essence, and potential directions for future research are indicated. The entire article is organized in a way that facilitates understanding of the topic and effective absorption of research results.

2 Related Works

The literature review provided insights into various aspects of sign language translation technologies. The focus lies on translating spoken language into sign language and vice versa. Noteworthy approaches include the utilization of avatars for recognizing sign language poses and translating through talking faces, as described in [23]. Additionally, research emphasizes the development of two-way communication systems that translate spoken languages into sign languages and vice versa, exemplified in works like [7, 29, 39]. In the realm of recognizing and translating sign language into spoken languages, innovative solutions include an AI-based approach for capturing sign language [34], a crowdsourcing platform to address the unavailability of annotated datasets [33], and an automatic sign language synthesis system based on machine translation advancements [35]. Real-time motion recognition systems, such as the one using electromyography signals [36], have shown high accuracy in recognizing American Sign Language (ASL) movements.

Two-way communication, crucial for smooth interactions between deaf individuals using sign language and hearing individuals using spoken language, has been a significant area of research. Projects like the European initiative [29] aim to develop technology for automatic translation of sign languages into spoken languages and vice versa, focusing on languages such as English, Irish, Dutch, and Spanish. Another notable effort is the EXTOL project [7], dedicated to translating British Sign Language into English and creating a functional machine translation system for any sign language. The translation of spoken languages into sign languages is explored extensively, with a focus on Arabic sign language [2], Mexican Sign Language [4], and Chinese Sign Language [39]. These studies involve developing dictionaries, avatars, and structured language models for various sign languages. Additionally, evaluations of sign language translation systems, such as for Portuguese Sign Language (LIBRAS) [12], have been conducted, shedding light on grammatical considerations within the deaf community.

In sign language technology research, a focus on improving systems, especially in recognition, production, and animation, is evident [10,14]. Researchers are actively developing software to create authentic sign language gestures, facial expressions, and body movements, exploring motion capture for realistic animations [3,30]. Language-specific advancements include a proposed system translating English text into Indian Sign Language using a 3D avatar [18]. This approach utilizes an ISL parser for real-time representation, enhancing dynamic communication. The Indian Sign Language Dictionary, bilingual for English and Hindi, employs the Hamburg notation system and SIGML with WebGL for 3D avatar animations [19]. Innovative tools like Kazoo's and Paul's avatars aim for automated content synthesis [6,10]. Educational applications include adding sign language translations to digital mathematical materials [14]. The SignGAN system [30] generates realistic sign language videos, addressing motion blur issues.

Challenges in sign language generation, such as modality differences and limited resources, are explored [37]. Non-manual sign challenges are discussed from linguistic, computer graphics, and sign language representation perspectives [38]. Addressing dataset unavailability, a crowdsourcing platform captures sign language [34]. To enhance communication, methods using machine learning for automatic calculation of key values and innovative techniques for facial expression presentation are proposed [1,15]. A parametric model for facial expression synthesis with 3D avatars contributes to field advancements [13].

In situations requiring effective communication for understanding and expressing thoughts, such as business meetings, school activities, or medical consultations, the translation from the national language into sign language plays a crucial role. Advancements in technologies, such as mobile applications and interactive screens, offer new possibilities for faster and more precise translations, facilitating improved communication between deaf and hearing individuals [16]. Automatic translation of natural language into sign language holds promise for enhancing the quality of education for the deaf. Tools enabling access to educational content, such as the Mexican Sign Language Avatar, utilizing NLP and automatic translation, present textbook content in sign language [4]. In the realm of mathematics education, e-learning systems and 3D avatars are employed to aid Arab deaf sign language students and enhance digital math education materials [14,31]. A system supporting independent learning of English Sign Language has also been developed, incorporating a neural network for classifying signs recorded with a webcam [26].

Educational efforts extend globally, with projects like the Turkish initiative utilizing 3D avatars to assess the effectiveness of avatar-based tutoring compared to text-based learning tools [40]. Dictionaries in various sign languages, including English, Irish, Arabic, Indian, and Portuguese, further contribute to educational resources [2,10,11,18,19,21].

The pandemic underscored the importance of accessibility to medical care for deaf individuals. Dutch researchers explored the potential of automatic translation of text into sign language, focusing on COVID-related medical consultations. While avatars were found advantageous in terms of flexibility and scaling, concerns were raised about lower realism and understanding compared to human video translation [27,28]. Patient comfort and acceptance of virtual advisors were found to vary depending on the nature of the interaction, with greater acceptance in general areas compared to more personal topics [5,8,17]. In the context of safety, efforts were made to develop avatars for disaster messages, utilizing voice notations and investigating motion capture methods. Challenges included collecting data on emotional expression and facial expressions during the creation of a 3D avatar from a 2D video [22]. Another example involves the development of an avatar for a machine translation system, translating real-time messages for Swiss Federal Railways, utilizing JASigning software for avatar animations [9].

3 Project *Avatar2PJM*

The research is part of the *Avatar2PJM* project (Project: Framework of an automatic translator into the Polish Sign Language using the avatar mechanism, The National Centre for Research and Development, GOSPOSTRATEG-IV/0002/2020). This project aims to develop a solution for translating speech from Polish into Polish Sign Language using avatar and artificial intelligence methods. The innovation of this solution lies in the inclusion of emotions and non-verbal elements in the visualisation of gestures.

A primary objective of the project is to create a method for translating Polish into Polish Sign Language through the application control mechanism of an avatar. The sign language avatar serves as a computer-generated representation (animation) of linguistic phenomena. By referencing appropriate video-recorded material, it becomes feasible to animate any described speech. Motion Capture (MoCap) sessions were employed for this purpose, a technique commonly used in computer games to realistically replicate three-dimensional movements of actors (refer to Fig. 1). In the context of sign language avatars, MoCap facilitates the replication of sign language signs, enhancing comprehension of the communicated content. From the animator's standpoint, sign language signs involve geometric positions and movements.

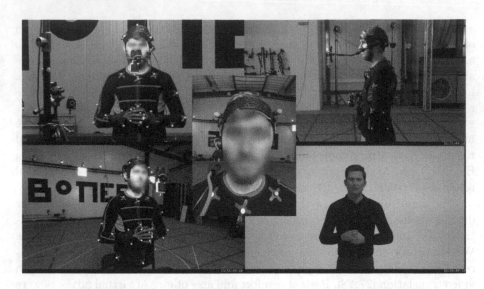

Fig. 1. MoCap recordings as part of the *Avatar2PJM* project.

A message conveyed in sign language encompasses both the signs themselves and various supplementary information, as the physical expression results from concurrent linguistic and extra-linguistic processes. When generating computer-generated animations, consideration is given to the emotional context of the expression, as well as phenomena like accurate mouth movements and voiceless speech inherent in sign language communication. Notably, the facial expressions of the sign language interpreter and the information they convey play a crucial role. These elements are also vital in the context of the data required for developing the interpreting module.

The material obtained during Motion Capture (MoCap) sessions is utilized to fuel the animation module and furnish an input dataset for the translation module using machine learning techniques. To achieve this, the collection of recordings undergoes an annotation process, describing individual sign language elements at specific intervals. This encompasses sign units, lexical interpretations (lemmas, lexemes), and information related to the non-manual aspects of the sign. Since the interpreter's face is a key element of annotation and the process is time-intensive, efforts were made to explore the feasibility of automatically recognizing the interpreter's facial expressions. The implementation of automatic annotation holds the potential to significantly enhance and expedite the annotator's work. The article presents partial findings from the research conducted in this domain.

A projected outcome of the project involves pilot testing selected online information services offered by public administrations, employing the avatar showcased in Fig. 2. Widespread implementation of automatic translation mechanisms in public online systems represents a constructive stride toward enhancing digital public administration accessibility. Additionally, the project team examines

Fig. 2. Actual avatar prepared for testing the *Avatar2PJM* project.

the professional potential of deaf individuals and their satisfaction with interactions with public administration both pre- and post-implementation of the
virtual interpreter. This investigation aims to identify social and economic barriers faced by deaf individuals in their dealings with administration and the job
market. The study will explore the vocational potential of deaf individuals and
methods to optimize data capture for maximal vocational activation effects. Ultimately, the project's results will contribute to sustainable efforts in eliminating
barriers for users of Polish Sign Language.

4   The Translation Model

The developed model is based on a bidirectional recurrent neural network (RNN),
hereinafter referred to as bidirectional RNN or RNN. The choice of this architecture is due to its ability to effectively analyze the relationships between key
words in sentences, and the possibility of analysis in both directions, which is
important for complex sentence structures. It should be noted, however, that this
advantageous feature lengthens the learning process and potentially increases the
risk of making mistakes in the case of longer or more complex sentences.

The final layer architecture of the bidirectional RNN model is shown in
Fig. 3. The sequential model starts with a Polish word embedding layer, which
transforms tokens into vectors of lower dimensionality. Another element of the
model is the *LearningRateScheduler* callback function, which aims to regulate the learning rate during the learning process. This mechanism, known as

Learning Rate Annealing, accelerates the initial learning epochs and then stabilizes them in later stages, positively affecting the overall quality of model generalization. In this case, the *LearningRate* value decreases by 1.25 every 20 epochs, excluding the first epoch.

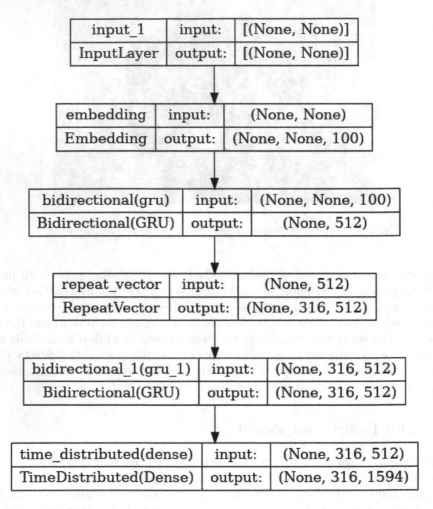

Fig. 3. Architecture diagram of the translation model of the *Avatar2PJM* project.

It is worth emphasizing the important role of the data tokenization process. Two tokenizers were used: one for the Polish language with the *char_level=false* parameter (tokenization at the word level) and the other for the sign language animation IDs with the parameters *split=' '* and *filters='',* where split divides tokens by white space characters, and empty filters disables special character filters. This procedure allows for the correct tokenization of animation IDs, which may contain special characters such as underscores or hyphens.

5 Data Quality of the Training Set

In this study, the data used to train and evaluate the Polish to Polish Sign Language translation model was provided in the form of a JSON file that contained a list of sentence pairs. Each pair consisted of one sentence in Polish and the corresponding animation IDs representing the appropriate translation into sign language. The main goal was to enable the learning model to generalize, be able to correctly predict new, unknown data, and adjust the optimization of weights during training.

During the data preparation stage, three iterations were carried out (marked as *Set* 1, *Set* 2 and *Set* 3), which successively expanded the previous version of the set with additional pairs of training sentences. Detailed information about each data set is presented in the Table 1. This table analyzes key criteria for each version of the set, such as:

- *number of all training pairs* – the total count of training sentence pairs in each dataset, indicating the volume of examples used for model training,
- *number of all Polish words* – the total count of Polish words present in the datasets, reflecting the linguistic complexity of the training data,
- *number of unique Polish words* – the count of distinct Polish words within the datasets, offering insights into the diversity and richness of the Polish vocabulary,
- *number of all animation IDs* – the total count of animation IDs used in the datasets, providing information about the variety and quantity of sign language representations,
- *number of unique animation IDs* – the count of unique animation IDs, reflecting the diversity and specificity of sign language expressions.

This data structure allows for a precise understanding of the characteristics of each set and provides the basis for further analysis on the performance of the translation model.

Table 1. Characteristics of training datasets.

Classification criteria	Set 1	Set 2	Set 3
number of all training pairs	376	554	801
number of all Polish words	8 557	16 519	26 866
number of unique Polish words	1 969	3 620	5 517
number of all animation IDs	10 779	17 107	25 306
number of unique animation IDs	708	774	1 594

An analysis of the data presented in Table 1 shows a significant increase in the number of all training pairs between *Set* 2 and *Set* 1, as well as between *Set* 3 and *Set* 2, reaching 47% and 45%, respectively. Similar upward trends are observed in the number of all word pairs, where the increase between *Set* 2 and *Set* 1 is 93%, and between *Set* 3 and *Set* 2 - 63%. Analyzing unique Polish words, there is a significant increase of 83% between *Set* 2 and *Set* 1, and an increase of 52% between *Set* 3 and *Set* 2. Another significant observation concerns the number of animation IDs, which increased by 59% between *Set* 2 and *Set* 1, and by 48% between *Set* 3 and *Set* 2. Also of particular interest is the increase in total animation IDs, which is 59% between *Set* 2 and *Set* 1, and 48% between *Set* 3 and *Set* 2. It is worth noting the smaller increase in the number of unique animation IDs, only 9% between *Set* 2 and *Set* 1, which could potentially affect its generalization ability compared to *Set* 3. However, the greatest increase, by as much as 106%, is observed between *Set* 3 and *Set* 2, which is an area with greater potential for exploration and acquiring new patterns.

The analysis of selected criteria was aimed at assessing the diversity of data and the model's ability to generalize depending on the growing amount of available information. It is worth emphasizing that when analyzing the data, issues related to the length or distribution of sentences were omitted. Due to the specificity of sign language, where "sentences" are represented by animation IDs, traditional length metrics do not adequately reflect the actual signing time or sentence structure in this context. Therefore, the main emphasis was placed on parameters related to the number of words and diversity, which are crucial for the effectiveness and generalization of the translation model. The analysis of the above data leads to the conclusion that each set is characterized by a greater number of Polish words than unique sign animation IDs. This important observation provides the basis for further reflection on data asymmetry in the context of the translation process. Ultimately, adding new pairs of training sentences and expanding the vocabulary in both Polish and Sign Animation ID is a key element in the data enrichment process. Analyzing the graphs of layers and functions in the tensorboard should allow for a better understanding of the impact of these changes on the translation quality and enable further improvement of the model.

6   Experimental Analysis and Model Variance Assessment

In order to explore the potential of pre-trained embedding layers, an experiment was conducted by including an embedding layer trained using the word2vec algorithm, based on the Polish Wikipedia, into the model analysis. The experiment aimed to evaluate the impact of this additional layer on the performance of the translation models. However, initial results proved unsatisfactory, with a drop in model accuracy of approximately 6 percentage points, representing a 7% reduction. Analyzing the characteristics of the models, rapid convergence was observed with moderately satisfactory results, which suggested a lack of sufficient variance in the model architecture.

Figure 4 shows the accuracy plot of the validation set for the model on *Set* 2 with learning embedding or fixed embedding depending on the epochs. The light blue line represents the learning embedding model, while the green line is the fixed embedding model that did not participate in the training loop involving Polish to Polish Sign Language (PJM) translations. The training process was carried out on various data sets, gradually enriched with additional data, which significantly influenced the performance of the models.

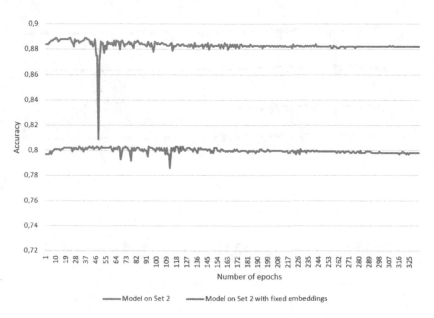

Fig. 4. Accuracy on the validation set for for the model on Set 2 with learning embedding or fixed embedding across epochs.

Figure 5 shows models with identical architecture with learning embeddings, but trained on different data sets. The dark blue model was trained on *Set* 1 and the light blue model on *Set* 2. Similarly, the red and green lines represent models with the same solid embedding architecture but with different datasets, where the model marked with the green line was trained on *Set* 2, and the red line on *Set* 3. During the analysis of the obtained accuracy values depending on the epochs, it was observed that the expansion of the data set contributed to increasing the accuracy of the models on the training set, increasing the value of the metric by over 2%. However, the introduction of a previously trained embedding resulted in a decrease in the function values on the validation set, which is visible as light blue and green lines.

Additionally, it can be noticed that adding previously trained embeddings had a negative impact on the value of the function on the validation set, especially for models on *Set* 1 and *Set* 2 (light blue and green lines). This decrease may be related to a limitation in the flexibility of the model, introducing some rigidity in the word representations. Nevertheless, despite this negative effect on the validation set, experiments indicate that the models on the training set use previously trained embeddings, which emphasizes the importance of adapting the model to the specifics of the validation set. However, expanding the data set has a positive effect on the results on the validation set, which can be observed by analyzing models moving from *Set* 1 to *Set* 2 (dark blue and light blue lines), as well as models moving from *Set* 2 to *Set* 3 (green and red lines).

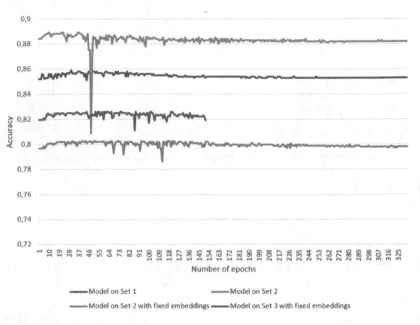

Fig. 5. Accuracy of the validation set for selected models across epochs trained on various datasets. (Color figure online)

Also of interest is the observation that the projected issues of a small increase in unique animation IDs in *Set* 2 and a large increase in *Set* 3 did not significantly impact the feature value. The increase in the accuracy value for the model on *Set* 2 (light blue line) compared to the model on *Set* 1 (dark blue line) and the increase in the accuracy value for the model on *Set* 3 (red line) compared to the model on *Set* 2 (green line) suggest that adding new data, despite differences in embeddings, has a positive effect on the performance of models, which is important from the perspective of improving sign interpreting.

By analyzing the characteristic weight distributions in the tested models, interesting phenomena can be noticed. First, a larger relative spread of parameters can be identified in all models with "frozen" embeddings. This probably results from an attempt to correct the embedding weights using the weights of the next layer. This effect is particularly noticeable in the example of the distribution of the load term values for the GRU layer in the encoder (backward), comparing models with frozen embedding (pink graph) and learning embedding (orange graph), as shown in Fig. 6.

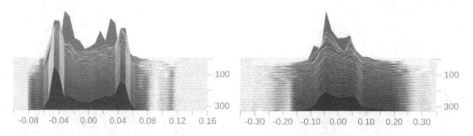

Fig. 6. Distribution of the load term values for the GRU layer in the encoder (backward) for the model with frozen embedding (pink graph - on the left) and for the model with learning embedding (orange graph - on the right). (Color figure online)

Second, unlike the bias terms, the weights for all GRU layers in all models remained approximately rectangular or bell-shaped, depending on the initialization. Figure 7 shows the distribution of weight values for the GRU layer in the encoder (forward) for the model with frozen embedding (pink graph - on the left) and the model with learning embedding (orange graph - on the right). These observations provide important information about the structure of weights in models, which may impact their ability to extract important features from training data. Analyzing these distributions is important for understanding the model training and optimization process.

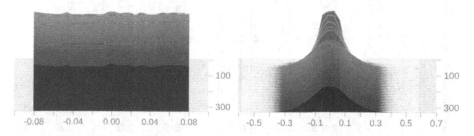

Fig. 7. Distribution of weight values for the GRU layer in the encoder (forward) for the model with frozen embedding (pink graph - on the left) and for the model with learning embedding (orange graph - on the right). (Color figure online)

7   Validating Model Translation Data

In the process of verifying the quality of translation, the use of algorithms based on measures of subtitle dissimilarity, such as the Levenshtein distance or the Hamming distance, was initially considered. It was planned to compare the animation ID sequences in the training set to those generated by the models for the corresponding sentences in Polish. However, the autoregressive architecture

Table 2. Actual results of sentence translation using the proposed approaches (the sentences are written in Polish).

Sentence in Polish	Model on Set 1	Model on Set 2	Model on Set 3
Zgłoś chęć głosowania korespondencyjnego	id_14, id_763, id_149	id_14	id_14, id_298, id_494
Do urzędu gminy, na terenie której mieszkasz po powrocie z zagranicy	id_714, id_14, id_623, id_14, id_714, id_837, id_14, id_623, id_837, id_714, id_623, id_714, id_811	id_14, id_383	id_14, id_40, id_8, id_137, id_507, id_851, id_654, id_383, id_572, id_5
Jeśli nie możesz dostać tych dokumentów elektronicznych, dołącz ich odwzorowanie cyfrowe, na przykład skany	id_106, id_235, id_369, id_577, id_670, id_770, id_854, id_14, id_852, id_365, id_295, id_11, id_593	id_14, id_11	id_106, id_369, id_14, id_854, id_365, id_434, id_593
Dowód osobisty MUSI mieć każdy pełnoletni, który mieszka w Polsce	*id_646, id_258, id_237, id_267, id_646, id_237, id_283, id_258, id_685, id_74*	id_646, id_685, id_237, id_559	id_14, id_267
Jeśli NIE jesteś obywatelem państwa członkowskiego UE albo EFTA oraz NIE jesteś członkiem rodziny wymienionego cudzoziemca, NIE MOŻESZ się zameldować przez internet	id_106, id_14, id_646, id_339, id_294, id_490, id_441, id_267, id_819, id_338, id_646, id_54, id_40, id_14, id_410, id_845, id_819, id_14, id_572, id_568, id_507, id_74, id_854	id_106, id_14, id_646, id_74, id_339	id_106, id_14, id_339, id_819, id_845, id_646, id_74
Sprawdź, jak założyć profil zaufany lub jak korzystać z dowodu	id_14, id_818, id_345, id_802, id_267, id_777, id_188, id_862	id_14, id_345, id_777	id_14, id_818, id_345, id_705, id_188, id_14
Przez internet	id_572, id_365	id_14	id_572, id_365
Pamiętaj, że pełnomocnik musi mieć przy sobie dokument tożsamości	id_14, id_401, id_646, id_607, id_233, id_733, id_235, id_205, id_22, id_39	id_646, id_447, id_695, id_39	id_353
ty możesz zrobić to osobiście	*id_646, id_562, id_646, id_237, id_283*	id_14	id_14, id_401, id_447, id_235, id_205, id_39
Zgłoś wymeldowanie. Szczegóły znajdziesz w sekcji Gdzie składasz wniosek	id_208, id_14, id_474, id_504, id_479, id_572, id_283, id_14, id_585	id_14	id_14, id_572
Pamiętaj, żeby się przygotować	*id_14, id_401, id_467, id_509, id_79, id_14*	id_14	id_14, id_298, id_494

of the translation model resulted in a drastic reduction in the effectiveness of these algorithms as the sequence length increased.

Given the above-mentioned difficulties and the limited amount of available data, the decision was made to involve sign language experts. For this purpose, a simple graphical interface was developed in the form of a web application, enabling the introduction of sentences in Polish and then translating them into IDs (which are an indication for appropriate animation) in the JSON format (in Table 2 you can see examples sentences and then the ID to animate). These results could then be used to communicate with sign language experts, maintaining an ongoing open dialogue about the effectiveness of the model-generated translations.

In Table 2, column 1 presents actual sentences written in Polish, which came from official websites. The results of translation into Polish Sign Language (PJM) obtained by the analyzed models based on three datasets (*Set* 1, *Set* 2 and *Set* 3) are respectively presented as three consecutive columns in Table 2. It is worth noting that the model on *Set* 2 and the model on *Set* 3 do not cover the complete translation and, as a result, remain incomprehensible to the recipient.

However, the use of a model based on set 1 allows for obtaining good translation results, despite the difficulty of the problem and the very limited amount of data. In this case, in 11 randomly selected sentences, the experts concluded that:

- 4 sentences were very well understandable (bold text in Table 2),
- 2 sentences were rated as understandable (underlined text in Table 2),
- 3 sentences were rated as requiring improvement – ambiguous assessment by experts (italic text in Table 2),
- 1 sentence has been rated as incorrectly translated,
- 1 sentence contained too many words unknown to the model, which made a reliable assessment impossible.

When analyzing selected sentences for translation, it is worth paying attention to problems with the quality of the training set. In several cases, words indicate the lack of their equivalents in the animation ID, which is a significant challenge to improve to increase the quality of translations. Additionally, despite some sentences being translated correctly, the translators' ratings were not always consistent, suggesting potential semantic problems or ambiguities and interpretations - in such cases, we marked the sentences as requiring improvement.

The dark blue line in Fig. 5 illustrates the quality of this model, while the other models show a deterioration in the quality of translations after the introduction of Polish permanent embeddings, which is visible. Many sentences were shortened by over-adaptation, and common animation IDs such as id_14 (*you*) were frequently repeated.

8   Conclusions

This article focuses on assessing the efficiency of a model translating strings of characters from Polish into Polish Sign Language. Sign language interpretation was based on verbal data, referred to as animation identifiers (animation IDs), which identified specific sequences of symbols in sign language.

The aim of our research was to comprehensively assess the efficiency of a model translating Polish text into Polish sign language. Through collaboration with experts, we aim to pinpoint specific performance issues, with a particular focus on identifying irregularities, illogicalities, and inconsistencies in the generated sentences. The ultimate objective is to offer recommendations for enhancing the overall quality of model translations. Drawing from the analysis of problems in the training data and valuable insights from experts, we plan to implement strategic modifications to the model. This approach is geared towards ensuring continuous development and improvement in the translation process between Polish and sign language. Additionally, our research seeks to provide recommendations aimed at further elevating the quality of model translations.

Initially, it was assumed that the quality could be verified using algorithms comparing measures of subtitle dissimilarity, such as the Levenshtein distance or the Hamming distance. These algorithms were supposed to compare animation IDs sequences in the training set with those generated by the model for the same sentences in Polish. However, due to the non-autoregressive architecture of the translation model, this methodology was rejected. The model's autoregressive nature means that even in the case of a correct translation, the probability of two translations overlapping decreases exponentially with the length of the sequence, which would result in a dramatic underestimation of the real performance of the model.

Due to the above difficulties and the small amount of data, it was decided to use the help of experts in the field of sign language. A simple graphical user interface (GUI) was created in the form of a web application, enabling the entry of sentences in Polish and then translating them into the animation IDs in the JSON format. This data could then be transferred to the API that generated specific signs in Polish Sign Language. This solution enabled interaction with experts and an open dialogue about the results and effectiveness of model translation.

Analysis of the results revealed incorrect operation of the model, frequent illogical and inconsistent output sentences, especially when translated into words from outside the training set. Low data volume, low quality and nonrepresentativeness were also identified as reasons for poor model performance, mentioned by translators who noticed that some randomly selected training examples were not correct translations.

Moving forward, addressing these issues will require strategic modifications to the model, informed by insights from both computational analysis and expert feedback. By prioritizing data quality and diversity, and fostering ongoing collaboration with domain experts, we aim to advance the translation capabilities between Polish and sign language, ensuring greater accuracy and relevance in real-world applications.

Acknowledgments. This research was funded by the framework of an automatic translator into the Polish Sign Language using the avatar mechanism, The National Centre for Research and Development, grant number GOSPOSTRATEG-IV/0002/2020.

Disclosure of Interests. The authors have no competing interests to declare that are relevant to the content of this article.

References

1. Al-Khazraji, S., Berke, L., Kafle, S., Yeung, P., Huenerfauth, M.: Modeling the speed and timing of American sign language to generate realistic animations. In: Proceedings of the 20th International ACM SIGACCESS Conference on Computers and Accessibility, pp. 259–270 (2018). https://doi.org/10.1145/3234695.3236356
2. Aliwy, A.H., Ahmed, A.A.: Development of Arabic sign language dictionary using 3D avatar technologies. Indones. J. Electr. Eng. Comput. Sci. **21**(1), 609–616 (2021). https://doi.org/10.11591/ijeecs.v21.i1.pp609-616
3. Angga, P.A., Fachri, W.E., Elevanita, A., Agushinta, R.D., et al.: Design of chatbot with 3D avatar, voice interface, and facial expression. In: 2015 International Conference on Science in Information Technology (ICSITech), pp. 326–330. IEEE (2015). https://doi.org/10.1109/ICSITech.2015.7407826
4. Barrera Melchor, F., Alcibar Palacios, J.C., Pichardo-Lagunas, O., Martinez-Seis, B.: Speech to Mexican sign language for learning with an avatar. In: Martínez-Villaseñor, L., Herrera-Alcántara, O., Ponce, H., Castro-Espinoza, F.A. (eds.) MICAI 2020. LNCS (LNAI), vol. 12469, pp. 179–192. Springer, Cham (2020). https://doi.org/10.1007/978-3-030-60887-3_16
5. Bouillon, P., David, B., Strasly, I., Spechbach, H.: A speech translation system for medical dialogue in sign language-questionnaire on user perspective of videos and the use of avatar technology. In: 3rd Swiss Conference on Barrier-free Communication (BfC 2020), p. 46 (2021). https://doi.org/10.21256/zhaw-3001
6. Braffort, A., Filhol, M., Delorme, M., Bolot, L., Choisier, A., Verrecchia, C.: Kazoo: a sign language generation platform based on production rules. Univ. Access Inf. Soc. **15**, 541–550 (2016). https://doi.org/10.1007/s10209-015-0415-2
7. Cormier, K., Fox, N., Woll, B., Zisserman, A., Camgöz, N.C., Bowden, R.: ExTOL: automatic recognition of British sign language using the BSL corpus. In: Proceedings of 6th Workshop on Sign Language Translation and Avatar Technology (SLTAT) 2019. Universitat Hamburg (2019). https://openresearch.surrey.ac.uk/esploro/outputs/99514750802346
8. De Maria Marchiano, R., et al.: Translational research in the era of precision medicine: where we are and where we will go. J. Pers. Med. **11**(3), 216 (2021). https://doi.org/10.3390/jpm11030216
9. Ebling, S., Glauert, J.: Building a Swiss German sign language avatar with JASigning and evaluating it among the deaf community. Univ. Access Inf. Soc. **15**, 577–587 (2016). https://doi.org/10.1007/s10209-015-0408-1

10. Filhol, M., McDonald, J.C.: Extending the AZee-Paula shortcuts to enable natural proform synthesis. In: sign-lang@ LREC 2018, pp. 45–52. European Language Resources Association (ELRA) (2018). https://www.sign-lang.uni-hamburg. de/lrec/pub/18024.pdf
11. Galea, L.C., Smeaton, A.F.: Recognising Irish sign language using electromyography. In: 2019 International Conference on Content-Based Multimedia Indexing (CBMI), pp. 1–4. IEEE (2019). https://doi.org/10.1109/CBMI.2019.8877421
12. Garcia, L.S., et al.: Deaf inclusion through Brazilian sign language: a computational architecture supporting artifacts and interactive applications and tools. In: Antona, M., Stephanidis, C. (eds.) HCII 2021. LNCS, vol. 12769, pp. 167–185. Springer, Cham (2021). https://doi.org/10.1007/978-3-030-78095-1_14
13. Gonçalves, D.A., Baranauskas, M.C.C., dos Reis, J.C., Todt, E.: Facial expressions animation in sign language based on spatio-temporal centroid. In: International Conference on Enterprise Information Systems, pp. 463–475 (2020). https://api. semanticscholar.org/CorpusID:219328598
14. Hayward, K., Adamo-Villani, N., Lestina, J.: A computer animation system for creating deaf-accessible math and science curriculum materials. In: Eurographics (Education Papers), pp. 1–8 (2010). https://doi.org/10.2312/eged.20101009
15. Johnson, R.: Towards enhanced visual clarity of sign language avatars through recreation of fine facial detail. Mach. Transl. **35**(3), 431–445 (2021). https://doi. org/10.1007/s10590-021-09269-x
16. Kipp, M., Nguyen, Q., Heloir, A., Matthes, S.: Assessing the deaf user perspective on sign language avatars. In: The Proceedings of the 13th International ACM SIGACCESS Conference on Computers and Accessibility, pp. 107–114 (2011). https://doi.org/10.1145/2049536.2049557
17. Kruk, D., Mętel, D., Gawęda, Ł, Cechnicki, A.: Implementation of virtual reality (VR) in diagnostics and therapy of nonaffective psychoses. Psychiatr. Pol. **54**(5), 951–975 (2020). https://doi.org/10.12740/pp/onlinefirst/113437
18. Kumar, P., Kaur, S.: Sign language generation system based on Indian sign language grammar. ACM Trans. Asian Low-Resour. Lang. Inf. Process. (TALLIP) **19**(4), 1–26 (2020). https://doi.org/10.1145/3384202
19. Kumar, P., Kaur, S., et al.: Online multilingual dictionary using Hamburg notation for avatar-based Indian sign language generation system. Int. J. Cogn. Lang. Sci. **12**(8), 1117–1124 (2018). https://doi.org/10.5281/zenodo.1474397
20. Liddell, S.K.: American sign language syntax. In: American Sign Language Syntax. De Gruyter Mouton (2021). https://books.google.pl/books?id=04iFEAAAQBAJ
21. Lima, T., Rocha, M.S., Santos, T.A., Benetti, A., Soares, E., de Oliveira, H.S.: Innovation in learning – the use of avatar for sign language. In: Kurosu, M. (ed.) HCI 2013. LNCS, vol. 8005, pp. 428–433. Springer, Heidelberg (2013). https://doi. org/10.1007/978-3-642-39262-7_49
22. Martin, P.M., Belhe, S., Mudliar, S., Kulkarni, M., Sahasrabudhe, S.: An Indian sign language (ISL) corpus of the domain disaster message using avatar. In: Proceedings of the Third International Symposium in Sign Language Translations and Technology (SLTAT-2013), pp. 1–4 (2013). https://www.academia.edu/download/ 46998419/SLTATElsevierJOURNAL.pdf
23. Mazumder, S., Mukhopadhyay, R., Namboodiri, V.P., Jawahar, C.: Translating sign language videos to talking faces. In: Proceedings of the Twelfth Indian Conference on Computer Vision, Graphics and Image Processing, pp. 1–10 (2021). https://doi.org/10.1145/3490035.3490286

24. Patil, A., Kulkarni, A., Yesane, H., Sadani, M., Satav, P.: Literature survey: sign language recognition using gesture recognition and natural language processing. In: Sharma, N., Chakrabarti, A., Balas, V.E., Bruckstein, A.M. (eds.) Data Management, Analytics and Innovation. LNDECT, vol. 70, pp. 197–210. Springer, Singapore (2021). https://doi.org/10.1007/978-981-16-2934-1_13

25. Probierz, B., Kozak, J., Piasecki, A., Podlaszewska, A.: Sign language interpreting-relationships between research in different areas-overview. In: 2023 18th Conference on Computer Science and Intelligence Systems (FedCSIS), pp. 213–223. IEEE (2023). https://doi.org/10.15439/2023F2503

26. Rajendran, R., Ramachandran, S.T.: Finger spelled signs in sign language recognition using deep convolutional neural network. Int. J. Res. Eng. Sci. Manag. 4(6), 249–253 (2021). https://journal.ijresm.com/index.php/ijresm/article/view/894

27. Roelofsen, F., Esselink, L., Mende-Gillings, S., De Meulder, M., Sijm, N., Smeijers, A.: Online evaluation of text-to-sign translation by deaf end users: some methodological recommendations (short paper). In: Proceedings of the 1st International Workshop on Automatic Translation for Signed and Spoken Languages (AT4SSL), pp. 82–87 (2021). https://aclanthology.org/2021.mtsummit-at4ssl.9

28. Roelofsen, F., Esselink, L., Mende-Gillings, S., Smeijers, A.: Sign language translation in a healthcare setting. In: Proceedings of the Translation and Interpreting Technology Online Conference, pp. 110–124 (2021). https://aclanthology.org/2021.triton-1.13

29. Saggion, H., Shterionov, D., Labaka, G., Van de Cruys, T., Vandeghinste, V., Blat, J.: SignON: bridging the gap between sign and spoken languages. In: Alkorta, J., et al. (eds.) Proceedings of the Annual Conference of the Spanish Association for Natural Language Processing: Projects and Demonstrations (SEPLN-PD 2021) Co-located with the Conference of the Spanish Society for Natural Language Processing (SEPLN 2021), Málaga, Spain, 21–24 September 2021, p. 21-5. CEUR Workshop Proceedings, Aachen. CEUR Workshop Proceedings (2021). http://hdl.handle.net/10230/52242

30. Saunders, B., Camgoz, N.C., Bowden, R.: Everybody sign now: translating spoken language to photo realistic sign language video. arXiv preprint arXiv:2011.09846 (2020). https://doi.org/10.48550/arXiv.2011.09846

31. Shohieb, S.M.: A gamified e-learning framework for teaching mathematics to Arab deaf students: supporting an acting Arabic sign language avatar. Ubiquit. Learn. Int. J. 12(1), 55–70 (2019). https://doi.org/10.18848/1835-9795/CGP/v12i01/55-70

32. Smith, R., Nolan, B.: Manual evaluation of synthesised sign language avatars. In: Proceedings of the 15th International ACM SIGACCESS Conference on Computers and Accessibility, pp. 1–2 (2013). https://doi.org/10.1145/2513383.2513420

33. Soudi, A., Van Laerhoven, K., Bou-Souf, E.: AfricaSign – a crowd-sourcing platform for the documentation of stem vocabulary in African sign languages. In: Proceedings of the 21st International ACM SIGACCESS Conference on Computers and Accessibility, pp. 658–660 (2019). https://doi.org/10.1145/3308561.3354592

34. Stefanidis, K., Konstantinidis, D., Kalvourtzis, A., Dimitropoulos, K., Daras, P.: 3D technologies and applications in sign language. In: Recent Advances in 3D Imaging, Modeling, and Reconstruction, pp. 50–78 (2020). https://doi.org/10.4018/978-1-5225-5294-9.ch003

35. Stoll, S., Camgoz, N.C., Hadfield, S., Bowden, R.: Text2Sign: towards sign language production using neural machine translation and generative adversarial networks. Int. J. Comput. Vis. 128(4), 891–908 (2020). https://doi.org/10.1007/s11263-019-01281-2

36. Tateno, S., Liu, H., Ou, J.: Development of sign language motion recognition system for hearing-impaired people using electromyography signal. Sensors **20**(20), 5807 (2020). https://doi.org/10.3390/s20205807
37. Wolfe, R.: Sign language translation and avatar technology. Mach. Transl. **35**(3), 301–304 (2021). https://doi.org/10.1007/s10590-021-09270-4
38. Wolfe, R., et al.: State of the art and future challenges of the portrayal of facial nonmanual signals by signing avatar. In: Antona, M., Stephanidis, C. (eds.) HCII 2021. LNCS, vol. 12768, pp. 639–655. Springer, Cham (2021). https://doi.org/10.1007/978-3-030-78092-0_45
39. Xiao, Q., Qin, M., Yin, Y.: Skeleton-based Chinese sign language recognition and generation for bidirectional communication between deaf and hearing people. Neural Netw. **125**, 41–55 (2020). https://doi.org/10.1016/j.neunet.2020.01.030
40. Yorganci, R., Kindiroglu, A.A., Kose, H.: Avatar-based sign language training interface for primary school education. In: Workshop: Graphical and Robotic Embodied Agents for Therapeutic Systems (2016). https://api.semanticscholar.org/CorpusID:31599382

Methods of Solving Business

Sustainable Smart Cities: A Comprehensive Framework for Sustainability Assessment of Intelligent Transport Systems

Alisa Lorenz[1,2]([envelope]) [iD], Nils Madeja[1] [iD], and Christian Leyh[1] [iD]

[1] Technische Hochschule Mittelhessen – THM Business School, Wiesenstr. 14, 35390 Giessen, Germany
{alisa.lorenz,nils.madeja,christian.leyh}@w.thm.de
[2] University of Cologne, Albertus-Magnus-Platz, 50923 Cologne, Germany

Abstract. This paper is an extended version of a previously published paper [22], which proposes a framework for assessing the sustainability impact of intelligent transport systems (ITS). Building on this research, this paper shows the practical application of the framework by assessing three exemplary ITS projects and discussing potential future use. Due to the increasing relevance of ITS to improve the efficiency of transport in highly congested areas, this framework has high practical relevance for smart mobility initiatives and (future) smart cities. Municipalities increasingly recognize their responsibility for creating a sustainable environment for citizens in the face of challenges like overpopulation, land shortage, and climate change. Nevertheless, many ITS initiatives still mainly focus on technical solutions and overlook their impact on sustainability despite the relevance for the environment, society, and economy. This paper bridges the gap between technical applications and their impact on sustainability by proposing a framework for assessing the sustainability of ITS applications and initiatives. It discusses and analyzes different perspectives on the complex concepts of sustainability and ITS to derive a set of Sustainable Development Goals (SDGs) that can be targeted by ITS in one central framework. Besides this theoretical contribution, this paper focuses on demonstrating the practical use of the framework with a diverse set of projects. Hence, this work bridges two fundamental perspectives for further research and supports decision-makers in choosing ITS initiatives that contribute to both smart mobility and sustainability.

Keywords: Smart City · Smart Mobility · Smart Traffic Management · Intelligent Transport Systems · Sustainability

1 Introduction

This article is an extension of work originally presented in the Proceedings of the 18th Conference on Computer Science and Intelligence Systems [22].

Smart mobility refers to a wide range of data-driven concepts that help move individuals, groups, or objects across different locations, shaping both our present and future

E. Ziemba et al. (Eds.): FedCSIS-ITBS 2023/ISM 2023, LNBIP 504, pp. 205–223, 2024.
https://doi.org/10.1007/978-3-031-61657-0_10

[10]. Considering the complex challenges of the current decade, such as overpopulation, demographic change, globalization, space shortage, and dense traffic, cities aim to stay attractive to their citizens and provide a livable environment [5, 23]. With over 50% of the global population living in urban areas, their citizens can especially profit from the opportunities of smart traffic management and the management of high traffic volume in congested environments [9]. Simultaneously, the environmental and social challenges driven by climate change raise the need for municipalities to take responsibility and counteract the negative aspects of these challenges on their citizens. Consequently, more cities aim to use the advances of digitalization to create value for smart and sustainable mobility of citizens [2, 3, 18, 24]. Some researchers even point out that cities cannot become smart without being sustainable, making sustainability an important factor in smart city projects [34].

Intelligent transport systems (ITS) provide a set of technical applications and aim to provide innovative services for different modes of transport and traffic management [8, 10, 19]. They empower citizens to make better decisions regarding their mobility and enable safer and better-coordinated transport networks. Since road traffic is responsible for about 65% of the CO_2 emissions in cities and is likely to increase in the future, ITS promise to mitigate the negative effects of traffic on the environment [4]. However, while sustainability is a key factor in smart mobility initiatives, many ITS projects are still mainly focused on technical criteria and measures and do not seem to analyze their impact on sustainability [7, 20, 27].

Therefore, we target the intersection of sustainability and ITS in this paper. We analyze the Sustainable Development Goals (SDGs) defined by the United Nations (UN) to determine which goals, targets, and indicators have implications for the development of ITS in the context of smart mobility towards a sustainable smart city. Specifically, we explore different perspectives on ITS and relate them to the SDGs to answer the following question:

Which Sustainable Development Goals, targets, and indicators are relevant for assessing the sustainability of intelligent transport systems?

To answer this question, we review the relevant literature and combine it with international agreements and resolutions to derive a framework for assessing the effectiveness of ITS strategies on sustainability. Further, we demonstrate the practical use of this framework by assessing three exemplary German ITS projects. This paper is structured as follows. First, we define the term intelligent transport systems and set it into the context of smart cities and sustainability. We then develop our framework based on the literature, demonstrate its use, and describe the implications for further research and practice.

With our research, we contribute to the research fields of sustainable smart cities and mobility while also providing practical implications for sustainable ITS. Through our findings, we aim to inspire municipal decision-makers and technical leaders to consider sustainability factors to build data-driven solutions that have a positive impact on society and nature. In fact, we are currently facing this specific challenge in a project for data-driven traffic management funded by the German Federal Ministry for Digital and

Transport[1]. Hence, we want to share our approach to support other cities considering or planning ITS projects.

2 Theoretical Background

2.1 Smart Cities and Smart Mobility

With the trend of urbanization and population growth, cities become increasingly populated while space and resources are limited. Urban areas will face challenges in meeting the needs of their growing populations in many sectors, such as housing, transportation, energy systems, education, and healthcare. These challenges lead to the need for sustainable development [11]. The concept of smart cities has been evolving in the last decade. It aims to enhance quality of life in urban areas by using the opportunities of information and communication technologies (ICT), hardware, algorithms, and data to create a positive impact on life in cities [24].

Smart cities are characterized by the six areas *smart economy, smart people, smart governance, smart environment, smart living,* and *smart mobility,* which are all inter-linked [13]. Smart mobility is an especially relevant building block of smart cities. The improvement of mobility with technical advances can save resources, increase efficiency, and provide accessibility [9]. More specifically, smart mobility is defined as "a set of coordinated actions addressed at improving the efficiency, the effectiveness and the environmental sustainability in cities," which is characterized by transport and the use of information and communication technology [2]. It further consists of local accessibility, (inter-)national accessibility, availability of ICT infrastructure, and sustainable, innovative and safe transport systems [13]. Smart mobility has direct implications for fulfilling the Sustainable Development Goals defined by the UN and will contribute to the future of city planning and logistics [25]. However, research still shows gaps regarding the consideration of potential sustainability factors that directly affect citizens, e.g., air quality [31]. The field of smart mobility therefore holds significant potential for future research aimed at creating more sustainable cities.

2.2 Smart Traffic Management and Intelligent Transport Systems

Various terms are employed to denote the technical applications, data-driven services, and conceptual advances for data-driven traffic management. The most frequently used terms are intelligent transport systems, smart traffic management, transport/travel demand management, and smart mobility management. Though not completely congruent, these terms are used interchangeably and exhibit a high semantic overlap. In this paper, we consistently use the term intelligent transport systems (ITS) since it has been researched for more than two decades [1] and is used by the UN and European Parliament [8].

---

[1] This research is in part funded by the German Federal Ministry for Digital and Transport in the context of the "VLUID" project, an Abbreviation for the German term "traffic management solutions for complex reconstruction scenarios based on intelligent data analysis".

ITS are defined as all technical solutions and construction concepts related to traffic [10]. The UN Economic Commission for Europe (UNECE) further describes them as "a set of procedures, systems and devices that enable (a) improvements in the mobility of people and transportation of passengers and goods, through the collection, communication, processing and distribution of information and (b) the acquisition of feedback on experience and a quantification of the results gathered" [32]. The European Parliament defines ITS in a slightly more generalized manner as communication systems that provide services related to different modes of transport and traffic management. These systems support a safer, more coordinated, and smarter use of transport networks for users [8]. All definitions, however, share the common goal of technology-based and data-driven traffic management, aiming to improve mobility. ITS further consist of various tools based on information and communication technology and support the concept of smart mobility [19]. Examples for specific applications are traffic light control systems or analytical tools that influence transport management.

In addition to various definitions, several perspectives on ITS focus on different means and needs. In Fig. 1, we summarize four of the most prominent perspectives and definitions. In the following, we describe them in more detail for a broad understanding of the concept.

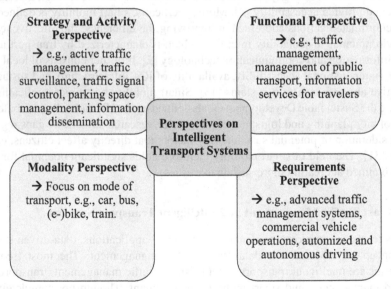

Fig. 1. Perspectives on intelligent transport systems, own illustration derived from [6, 10, 14, 19, 32].

The strategy and activity perspective on ITS [6, 14] is defined by the US Department of Transportation and provides the broadest and most granular perspective. It is focused on ITS strategies and details them in activities. Depending on the publication, 16 to 26 related activities are defined. The strategies and sample activities are:

- Traffic management and operations (e.g., traffic surveillance, traffic signal control, speed and intersection warning systems, and bicycle and pedestrian crossing enhancements),
- Road weather management operations (e.g., road weather information systems, winter roadway operations),
- Maintenance and construction management (e.g., coordination activities for construction management, work zone management),
- Incident and energy management (e.g., emergency management, emergency vehicle routing), and
- Public transportation management (e.g., electronic fare collection and integration, multimodal travel connections, transit surveillance).

The functional perspective [19] on ITS describes functions of ITS, such as management or information provision, consisting of:

- Traffic management,
- Management of public transport,
- Management of cargo transport and fleet of vehicles,
- Traffic safety management and monitoring systems for violation of regulations,
- Management of road incidents and emergency services,
- Information services for travelers and electronic payment services, and
- Electronic systems for collecting tolls for road use.

Some of these functions also overlap with the activities from the strategy and activity perspective, indicating the lack of a clear separation of the different perspectives. According to this definition, ITS operation is particularly focused on information collection from different systems, processing of this information, and the provision of related recommendations.

The requirements perspective [10] focuses on requirements profiles, and specific technical systems. Again, there are overlaps to both the strategic and functional perspectives. The related systems are:

- Advanced Traffic Management (ATMS),
- Advanced Traveler Information (ATIS),
- Advanced Vehicle Control (AVCS),
- Commercial Vehicle Operations (CVO),
- Advanced Public Transportation (APTS),
- Rural Transportation (ARTS),
- Automized and Autonomous Driving,
- Intelligent Traffic Data (Smart Traffic), and
- Vehicle Networks (Connected Vehicles).

These systems have a direct impact on activities such as emergency management, information management, and innovation management.

While the previous perspectives provide a more generic view, ITS can also be categorized according to the modes of transport they address. That leads to the modality perspective [10], comprising:

- (Motor) car traffic,

- Public transport (bus, train, city train, subway),
- (e-)Bike,
- Motorcycle,
- Plane, or
- Vessel.

The modal split is especially important in relation to sustainable solutions. However, unlike the previous ones, this perspective does not present activities or strategies. In summary, every perspective provides a slightly different view on ITS, with a common focus on more efficient, safe, and sustainable intelligent traffic management and consideration of the modal split.

2.3 Sustainability and the SDGs

Sustainability is a broad concept that is not easily defined, yet it is becoming an increasingly important research field. Previous research has found that researchers use four key concepts of sustainability:

1) a set of social and ecological criteria that guide human action,
2) a vision which is realized through a particular (social and ecological) reference system,
3) an object, thing or phenomenon that happens in certain social-ecological systems, and
4) an approach to include social and ecological variables in an activity, process, or human product [28].

All four concepts align in the social and ecological aspects in the definition of sustainability. In the context of software engineering, sustainability it can be defined as the "creation and upkeep of software systems in a way that is ethical and morally righteous, commercially viable, and technologically practicable" [15]. This includes effects on the environment, society, and economy. Other researchers have constructed sustainability with 16 variables that contribute to the four components of ecological, economic, socio-cultural, and political sustainability in the context of enterprises [35].

In the process of formulating a broad but also specific definition of sustainability, the Sustainable Development Goals provide more general guidance. In 2015 the UN formally acknowledged the need for transformative change towards sustainability and defined 17 sustainable development goals (SDGs). The resulting resolution defines sustainability as "meeting the needs of the present without compromising the ability of future generations to meet their own needs" by considering environmental concerns, social aspects, and economic development [11]. According to this definition, sustainability encourages growth and technological progress by focusing on people's needs while also ensuring that choices in the present do not exhaust resources needed in the future. All 17 goals are interdependent, and they are defined by a total of 169 targets. The progress for achieving these targets can be tracked by 231 unique indicators (ibid). The goals are set to be achieved by 2030 and have universal relevance, as they have been aligned between all 191 UN member nations and thus represent a collective understanding of sustainability.

Current research further highlights the complex relationship between ICT and sustainability while showing that it is important to measure the impacts of ICT on sustainability. Especially challenging in this context is the alignment between the concepts of digitalization, ICT, digital sustainability, and digital transformation [16]. In general, previous research has found a positive association between ICT use and sustainable development, defined as contributing to social, economic, and environmental aspects. However, such research focused on the country-level sustainability impacts and not on how individual ICT can contribute to sustainability, especially in cities [17].

Many of the SDGs build an important foundation for the progress towards smart mobility. The application of traffic-related technology and smart services in cities reflects the original idea of smart mobility. However, smart mobility also calls for a balance of technology with the needs of citizens that are reflected by the sustainability factors [29]. Recent research shows that there is a high potential for analyzing the contribution of smart cities to achieve sustainable development [30]. Some researchers even go as far as to point out that cities cannot become smart without being sustainable, making sustainability an important factor in smart city projects [33]. Further, researchers have covered ICT adoption for sustainable development in the industry context, highlighting the link between ICT and sustainability [36]. In contrast, while sustainability is considered an important aspect, researchers have found that it does not (yet) influence ICT infrastructure decision making in companies [26]. However, sustainability is especially important in smart city projects due to the global challenges in urban development. More specifically, smart cities a) usually aim to integrate technology to improve the quality of life and reduce the impact of urbanism on the environment [30] and b) are usually funded by state funds and are hence linked with a responsibility towards citizens as taxpayers and stakeholders. As pointed out, smart mobility especially has the potential to improve sustainability in cities.

In summary, the presented literature shows that sustainability is important for smart mobility in smart cities. While there are many perspectives on sustainability, the Sustainable Development Goals provide a broad view while being aligned between the countries of the UN. Therefore, we aim to provide a framework of the important SDGs that relate to ITS in order to assess related projects and support decision-making in smart mobility initiatives.

3 Research Methodology

3.1 Method Overview

In the previous section, we showed the need for ITS that are not only smart but also sustainable. However, to our knowledge, no frameworks exist to help researchers and decision-makers assess whether and how smart traffic management measures contribute to sustainability. Therefore, we dedicate this research to analyzing the various perspectives on ITS and bringing them into the context of the SDGs. To answer our research question, we combine the Sustainable Development Goals, their targets, and related indicators in a framework that shows the sustainability factors ITS can influence. Based on the relevant literature on sustainability, smart mobility, and ITS, we conduct conceptual development in our study. Besides scientific literature, we also include international agreements and recommendations regarding development for several reasons: First, UN resolutions can be seen as universally relevant because 191 states from the world community have committed to their achievement. Recommendations by the UNECE are similarly relevant and, while not legally binding, provide a more detailed view than the resolutions. While other conceptualizations of sustainability are discussed in the literature section of this article, the SDGs provide the most detailed view, encompassing various social, economic, political, and ecological perspectives. Second, we aim to ground our framework on existing work while developing a new concept through the combination of several perspectives. An exploration of the literature can provide different views and serve as a foundation for developing a unified understanding. Third, combining scientific literature with international agreements allows for both rigorous and relevant contributions. The detailed process of the framework development is described in the following section.

3.2 Framework Development

In the following, we detail the process of our framework development and explain how we combined the SDGs with perspectives from ITS, filtered and refined them across different stages, and finally brought them together for a central view. Figure 2 summarizes this process and shows how both strands are first considered individually and then merged into the final framework.

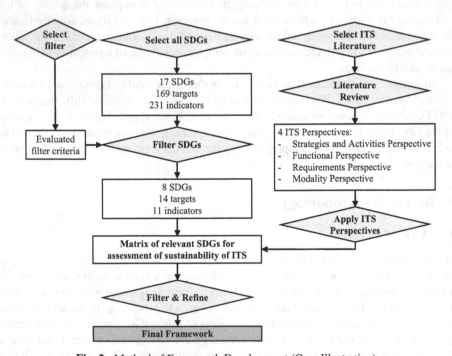

Fig. 2. Method of Framework Development (Own Illustration)

3.3   Determination of Relevant Sustainable Development Goals

To determine the relevant SDGs for our framework and their relation to ITS, we searched for key terms in the resolutions A/RES/70/1 as the original 2030 Agenda for Sustainable Development and A/RES/71/313, which additionally contains the later-adopted indicators to the goals [11, 12]. We began with all 17 goals, 169 targets, and 231 indicators (248 indicators including duplicates) and filtered them according to the terms in Table 1. We determined the terms according to the perspectives of ITS described in the previous section and used collective terms, e.g., "transport," for all related terms. We added terms that focus on cities since we used them as the application context of our study. Additionally, we added the pollution perspective as a result of traffic and as one goal of ITS. The detailed rationale behind the terms can also be found in Table 1.

The resulting set contained eight goals, 16 targets, and 16 indicators. We then eliminated two further targets and five indicators. First, we ruled out target 14.1 because it is related to marine pollution, which falls outside the scope of our framework that focuses on traffic on land. We also excluded two indicators that contained the term "urban" as a description for the measurement process and therefore did not apply in terms of content (indicators 1.1.1., 4.5.1, 11.6.1). Finally, we also excluded goal 12.c and indicator 12.c.1 because they are related to subsidies that are not decided on the level of municipalities and therefore not in the scope of ITS in the context of smart cities. Afterward, we added the superordinated targets or goals related to targets or indicators since they would not apply to the search terms. Hence, we did not add indicators to related targets when they did not apply to the criteria, leaving some indicators blank. From these constraints, we derived eight goals, 14 targets, and 11 indicators that we applied to different perspectives on ITS.

Table 1. Filter Terms for Sustainable Development Goals, Targets, and Indicators

Term	Rationale
"traffic", "transport"	Direct relation to the traffic component of ITS
"air", "pollution", "air pollution", "greenhouse gas", "emission(s)"	Direct relation to the consequences of (motorized) traffic and traffic density as well as the goal of ITS to mitigate the effects on the environment with data-driven systems and technology
"urbanization", "urban", "urban planning", "city", "cities"	Application context of a (smart) city
"fuel", "fossil fuel"	Resources for motorized traffic, which is the dominant form of traffic in cities
"car", "bike", "bicycle", "public transport", "train", "pedestrian", "walk(ing)"	Relation to modes of transport on land that are part of ITS

3.4 Perspectives of Intelligent Transport Systems

After the preselection of relevant SDGs, we determined the relevant ITS dimensions. As presented in the literature review, multiple perspectives of ITS overlap and align in some parts but still provide different views and concepts. In general, we opted for the UNECE definition, which contains the aspects of improvements in the mobility of people, transportation of passengers and goods, and the collection, communication, processing, and distribution of information. Additionally, the definition includes the acquisition of feedback on experience and quantification of the gathered results. Based on this definition, we aimed to equally consider all four perspectives on ITS derived from the literature and presented in Fig. 1. We decided against choosing only one of the perspectives in order to include SDGs that are relevant but do not relate to all perspectives. By using several perspectives, we further aim for more transparency, a broader view, and stability in the evaluation to assess the SDGs for developing our final framework.

3.5 Combination of SDGs and ITS

After filtering the relevant SDGs and determining the ITS perspectives, we combined both dimensions in a matrix. By doing this, we analyzed how the measure of each of the ITS perspectives could contribute to sustainability targets and indicators. We distinguished the impact in direct contributions to a target or indicator and indirect contributions to indicate a lower relevance. After analyzing each relation, we summarized the findings in a central framework and determined whether ITS primarily or secondarily impacts a target or indicator.

4 Research Findings

4.1 Final Framework

From the analysis performed, we were able to determine six main sustainability indicators and eight targets that relate to a total of six Sustainable Development Goals and are primarily influenced by ITS. The remaining five indicators and five targets can be influenced by ITS but probably with lower intensity. Therefore, they were marked as indirectly influenced. The final framework is displayed in Tables 2 and 3.

While SDG 11, "Sustainable Cities and Communities," is the most represented goal in the framework with the highest number of related targets and indicators, the other goals are equally relevant. Our framework also highlights goals that do not relate directly to traffic, like SDG 7, "Affordable and Clean Energy," or SDG 6, "Clean Water and Sanitation" but still might have an impact on the SDGs. In general, the framework does not prioritize or weight certain SDGs.

Our framework provides an overall view of the most important SDGs as a recommendation for researchers and practitioners to consider when developing intelligent transport systems. It further emphasizes that there is not only one perspective on sustainability and that ITS solutions could target sustainability in multiple areas. Some measures might also contribute to multiple SDGs at the same time, e.g., targeting indicator 9.4.1, "CO2 emission per unit of value added," might also have a positive impact on indicator 13.2.2, "Total greenhouse gas emissions per year," due to the general reduction of emissions.

Table 2. Final Assessment Framework: Primary impact of ITS on relevant SD goals, targets, and indicators

SDG	SDG Target/Indicator
Goal 3: Good Health and Well-Being	3.6 Halve the number of global deaths and injuries from road traffic accidents 3.6.1 Death rate due to road traffic injuries 3.9 Substantially reduce the number of deaths and illnesses from hazardous chemicals and pollution and contamination 3.9.1 Mortality rate attributed to household and ambient air pollution
Goal 6: Clean Water and Sanitation	6.3 Improve water quality by reducing pollution, eliminating dumping, and minimizing release of hazardous chemicals and materials
Goal 7: Affordable and Clean Energy	7.1 Ensure universal access to affordable, reliable, and modern energy services 7.1.2 Proportion of population with primary reliance on clean fuels and technology
Goal 9: Industry, Innovation and Infrastructure	9.4 Upgrade infrastructure and retrofit industries to make them sustainable, with increased resource-use efficiency and greater adoption of clean and environmentally sound technologies and industrial processes 9.4.1 CO_2 emission per unit of value added
Goal 11: Sustainable Cities and Communities	11.2 Provide access to safe, affordable, accessible, and sustainable transport systems for all, improving road safety, notably by expanding public transport 11.2.1 Proportion of population that has convenient access to public transport, by sex, age, and persons with disabilities 11.6 Reduce the adverse per capita environmental impact of cities; special attention to air quality 11.6.2 Annual mean levels of fine particulate matter (e.g. PM2.5 and PM10) in cities (population weighted) 11.b Increase the number of cities/settlements adopting and implementing policies and plans towards inclusion, resource efficiency, mitigation and adaptation to climate change, resilience to disasters, and develop and implement (…) holistic disaster risk management at all levels
Goal 12: Responsible Consumption and Production	12.4 Environmentally sound management of chemicals and all wastes and reduce their release to air, water, and soil

4.2 Using the Framework

Researchers and practitioners can use our framework to reflect upon projects and initiatives related to intelligent transport systems and sustainability. While it might not be

Table 3. Final Assessment Framework: Secondary impact of ITS on relevant SD goals, targets, and indicators

SDG	SDG Target/Indicator
Goal 11: Sustainable Cities and Communities	11.3 Enhance inclusive and sustainable urbanization and capacity for participatory, integrated, and sustainable human settlement planning and management 11.3.2 Proportion of cities with a direct participation structure of civil society in urban planning and management 11.7 Provide universal access to safe, inclusive, and accessible green and public spaces 11.7.1 Average share of the built-up area of cities that is open space for public use for all, by sex, age, and persons with disabilities 11.a Support positive economic, social and environmental links between urban, peri-urban, and rural areas by strengthening development planning 11.a1 Number of countries that have national urban policies or regional development plans that respond to population dynamics and ensure balanced territorial development
Goal 13: Climate Action	13.2 Integrate climate change measures into national policies, strategies, and planning 13.2.2 Total greenhouse gas emissions per year
Goal 16: Peace, Justice, and Strong Institutions	16.1 Significantly reduce all forms of violence and related death rates everywhere 16.1.4 Proportion of population that feel safe walking alone around the area they live after dark

possible to consider every factor equally, the framework serves as a starting point to create awareness of sustainability targets and indicators in the context of ITS.

Derived from one of our current ITS projects in cooperation with the German city of Wetzlar, Fig. 3 shows the different phases in which our framework can be used to assess the contribution of ITS projects to sustainability. We recommend using it as a checklist to determine whether at least one of the goals, targets, or indicators is addressed with the planned initiative. The framework is best used in the planning phase of new ITS projects to determine possible sustainability goals, targets, and indicators that might play a role in the related projects. Nevertheless, practitioners can also use the framework along the project to assess whether the individual solution approaches still fit the SDGs or to conduct a final evaluation that compares the contribution in relation to the initial strategy. Throughout initiatives, the framework can help in make the general assessment of the contribution to the sustainability of software solutions more transparent and provide a more complete view at different stages.

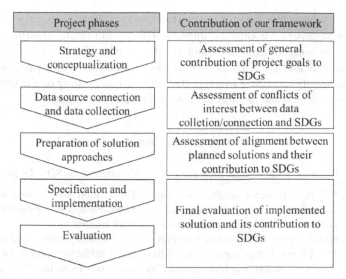

Project phases	Contribution of our framework
Strategy and conceptualization	Assessment of general contribution of project goals to SDGs
Data source connection and data collection	Assessment of conflicts of interest between data colletion/connection and SDGs
Preparation of solution approaches	Assessment of alignment between planned solutions and their contribution to SDGs
Specification and implementation	Final evaluation of implemented solution and its contribution to SDGs
Evaluation	

Fig. 3. Use of the framework in different project phases (Own Illustration)

To demonstrate the use of our framework, we chose three exemplary projects to assess their contribution to sustainability. All three projects are part of the "Emmett" network, which connects projects funded by the German Federal Ministry for Digital and Transport. We decided on this platform as a source for exemplary projects since the author's project is also associated with this funding and initiative. All three projects are already completed and were listed in the category of "sustainable" projects by the Emmett network. In the following, we will briefly discuss the projects "PAMIR," "SAUBER," and "ECOSense," which all differ in their target goal as well as in their contributions to sustainability, demonstrating the need for a broad framework (Table 4). We explicitly do not evaluate or rate the projects but rather show a qualitative representation of our framework.

The PAMIR project installed a system for reserving parking spots in advance at selected park-and-ride car parks to improve the planning of multimodal travel routes and promote the use of public transport as part of such a route [37]. Although the project is listed as "contributing to sustainability" on the related project page, there is no description or explanation included as to how it does this. Applying the project description and closing report to our framework, we concluded that it contributes to SDG 11.2 by providing safe and accessible access to (sustainable) transport systems, e.g. public transport like trains. Additionally, it aligns with 11.2.1 by facilitating easier route planning, thereby increasing the population with access to such options. Further, the project indirectly contributes to SDGs 11.6 and 13.2.2 by promoting the use of public transport and eventually reducing the environmental impact of individual transport in cities. In sum, the project contributes to several sustainability goals, targets, and indicators and can hence be considered as being sustainable.

The second exemplary project is SAUBER which targets pollution in cities by collecting current environmental data and using artificial intelligence to predict future air quality [38]. By doing this, the project aims to identify polluted areas early to mitigate or even prevent negative environmental impacts. This project clearly contributes to SDGs 3.9 and 3.9.1 by mitigating pollution and its effects on health and well-being. It further contributes to indicator 13.2.2 by aiming to reduce emissions in highly polluted areas. It also could indirectly contribute to targets 6.3 and 12.4, depending on the links between the pollution evaluated and its links to clean water and production.

Table 4. Exemplary application of the framework

Project	Relation to SDG Target/Indicator	Contribution to SDG Target/Indicator
PAMIR	11.2 Provide access to safe, affordable, accessible, and sustainable transport systems for all, improving road safety, notably by expanding public transport 11.2.1 Proportion of population that has convenient access to public transport, by sex, age, and persons with disabilities 11.6 Reduce the adverse per capita environmental impact of cities; special attention to air quality 13.2.2 Total greenhouse gas emissions per year	The solution provides safe and accessible access to public transport for more citizens The solution promotes and supports the use of public transport and makes it more convenient, therefore helping to reduce total emissions
SAUBER	3.9 Substantially reduce number of deaths and illnesses from hazardous chemicals and pollution and contamination 3.9.1 Mortality rate attributed to household and ambient air pollution 13.2.2 Total greenhouse gas emissions per year 6.3 Improve water quality by reducing pollution, eliminating dumping, and minimizing release of hazardous chemicals and materials 12.4 Environmentally sound management of chemicals and all wastes and reduce their release to air, water, and soil	The solution mitigates pollution in general and predicts future air quality to prevent highly polluted areas
ECOSense	3.6 Halve the number of global deaths and injuries from road traffic accidents 3.6.1 Death rate due to road traffic injuries 11.2 Provide access to safe, affordable, accessible and sustainable transport systems for all, improving road safety, notably by expanding public transport	The solution helps to identify and mitigate potential threats on bike roads The solution promotes and supports more sustainable mode of transport

The third project ECOSense aimed to develop and evaluate a platform to collect data on bicycle usage [39]. Through the collection and analysis of cyclists' data, they wanted to help city planners to gain a better understanding of the needs of cyclists, thereby enabling more effective planning of the bicycle infrastructure within cities. Such data includes information on infrastructure, road safety and the environment. This project contributes to SDGs 3.6 and 3.6.1 by identifying potential threats for cyclists, helping cities make their roads safer. It further indirectly contributes to SDG 11.2 by improving road safety and promoting a sustainable mode of transport. Summarizing those three examples, we can say that sustainable ITS solutions could contribute to multiple SDGs.

5 Discussion of Findings

Our framework targets the gap between the development of ITS applications and concerns regarding sustainability. While sustainability is a broadly defined term, we narrowed it down in the literature review and specified it further in the development process of our evaluation framework. Furthermore, while there are already guidelines on how to measure the achievement of SDGs on a global level (e.g., per country), there are no guidelines for measuring them on an individual level. With our final framework, we were able to answer our research question: Which Sustainable Development Goals, targets, and indicators are relevant for assessing the sustainability of intelligent transport systems?

The specific contributions to sustainability can still vary between initiatives which makes a broad and more general framework like ours a necessity. For now, we decided against weighting individual SDGs because of this span and variety between contributions. However, we advocate for the requirement that initiatives, which claim to contribute to sustainability must specify precisely how their projects contribute to SDGs. Of course, initiatives can never fully fit all sustainability criteria, but projects and ITS solutions should at least contribute to one of the SDGs if they claim to be sustainable. This would foster transparency and communicate the contributions of such projects more clearly. Since many ITS projects are funded by public funds, they further have a responsibility to consider sustainability factors. Governments are funded by taxpayers, who are citizens of cities and therefore central stakeholders of such projects.

This framework can serve as a starting point for assessments of sustainability and certainly allows for extension. One aspect will be to prioritize contributions to sustainability and expand the framework to an instrument for decision-making.

6 Conclusion

In this paper, we described the need for more sustainable actions in the mobility sector and pointed out that previous ITS projects and research seemed to lack the consideration of sustainability factors. We further argued that municipalities have a particular responsibility towards sustainability, given their role as decision-makers for their citizens, who, eventually, should benefit from ITS solutions. We developed a framework that considers both different ITS perspectives and sustainability factors. This framework determined which Sustainable Development Goals, targets, and indicators are relevant for assessing the sustainability of intelligent transport systems, and it should be considered when developing ITS strategies. We further showed how our framework can be used to assess the sustainability impact along different project phases and assessed three exemplary German ITS projects.

In summary, our research contributes to the research fields of sustainable smart cities and smart mobility in the practical context of sustainable ITS. For practitioners, we provide an easy-to-use framework that can be adjusted to individual needs. We further showed the practical use of the framework as a blueprint for further assessments. With this, we aim to enable decision-makers to assess the sustainability impact of individual ITS projects or measures. This research employs an interdisciplinary approach, combining technical considerations and sustainability aspects while identifying avenues for further investigation. We advocate considering the impacts of sustainability in future ICT research.

While we aimed for a broad and deep analysis in the creation of our framework, we would like to address some limitations in the approach and implications for future work.

First, one challenge of a literature review is including both relevant and novel literature as well as considering established "basic" literature. Despite our diligence in the selection process, we cannot claim to have a complete overview. Further, we recognize that other researchers might choose different publications. Additionally, the selection of the four perspectives on ITS might be influenced by subjective perception. As discussed in the literature review, there are many different terms for and perspectives on ITS. One reason might be the interdisciplinary character of ITS, where different perspectives from traffic engineering, traffic planning, business administration, and information systems intersect. We see the potential for future work in attempting to find one definition of ITS that includes all perspectives, thereby fostering a common transdisciplinary understanding.

Second, the inclusion and exclusion criteria of the relevant Sustainable Development Goals were chosen with the application context in mind but are nevertheless subjective and offer room for discussion. Using various search terms could produce diverse result sets and potentially influence the composition of the final matrix. Further, there might be additional SDGs that do not have a direct relation to ITS but might still be considered when developing such systems. For example, SDG target 16.7 calls for ensuring responsive, inclusive, participatory, and representative decision-making at all levels. From a more social perspective, inclusive decision-making in choosing and developing ITS measures, e.g., by including citizens, could also contribute to this target. While we do not consider the development process of the applications or social factors in our analysis, our framework is easily adjustable and could include these factors in the future or be enhanced for projects with special emphasis on these dimensions.

Third, we recognize that the assessment of each SDG in relation to ITS might be subjective. We conducted the assessment to the best of our knowledge and based it on the descriptions of each SDG, target, and goal. However, other researchers might have rated the criteria differently. In future work, the rating could be enhanced with more expertise by including more researchers.

Fourth, our framework shows the criteria for assessing ITS from a qualitative perspective but does not provide quantitative measurement criteria. The UN does provide some implications for measurement in its definition of indicators. However, they are on a rather high level and need to be adjusted to and detailed for the specific context. Therefore, we suggest a follow-up study on developing a specific measurement for assessing ITS quantitatively. A central index that incorporates and balances all indicators would facilitate comparability between projects and measures. Furthermore, we aim to combine the results from this framework with our previously developed instrument to evaluate data-driven traffic management applications [21]. In this work, we included criteria to evaluate sustainability, e.g., on an environmental level. By combining both approaches we aim to develop a more robust and extensive evaluation instrument.

To summarize, our framework can support decision-makers in municipalities by providing an approach to assess their selected or planned ITS initiatives regarding sustainability factors. This could help policymakers, planners, and citizens make more conscious decisions towards a higher quality of living in cities and contribute to the economy, society, and nature at the same time. Hence, we call for municipal traffic management that is not only smart but also sustainable to contribute to a livable future.

References

1. Andersen, J., Sutcliffe, S.: Intelligent transport systems (ITS) - an overview. IFAC Proc. Vol. **33**(8), 99–106 (2000). https://doi.org/10.1016/S1474-6670(17)37129-X
2. Benevolo, C., Dameri, R.P., D'Auria, B.: Smart mobility in smart city. In: Torre, T., Braccini, A.M., Spinelli, R. (eds.) Empowering Organizations. LNISO, vol. 11, pp. 13–28. Springer, Cham (2016). https://doi.org/10.1007/978-3-319-23784-8_2
3. Chan, F., Chan, H.: Recent research and challenges in sustainable urbanisation. Resour. Conserv. Recycl. **184**, 106346 (2022). https://doi.org/10.1016/j.resconrec.2022.106346
4. Chapman, L.: Transport and climate change: a review. J. Transp. Geogr. **15**(5), 354–367 (2007). https://doi.org/10.1016/j.jtrangeo.2006.11.008
5. Chen, T., Ramon Gil-Garcia, J., Gasco-Hernandez, M.: Understanding social sustainability for smart cities: the importance of inclusion, equity, and citizen participation as both inputs and long-term outcomes. J. Smart Cities Soc. **1**(2), 135–148 (2022). https://doi.org/10.3233/SCS-210123
6. Clark, J., Neuner, M., Sethi, S., Bauer, J., Bedsole, L., Cheema, A.: Transportation Systems Management and Operations in Action. U.S. Department of Transportation. Federal Highway Administration, Washington, D.C. (2017)
7. Devi, T., Alice, K., Deepa, N.: Traffic management in smart cities using support vector machine for predicting the accuracy during peak traffic conditions. Mater. Today Proc. **62**(7), 4980–4984 (2022). https://doi.org/10.1016/j.matpr.2022.03.722
8. European Parliament: Directive 2010/40/EU of the European Parliament and of the Council of 7 July 2010 on the framework for the deployment of Intelligent Transport Systems in the field of road transport and for interfaces with other modes of transport (2010)
9. Faria, R., Brito, L., Baras, K., Silva, J.: Smart mobility: a survey. In: 2017 International Conference on Internet of Things for the Global Community (IoTGC), pp. 1–8. IEEE (2017). https://doi.org/10.1109/IoTGC.2017.8008972
10. Flügge, B.: Smart Mobility – Connecting Everyone. Springer, Wiesbaden (2017). https://doi.org/10.1007/978-3-658-15622-0

11. General Assembly of the United Nations: Global indicator framework for the Sustainable Development Goals and targets of the 2023 Agenda for Sustainable Development. A/RES/71/313 (2017)
12. General Assembly of the United Nations: Transforming our World: The 2030 Agenda for Sustainable Development. A/RES/70/1 (2015)
13. Giffinger, R., Haindlmaier, G.: Smart cities ranking: an effective instrument for the positioning of the cities? ACE: Archit. City Environ. **4**(12), 7–26 (2010). https://doi.org/10.5821/ace. v4i12.2483
14. Grant, M., Noyes, P., Oluyede, L., Bauer, J., Edelman, M.: Developing and Sustaining a Transportation Systems Management & Operations Mission for Your Organization. A Primer for Program Planning. U.S. Department of Transportation, Reston, Washington, Boulder (2017)
15. Gupta, V., Rubalcaba, L., Gupta, C., Hanne, T. (eds.): Sustainability in Software Engineering and Business Information Management. Springer, Cham (2023). https://doi.org/10.1007/978-3-031-32436-9
16. Hassmann, T., Westner, M.: Conceptualizing sustainability in the context of ICT. A literature review analysis. In: Ganzha, L., Maciaszek, L., Paprzycki, M., Ślęzak, D. (eds.) Communication Papers of the 18th Conference on Computer Science and Intelligence Systems, vol. 37, pp. 121–129 (2023). https://doi.org/10.15439/2023F5720
17. Jayaprakash, P., Pillai, R.: The role of ICT for sustainable development: a cross country analysis. In: ICIS 2019 Proceedings, 11 (2019)
18. Jonathan, G.M.: Digital transformation in the public sector: identifying critical success factors. In: Themistocleous, M., Papadaki, M. (eds.) EMCIS 2019. LNBIP, vol. 381, pp. 223–235. Springer, Cham (2020). https://doi.org/10.1007/978-3-030-44322-1_17
19. Kos, B.: Intelligent transport systems (ITS) in smart city. In: Suchanek, M. (ed.) Challenges of Urban Mobility, Transport Companies and Systems: 2018 TranSopot Conference, pp. 115–126. Springer, Cham (2019). https://doi.org/10.1007/978-3-030-17743-0_10
20. Li, Z., Al Hassan, R., Shahidehpour, M., Bahramirad, S., Khodaei, A.: A hierarchical framework for intelligent traffic management in smart cities. IEEE Trans. Smart Grid **10**(1), 691–701 (2019). https://doi.org/10.1109/TSG.2017.2750542
21. Lorenz, A., Madeja, N., Leyh, C.: A framework for assessing the sustainability of intelligent transport systems in the smart city context. In: Ganzha, L., Maciaszek, L., Paprzycki, M., Ślęzak, D. (eds.) Proceedings of the 18th Conference on Computer Science and Intelligence Systems, vol. 35, pp. 161–169 (2023). https://doi.org/10.15439/2023F6002
22. Lorenz, A., Madeja, N., Cifci, A.: An instrument for evaluating data-driven traffic management applications in the context of digital transformation towards a smart city. In: Carroll, N., Nguyen-Duc, A., Wang, X., Stray, V. (eds.) Software Business: 13th International Conference, ICSOB 2022, Bolzano, Italy, November 8–11, 2022, Proceedings, pp. 3–18. Springer, Cham (2022). https://doi.org/10.1007/978-3-031-20706-8_1
23. Morabito, V.: Big data and analytics for government innovation. In: Morabito, V. (ed.) Big Data and Analytics, pp. 23–45. Springer, Cham (2015). https://doi.org/10.1007/978-3-319-10665-6_2
24. Al Nuaimi, E., Al Neyadi, H., Mohamed, N., Al-Jaroodi, J.: Applications of big data to smart cities. J. Internet Serv. Appl. **6**(1), 25 (2015). https://doi.org/10.1186/s13174-015-0041-5
25. Paiva, S., Ahad, M., Tripathi, G., Feroz, N., Casalino, G.: Enabling technologies for urban smart mobility: recent trends, opportunities and challenges. Sensors **21**(6), 2143 (2021). https://doi.org/10.3390/s21062143
26. Sacchero, S., Molla, A.: Environmental considerations in ICT infrastructure decision making. In: ACIS 2009 Proceedings - 20th Australasian Conference on Information Systems, pp. 1066–1075 (2009)

27. Saikar, A., Parulekar, M., Badve, A., Thakkar, S., Deshmukh, A.: TrafficIntel: smart traffic management for smart cities. In: 2017 International Conference on Emerging Trends and Innovation in ICT (ICEI), Pune, pp. 46–50 (2017). https://doi.org/10.1109/ETIICT.2017.797 7008

28. Salas-Zapata, W.A., Ortiz-Muñoz, S.M.: Analysis of meanings of the concept of sustainability. Sustain. Dev. **27**(1), 153–161 (2019). https://doi.org/10.1002/sd.1885

29. Soeiro, D.: Smart cities, well-being and good business: the 2030 agenda and the role of knowledge in the era of industry 4.0. In: Matos, F., Vairinhos, V., Salavisa, I., Edvinsson, L., Massaro, M. (eds.) Knowledge, People, and Digital Transformation: Approaches for a Sustainable Future, pp. 55–67. Springer, Cham (2020). https://doi.org/10.1007/978-3-030-40390-4_5

30. Toli, A., Murtagh, N.: The concept of sustainability in smart city definitions. Front. Built Environ. **6**, 77 (2020). https://doi.org/10.3389/fbuil.2020.00077

31. Tomaszewska, E., Florea, A.: Urban smart mobility in the scientific literature—bibliometric analysis. Eng. Manag. Prod. Serv. **10**(2), 41–56 (2018). https://doi.org/10.2478/emj-2018-0010

32. United Nations Economic Commission for Europe: Intelligent Transport Systems (ITS) for sustainable mobility, Geneva (2012)

33. Yigitcanlar, T., Kamruzzaman, M., Foth, M., Sabatini-Marques, J., da Costa, E., Ioppolo, G.: Can cities become smart without being sustainable? A systematic review of the literature. Sustain. Cities Soc. **45**, 348–365 (2019). https://doi.org/10.1016/j.scs.2018.11.033

34. Yigitcanlar, T.: Smart cities: an effective urban development and management model? Aust. Planner **52**(1), 27–34 (2015). https://doi.org/10.1080/07293682.2015.1019752

35. Ziemba, E.: Exploring levels of ICT adoption and sustainable development – the case of polish enterprises. In: 2019 Federated Conference on Computer Science and Information Systems (FedCSIS), Leipzig, pp. 579–588. IEEE (2019). https://doi.org/10.15439/2019F145

36. Ziemba, E.: Synthetic indexes for a sustainable information society: measuring ICT adoption and sustainability in polish enterprises. In: Ziemba, E. (ed.) Information Technology for Management. Ongoing Research and Development: 15th Conference, AITM 2017, and 12th Conference, ISM 2017, Held as Part of FedCSIS, Prague, Czech Republic, September 3-6, 2017, Extended Selected Papers, vol. 311, pp. 151–169. Springer, Cham (2018). https://doi.org/10.1007/978-3-319-77721-4_9

37. Emmett: Über ECOSense. https://emmett.io/project/erfassung-und-analyse-von-radverkeh rsdaten-zur-unterstuetzung-der-infrastrukturoptimierung. Accessed 05 Jan 2024

38. Emmett: Über PAMIR. https://emmett.io/project/stellplatzfeine-parkplatzbelegungsinf ormation-und-parkplatzreservierung-fuer-ein-komfortableres-multimodales-reisen#info. Accessed 05 Jan 2024

39. Emmett: Über SAUBER. https://emmett.io/project/satellitenbasiertes-system-zur-anzeige-prognose-und-simulation-von-luftschadstoffen-fuer-eine-nachhaltige-stadt-und-regionale ntwicklung. Accessed 05 Jan 2024

Brand Dynamics and Social Media Strategies During the Russia-Ukraine War: Insights from Poland

Magdalena Grzanka and Artur Strzelecki[✉] [iD]

University of Economics in Katowice, Katowice, Poland
`artur.strzelecki@ue.katowice.pl`

Abstract. This study investigates the significant shift in social media and brand management due to the outbreak of the war in Ukraine in 2022, focusing particularly on how companies' social media posts and strategies evolved in response to the conflict and its impact on user attitudes. The research explores the changing dynamics of social media engagement by companies and the public during the war, examining the role of social media in shaping public perceptions and responses to the conflict and the effect of companies' online activities on their relationships with users and consumers. Utilizing data from platforms like Facebook, Instagram, and Twitter, the study also incorporates a survey conducted among the Polish community to evaluate consumer opinions about corporate actions on social media during the crisis. The findings reveal a paradigm shift in brand communication and management on social media, highlighting the expectation of users for companies to address social and political issues and the demand for brands to withdraw from the Russian market as a show of support for Ukraine. The study also explores into the practical implications of social media crisis management, underscoring the need for brands to monitor online platforms, respond promptly and transparently, offer solutions, and have a crisis management plan.

Keywords: Social media · Brand management · Ukraine War · Company engagement · User attitudes

1 Introduction

In recent years, social media has become an increasingly important platform for brands to reach and engage with their customers. With the proliferation of social media networks and the widespread use of mobile devices, consumers are now able to access and interact with brands in real time, anywhere, and anytime. This has led to a shift in the way that brands manage their online presence and reputation, as well as the way that they communicate and interact with their customers.

In 2022, the outbreak of the war in Ukraine caused a significant shift in social media and brand management. By the end of February 2022, companies abruptly altered the content they were posting on social media [29]. Companies that had not previously shared their social or political views on social media were required to take a side in the

E. Ziemba et al. (Eds.): FedCSIS-ITBS 2023/ISM 2023, LNBIP 504, pp. 224–241, 2024.
https://doi.org/10.1007/978-3-031-61657-0_11

conflict—either the side of Ukraine or the side of the Russian state—which initiated the war [42]. The lack of involvement of a brand in helping Ukraine was often criticized by social media users, who had previously been willing to buy products from the company. During the war in Ukraine, social media users worldwide identified with the people affected by the war in Ukraine and demanded that brands withdraw from the Russian market.

In times of war, an increasing number of social media users began to believe that companies should openly address social and political issues and share their own views on the actions of the Russian state. The start of the war in Ukraine forced many companies to change the way they conducted their social media activities [2]. The war conflict required companies to adopt a new strategy and change the way they communicated with social media users, where consumer views of a particular brand are most often expressed. Numerous companies have decided to limit their social media activity and relinquish their standard Internet activity. Many of them provided immediate help to Ukraine and expressed their support for the eastern community with posts published on their social media. Companies began to organize aid campaigns and money collections, which they had provided about on their social media. Those who had not previously published posts on social media were now forced to do so to express their support for Ukraine and to inform about the actions taken in this regard. The start of the war in Ukraine led to a change in the way brands communicated with their customers and the way they conducted their social media activities [50].

According to Wirtualnemedia.pl., in the first days of the war conflict in Ukraine, approximately 900,000 posts appeared on social media calling for help for the Eastern neighbors. The majority of these publications appeared on the social networking site Facebook (approximately 43%), and on Twitter (approximately 38%) [57]. With the start of the war, social media was dominated by posts related to help for Ukraine. After the Russian attack on Ukraine, a significant decrease in the number of ads published on Facebook was observed; on February 28, 2022, the number of ads on this social networking site decreased by 73% compared to the previous highest result in that month [56]. At the end of February 2022, ads on social media were mainly suspended, but posts that had been planned several months earlier and had to be published by brands on the internet could still be observed. These were posts from companies that had already been contracted in the past and had to be completed according to the company's regulations. These posts included the results of organized contests, planned events, or webinars [31]. There were also companies that completely suspended their social media business during the war crisis. These actions mainly resulted from the concern of brands about the reactions of consumers to the company's further actions on the internet during the war in Ukraine. Some companies remained active on their social media platforms but chose to disable comments in their posts. Such behavior did not win the sympathy of consumers. These actions were perceived by social media users as insincere, and silence was treated as an attempt to mask the brand's opinion on the war in Ukraine. The situation changed at the end of March 2022 when companies began to publish posts on social media again, but these changes were mainly related to the companies' involvement in activities supporting Ukraine. The war in Ukraine had a significant impact on the way brands communicated with their customers and changed their social media activities.

The war in Ukraine in 2022 had significant impacts on social media and brand management, as well as on how companies and users engaged with each other on social media platforms [46]. In this research, we explore how social media and brand management changed in response to the war, how companies' social media posts and strategies evolved during this time, and how users' attitudes toward these efforts were impacted. Additionally, we will examine the role that social media played in shaping public perceptions of and responses to the war and how companies' social media engagement during this time affected their relationships with users and consumers. The study relies on data from social media platforms such as Facebook, Instagram, and Twitter [27].

This paper is organized as follows: after the introduction, there is a literature review which consists of the impact on the economy, financial markets, mental health, and social media. The next section describes the methods used in this study, followed by the results section. The results focus on brands' activities in social media and the study group from our survey. The discussion section highlights the outcomes of the study and emphasizes the practical contributions. The study concludes with the conclusion section.

2 Literature Review

Current studies on the Russia-Ukraine war focus on several major areas, such as its impact on the economy and finance. More detailed studies demonstrate changes in the behavior of individuals who are impacted by the war. Changes in social media usage have also been observed.

2.1 Impact on the Economy

Extensive research on the implications of the Russia-Ukraine War has revealed its profound impact on global economic sectors, especially sustainable development, food security, and financial markets. Recent works emphasize how the conflict has exacerbated poverty and hunger in Africa and the MENA region. They highlighted disruptions in global supply chains, inflation, and price hikes due to war and sanctions, hindering regions' progress toward achieving sustainable development goals [32]. These studies focus on regional vulnerability to food insecurity due to the dependence of these regions on food imports [1].

The economic costs of the Russia–Ukraine war are estimated at a 1% reduction in global GDP and significant contractions in the European, Russian, and Ukrainian economies. This creates challenges faced by policymakers in balancing growth and inflation [28]. Implications of the war for global food security have affected global food systems and supply chains, particularly impacting wheat and corn exports and thereby exacerbating food insecurity in regions reliant on imports from Ukraine and Russia [7].

The cascading failure model used to assess the impact of the war on global energy and cereal trade networks is highlighted [59]. There is evidence on how the war changed public support for clean energy policies. An increase in public support for clean energy policies has been revealed in European countries since the war, indicating a shift in perception toward energy independence and reduced reliance on fossil fuels [47]. The impacts on clean energy, conventional energy, and metal markets suggest a shift toward renewable energy investments and varied effects on metal markets, underlining the geopolitical significance of Russia in these sectors [52].

Some studies advocate for a transformation in the global food system in response to war-induced disruptions. They propose measures such as shifting toward healthier diets, increasing legume production, and reducing food waste to address both immediate and long-term challenges in food security and sustainability [41]. The conflict is analyzed through resource dependency theory, highlighting strategic concerns over energy resources and markets as significant factors in the war's inception [22]. There are also notable shifting dynamics between oil and other financial assets during the war. Market behavior and risk management are changing during periods of geopolitical conflict [3].

2.2 Impact on the Finance Markets

The literature on the financial impacts of the Russia-Ukraine War provides comprehensive insights into global market reactions and the valuation of specific sectors. Some analyses employ data from thousands of firms worldwide, revealing that European firms and those with high trade dependence on Russia experienced lower returns, while industries such as oil, gas, and military saw higher returns [49]. Another study quantified the aggregate cost of the war on European firms using high-frequency stock data and structural models. It shows decreased corporate security prices, increased asset volatility, and heightened default risks, especially for firms with significant Russian economic ties [8].

In a different sector, the impact of the conflict on tourism stocks was analyzed using the event study method. A study revealed that the war's effect varied across firms, with American tourism firms experiencing positive returns on certain days, contrasting with Asian firms' mixed responses [35]. Similar work has explored the effects of conflicts on global currencies, observing significant regional variations. European currencies generally depreciated against the USD, while Pacific currencies appreciated [10]. Another study employs event study, cross-sectional, and network analyses to understand EU market reactions. It observes adverse impacts on stock market indices, influenced by geographic proximity and market efficiency, and highlights the interconnectedness between EU stock markets [25]. Finally, two additional studies extend the analysis to fintech, environmental, social and government, renewable energy indices, and commodities. El Khoury et al. [24] showed that these indices are net transmitters of connectedness in developed countries, while Izzeldin et al. [19] compared the impact of war on financial markets to that of other significant events, such as the COVID-19 pandemic, revealing unique market dynamics in response to geopolitical crises.

2.3 Impact on Mental Health

The literature on the impact of the Russian-Ukrainian War on healthcare and mental health reveals profound challenges and coping strategies among affected populations. There are dire consequences for individuals with chronic diseases due to disrupted healthcare infrastructures in Ukraine, emphasizing the critical situation for those requiring regular treatments such as dialysis and the struggles of refugees in accessing necessary medical care [37]. Similarly, another study demonstrated the efficacy of social media-based therapies such as drama, music, and art in reducing PTSD symptoms among evacuees, with drama therapy showing the most significant benefit, suggesting the potential of these digital interventions in managing mental health in crisis contexts [13]. Further research on the psycho-emotional impact of the war on university students and personnel in Ukraine reveals considerable mental health deterioration, such as depression, exhaustion, and increased substance use, with more severe effects on students than personnel and greater impacts on females [26]. Additional studies have shown high prevalence rates of mental health symptoms such as anxiety, depression, and insomnia among Ukrainians, highlighting the critical need for mental health support and effective coping strategies during such conflicts [58].

2.4 Impact on Social Media

In the literature on the impacts of social media and public opinion during the Russia-Ukraine conflict, several studies offer diverse insights. Research on the Ukrainian government's ban on Russian social media platforms such as VKontakte reveals a significant reduction in platform activity postban, regardless of users' political affiliations [14]. Similarly, the exploration of Twitter content related to the conflict indicates varied global opinions, with a notable emphasis on support for Ukraine. The study of "user-generated content" highlights the role of unverified accounts in propagating opinions, although verified accounts have greater impact on engagement [33]. Moreover, comparative analysis of Weibo and Twitter posts reveals distinct cultural and ideological influences on the portrayal of the conflict, emphasizing unified public sentiment favoring humanitarianism across platforms [51].

Furthering this exploration, a study distinguishes between human and bot account activities on Twitter, revealing significant differences in engagement and political stances. Their findings highlight the nuanced roles of bots in shaping online narratives during conflict [45]. Similarly, another study on pro-Russian propaganda on social media during the 2022 invasion of Ukraine underscores the critical role of bots in spreading propaganda, offering insights into modern information warfare tactics [12]. Complementing these perspectives, another study analyzes public sentiment toward economic sanctions using a vast array of Facebook posts. Their research reveals the complex interplay between public sentiment, government stances, and geopolitical positions, highlighting the fragmented nature of public opinion in international conflicts [34]. The conducted literature review reveals that there is a gap that this study aims to fill. The gap pertains to studying the change in brand management on social media during the conflict.

Based on the literature review, the following research questions are formulated:

1. How did social media and brand management change in response to the war in Ukraine in 2022?
2. How did companies' social media posts change during the war in Ukraine in 2022?
3. How did users' attitudes toward companies' social media engagement change during the war in Ukraine in 2022?

3 Method

For this study, we used a social media review and survey. In the social media review, we conducted an analysis of the actions taken by several different Polish companies following the occurrence of the War crisis. We primarily analyzed posts from the Twitter and Facebook accounts of well-known Polish companies. This was done using convenient sampling supported by news outlets. We described the actions taken by brands operating in Poland, such as Rossmann, ING, and InPost, as well as noting the absence of actions performed by Leroy Merlin. Survey research is a method of collecting information from a sample of individuals using structured questionnaires or interviews. To verify consumers' opinions about the actions taken by companies on social media during the war crisis in Ukraine, we decided to conduct a study among the Polish community [30]. This study took the form of a questionnaire survey in the Polish language and aimed to identify consumers' feelings and observations about daily brand image management compared to those experienced during the war crisis, which affected the Ukrainian community in 2022. The survey questionnaire was prepared using Google Forms software and was made available from March to April 2022. The survey was fully anonymous, and anyone interested could fill it out. To gather as many responses as possible, we made the questionnaire available on social media, especially on themed groups on the Facebook social networking site. The aim of the survey was to conduct a public opinion review on the perceptions of companies on social media and the activities of companies on social media during the war in Ukraine.

The study was conducted in accordance with the Declaration of Helsinki and approved by the Faculty Research Ethics Committee of the University of Economics in Katowice, Poland; Approval code: 135890, and date: April 3, 2022. Informed consent was obtained from each participant at the beginning of the survey. The statement was as follows: "By taking part in this study, you agree to allow us to collect data about managing brand image on social media during the war crisis in Ukraine. These data will help us better understand brand management during this crisis and will be kept strictly confidential. You may withdraw from the study at any time by contacting us."

In the survey, 150 respondents participated [15]. The questionnaire was completed by both women and men. The majority of the individuals surveyed were women (114 of whom were 76%). The questionnaire was published on social media platforms and influenced a large percentage of the respondents who were young—mostly school or university students. The number of respondents aged less than 18 years and older than 56 years was minimal. The largest number of people who participated in the survey were aged 18 to 26 years—85.3% of whom were 128 respondents. The next largest group of people participating in the survey were those aged 27–35 years (16 respondents). Three people were aged 36–55, two people were aged 18–1.3%, and one person was aged older than 56 years.

4 Results

4.1 Brands' Activities in Social Media During the Ukraine War Crisis

The onset of the war crisis in Ukraine changed the way brands were managed on social media. In the early days of the war, companies were constantly seeking new ways to build their brand image on social media. They tried to help their eastern neighbors and kept the public informed about it on social media. Companies chose different ways to support Ukraine. Brands supported refugees, organized financial and material collections, fought against disinformation, and used social media profiles as a place to publish reliable information from around the world. Some companies also decided to withdraw Russian products from their own range, suspend production, or ultimately cease operations in Russia [44]. As the war in Ukraine began, companies from various industries began to assist their eastern neighbors. Brands on social media platforms called for support for refugees and documented their efforts to help Ukraine. Similar strategies were adopted by well-known celebrities and influencers, who were often associated with a particular brand as a result of a campaign or promotion of goods. While helping their eastern neighbors, companies did not forget about maintaining the good reputation of their brand [48]. An important step during the war crisis in Ukraine was the fight against disinformation. Many companies decide to run a certain type of news service on their social media platforms [14]. This activity was intended to eliminate fake news and reduce panic among people [30]. A new service called VPolshchi.pl was created by Virtual Poland in response to the onset of the war crisis in Ukraine [55]. The VPolshchi.pl service was intended to correct false information. VPolshchi.pl features current information on the military actions being carried out in Ukraine and the most important news related to the ongoing war. The news in this service is conveyed in Ukrainian and is intended to be helpful to the Ukrainian community. This news focuses on delivering accurate information about the current situation in Ukraine and informing about organized aid efforts [48].

During the war in Ukraine, a significant number of refugees sought shelter in various countries, including Poland. Both individuals and businesses extended their support to these refugees through financial and material assistance. Companies organized campaigns to collect funds, food, clothing, medical supplies, hygiene products, and children's accessories for their eastern neighbors. Special hashtags and discount codes were created, where the use of such codes resulted in a specified amount of money being donated for the benefit of aiding Ukraine. These campaigns effectively encouraged consumers to participate in helping refugees. One notable example is Rossmann Pharmacy, which has actively supported its eastern neighbor since the war's onset. They organized an aid campaign by offering a special 40% coupon for selected products to those who wished to support Ukrainian refugees. The company emphasized that this campaign was not merely a promotion but also aimed to raise awareness among consumers. The discount was provided to individuals who would donate the purchased products to the refugees. This coupon was valid until March 8, 2022, and covered various hygiene products and children's accessories. The coupon was exclusively available to users of Rossmann's mobile application and could only be used once [20].

The coffee roaster KawePale also joined the aid action for Ukraine. A post appeared on Instagram announcing the campaign organized by the brand. The company created a universal discount code for use in the company's online store [23]. The use of this discount code contributes 15% of the sales of the company's ordered coffees to the Polish Humanitarian Action. Polish humanitarian action supported both people in Ukraine during the ongoing war and refugees coming to Poland [40]. To help Ukraine, companies organized their own collections or transferred funds to the existing collections. Information about the ongoing campaigns was announced on the social media portals of companies and among employees of the network who had the opportunity to become involved in the assistance and show solidarity with Ukraine. These activities were undertaken by one of the Polish banks, ING Bank Slaski SA. On their Facebook profile, the bank posted information about a fundraising campaign for the Ukrainian community in connection with the ongoing war [16]. In addition, the bank declared that it would not only transfer the collected funds to help Ukraine but also double the amount collected.

InPost, one of the main logistics and transportation operators in Poland, also decided to help the Ukrainian community. The company decided to use its resources to help with the delivery of products collected as part of the aid campaigns organized throughout the country for Ukraine. The brand was informed about its decision on the Facebook social media platform [18]. The logistics operator InPost not only organized product deliveries to the eastern border but also participated in numerous charitable collections supporting refugees from Ukraine. The company entered into cooperation with the Polish Red Cross. InPost helped the PCK in the transportation of medical equipment, dressings, medicines, hygienic and medical supplies, and food products. Together with the Melissa brand, the company developed aid packages that were available for purchase through the InPost mobile application. Those willing to help the Ukrainian community purchased these packages, and the company delivered the goods to those in need in Ukraine. This transport was free of charge and was intended to support the Ukrainian community. In addition, to support refugees' lives outside their homeland, the InPost brand created a Ukrainian language version of the mobile application, InPost Mobile [17]. Communication service providers also supported people from Ukraine, initiating the creation of free starters for people from Ukraine. One of the mobile operators that supported Ukraine was the Plus Poland Company [48]. On Twitter, the company announced information about the organized action related to free starters for every person from Ukraine. This starter included a free package of 500 min and 10 GB for 30 days and required the person interested in showing their residence card or passport at the sales point [39].

During the Ukraine war crisis, a group of companies emerged that, after approximately two months of the war, still did not declare the withdrawal of their brand from the Russian market. This group included Leroy Merlin, Auchan, and Nestle. In April 2022, the opinions of internet users about these companies were critical. These brands were regularly boycotted on the internet, and previous customers of these businesses stopped purchasing products from their offerings [6]. The consequences of not leaving the Russian market, for example, affected the Leroy Merlin brand. Internet users were calling for a continuous boycott of this company on the internet, and social media users formulated a special hashtag, #boycottleroymerlin, calling for the cessation of using the services offered by this company. Newer graphics appearing on the internet showed the disapproval of social media users. The Russian market was not abandoned by the Auchan hypermarket chain either. As a result of the companies' approach to the events taking place in Ukraine, a petition was issued by the National Boycott of Leroy Merlin, calling for the dismissal of the Polish management of the Leroy Merlin and Auchan chains [11]. Internet users described these companies as being cowardly and unworthy of imitation. Strikes were being organized under the stationary stores of the companies, calling for help for the Ukrainian community and the withdrawal of brands from the Russian market. Like with the company Leroy Merlin, the company Auchan tried to alleviate the tense situation it is facing. On March 11, 2022, the Polish branch of the company informed the social media site Facebook about the assistance organized for the Ukrainian community and declared that it has no influence on the decision of the parent company regarding the conduct of business in the Russian Federation [4]. In view of the expression of solidarity with Ukraine, the company hoped for a gradual easing of the consumer boycott. The effect of the message shared online was the opposite, and approximately twelve thousand negative reactions and comments directed at the Leroy Merlin Company were recorded under the published post [27].

4.2   Survey Study Group

The respondents were asked about their attention given to businesses' online activity during the war crisis in Ukraine and its impact on brand posts on social media. The survey items are presented in Tables 1, 2, 3, 4 and 5. Of the total number of respondents, 63 indicated paying attention to companies' posts during the war, with 36 showing significant interest. On the other hand, 31 respondents stated that they did not pay attention to these posts, and one person explicitly ignored business posts during the war. Additionally, 19 respondents were uncertain and chose the "Difficult to say" response (Table 1).

Table 1. Respondents' assessment of posts by brands on social media during the war in Ukraine

Statement	Answer				
	No	Rather not	Difficult to say	Rather yes	Yes
I pay attention to the actions taken by companies in social media during the war in Ukraine	0.6%	20.7%	12.7%	42%	24%
I notice a change in the posts published by brands on social networks as a result of the war in Ukraine	1.3%	18.7%	14%	40.6%	25.4%

The respondents observed both the actions taken by companies on social media during the war crisis in Ukraine and the changes in their posts. Of the respondents, 63 and 36 definitely noticed a difference in the behavior of brands on social media during the war. Only 32 respondents did not perceive any changes in the companies' social media posts following Russia's aggression against Ukraine. Additionally, 19 respondents found it challenging to provide a clear answer to this question (Table 1). Furthermore, the war in Ukraine led to the emergence of numerous negative consumer opinions about specific brands on the internet. Among the surveyed respondents, 104 individuals confirmed seeing criticism directed at companies on social media in relation to the ongoing war in Ukraine. Conversely, 46 respondents did not notice any negative opinions about companies on the internet concerning the war's impact on the Ukrainian community (Table 2).

Table 2. Opinions of users about companies on social media during the war crisis in Ukraine

Statement	Answer	Count
I notice negative opinions about companies appearing in social media during the time of war crisis in Ukraine	Yes	69.3%
	No	30.7%
I comment on content posted by companies' relationship on social media with the war in Ukraine	Yes	9.3%
	No	90.7%

During the war in Ukraine, respondents noticed negative comments about companies on social media, but they rarely shared their own opinions or comments about brand posts. Only 14 respondents confirmed commenting on content posted by companies on social media regarding the war in Ukraine. On the other hand, 136 respondents stated that they did not express their views on the internet about the actions of companies during the war crisis in Ukraine (Table 2). The respondents were also asked to provide their opinions on companies' social media activity during the war in Ukraine. A significant number of respondents (98) believed that brands should not engage in standard activity, 21 had different views, and 31 marked the response as "difficult to say" (Table 3).

The respondents unanimously agreed that businesses should deliver continuous updates on social media regarding their actions in response to the ongoing war in Ukraine, including providing material and financial aid to refugees. This view was shared by the majority, with 97 respondents expressing this opinion. Additionally, 108 respondents believed that businesses should support Ukraine on social media, while only 12 disagreed with this statement (Table 3). The surveyed individuals also believed that businesses should provide social media information about the withdrawal of Russian products from their own offerings—123 responses of this type were given. According to the respondents, it is important for companies to involve their brand's consumers in actively helping Ukraine and its refugees. Companies should also pay more attention to comments made about posts by brands on social media, especially during the ongoing crisis in Ukraine (111 responses). As claimed by the respondents, businesses should feel obligated to help the Ukrainian community and appeal for help among the followers gathered on social media networks (96 responses) (Table 4).

Table 3. Respondents' assessment of statements about companies on social media and the war in Ukraine

Statement	Answer				
	No	Rather not	Difficult to say	Rather yes	Yes
During the war in Ukraine, companies should not conduct standard activity in social media	34.7%	30.7%	20.6%	10%	4%
Companies should inform via social media about the current actions of the brand taken in the era of the war crisis	4.6%	12.7%	18%	40%	24.7%
Businesses should show support for Ukraine on social media	2.7%	5.3%	20%	37.3%	34.7%

Table 4. Respondents' assessment of the statements regarding the actions of brands during the war in Ukraine

Statement	Answer				
	No	Rather not	Difficult to say	Rather yes	Yes
Companies should inform on social networks about the withdrawal of Russian products from its own offer	2.7%	4.7%	10.6%	34.7%	47.3%
Companies should pay attention to comments posted by followers on social networks during the war crisis in Ukraine	4%	6%	16%	35.3%	38.7%
Companies should involve followers in aid for Ukraine	5.3%	6.7%	24%	40.6%	23.4%

The survey respondents showed a keen interest in the support demonstrated by companies on social media for Ukraine. Of the respondents, 104 expressed concern and engagement with this issue. The respondents were aligned in their demand for businesses to provide assistance to Ukraine, but not all respondents were discouraged from purchasing products from brands that did not take decisive action regarding the war in Ukraine. The responses were divided regarding the question of purchasing products from brands that lacked solidarity with Ukraine. Fifty-eight respondents indicated that they would still purchase products from such brands, while 51 respondents held the opposite opinion. However, the responses were almost evenly distributed regarding consumer reluctance to purchase products from companies that did not criticize Russia's aggression against Ukraine. For this question, 53 respondents answered affirmatively, while 72 respondents had a negative response. Furthermore, a decisive majority of the respondents expressed their intention to continue following the social media profiles of brands that do not show support for Ukraine, with 100 respondents confirming this. However, 28 respondents found it challenging to provide a definitive answer, and 22 respondents were prepared to stop following such businesses on social media (Table 5).

Table 5. Respondents' assessment of the statements about the war in Ukraine and the activities of brands online

Statement	Answer				
	No	Rather not	Difficult to say	Rather yes	Yes
I pay attention to the support shown in social media by companies for Ukraine	8,7%	11,3%	10,7%	40,6%	28,7%
No firm action by the company in the relationship with the conflict in Ukraine discourages the purchase of products of a given brand	20%	28%	16,7%	20%	15,3%
I will resign from following the profile of a company in social media that does not show support for Ukraine	35.4%	31.3%	16.7%	9.3%	5.3%
I will resign from buying products of a specific brand that is not in solidarity with Ukraine	16.7%	22%	27.3%	22%	12%

5 Discussion

The study addressed issues related to the change in brand image management due to the war crisis in Ukraine and the new reality that modern businesses had to find themselves in. The study of the activities of businesses and brand image management in social media was based on a developed questionnaire survey that was made available on social media portals. One hundred fifty people participated in the study, expressing their own opinions on social media and their impact on brand image, even in the face of the war crisis in Ukraine. The analysis focused on the behavior and views of modern consumers in relation to the actions taken by companies on social media.

During the war crisis in Ukraine, businesses sought to provide assistance to their eastern neighbors and ensured support for refugees both materially and financially. The responses confirmed that consumers pay close attention to the activities of companies on social media, and these actions significantly impact the brand perception of customers. The surveyed individuals base their opinions on the products offered by brands and the reputation of the companies on the opinions of other users. In addition, due to Russia's aggression toward Ukraine, respondents experienced a significant change in the themes of posts published on social media and encountered more negative comments directed toward contemporary businesses. These negative comments are mainly directed toward companies that have not yet decided to withdraw their brand from the Russian market and have not withdrawn Russian products from their own offerings (as of the date of the survey). Respondents confirmed that, in their opinion, businesses should not conduct their usual activities on social media during the ongoing war crisis in Ukraine, and some of those surveyed replied that they would refrain from purchasing products from a company that is not supportive of Ukraine.

We have found the following answers to the research questions. The war in Ukraine in 2022 had a significant impact on social media and brand management, as companies were required to take a side in the conflict and express their views on social and political issues. This led to a change in the way that companies conducted their social media activities and communicated with their customers (Research question 1). During the war in Ukraine in 2022, companies' social media posts changed as they were required to take a side in the conflict and express their views on social and political issues. Many companies also limited their social media activity or changed the way they communicated with their customers to show their support for Ukraine (Research question 2). Users' attitudes toward companies' social media engagement changed during the war in Ukraine in 2022, as they began to expect companies to openly address social and political issues and share their views on the actions of the Russian state. Social media users also demanded that brands withdraw from the Russian market and show their support for Ukraine through their engagement with companies on social media (Research question 3).

The results from the survey confirm the actions observed in the social media review. When a company decided to leave the Russian market, it was generally viewed positively. Respondents mostly commended such decisions. However, on the other hand, if a company chose not to leave the Russian market, it faced negative feedback from social media users. This observation was also supported by the data from the study.

Brand management during a war crisis is strongly related to management on social media during a crisis [5]. Social media crisis management involves taking steps to mitigate the negative impact of a crisis on companies' reputation and relationships with stakeholders and has the following managerial implications [21]. First, brand management during a crisis involves monitoring social media platforms. Keeping an eye on social media platforms is crucial for identifying and responding to potential crisis situations [9]. Social media monitoring tools can be used to track mentions of a brand and alert individuals to any negative or potentially crisis-causing content. This allows the brand to assess the situation and take appropriate action quickly.

Second, the response needs to be made quickly. When a crisis arises, it is important to respond quickly to mitigate any negative impact on the brand's reputation. This helps to demonstrate that the brand is at the top of the situation and is taking it seriously. A timely response also allows us to provide information and address any concerns that stakeholders may have [53]. Third, communication needs to be transparent. In a crisis situation, it is important to be open and transparent in brand communication. This helps to build trust with stakeholders and shows that brand is taking responsibility for the situation. A brand would like to avoid trying to hide or downplay the issue, as this can often do more harm than good [36].

Fourth, if appropriate, it can be helpful to offer solutions or take steps to resolve the crisis. This finding shows that a brand is actively working to address an issue and helps to demonstrate its commitment to solving problems. It may also help to reassure stakeholders that the brand is taking the situation seriously and is working to fix it [54]. The fifth way is to use social media to improve brands' advantages. Social media can be a powerful tool for crisis management, as it allows brands to quickly and easily communicate with a large audience. Brands could use these tools to share updates and information about the crisis as well as to provide support to stakeholders. A brand can also use social media to address any concerns or questions that stakeholders may have [43]. Sixth, it is important to have a crisis management plan in place before a crisis occurs. This approach will help brands respond more effectively and efficiently when a crisis does arise. A crisis management plan should outline the steps that a brand will take to identify and respond to a crisis, as well as the resources and personnel brand needed to manage the situation effectively [38].

6 Conclusions

This research has shown that the start of the war in Ukraine in 2022 significantly impacted the way that brands managed their social media presence and interacted with their customers. Companies that had previously not shared their social or political views on social media were required to take a side in the conflict and faced criticism from consumers if they did not support Ukraine. Consumers began to expect brands to openly address social and political issues and demanded that companies show support for Ukraine or withdraw from the Russian market. This led to a decrease in advertising on social media, as well as a suspension of business by some companies. However, there were also companies that remained active on social media and sought to address the war crisis through actions such as aid campaigns and money collections. The war in Ukraine ultimately changed the way that brands communicated with their customers and conducted their social media activities.

There are several limitations to consider. The first is the time period. The study focuses on events that occurred in 2022, which may not be representative of the current state of social media and brand management. The second is geographical scope. The study focuses on the impact of the war in Ukraine on social media and brand management, which may not be applicable to other countries or regions. The third is the causal relationship. The study suggested that the start of the war in Ukraine caused changes in the way brands managed their social media presence, but it is not clear if this was the only factor that contributed to these changes. Other factors, such as changes in consumer behavior or the adoption of new social media platforms, may also have played a role. The fourth group includes data sources. The study relies on data from social media platforms such as Facebook, Instagram, and Twitter, which may not be representative of the entire population or all social media activity. The fifth factor is the sample size. The study does not specify the sample size of the companies analyzed, so it is not clear how representative the findings are of all companies that were active on social media during the war in Ukraine. Finally, the study is focused on the specific context of the war in Ukraine, so it is not clear how applicable the findings are to other situations or contexts.

Future research could explore the long-term effects of the war in Ukraine on brand management on social media. It would also be interesting to compare the responses of different types of companies to the war conflict and how their social media strategies were impacted. Additionally, further research could examine the impact of other significant global events on the way that brands use social media to communicate with their customers.

References

1. Abay, K.A., et al.: The Russia-Ukraine war: implications for global and regional food security and potential policy responses. Glob. Food Sec. **36**, 100675 (2023). https://doi.org/10.1016/j.gfs.2023.100675
2. Abbassi, W., et al.: What makes firms vulnerable to the Russia-Ukraine crisis? J. Risk Financ. **24**(1), 24–39 (2023). https://doi.org/10.1108/JRF-05-2022-0108
3. Adekoya, O.B., et al.: Does oil connect differently with prominent assets during war? Analysis of intra-day data during the Russia-Ukraine saga. Resour. Policy **77**, 102728 (2022). https://doi.org/10.1016/j.resourpol.2022.102728
4. AdMonkey: Internauci wzywają do bojkotu firm, które nie wycofały się Rosji. Najczęściej w tym kontekście pojawia się Leroy Merlin. https://admonkey.pl/internauci-wzywaja-do-bojkotu-firm-ktore-nie-wycofaly-sie-rosji-najczesciej-w-tym-kontekscie-pojawia-sie-leroy-merlin-analiza-sentione/. Accessed 25 Nov 2022
5. Alexander, D.E.: Social media in disaster risk reduction and crisis management. Sci. Eng. Ethics **20**(3), 717–733 (2014). https://doi.org/10.1007/s11948-013-9502-z
6. Badowski, M.: Bojkot firm, które nie wycofały się z Rosji. W tym kontekście najczęściej pojawia się market budowlany Leroy Merlin. https://strefabiznesu.pl/bojkot-firm-ktore-nie-wycofaly-sie-z-rosji-w-tym-kontekscie-najczesciej-pojawia-sie-market-budowlany-leroy-merlin/ar/c3-16240353. Accessed 25 Nov 2022
7. Behnassi, M., El Haiba, M.: Implications of the Russia-Ukraine war for global food security. Nat. Hum. Behav. **6**(6), 754–755 (2022). https://doi.org/10.1038/s41562-022-01391-x
8. Bougias, A., et al.: Valuation of European firms during the Russia-Ukraine war. Econ. Lett. **218**, 110750 (2022). https://doi.org/10.1016/j.econlet.2022.110750
9. Buzoianu, C., Bîră, M.: Using social media listening in crisis communication and management: new methods and practices for looking into crises. Sustainability. **13**(23), 13015 (2021). https://doi.org/10.3390/su132313015

10. Chortane, S.G., Pandey, D.K.: Does the Russia-Ukraine war lead to currency asymmetries? A US dollar tale. J. Econ. Asymmetries **26**, e00265 (2022). https://doi.org/10.1016/j.jeca.2022.e00265
11. dlahandlu.pl: Aktywiści domagają się dymisji polskich zarządów Leroy Merlin i Auchan. https://www.dlahandlu.pl/detal-hurt/wiadomosci/aktywisci-domagaja-sie-dymisji-polskich-zarzadow-leroy-merlin-i-auchan,107660.html. Accessed 25 Nov 2022
12. Geissler, D., et al.: Russian propaganda on social media during the 2022 invasion of Ukraine. EPJ Data Sci. **12**(1), 35 (2023). https://doi.org/10.1140/epjds/s13688-023-00414-5
13. Gever, V.C., et al.: Comparing the effect of social media-based drama, music and art therapies on reduction in post-traumatic symptoms among Nigerian refugees of Russia's invasion of Ukraine. J. Pediatr. Nurs. **68**, e96–e102 (2023). https://doi.org/10.1016/j.pedn.2022.11.018
14. Golovchenko, Y.: Fighting propaganda with censorship: a study of the Ukrainian ban on Russian social media. J. Polit. **84**(2), 639–654 (2022). https://doi.org/10.1086/716949
15. Grzanka, M., Strzelecki, A.: Change of brand management in social media during the Russia-Ukraine war: findings from Poland. In: Ganzha, M. et al. (eds.) Proceedings of the 18th Conference on Computer Science and Intelligence Systems, pp. 253–258. Warsaw (2023). https://doi.org/10.15439/2023F3585
16. ING Polska: Wasza pomoc i zaangażowanie chwytają za serce! Zebraliście już ponad 5 mln zł na pomoc Ukrainie. My – zgodnie z obietnicą. https://www.facebook.com/INGPolska/photos/a.147932405240208/5395147673851962/. Accessed 01 Apr 2022
17. InPost.pl: Pomoc dla Ukrainy – transport produktów samochodami InPost. https://inpost.pl/aktualnosci-pomoc-dla-ukrainy-transport-produktow-samochodami-inpost. Accessed 25 Nov 2022
18. InPost: Wykorzystując nasze zaplecze logistyczne i flotę transportową pomagamy dostarczyć duże ilości produktów zebranych w ramach akcji i zbiórek organizowanych na. https://www.facebook.com/paczkomatkurier/posts/10159671676527999. Accessed 28 Feb 2022
19. Izzeldin, M., et al.: The impact of the Russian-Ukrainian war on global financial markets. Int. Rev. Financ. Anal. **87**, 102598 (2023). https://doi.org/10.1016/j.irfa.2023.102598
20. Jankowski, J.: Kupon -40 proc. dla osób, które chcą wesprzeć uchodźców z Ukrainy. https://www.rossmann.pl/firma/pl-pl/biuro-prasowe/informacja/kupon-40-proc-dla-osob-ktore-chca-wesprzec-uchodzcow-z-ukrainy,729051. Accessed 25 Nov 2022
21. Jin, Y., et al.: Examining the role of social media in effective crisis management. Commun. Res. **41**(1), 74–94 (2014). https://doi.org/10.1177/0093650211423918
22. Johannesson, J., Clowes, D.: Energy resources and markets - perspectives on the Russia-Ukraine War. Eur. Rev. **30**(1), 4–23 (2022). https://doi.org/10.1017/S1062798720001040
23. Kawepale: Pomoc dla Ukrainy! Za naszą granicą rozgrywa się koszmar, którego boi się każdy z nas. Dlatego szczególnie teraz jest niezwykle. https://www.instagram.com/p/CbIJXqCod-A/. Accessed 15 Mar 2022
24. El Khoury, R., et al.: Spillover analysis across FinTech, ESG, and renewable energy indices before and during the Russia-Ukraine war: international evidence. J. Int. Financ. Manag. Account. **34**(2), 279–317 (2023). https://doi.org/10.1111/jifm.12179
25. Kumari, V., et al.: Are the European union stock markets vulnerable to the Russia-Ukraine war? J. Behav. Exp. Financ. **37**, 100793 (2023). https://doi.org/10.1016/j.jbef.2023.100793
26. Kurapov, A., et al.: Toward an understanding of the Russian-Ukrainian war impact on university students and personnel. J. Loss Trauma **28**(2), 167–174 (2023). https://doi.org/10.1080/15325024.2022.2084838
27. Leroy Merlin Polska: Drodzy, jako Leroy Merlin Polska mamy wpływ na to co robimy w Polsce, dlatego nasze działania koncentrują się na pomocy. https://www.facebook.com/LeroyMerlinPolska/posts/4958165310968473/. Accessed 11 Mar 2022
28. Liadze, I., et al.: Economic costs of the Russia-Ukraine war. World Econ. **46**(4), 874–886 (2023). https://doi.org/10.1111/twec.13336

29. Lim, W.M., et al.: What is at stake in a war? A prospective evaluation of the Ukraine and Russia conflict for business and society. Glob. Bus. Organ. Excell. **41**(6), 23–36 (2022). https://doi.org/10.1002/joe.22162
30. Majerczak, P., Strzelecki, A.: Trust, media credibility, social ties, and the intention to share information towards verification in an age of fake news. Behav. Sci. (Basel) **12**(2), 51 (2022). https://doi.org/10.3390/bs12020051
31. Małkowska-Szozda, A.: Z powodu wojny firmy ograniczyły lub zmieniły aktywność w social mediach. https://www.press.pl/tresc/69789,z-powodu-wojny-firmy-ograniczyly-lub-zmienily-aktywnosc-w-social-mediach. Accessed 28 Nov 2022
32. Mhlanga, D., Ndhlovu, E.: The implications of the Russia-Ukraine War on sustainable development goals in Africa. Fudan J. Humanit. Soc. Sci. **16**(4), 435–454 (2023). https://doi.org/10.1007/s40647-023-00383-z
33. Mir, A.A.: Exploring the perceived opinion of social media users about the Ukraine-Russia conflict through the naturalistic observation of tweets. Soc. Netw. Anal. Min. **13**(1), 1–13 (2023). https://doi.org/10.1007/s13278-023-01047-2
34. Ngo, V.M., et al.: Public sentiment towards economic sanctions in the Russia-Ukraine war. Scott. J. Polit. Econ. **69**(5), 564–573 (2022). https://doi.org/10.1111/sjpe.12331
35. Pandey, D.K., Kumar, R.: Russia-Ukraine War and the global tourism sector: a 13-day tale. Curr. Issues Tour. **26**(5), 692–700 (2023). https://doi.org/10.1080/13683500.2022.2081789
36. Pfeffer, J., et al.: Understanding online firestorms: negative word-of-mouth dynamics in social media networks. J. Mark. Commun. **20**(1–2), 117–128 (2014). https://doi.org/10.1080/13527266.2013.797778
37. Piccoli, G.B., et al.: The impact of the Russian-Ukrainian war for people with chronic diseases. Nat. Rev. Nephrol. **18**(7), 411–412 (2022). https://doi.org/10.1038/s41581-022-00574-z
38. du Plessis, C.: Social media crisis communication: enhancing a discourse of renewal through dialogic content. Public Relat. Rev. **44**(5), 829–838 (2018). https://doi.org/10.1016/j.pubrev.2018.10.003
39. Plus Polska: #Plus poszerza wsparcie. Darmowy starter dla każdego, kto rejestruje się w punkcie sprzedaży na ukraiński paszport lub kartę pobytu. https://twitter.com/Plus_Polska/status/1498999195252006919. Accessed 02 Mar 2022
40. Polska Akcja Humanitarna: UKRAINA. Pomóżmy ludziom w strefie konfliktu. https://www.pah.org.pl/sos-ukraina/. Accessed 25 Nov 2022
41. Pörtner, L.M., et al.: We need a food system transformation—in the face of the Russia-Ukraine war, now more than ever. One Earth **5**(5), 470–472 (2022). https://doi.org/10.1016/j.oneear.2022.04.004
42. Ratten, V.: The Ukraine/Russia conflict: geopolitical and international business strategies. Thunderbird Int. Bus. Rev. **65**(2), 265–271 (2023). https://doi.org/10.1002/tie.22319
43. Rauschnabel, P.A., et al.: Collaborative brand attacks in social media: exploring the antecedents, characteristics, and consequences of a new form of brand crises. J. Mark. Theory Pract. **24**(4), 381–410 (2016). https://doi.org/10.1080/10696679.2016.1205452
44. Sakas, D.P., et al.: Social media strategy processes for centralized payment network firms after a war crisis outset. Processes **10**(10), 1995 (2022). https://doi.org/10.3390/pr10101995
45. Shen, F., et al.: Examining the differences between human and bot social media accounts: a case study of the Russia-Ukraine War. First Monday **28**(2) (2023). https://doi.org/10.5210/fm.v28i2.12777
46. Smart, B., et al.: #IStandWithPutin versus #IStandWithUkraine: the interaction of bots and humans in discussion of the Russia/Ukraine War. In: Hopfgartner, F., Jaidka, K., Mayr, P., Jose, J., Breitsohl, J. (eds.) Social Informatics. Lecture Notes in Computer Science, vol. 13618, pp. 34–53. Springer, Cham (2022). https://doi.org/10.1007/978-3-031-19097-1_3

47. Steffen, B., Patt, A.: A historical turning point? Early evidence on how the Russia-Ukraine war changes public support for clean energy policies. Energy Res. Soc. Sci. **91**, 102758 (2022). https://doi.org/10.1016/j.erss.2022.102758
48. Sułkowski, Ł., et al.: Perception of patriotic entrepreneurship in Poland and Ukraine. Entrep. Bus. Econ. Rev. **10**(3), 167–190 (2022). https://doi.org/10.15678/EBER.2022.100310
49. Sun, M., Zhang, C.: Comprehensive analysis of global stock market reactions to the Russia-Ukraine war. Appl. Econ. Lett. **30**(18), 2673–2680 (2023). https://doi.org/10.1080/13504851.2022.2103077
50. Talabi, F.O., et al.: The use of social media storytelling for help-seeking and help-receiving among Nigerian refugees of the Ukraine-Russia war. Telemat. Inform. **71**, 101836 (2022). https://doi.org/10.1016/j.tele.2022.101836
51. Tao, W., Peng, Y.: Differentiation and unity: a cross-platform comparison analysis of online posts' semantics of the Russian-Ukrainian War based on Weibo and Twitter. Commun. Publ. **8**(2), 105–124 (2023). https://doi.org/10.1177/20570473231165563
52. Umar, M., et al.: Impact of Russian-Ukraine war on clean energy, conventional energy, and metal markets: evidence from event study approach. Resour. Policy **79**, 102966 (2022). https://doi.org/10.1016/j.resourpol.2022.102966
53. Veil, S.R., et al.: A Work-in-process literature review: incorporating social media in risk and crisis communication. J. Contingencies Cris. Manag. **19**(2), 110–122 (2011). https://doi.org/10.1111/j.1468-5973.2011.00639.x
54. Wang, Y., Laufer, D.: How does crisis management in China differ from the West?: A review of the literature and directions for future research. J. Int. Manag. **26**(1), 100708 (2020). https://doi.org/10.1016/j.intman.2019.100708
55. Wirtualna Polska: VPolshchi.pl - nowy serwis WP specjalnie dla Ukraińców. https://wiadomosci.wp.pl/vpolshchi-pl-nowy-serwis-wp-specjalnie-dla-ukraincow-6741912413551104a. Accessed 27 Feb 2022
56. Wirtualnemedia.pl: Netto, Rossmann, Stokrotka, Polomarket i Topaz wycofują rosyjskie produkty ze swoich sklepów. https://www.wirtualnemedia.pl/artykul/bojkot-rosyjskich-produktow-sklepy-wycofuja-netto-rossmann-stokrotka-polomarket-topaz. Accessed 25 Nov 2022
57. Wirtualnemedia.pl: Prawie 900 tysięcy postów w social mediach o pomocy Ukrainie. https://www.wirtualnemedia.pl/artykul/prawie-900-tysiecy-postow-w-social-mediach-o-pomocy-ukrainie. Accessed 25 Nov 2022
58. Xu, W., et al.: Mental health symptoms and coping strategies among Ukrainians during the Russia-Ukraine war in March 2022. Int. J. Soc. Psychiatry **69**(4), 957–966 (2023). https://doi.org/10.1177/00207640221143919
59. Zhou, X.Y., et al.: Influence of Russia-Ukraine War on the global energy and food security. Resour. Conserv. Recycl. **188**, 106657 (2023). https://doi.org/10.1016/j.resconrec.2022.106657

Opportunities and Obstacles of Using Gamification in the Recruiting Process

Jasmin Zerrer, Ralf Christian Härting[✉] [iD], and Maren Gerst

Aalen University of Applied Sciences, Aalen, Germany
{jasmin.zerrer,maren.gerst}@kmu-aalen.de,
ralf.haerting@hs-aalen.de

Abstract. Digitalization is transforming the world of work completely. With the evolution of the recruitment process in the digital era, organizations are increasingly embracing innovative strategies to attract and engage candidates effectively. A suitable tool for this purpose is the use of Gamification. Gamification focuses primarily on generation Y and Z, because they grew up in the age of digitalization. This study uses a qualitative empirical research approach according to Mayring and is based on a detailed literature review. The research design relies on expert interviews with Human Resource (HR) professionals who provide insights into the practical implications of integrating Gamification into the recruitment process. Companies that implement Gamification benefit from an improvement in employer attractiveness, an increase in applicant quality and the optimization of processes to achieve higher efficiency. At the same time, the implementation of Gamification is associated with a number of obstacles. The requirements for digitization and data protection are becoming more complex for companies. In addition, Gamification can be particularly off-putting for older applicants, making it difficult to define a suitable target group. This study delves into the multifaceted realm of Gamification within the recruiting landscape, investigating its opportunities and obstacles amid the ongoing wave of digitalization. The collected data generated through interviews will be analyzed and evaluated. Based on the results, eleven hypothesis concerning the positive and negative influences of Gamification in recruitment are derived.

Keywords: Gamification · Digitalization · Recruiting · Recruiting Process · Potentials · Obstacles · Qualitative Study · Literature Review · Expert Interviews

1 Introduction

Wrong decisions in the recruiting process can cause excessive costs for companies. For this reason, it is necessary to introduce a process that efficiently selects suitable candidates. To achieve this, recruiters can use different tools and methods. One relatively new tool, which is not very advanced, especially in German companies, is the use of Gamification. Playing games in a business context is still fairly new. Especially, the use of Gamification in Recruiting is still unfamiliar to many companies [2]. In general, the recruitment process is about identifying and classifying the potential of human resources

E. Ziemba et al. (Eds.): FedCSIS-ITBS 2023/ISM 2023, LNBIP 504, pp. 242–260, 2024.
https://doi.org/10.1007/978-3-031-61657-0_12

for hiring staff and using this knowledge in an effective way [6]. Recruiting is a continuous process and is divided into five phases: Planning human resources, defining the strategy, evaluating recruitment sources, implementing recruitment methods and strategies, as well as feedback and monitoring. The objective is to identify and select the most suitable candidates for the advertised job position. A well-planned and well-structured recruitment process is essential for a company to acquire high-quality applicants [19]. Also, large organizations such as PwC, Google, L'Oréal, the US Army and the British Intelligence Service already utilize gamified tools [1]. The current literature does not contain any research studies that have dealt intensively with the different opportunities and obstacles of Gamification, especially in the process of recruiting. This qualitative study is intended to formulate hypotheses that will be verified in a quantitative study in the next step. The aim is to close the research gap in the current literature. First a literature review is conducted to explain the concept and present Gamification as a recruiting tool. The potential target group is identified as well as the benefits and challenges that have been summarized from the literature. It is followed by a detailed description of the methodology and the findings of the research study. Finally, the study results have been compared and discussed with the findings from the literature research.

2 Literature Review

Playing is exciting, motivating and has a positive effect on teamwork. Playing is an essential part of human nature and has become a growing trend in society. Game elements, consciously and unconsciously, accompany people's private and working environments. They primarily aim to increase the motivation for a variety of activities in order to maximize the quantity and quality of the corresponding activity's output [18]. The research question has not been answered exactly in the literature until now. Only a small number of studies can be used to derive possible benefits and challenges, which are described in the literature research.

2.1 Concept of Gamification

Gamification is one of the most significant developments of the 21st century and includes new technological developments such as big data, robotics, artificial intelligence and advances in computing [9]. But until now, there is still no standardized definition that describes the term Gamification universally. Different opinions exist regarding the meaning of this term. For the first time, the term "Gamification" was used by several players at the end of 2010. Today, the definition is still very controversial, and many game designers and user experience designers utilize alternative terms such as "Gameful Design" or "Gamefulness" [3]. The definition by Deterding is currently the most popular one, because it describes Gamification as the use of game design elements in a non-game context [4]. Huotari and Hamari (2012) disagree with Deterding's definition, as they believe that the focus should be more on the user's experience. They describe Gamification as a process in which opportunities for playful experiences are added to a service in order to support the overall value creation of users [10]. Werbach (2014) redefines Gamification as a process that makes activities more game-like. According to this definition, it is not necessary to define a point where the designed system transitions into Gamification, such as in Deterding's definition [20]. Seaborn and Fels (2015) understand Gamification as the selective integration of gaming elements into an interactive system without a finished game as a product. For this reason, it is not possible to determine whether a particular empirical system is just a gamified application or only a game without referring to the intentions of the designers or the experiences and actions of the players [4, 5]. In the context of this research, the definition of Deterding is used, as it is the most widespread term, and the recruiting process involves the use of game design elements in a non-game context.

2.2 Gamification as a Digital Recruiting Tool

Due to the close connection between Gamification and recruiting, the term "Recrutainment" has emerged, which is frequently mentioned in the literature. Recrutainment refers to the fusion of cognitive assessment methods, aptitude assessment and gamification elements, which are integrated into a company's recruiting process [14]. Gamification is used to make job interviews more engaging, interactive and successful. This automated method is used in practice to evaluate an applicant on a comprehensive level and assess their ability to perform the required job role in the required manner [16]. The concept of Gamification is an interaction between psychology and user experience design [6]. The idea behind this is to create a game-based solution that has several challenges that are relevant to the vacant job position. For this reason, the recruitment game must give a realistic impression of the position type and the pre-selection process [16]. Special game techniques are used to increase the engagement and enjoyment of employees in a specific game environment. The mechanisms used are directly linked to the availability of a specific reward. For example, if the players complete a task in a limited time, they receive a reward depending on the level of difficulty. This makes Gamification an effective tool for influencing and motivating potential job candidates [7]. Employees' basic needs are addressed through the use of Gamification, such as receiving a reward, the desire for success, striving for superiority in competitions, or projecting a certain self-image and increasing their own popularity [12]. Gamified (online) assessments are one possibility for personnel selection. In a gamified assessment, applicants are exposed to a game-like environment or a virtual world. The virtual world can look like a real working environment, and the employees can be represented by avatars. In this way, job-relevant behaviors are triggered in situations that could also occur in a real workplace. Gamified assessments or Serious Games do not necessarily have to represent a realistic, work-related scenario. Gamification can be integrated into the recruitment process in two ways: Either as a one-to-one assessment of employees or as an extension of existing situational tests by adding game elements. By integrating game elements into the selection process, it is possible to reduce cheating to improve the quality of the information provided by applicants and the predictability of job performance. At the same time, transparency, fun and interaction are encouraged [23]. In addition, the game elements can be integrated into psychometric tests, to test situational awareness and to better assess the soft skills of applicants [13].

2.3 Potential Target Groups of Gamified Recruiting Processes

Based on their knowledge of advanced technologies and computer skills, people can be classified into specific generations. On the one hand, there are the "Baby Boomers". This generation includes everybody born between 1946 and 1964. Generation X was born between 1964 and 1976, and Generation Y between 1977 and 1994. Generation Z consists of all those born since 1995 [22] and is also known as "Digital Natives". They represent the first generation that grew up completely with digitalization. From an early age, this generation played on their parents' smartphones and notebooks. Dealing with digital media and technology is a normal part of their daily lives. The previous Generation Y, on the other hand, only came into contact with new technologies in their childhood or adolescence. But they were able to acquire media skills through the development of social networks like Facebook. Both generations are clearly different in their communication behavior. While the communication of Generation Z is more online, the communication of Generation Y is a mixture of online and in-person [21]. However, both generations like to use modern technologies and spend a lot of time on social networks. In that context Gamification might be a promising recruiting strategy for this target group. It can attract numerous potential applicants to the company [17]. Many companies face with the issue that they still using recruitment methods specific to Generation X and Generation Y. These methods mainly include personality tests, tests of logical thinking, attitude tests and mental capabilities, as well as a personal interview. These recruitment measures are no longer up to date for Generation Z. This means that the HR department will have to deal more and more with new recruiting tools in the future [22].

2.4 Benefits and Challenges of Gamification

The most important role of the recruiter is to identify talents and ensure that the candidate's skills match closely with the company's requirements and culture. The use of Gamification during the recruitment process has several benefits [11]. Gamified recruiting tools can help to increase the attractiveness of the application process and the company itself for potential candidates. The aim is also to win more younger applicants and, at the same time, achieve better candidate results. In this way, the applicants who fit best into the company environment can be selected [14]. For candidates from Generation Y and Z in particular, it is an exciting opportunity to show their skills [22]. The competition within the game keeps applicants hungry for more and motivated to achieve the maximum score/reward in the game to quickly reach the next level. Gamification allows companies to attract and engage a variety of applicants, in addition to other types of recruitment. From an HR perspective, evaluating the skills and qualifications of a large talent pool after the game is a possibility to select only the best ones who have successfully shown their suitability and value to the organization [10]. The use of Gamification also allows the company to test specific skills and competences, such as time management, creativity and innovative thinking, before a hiring decision is made. In this way, unsuitable applicants can be easily identified at the initial stage, which can speed up the whole recruiting process. Companies benefit from being able to predict an applicant's potential performance in the intended position using a gamified personnel selection tool. In contrast to other recruiting methods, such as traditional personality tests, Gamification allows for more targeted statements about the personality and behavior of a potential candidate. With traditional personality tests, there is a high probability that candidates will change their behavior by giving suitable answers to the recruiters' questions. Game elements and virtual games make it more difficult for applicants to fake or embellish their behavior in the recruiting process. This improves the authenticity of the test participants and contributes to a more reliable prediction of potential job performance [8]. A challenge is that Gamification is perhaps only a short-term trend. Gamification opponents argue that it is also pointless to turn everything into a game. The tricky thing is that a reward system like Gamification initially promises to increase engagement. In the short term, this is true. In the long term, employees will only conduct a certain activity because of the reward. While people do lots of things voluntarily and out of their own motivation, companies use Gamification to control intrinsically motivated behavior with extrinsic rewards. This only achieves the opposite. The Extrinsic incentives cause intrinsic motivation to be undermined, and activities are only carried out because of potential rewards and not out of real interest in the company [23]. Another obstacle is that Gamification addresses a specific target group. For generations like the "Baby Boomers", this type of recruiting process is a rather challenging experience that discourages them from participating [22].

The opportunities and obstacles identified during the literature research are presented within the framework in Fig. 1.

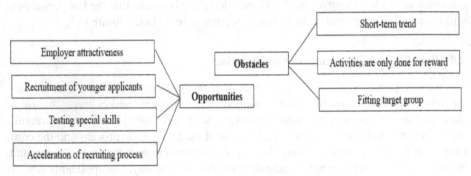

Fig. 1. Framework based on Literature Review.

3   Research Methodology

This empirical investigation is based on a qualitative research design (see Fig. 2). The literature research has shown that there are less specific research works on the benefits and obstacles of Gamification in recruiting for applicants and companies. Only publications on Gamification in general or in relation to the field of Human Resources have been published. Because the topic plays, an important role, especially in today's age of digitalization, this study aims to close this gap. Semi-structured expert interviews were conducted to collect relevant data. These data were transcribed and coded using the software MAXQDA. This allowed the development of hypothesis and the derivation of a hypothesis model. The creation of the hypothesis model forms the framework for subsequent quantitative research, in which the hypotheses can be verified. The results were interpreted and discussed with the findings from the literature review.

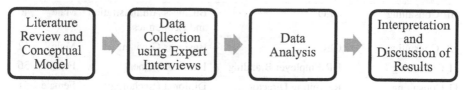

Fig. 2. Research Design.

3.1 Data Collection

Using the knowledge gained from the literature research, expert interviews are used for the data collection. First, it is explained how the target group was defined, and an overview of all interview participants is given. After that, the structure of the questionnaire is explained in more detail. In order to avoid overlaps and errors, two pre-tests were carried out before the interviews started. Afterward, the steps for acquiring participants and conducting expert interviews are described in more detail (see Fig. 3).

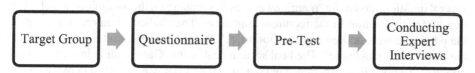

Fig. 3. Process of Data Collection.

The target group for the interviews includes HR experts which have already implemented Gamification in their recruiting process and HR Consultants, who are offering Gamification solutions for recruiting processes. Participants from different functional domains were interviewed to attain a more comprehensive understanding of the situation and to mitigate individual biases. The survey was limited to German companies, and in total, 11 semi-structured interviews were conducted. The participants in this study consist of five female and six male interviewees. They were between 36 and 55 years old and had an average of five years of experience with Gamification. The following Table 1 gives a summary of all interview participants.

The questionnaire consists of 33 questions, which have been divided into five categories. Because the literature research did not provide any specific findings about the benefits and obstacles of using Gamification in the recruiting process, the questions were formulated in a way that the experts could answer as openly and freely as possible in order to obtain the maximum amount of relevant information.

During the first section of the interview, the experts answered demographic questions such as gender, age, academic background and some questions about the company. In

Table 1. Overview of Interview Participants.

Industry Sector	Professional Field	Academic Background	Gender	Age
HR Consulting	CEO Managing Director	Business Administration	Male	49
HR Consulting	CEO	Business Administration and Economics	Male	40
HR Consulting	CEO	Business Graduate	Male	52
IT Consulting	HR Employer Branding	Int. Management	Female	36
IT Consulting	Recruiting Director	Diploma Psychology	Female	51
IT Consulting	HR Employer Branding	Business Administration	Female	55
Transport/ Logistics	Head of Recruiting	Diploma Psychology	Female	47
Industrial Solutions	Head of int. Recruiting	Int. Recruiting	Male	36
Automotive	Director HR for USA and EU	Business Economist	Male	36
Consumer Goods	CEO	Business Administration	Male	36
Construction Industry	Head of HR	Management	Female	37

the second section, they were asked about the "status of digitalization" in their company in general and then specifically about the recruitment process. The third section contains several questions about the "recruiting process", focusing on the area of personnel selection and digitalization in the recruitment process. The challenges in recruiting during the pandemic were addressed in section four "Changes in the recruiting process due to the coronavirus pandemic". The final section dealt with "Gamification in the recruiting process". The practical experience of Gamification in HR was surveyed here. The questionnaire was developed to identify important framework conditions for the introduction of Gamification, as well as possible opportunities and obstacles. Before the questionnaire was sent out to the participants, a pre-test was carried out to check the comprehensibility of the questions and eliminate overlaps in content. The pre-test proved to be successful, so no subsequent adjustments had to be made to the questionnaire. The data collection took place from January 2022 to February 2022. LinkedIn was used to acquire participants. The response rate was very low. Only 11 out of 134 contacted experts agreed to be interviewed. This shows that the topic of Gamification is currently rarely implemented, especially in small and medium-sized companies, as not many enterprises are familiar with this new type of recruitment. Through their participation in the interview, the experts wanted to contribute to advancing research in this area. The questionnaire was sent out a few days before the interview to give the participants the possibility to prepare themselves. For the interviews, the experts were interviewed via the platform Zoom and digitally recorded. The duration of the interviews was between 40 and 75 min. The answers were later transcribed, coded and analyzed in the original German language.

3.2 Data Analysis

After the data collection was completed, an analysis of the gathered data was carried out in order to present the results using a hypothesis model. The recorded audio files were transcribed using the MAXQDA transcription program. MAXQDA is a supporting software program for qualitative research that is especially well suited for the transcription and analysis of interviews. During the transcription, care was taken to make sure that all personal data were completely anonymized. The transcription was done in the original German language. Only non-verbal speech elements were omitted. Ambiguous passages, e.g., due to background noises, were eliminated, and the existing dialect was translated into the written German language. After transcribing the semi-structured interviews, the data was analyzed using Mayring's coding method for building inductive categories.

The coding process was divided into five steps. At the beginning, all transcripts were reviewed one after the other, and statements were paraphrased. Codes and subcodes were defined and then assigned to the respective text sections. If a text section could not be assigned to any of the existing codes, a new code was created. In this way, the codes were expanded step by step. After the first four transcripts were coded, the first reduction process took place, in which the existing codes were combined into categories. After that, the coding process was completed, and the second reduction process started after the last transcript. This involved checking again whether any codes could be combined into categories. Finally, the category system was checked again. This includes testing the initial source material and verifying whether the established category system suitably reflects what the interviewees stated during the interviews (see Fig. 4).

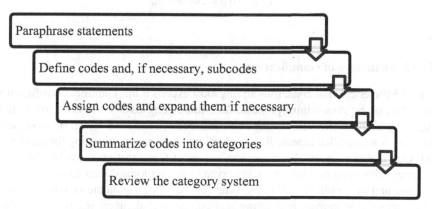

Fig. 4. Coding process for creating inductive categories.

A total of 525 codes were generated from all 11 interviews. These codes were summarized in the last step of coding into 473 codes. The generated code segments were used to present and describe the results. In addition, the codes are also used to underline important statements from the interviews with meaningful citations.

4 Research Findings

Consistently following the coding process, the identified codes have been grouped into 11 categories. Five categories represent the opportunities, and six categories represent the challenges of Gamification in the recruiting process. The results are illustrated in a hypothesis model (see Fig. 5).

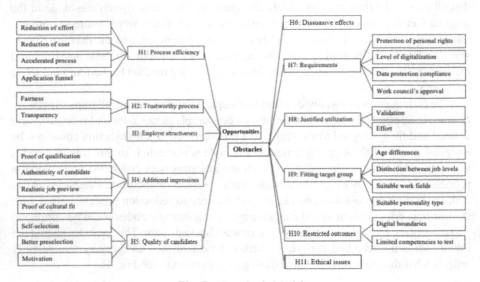

Fig. 5. Hypothesis Model.

4.1 Opportunities of Gamification

Process Efficiency. The consensus among most experts is that Gamification offers time-saving benefits by streamlining processes and automating tasks more efficiently. Initially, integrating Gamification into recruitment may require additional effort. However, as the same positions are filled repeatedly, standardization occurs, minimizing the extra work-load. One expert suggests that the effectiveness of Gamification is evident in process efficiency. This effectiveness can be observed over a prolonged interaction between the company and the applicant, allowing time for assessing candidate suitability without undue pressure. Moreover, integrating real-company challenges into the game allows applicants to demonstrate problem-solving skills. Utilizing tools such as Gamification to target large groups of applicants with similar profiles can result in a cost reduction. The adoption of Gamification in mass processes with scaling potential pays off quickly. In this scenario, recruiting costs are reduced as the involvement of managers or special-ists is not necessary anymore. Additionally, gamified approaches can help minimize the subsequent costs associated with hiring mistakes. Gamification has an accelerating effect due to standardization and automation. Some experts stated that a faster decision-making contributes to this. Additionally, the feature of pre-selection accelerates the process as well. According to the interviews, Gamification serves the purpose of an application funnel. In mass applications, performance diagnostics lead to a faster preselection. The company can provide certain answers to the applicants to prioritize more effectively which candidates are invited for a personal interview. Mostly, it saves the companies from screening many application documents as well as conducting unnecessary interviews. Gamification in recruiting involves standardization, automatization, and more effective preselection. As a result, companies can design their recruiting processes more efficiently.

H1: Gamification has a positive impact on process efficiency in the recruiting process.

Trustworthy Process. Since Gamification is the packaging of suitability diagnostics, it provides a more objective basis for evaluation. Nearly every expert stated that fairness is included in the consideration of applicants by lowering recruiting bias. The fact that each applicant knows they must overcome a hurdle increases fairness. Competencies are captured in a way that ensures equal opportunities. Most experts agreed that Gamification provides transparency in recruiting, because of its objectivity. This is most evident in the applicant's qualifications and performance. Therefore, the results achieve transparency in the decision-making process. However, many experts have stated, that transparency only exists when there is enough data from which to draw comparisons. To ensure transparency on the applicant side, a report is required, which includes information about the skills, the selection criteria and the progress achieved. Another requirement is a clear communication about the process flow. Gamification in recruiting involves objectivity through transparent qualifications and performance. The exclusion of recruiting bias ensures fairness.

H2: Gamification has a positive impact on a trustworthy process in the recruiting process.

Employer Attractiveness. The consensus among most experts is that Gamification contributes to enhancing the company's image. Currently, it provides an opportunity to differentiate oneself from competitors through innovation. This allows the company to position itself as a forward-thinking digital employer, thereby increasing motivation among prospective employees. The interactive nature of gamified tasks creates a candidate experience that positively impacts potential applicants. Furthermore, the targeted approach of gamified assessments appeals to specific demographic groups, serving as a marketing tool to attract a larger pool of applicants. Introducing Gamification in recruiting creates a candidate experience and digital presence that strengthens employer branding.

H3: Gamification has a positive impact on employer attractiveness in the recruiting process.

Additional Impressions. One opportunity of Gamification is the proof of certain qualifications. Most interviewees agreed that different competencies can be verified, dependent on the adaptation of the gamified assessment. In this context, stated competencies can be compared with those that actually exist. Furthermore, gamified assessments are also suitable for identifying the cultural fit and competence for a job. Regarding the action behavior, concentration and attention span can be evaluated, which allows conclusions about the psychological security of the applicant. Regardless of oral expression, the results showed that additional skills and hidden talents can be captured. The applicant' skills are presented in a separate way. Gamification creates immersive situations that engage the capacities of the brain. The applicant has no time to think, but must act spontaneously. The gamified tasks provide information about the action competence as well as personality traits. Overall, the behavior of the applicant is more significant. In the interviews, there is an agreement that Gamification provides the packaging for a realistic job preview. The use of virtual reality in the presentation of the job offers a realistic self-assessment for the applicant. Gamification promotes the accuracy of expectations by experiencing and assessing a workday. The applicant is assured of the job requirements, the workplace and the company's products. Most experts claim that Gamification significantly minimizes the risk of termination after hiring. The interviewees mentioned that Gamification could be used to identify the cultural fit of the applicant. At the same time, the candidate gets the chance to assess the company environment. The organization can derive the cultural characteristics from the employer value proposition and prove them. Furthermore, Gamification is also capable of splitting the cultural fit into subcultures with the required team competencies for singular target groups. Companies can implement Gamification in recruiting to test certain qualifications and offer a realistic job preview in advance.

H4: Gamification has a positive impact on additional impressions in the recruiting process.

Quality of Applicants. The use of Gamification in self-assessment is most effective. The risk of making the wrong decision is reduced for the company and the applicant. Therefore, the majority of interviewees favor Gamification in career orientation to show the applicant which job is suitable. In addition, there is clarity of expectation, because the applicant actively engages with the job. The transparency of the required skills encourages self-selection. The findings show that Gamification is especially suitable at the beginning of the recruiting process. In the sense of pre-selection, it can be applied as early as the job advertisement. As a result, only those who are suitable for the job will apply. Experts agree that Gamification can filter out qualifications in advance. A certain level of qualification is assumed, and if job candidates do not reach it, they are not considered further. A more efficient pre-selection is achieved since the skills do not have to be tested again later. Gamification is an authentic self-assessment, which leads to dropouts and thus to a better pre-selection. The experts mentioned that Gamification increases the motivation through various factors. When used as a marketing tool, it increases motivation to apply. Furthermore, motivation is increased through active engagement in the game. The gamified journey increases appreciation because the applicant has to make an effort and is confronted with new challenges. Motivation is also achieved through a target-group-oriented approach. Due to the attractive design of the gamified elements, applicants go through a candidate experience that offers active testing and benchmarks. All interviewees agree that candidate experience motivates the applicants' motivation to work for the company. The application of Gamification in recruiting offers clarity to expectations and authentic self-assessment. Hence, wrong decisions are reduced.

H5: Gamification has a positive impact on the quality of applicants in the recruiting process.

4.2 Obstacles of Gamification

Dissuasive Effects. A shared concern for all interviewees was possible dropouts by suitable candidates due to gamified elements implemented in a recruiting process. Therefore, Gamification could have a considerable dissuasive effect on candidates. In this context, it was frequently stated that Gamification constitutes as an additional hurdle for candidates, and there might be a limited willingness to put that additional effort into a recruiting process. In consideration of the ongoing shortage of specialists in some work fields, the point is made that the risk of losing suitable candidates due to additional hurdles to competing companies with less extensive recruiting processes, might be too high for some companies and therefore further hampers the use of Gamification in recruiting. Moreover, it is mentioned that there are some reservations from candidates regarding the scientific respectability of gamified elements in recruiting, and their reflection on the overall company could consequently present a deterrent effect for some candidates. In addition to that, it is mentioned that some dropouts might also be related to a fear of failing the gamified elements. The level of personality that especially comes with digital Gamification could result in candidates feeling unappreciated and, as a result, dropping out of the process. The challenge, presenting itself, might be finding a balance in Gamification that does not have a dissuasive effect on the recruiting process.

H6: Dissuasive effects have a negative impact on Gamification in the recruiting process.

Requirements. Almost all interviewees agree that data protection regulations result in a high level of requirements for Gamification in recruiting. Only one interviewee states that data protection regulations need to be met in any recruiting process, and the implementation of Gamification does not add additional requirements towards data protection regulations. However, data protection regulations require clear communication with the candidates as well as communication with colleagues from intertwined departments. Within the scope of international recruiting processes, it is mentioned that it might be especially challenging since data protection regulations vary between countries. Many interviewees state that a certain level of digitalization is required for implementing Gamification in the recruiting process. Moreover, one interviewee states that the pressure of digitalization might even be the reason that Gamification receives increasing popularity in recruiting. The level of digitalization required is also imperative for integrating the collected data into existing systems and its further used in building a talent pool. Furthermore, it is vital to have automated processes in place to efficiently manage the high number of candidates taking part in a gamified recruiting process. For this reason, a certain degree of digitization is required to ensure success. In addition to that, all interviews have stated that Gamification in recruiting always requires personal rights. Consequently, a gamified recruiting process is required to always uphold personal rights policies, including clear communication with candidates. In German companies, the implementation of gamified elements in a recruiting process requires the approval of the work council. Whereas some interviewees suspect that this does not represent an additional challenge, more interviewees pointed out the opposite. Some more conservative companies might be especially wary of all things regarding digital processes, including Gamification. To receive the approval of the work council, it has been mentioned that the work council should be involved early in the decision-making process, and the idea needs to be presented deliberately and cautiously, taking possible negative attitudes into consideration. Because of these conditions, one interviewee thinks that the implementation of Gamification in recruiting might be easier in smaller companies like Startups without the additional challenge of getting the approval of the work council and a generally more open attitude towards innovation. Gamification in recruiting involves a multitude of legal, organizational and systematic requirements, particularly regarding data protection, digitalization, personal rights, and the approval of the work council. These requirements might present themselves as a challenge, that companies might not want to face, and therefore decide against Gamification in recruiting.

H7: Requirements have a negative impact on Gamification in the recruiting process.

Justified Utilization. All interviewees agree that the use of Gamification needs to be justified by valid utilization. Furthermore, most interviewees mentioned the connection between the gamified test and the future work, which validates the method of testing for the candidate. If the validation of using Gamification is not apparent, organizations must communicate the thoughts behind the implemented method to justify its use. In this context, some interviewees fear that Gamification might be used as an entertainment tool without having any actual validation or meaning. Moreover, there might not be a one-size-fits-all solution, and Gamification needs to fit the target group as well as the job field. If that is not given, using Gamification might have a negative effect on the recruiting process. In addition to that, the use of Gamification needs to reflect the organizational structure and the overall modernness of the organization. Having a modern recruiting approach with implemented Gamification elements, but a bureaucratic, outdated organizational structure, paints the wrong picture of the organization and therefore could result in a frustrated candidate. In this context, the use of Gamification is neither valid nor justified. Lastly, the quality of the gamified elements plays a part in a validated use of Gamification. Gamified elements that are of poor quality might convey the wrong image and wrong intent. These factors need to be considered to make Gamification valid and therefore, justify its implementation. All interviewees agreed that implementing Gamification into a recruiting process takes a lot of effort. In addition to time, this effort also involves excessive costs, especially in the implementation stage. There also might be more effort when Gamification is applied in regard of interface work, additional evaluation work, additional administrative efforts or additional reporting work. A shared apprehension is the justification of described high effort. Many interviewees suspect that Gamification is only worth the effort, when a certain number of candidates take part in the same process. One interviewee assumes that it is only worthwhile for bigger mid-sized enterprises or enterprises with resources to either develop themselves or buy fitting gamified elements. Although, another interviewee points out that owner-managed mid-sized enterprises might be more willing to put in that extra effort than bigger enterprises. Moreover, Gamification in recruiting might only be justifiable if it is profitable as well. Finding that limit when Gamification is justified in its effort presents a challenge for organizations. Therefore, to justify Gamification in recruiting the use needs to be valid and the effort put in needs to be reasonable for organizations.

H8: Justification of utilization has a negative impact on Gamification in the recruiting process.

Fitting Target Group. Most of the interviewees explain that Gamification might be more fitting for a younger generation of candidates. This is based on a possible higher gaming affinity of younger generations that grew up as digital natives. For the same reason, they might feel more comfortable in a digital Gamification setting than older generations would. Questioning the fit of Gamification for all job levels, most interviewees see more potential in using Gamification for recruiting junior positions, like trainees, interns or young professionals. However, it is also stated that since professionals and other higher positions also have a higher salary, it might be more economical to invest in Gamification for higher positions. Regarding the use of higher positions, it is nonetheless declared that higher levels also require a high level of Gamification quality. Furthermore, it has been mentioned that implementing Gamification for single positions, which can usually be found further up the hierarchy, is difficult. Lower levels often include more candidates and might be more suitable for Gamification from an economic viewpoint. Only a few interviewees stated that it does not depend on the job level at all. In this context, there might not be only one target group for Gamification regarding job levels, but distinctions between the levels need to be considered. Regarding the use of Gamification in different fields of work, it is mentioned multiple times that it might work best in job fields that involve a high level of numerical or technological understanding. In particular, IT is often listed as a job field with high potentials for Gamification, including jobs like data scientists or developers. However, it is mentioned that there is no distinction between academics and non-academics when using Gamification. In addition to that, it is stated that Gamification might not work as well for job fields with a high rate of repetitive work or for blue-collar workers. So, there might be only a few fields of work that fit as a target group for Gamification. Multiple text passages talk about a certain personality type that Gamification might work better for. This personality type has a preference for gaming, is motivated by gamified elements, and is likely to be found in gamers or chess players. It might further involve personality traits like performance or power orientation. Gamification can only be successful when a suitable target group is established. Companies might be challenged by finding a target group that fits for Gamification in recruiting. Age differences, distinctions between job levels, suitable fields of work, and even certain personality types need to be taken into consideration when trying to find the right target group.

H9: Target group fitting has a negative impact on Gamification in the recruiting process.

Restricted Outcomes. Gamification in recruiting usually occurs in a digital setting. In this context, it is mentioned multiple times that digital processes have boundaries that reflect Gamification. The fear is that, by losing one dimension in a digital setting, you only get limited results from digital Gamification. Next to facial expressions and gesticulations, senses could give additional insights on a candidate, might be restricted in digital settings. In addition to that, it is pointed out that a sense of chemistry might be lost and candidates might have limited insights into the workplace, leading to poor decision-making on both sides based on less information. Furthermore, technological issues could have a negative impact on a gamified recruiting process, and more innovation might be needed to assure life-like settings that do not limit the results of Gamification. Theoretically, Gamification can be used to test a variety of competencies, such as methodical, professional or social competencies. Most interviewees agree that not all these competencies can be adequately tested with gamified elements. Methodical competencies might be easier to evaluate in a gamified environment, and some potential is also seen in testing professional competencies. Especially challenging might be testing social skills in a gamified setting. High demands are placed on Gamification in order to be able to test social skills such as potential in group settings, extensive tests over a longer period of time, or working with avatars. Gamification is limited by digital settings and is unable to replace some interpersonal insights that result from more personal settings. Furthermore, Gamification might not be able to test all relevant competencies of candidates, only delivering limited results. The challenge, presenting itself, might be utilizing the potentials of Gamification within those limits.

H10: Restricted outcomes have a negative impact on Gamification in the recruiting process.

Ethical Issues. Ethical questions are discussed in all parts of business, and Gamification is no exception. Possible benefits for younger candidates in a gamified environment or implementing Gamification only for younger positions might raise issues regarding possible ageism. Another possible issue for the ethical utilization of Gamification might be accessibility for candidates with disabilities, like vision-impaired candidates. It has also been pointed out multiple times that there might be some underlying developer bias that presents unethical means. The values and attitudes of the person developing the gamified elements could be incorporated into the Gamification itself. This might be sustained by limiting courses of action within gamified elements. Furthermore, it is stated that algorithms autonomously deciding about a candidates' fate, could be prescribed as unethical. Lastly, a minimal relation to actual work assignments might also be unethical. Therefore, the challenge of implementing Gamification in recruiting is ensuring ethical utilization.

H11: Ethical issues have a negative impact on Gamification in the recruiting process.

5   Discussion of Findings

Gamification provides some opportunities as well as obstacles regarding its implementation in the recruiting processes of companies. Likewise, potential applicants can benefit from gamified recruiting processes on the one hand and, on the other hand, are facing new challenges, that must be overcome to get the offered job position. To implement Gamification successfully, it is necessary to fulfill a multitude of legal, organizational, and systematic requirements, particularly regarding data protection. Furthermore, it is essential to ensure a certain level of digitalization, which is required for implementing Gamification in the recruiting process. Implementing Gamification takes a lot of effort. In addition to time, this effort also involves high costs. To justify the effort, it must be established that gamified tests are scientifically valid and designed for a specific target group. Regarding the economical viewpoint, Gamification is appropriate for selecting candidates from many applicants. When developing gamified tests for recruiting processes, it must be ensured that underlying developer bias is excluded. As already emerged from the literature, the interviews also showed that Gamification is particularly suitable for younger applicants who have a higher affinity for games. This conclusion was also reached by J. Koivistro and J. Hamari [15]. Furthermore, the benefits of Gamification in recruiting are highly promising. Through Gamification both sides involved in the recruiting process can benefit from the added information given about the applicant and the vacant position. This leads to a better fit and a higher quality of suitable candidates, while simultaneously reducing fluctuation. In addition, this also promotes the opportunity for better self-selection by the candidates. When Gamification is already implemented in the recruiting process, even time savings can be generated, due to automated processes, accelerated decision-making and better pre-selection. If gamified tests are valid and follow a standardized process, Gamification can increase objectivity, due to the higher volume of collected data, which are considered during the evaluation. Gamification in recruiting processes can be used as a tool to increase the motivation of applicants, through active engagement of the candidates and a playful way to convey content alongside the recruiting process. The candidate experience can even lead to a higher attractiveness of the process and can have a positive effect concerning the employer branding of companies. A model of the opportunities and obstacles of Gamification in the recruiting process was developed, based on empirical data from German-speaking experts using the content analysis method, according to Mayring. The generated data show some important influencing factors like process efficiency, data protection, target groups, expenditure of cost and time, as well as the quality of applicants. Experts in the HR and Gamification environments have mentioned all of these factors repeatedly. Therefore, they can be considered as a good basis for the model. To extend the current scientific view of opportunities and obstacles of Gamification in recruiting, current researchers can use these results additionally. Comparing the hypothesis model from the expert interviews with the framework from the literature research, it can be clearly seen that the research on this topic was very limited. But in this empirical study, a comprehensive model was developed that includes the constructs from the framework identified at the beginning. Companies can benefit from this research by evaluating their level of digitalization and their personal fit for Gamification in their recruiting processes. Furthermore, this model can help to identify potential applicants based on their specific requirements and individual target groups. Besides looking at the opportunities of Gamification, this research demonstrates equally challenging aspects of Gamification, which can have a negative impact on the recruiting processes of companies.

6 Conclusion

First it can be determined that there are also obstacles for using Gamification in recruiting. It depends on the individual circumstances of a company whether Gamification is suitable and worthwhile, because not all professional groups and company sizes are well suited for this tool. Smaller companies, which have problems attracting employees due to high employee fluctuation, will not use Gamification to screen potential job applicants. The integration into the recruiting process is also associated with certain costs and efforts. Gamification will probably become more and more established in medium-sized and bigger companies in the next few years. Finally, it can be said that neither the opportunities nor the obstacles dominate. Opportunities for a company arise from an accelerated, more cost-effective and trustworthy process, a higher attractiveness of the company to candidates, additional impressions about applicants that would not be possible through a normal job interview and a higher quality of applicants. Obstacles include deterrent effects, especially for older applicants who are not familiar with technology, the high requirements for data protection and digitalization in the company, and justified utilization. Furthermore, it is difficult to address the right target group. There is the problem of ethical issues, and there are restricted outcomes.

This study will help companies that already use Gamification in their recruiting process to better understand and avoid obstacles. It is also intended to motivate companies that have not yet used gamification to integrate this tool into their recruiting process and offer an attractive application process for a younger target group. At the same time, the digitalization of the recruiting process enables companies to reduce costs for time- and cost-intensive standard tests. Gamification developers are given the opportunity to further optimize the tool based on the findings.

As this qualitative research focuses on a limited sample of experts, it is important to acknowledge certain limitations in this study. It is evident that not all German-speaking experts from different countries were included. The sample encompassed a range of perspectives from experts across different industries to ensure the reliability of the gathered information. Nevertheless, to validate this qualitative method utilizing Mayring's approach, a model validation using a representative quantitative method is necessary. The influencing factors identified in this study could serve as a suitable starting point for such validation. Expanding the evaluation of this model across multiple countries and exploring various aspects would present an excellent opportunity for future research. Within this framework, conducting a detailed investigation of individual German-speaking states and comparing German-speaking countries with others in the EU or internationally would be particularly interesting. In addition, only applicants from the Generation Z target group can be asked about the advantages and obstacles of gamification from an applicant's perspective.

References

1. Buil, I., Catalán, S., Martínez, E.: Understanding applicants' reactions to gamified recruitment. J. Bus. Res. **110**, 41–50 (2020). https://doi.org/10.1016/j.jbusres.2019.12.041

2. Clements, A.J., Ahmed, S., Henderson, B.: Student experience of gamified learning: a qualitative approach. In: Pivec, M., Gründler, J. (eds.) 11th European Conference on Game-Based Learning, pp. 88–94. ACPI (2017). ISBN 9781911218562
3. Dale, S.: Gamification: making work fun, or making fun of work? Bus. Inf. Rev. **31**(2), 82–90 (2014). https://doi.org/10.1177/0266382114538350
4. Deterding, S., et al.: From game design elements to gracefulness: defining ‚gamification. In: Proceedings of the 15th International Academic Mind Trek Conference: Envisioning Future Media Environments, Association for Computing Machinery, New York, USA, pp. 9–15 (2011). https://doi.org/10.1145/2181037.2181040
5. Deterding, S.: Gamification: designing for motivation **19**(4), 14–17 (2012). https://doi.org/10.1145/2212877.2212883
6. Durai, P.: Human Resource Management. Pearson Education India (2010). ISBN 9788131752814
7. Ērgle, D., Ludviga, I.: Use of gamification in human resource management: impact on engagement and satisfaction. In: 10th International Scientific Conference, Business and Management, Lithuania (2018). https://doi.org/10.3846/BM.2018.45
8. Gibson, D., Jakl, P.: Theoretical considerations for game-based e-learning analytics. In: Reiners, T., Wood, L.C. (eds.) Gamification in Education and Business, pp. 403–416. Springer, Cham (2015). https://doi.org/10.1007/978-3-319-10208-5_20
9. Härting, R.-C., et al.: Impact of the COVID-19 crisis on digital business models - contactless payments. In: Jezic, G., et al. (eds.) Agents and Multi-Agent Systems: Technologies and Applications 2021, Proceedings of 15th KES International Conference, vol. 241, pp. 143–153 (2021). https://doi.org/10.1007/978-981-16-2994-5_12
10. Huotari, K., Hamari, J.: Defining gamification: a service marketing perspective. In: Proceeding of the 16th International Academic Mind Trek Conference. Association for Computing Machinery, New York, USA, pp. 7–12 (2012). https://doi.org/10.1145/2393132.2393137
11. Joy Melwin, M.: An investigation into gamification as a tool for enhancing recruitment process. Ideal Res. **3**, 56–65 (2017). ISSN 2454-857X
12. Korn, O., Brenner, F., Börsig, J., Lalli, F., Mattmüller, M., Müller, A.: Defining recrutainment: a model and a survey on the gamification of recruiting and human resources. In: Freund, L.E., Cellary, W. (eds.) AHFE 2017. AISC, vol. 601, pp. 37–49. Springer, Cham (2018). https://doi.org/10.1007/978-3-319-60486-2_4
13. Küpper, D.M., Klein, K., Völckner, F.: Gamifying employer branding: an integrating framework and research propositions for a new HRM approach in the digitized economy. Hum. Resour. Manag. Rev. **31**(1), 100686 (2021). https://doi.org/10.1016/j.hrmr.2019.04.002
14. Lowman, G.H.: Moving beyond identification: using gamification to attract and retain talent. Ind. Organ. Psychol. **9**(3), 677–682 (2016). https://doi.org/10.1017/iop.2016.70
15. Nour, M., Rouf, A., Allman-Farinelli, M.: Exploring young adult perspectives on the use of gamification and social media in a smartphone platform for improving vegetable intake. Appetite **120**, 547–556 (2017). https://doi.org/10.1016/j.appet.2017.10.016
16. Obaid, I., Farooq, M.S., Abid, A.: Gamification for recruitment and job training: model, taxonomy, and challenges. IEEE **8**, 65164–65178 (2020). https://doi.org/10.1109/ACCESS.2020.2984178
17. Scheiner, C., Haas, P., Bretschneider, U., Blohm, I., Leimeister, J.M.: Obstacles and challenges in the use of gamification for virtual idea communities. In: Stieglitz, S., Lattemann, C., Robra-Bissantz, S., Zarnekow, R., Brockmann, T. (eds.) Gamification. PI, pp. 65–76. Springer, Cham (2017). https://doi.org/10.1007/978-3-319-45557-0_5
18. Staller, M.S., Koerner, S.: Beyond classical definition: the non-definition of gamification. SN Comput. Sci. **2**(2), 1–7 (2021). https://doi.org/10.1007/s42979-021-00472-4

19. Uggerslev, K.L., Fassina, N.E., Kraichy, D.: Recruiting through the stages: a meta-analytic test of predictors of applicant attraction at different stages of the recruiting process. Pers. Psychol. **65**(3), 597–660 (2012). https://doi.org/10.1111/j.1744-6570.2012.01254.x
20. Werbach, K.: (Re)Defining gamification: a process approach. In: Spagnolli, A., Chittaro, L., Gamberini, L. (eds.) PERSUASIVE 2014. LNCS, vol. 8462, pp. 266–272. Springer, Cham (2014). https://doi.org/10.1007/978-3-319-07127-5_23
21. Woods, S.A., et al.: Personnel selection in the digital age: a review of validity and applicant reactions, and future research challenges. Eur. J. Work Organ. Psychol. **29**(1), (2024). https://doi.org/10.1080/1359432X.2019.1681401
22. Yadav, A.: New age transportation system for smart city. Int. J. Adv. Innov. Res. **5** (2018). ISSN 2394-7780
23. Zerrer, J., Härting, R.-C., Gerst, M.: Potentials and challenges of gamification in recruiting. In: 18th Conference on Computer Science and Intelligence Systems, pp. 989–994 (2023). https://doi.org/10.15439/2023F4012

A Literature Review Based Insight into Agile Mindset Through a Lens of Six C's Grounded Theory Model

Necmettin Ozkan[1]([⊠]) [iD], Karen Eilers[2] [iD], and Mehmet Şahin Gök[1] [iD]

[1] Gebze Technical University, Kocaeli, Turkey
{n.ozkan2020,sahingok}@gtu.edu.tr
[2] Institute for Transformation, Hamburg, Germany
karen.eilers@in-transformation.com

Abstract. Agile approaches originated in software development. Due to their various advantages, they are being applied to many different industries and functions. Meanwhile, organizations face extreme challenges and obstacles in their Agile transformations and implementations. One of the major factors causing these challenges and obstacles relies on people related factors. As one of the critical human factors in Agile, Agile Mindset impacts all facets of behaviors and activities. Nevertheless, Agile Mindset-related matters are disregarded by several organizations and literature that focus on concrete and industrialized products of Agile. Motivated by this gap, we aimed to provide a thorough investigation of the research on Agile Mindset-related literature and modeled the obtained results by using Glaser's Six C's Grounded Theory coding family. Therefore, we aimed to provide a comprehensive insight into the Agile Mindset construct, which is new yet essential, required but hard to acquire, challenging to observe but important to notice, and cheap to disregard but at an excessive cost.

Keywords: Agility · Mentality · Mind-set · Being agile · Systematic Literature Review · SLR

1 Introduction

Attracted by its various advantages, organizations are transforming and facing extreme challenges in adapting to Agile [13, 14, 19, 54], mostly and mainly caused by the involved actor's mindset [16, 19, 64]. Humans are always one of the key elements that have a direct impact on their organizations and accomplishments of initiatives [11, 13, 19]. They are responsible for implementing Agile, regardless of the tools, methodologies, or frameworks used [32, 54]. Weinberg briefly states: "No matter how it looks at first, it's always a people problem" [61].

An increasing number of researchers have started to focus on internal aspects and the human side of agility [19]. Even though people-related issues' relevance and importance are evident in Agile adoptions, they are still largely disregarded by organizations [13, 19, 41, 54]. Similarly, the literature on Agile continues to emphasize engineering viewpoints,

© The Author(s), under exclusive license to Springer Nature Switzerland AG 2024
E. Ziemba et al. (Eds.): FedCSIS-ITBS 2023/ISM 2023, LNBIP 504, pp. 261–282, 2024.
https://doi.org/10.1007/978-3-031-61657-0_13

methods, and processes [31, 50] rather than the aspects pertaining to people. In addition to that, the industrialization effects driven by the Agile marketing and selling Agile™ products and "Fake Agile" to organizations have caused to prevent organizations from properly understanding the real and market-independent agility [7, 23, 31]. As a result, Agile teams are more commonly doing Agile rather than being agile [31].

The mindset which is one of the most important human factors reflects individuals' beliefs, assumptions, perceptions, conventions, attitudes, and conceptions, [3, 63]. It has an inherent impact on systems, processes, and tools that people design and use. It affects how people behave [55], make decisions [3], think, believe, and act [35], and consequently molds how organizations operate [3]. People bring their (agile) mentality to organizations, processes, and tools they design [49]. These all make it an important subject to research. Owing to its importance, the construct of mindset and its underlying major roles and implications are the subject of research in several fields, including information systems and beyond [45].

Agile Mindset, which prioritizes people, sits at the core of Agile [13, 21, 59], as Agile is mainly regarded as a social process [38]. Agility is often referred to as having an agile mindset [13, 34]. When compared to any technique, process, certification, system, platform, or organizational structure, Agile Mindset occupies a unique space [42, 64]. Targets cannot be attained by directly applying any Agile approach or without a mental shift [27]. Beyond the prescribed set of processes, methods, and rituals, the path to agility should begin with developing an appropriate and correct Agile Mindset, the spirit of agility [44, 64]. An agile culture should be built on an Agile Mindset [13]. "Without the right mindset, the methods are often adapted in an incorrect way and lose their purpose" [34]. Methods and practices can only lead to a shift in a degree of agility, and they alone do not guarantee being agile [16, 31, 34, 36, 57]. Consequently, living the key values, principles and mindset of agility is necessary for Agile organizations which are viewed as living systems, in information systems and beyond [13, 31, 34, 38, 57].

However, a lot of teams and organizations struggle to create an atmosphere that supports people's development of an Agile Mindset [55, 60]. Some Agile team members state that developing an Agile Mindset is the most challenging when moving to an agile company and they encounter several difficulties in fostering the development of an Agile Mindset [10, 17, 28]. Even more, it remains unclear what is meant by having an Agile Mindset and how the state of having Agile Mindset can be achieved [34].

Therefore, it is essential to look at the Agile Mindset construct that is concerned with significant application challenges and holds great importance in the field of information systems and beyond. Considering that research on this subject is still in its initial stages as of right now [19], this need becomes the driving force behind our study that attempts to provide a thorough investigation of the research by conducting a literature review and delivering results via a modeled view. Thus, our research objective (RO) is to investigate Agile Mindset-related literature and to model the results obtained from the literature by using Glaser's Six C's Grounded Theory coding family [24]. To have a more comprehensive representation of the construct and to provide it with additional inputs from a wider range of disciplines collected from every field, we preferred to go beyond software development, which heavily utilizes this construct.

This paper extends the conference paper [52]. The previous conference paper addresses the indicators, importance, definitions, characteristics, elements of Agile Mindset, activities for developing it and future directions of research on the topic. It also discusses the demographics of publications. The following are the major points that this paper broadens and deepens the conference paper: (1) The 82 Agile Mindset components found in the six research sources [19, 42, 43, 45, 55, 59] before in the previous conference paper were not elaborated there but now all such items have been investigated thoroughly in this work. (2) We revised our literature data extraction process according to the updated research objective. Accordingly, some of the previously included studies in the conference paper were excluded and some of those that were excluded in the previous study were included in this work (3) We extended our literature review by replaying our search procedure for recently published papers, which resulted in adding three new identified sources into the final set (4) We need to learn more about how Agile Mindset items contribute to Agile Mindset and how they are related to one another [19]. To do this, we utilized one of the theoretical coding families of grounded theory that is the Six C's, as the most pertinent theoretical code among others for conceptualization of the presence of Agile Mindset, unlike in the previous conference paper stating the results without any links between them. This coding family describes a category in terms of its Causes, Context, Contingencies, Consequences, Covariances, and Conditions dimensions and aids in the production and interpretation of the results [24].

In the rest of the paper, we give background information on the topic in Sect. 2. The research design overview, together with the research objective, paper selection and data extraction and synthesis procedure are covered in Sect. 3. The results are presented in Sect. 4. Section 5 delivers the discussions of our results. We present the study's conclusions and limitations in Sect. 6.

2 Background

2.1 Process of Agility

According to [48], Agile process begins with an expected or unforeseen, predicted, or unpredictable trigger, like any other process. The trigger could be an impending change, a realized change, or a requirement to generate necessary actions in anticipation of a potential change. Sensing and anticipating are the next steps. Diagnosing, filtering, and interpreting input data happens after detecting and anticipating the change [62]. After that, the entity decides what kind of answer to get ready for. The next action is to create a change as a response. In proactive activities, this stage occurs initially; in reactive behaviors, it occurs after the change occurs. Deliberately providing no response at all is also possible. The prepared response is put into action in the final phase. An organization might not be agile if it cannot sense and act promptly and appropriately [62], or when it senses and acts incorrectly or not rapidly enough which could be catastrophic for agility [5]. This definition indicates that the Agile process is heavily relied on human aspects and has a great deal of cognitivist, consciousness, and predictivity-related aspects from people. Because of this, dealing with critical thinking, decision-making, comprehension, and perception aspects that produce the most important asset in this process, the output, is critical to investigate and focus on. Those aspects are closely related to Agile Mindset of individuals.

2.2 Agile Mindset

Dictionaries define mindset as a mental and established set of attitudes, a cognitive understanding and interpretation of the environment, and a person's way of thinking and opinions [3, 8, 39]. Agile mindset is a particular personal attitude, way of thinking and behavior of both individuals and teams [44] embracing change, learning and self-development, with the goal of achieving a state of being agile [45, 53]. As "a way of thinking about things" [39] and "a person's way of thinking and their opinions" [8], it emphasizes collaboration among team members and adaptability to changing environments to be a high-performing team [55] which is necessary for the organization to survive in a changing marketplace [53].

Agile Mindset is an abstract, vague, intangible, and latent (invisible) construct, thus, difficult to measure, even to observe, and demonstrate [3, 17, 21, 23, 46], which makes the transformation and training of it the most difficult part [21, 23]. Thus, it is hard to prove and show when the transformation and training of it is successful. Even though, as an intangible and invisible asset, it influences various visible aspects [21], such as a successful Agile transformation [3].

Agile Mindset is a soft and dynamic asset, resource, and capability and a kind of trigger that can influence various tangible assets of organizations [3, 19, 21]. It is inherently a psychological, socio-cultural, and human-related matter [45, 46, 59]. Like other human-related assets, it presents complex interactions of social, cultural, and psychological perspectives of individuals with other people. This makes it challenging to understand, substitute, and emulate [3]. The nature of it also creates challenges for organizations in terms of finding and developing their Agile Mindset as an individual endeavor [3, 34].

Being abstract, vague, intangible, latent (invisible), and difficult to observe, and demonstrate construct [3, 17, 21, 23, 46], it is challenging to define Agile Mindset. Like the definitions of the term agility that have no consistent, complete, precise, and agreed definition yet [48], the current situation regarding the definitions of Agile Mindset remains unclear regarding what Agile Mindset is on various levels and perspectives [19, 34, 45]. Another issue with the previous Agile Mindset definitions is that people use different terms other than mindset to describe similar or identical constructs, such as Agile culture [45]. Regarding the key features of Agile Mindset, the most used source is the Agile Manifesto [6], exemplified in the study of [45], although the manifesto does not include a reference to mindset but just a certain overlap with the Agile Mindset construct [15, 23, 45]. Moreover, [23] proposes going beyond the manifesto and not solely relying on it for Agile Mindset in this regard.

2.3 Other Constructs Related to Agile Mindset

Agile leadership focuses primarily on empowering individuals in organizations to take on responsibility through a bottom-up strategy that includes transparency, leading, encouragement, inspiration, motivation, emotional intelligence, a shared vision, and collective decentralized decision-making [13, 53]. Agile workforce mostly concerns with behaviors, attitudes, and prerequisites of a workforce that is or is becoming agile and entails proactive, adaptive, and resilient behaviors of employees [53]. Agile people are those who have aptitude, know-how, and skills to proactively seek opportunities and who can quickly adjust to changing circumstances [53]. The Growth mindset theory of Carol Dweck [18] is related to Agile Mindset by some Agile practitioners. By focusing on the learning process, it reveals how a growth mindset rather than a fixed mindset can improve performance of individuals, foster self-esteem, and lead to accomplishment.

2.4 Grounded Theory and Six C's Model of Glaser

Grounded Theory (GT) is the systematic generation of theory from data analyzed by rigorous qualitative research method developed by sociologists Glaser and Strauss [12, 24]. With GT, we can investigate social interactions and behaviors, particularly in areas of inquiry that have not been thoroughly examined previously including those of Agile teams [30]. The goal of GT is to produce a theory, which is an integrated set of hypotheses, by continuously comparing data at progressively higher abstraction levels [30].

As soon as some data is gathered, the data analysis process, known as coding in GT, can start [30]. There are two types of coding in GT: Substantive coding and Theoretical coding. The substantive codes are "categories and properties of the theory which emerges from and conceptually images substantive area being researched [24]. Theoretical codes "implicitly conceptualize how the substantive codes will relate to each other as a modeled, interrelated, multivariate set of hypotheses in accounting for resolving the main concern" [24].

The Six C's coding family [24] is one of the common structures of theories that Glaser classifies as theoretical coding families used in GT. According to Glaser [24], the Six C's coding family describes a category in terms of its six dimensions (each starting with the letter C) encapsulating the core category at the center that is the "main theme" or "main concern or problem" [24]. Context refers to the setting and ambiance of the study. Condition outlines prerequisite factors [30] to manifest the consequent core concept [24]. The cause-consequence axis often stands out as a closely related duo in studies as causes that lead to the occurrence of the core category and outcomes or effects of its occurrence. The idea of contingency asserts that the concept depends on the contingent elements to occur [24]. Study [30] describes it as the moderating factors between causes and consequences. Covariance refers to correlations between various categories when one category changes with changes in another category [30].

3 Research Design

This research process has been undertaken as a Systematic Literature Review (SLR) based on the guidelines proposed by Kitchenham et al. [33]. The following section describes the implementation of this SLR. The research process starts with defining the research objective. After defining the search objective and searching in the Scopus and Web of Science (WoS) digital libraries, we gathered 1954 potentially relevant publications. For scanning the retrieved studies, we developed and applied inclusion/exclusion criteria and obtained a final pool of twenty-one sources. In addition, the references in the identified twenty-one studies were examined (backward snowballing) and two other related study were added. Finally, twenty-three studies were identified. After extracting the data from the sources, the obtained data were coded (Level 1/L1) and then grouped at Level 2 (L2) according to the model used. The results of this study were then analyzed, and the findings were discussed. The remainder of the section concerns the research objective, publication selection process, and data extraction and synthesis.

3.1 Research Objective

This study aims to review studies that focus on Agile Mindset. Thus, we set the main goals related to our research 1) identify the studies which focus totally or partly on Agile Mindset and 2) analyze and synthesize the studies' relevant results. We raise and investigate the research objective accordingly. Based on the research objective, we have maintained some contents from the previous conference paper and removed some data in the analysis stage. The removed data regards the definitions, characteristics of Agile Mindset, publication demographic-related data including country of authors, publication year, publication venue, authors' affiliation type, and paper citation, and future directions for research. We used the remaining data to identify the Six C's dimensions [24]. We thereby started by investigating the relevance of Agile Mindset from the data for different contexts, conditions, causes, consequences, contingencies, and covariance to address insights, which are necessary for organizations to build effective surroundings and concrete activities to achieve Agile Mindset for individuals. Consequently, we have identified our research objective (RO) as "*to investigate Agile Mindset related literature and to model the obtained results from the literature by using Glaser's Six C's Grounded Theory coding family*".

3.2 Publication Selection Process

The search process is the same as that conducted in the previous conference paper [52]. It follows the main procedure in [33] and as detailed out in Table 1, it includes Scopus and Web of Science (WoS) with the identified search strings, without any filter in the year range to gather a full overview. Based on the scope of this study, the search string is without any "population" related keyword referring to the application area, to access the largest population set of data.

The initial list obtained included duplicate records. After removing them, a total number of 1954 distinct peer-reviewed studies were reached. Based on the scope and context of our study, for the selection of papers, the propositions of inclusion criteria (IC) and exclusion criteria (EC) were specified and applied to those papers. The papers in English and fully or partially focusing on Agile Mindset in any field from conferences, workshops, journals, and book-chapters were included. Duplicate and extended papers and those not accessible by the authors were excluded.

During the application of inclusion/exclusion criteria, the papers were examined according to the procedure detailed in the previous conference paper [52] and the renewed RO in this study to identify whether they were within our scope. Every Agile practice, value, and principle is supposed to be theoretically and practically related to Agile

Table 1. Search strings and libraries.

Library	Place	Search strings	Number of Initial Results	Number of Selected
Scopus	TITLE-ABS-KEY	TITLE-ABS-KEY ("be* of agil*" OR "be* agil*" OR "agile mindset" OR "agile mind set" OR "agile mind-set" OR "agile mind" OR "agile mental" OR "agile mentality" OR "mental agility" OR "agility mindset" OR "agility mind set" OR "agility mind-set" OR "agility mind" OR "agility mental" OR "agility mentality") OR TITLE (("be" OR being OR becom* OR became) OR (mind* OR mental*) AND agil*) AND (LIMIT-TO (DOCTYPE, "cp") OR LIMIT-TO (DOCTYPE, "ar") OR LIMIT-TO (DOCTYPE, "ch")) AND (LIMIT-TO (LANGUAGE, "English"))	1706	21
WoS	All Fields	("be " OR being OR becom* OR became) AND agil* (Title) OR (mind* OR mental*) AND agil* (Title) OR ("be* of agil*" OR "be* agil*" OR "agile mindset" OR "agile mind set" OR "agile mind-set" OR "agile mind" OR "agile mental" OR "agile mentality" OR "mental agility" OR "agility mindset" OR "agility mind set" OR "agility mind-set" OR "agility mind" OR "agility mental" OR "agility mentality") (All Fields) and English (Languages) and Article or Proceeding Paper or Book Chapters (Document Types)	1105	15
Snowballing	References	–	–	2
Total in Distinct			1954	23

Mindset. Considering this, the content was excluded if it was not explicitly related to Agile Mindset in the paper. Regarding the search place and taking our inclusion criteria IC2 into account, we searched in meta-data and titles instead of the full texts. Finally, twenty-three papers were identified as relevant.

3.3 Data Extraction and Synthesis

The data extraction and synthesis process by applying detailed and thorough exam-
inations of the relevant studies and the quality assessment to validate the quality of
the selected candidate papers by ensuring each paper was of adequate standard were
done according to the procedure detailed in the previous conference paper [52] and the
updated RO in this study. We revised our literature data extraction process according
to the updated research objective. Accordingly, some of the previously included studies
in the conference paper were excluded and some of those that were excluded in the
previous study were included in this work. No studies existed lower than the threshold
score and no elimination regarding the quality assessment was done. This is most likely
due to the venue of publications being well-qualified and generally well-known.

Our study uses a content analysis method. We used a specific version of content
analysis, thematic content analysis. Content Analysis in general includes three stages:
selection of the focal texts, coding the texts, and interpreting the results of the coding [1].
The common steps in the processing of coding include transcription, coding, and category creation [14]. Transcription is the process of converting what is obtained through
interviews, observations, audio recordings, or field notes into text [14]. Regarding transcription, we used the papers' contents. For coding and category creation, we used the
method proposed by Glaser [24]. This GT method provides a three-level coding process
yielding categories at the end.

In our case, the raw data was extracted from the sources as-it-is, and then put into an
Excel file. Then those raw data were coded (L1). During this stage, it is seen that some
raw data items can serve for multiple L1 codes, then they are duplicated under different
L1 codes. Those codes were then grouped into L2 according to the model used. During
this grouping into L2, it was possible that some items were included in more than one
category in terms of their meanings (for example, the increase in performance could
be both a cause and a consequence). In this case, the context and meaning in which
the original study used the relevant item were considered. If such an insight was not
expressed and could not be inferred from the study directly, then the closest category to
which the relevant item would be suitable was selected by the authors. Our study has
been shaped around a main phenomenon (Agile Mindset) from the outline, rather than
focusing on discovering an emergent main phenomenon. Thus, the Level 3 item in our
model refers to Agile Mindset which is the main concept.

4 Findings

We present the results and findings of this SLR study concerning the identified RO. As
a result of our SLR, we identified relevant studies as [3, 6, 13, 16, 17, 19, 21, 23, 25, 26,
34, 37, 38, 42, 43, 45, 46, 53, 55–57, 59, 64].

After reaching the list of identified papers, the data from each paper were collected
as described in the Research Design section resulting in 282 items achieved. These items
were then coded into 96 distinct items (L1). These L1 items were then classified under
Six C's (L2) categories, according to their descriptions. As a result of this process, the
obtained tree is depicted in Fig. 1 (by using "https://miro.com" application) bearing

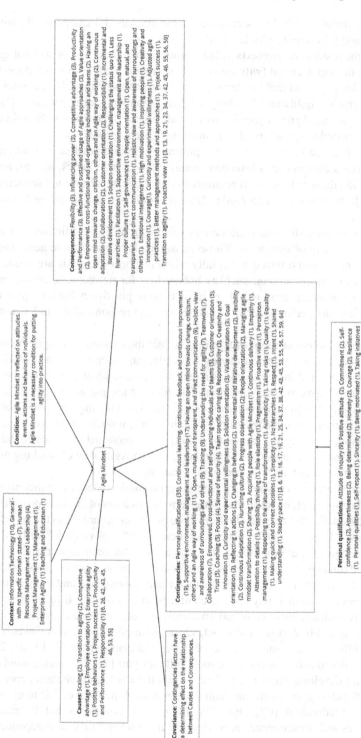

Fig. 1. The Model of Results Through the Six C's Grounded Theory

items names (L1), items' number of occurrence in the sources, L2 categories derived from those items and L3 category (Agile Mindset in our case).

According to the results, the **contexts** of the studies include information technology with ten papers at the top, General (with no specific domain stated) with seven papers, Human Resource Management and Leadership with four papers, Project Management, Management, Enterprise Agility and Teaching and Education with one paper each. This distribution shows, again, Agile is popular in the Information Technology discipline, meanwhile, it has started to spread to other management areas as well.

Agile Mindset is a necessary condition for putting Agile into practice, but we can only talk about its existence in **conditions** that require changes in attitudes, actions, and behaviors of individuals as reflections. It reminds us that Agile Mindset is not sufficient for being agile [3]; the existence of an Agile Mindset should activate people and cause some things to emerge.

Numerous studies have discussed the **causes** of having an Agile Mindset and its role in achieving a variety of outcomes. Those causes include competitive advantage to survive in a changing marketplace, especially when responses to crisis are needed, shift to agility, employee orientation such as onboarding for newcomers, attainment of enterprise agility, assisting team members in increasing positive behaviors, project success, productivity and performance of Agile teams, and responsibility, and scaling Agile.

When it comes to the **consequences** that may reflect the existence of Agile Mindset, having an Agile Mindset supports having a people, customer, value and solution orientation, and changes in thinking. Agile Mindset affects individual and team-related dimensions such as self-governance, leading to less hierarchies and more empowered, cross-functional, and self-organizing individuals and teams, having more responsibility, courage, high motivation, and collaboration. For individuals, it opens more avenues for creativity, innovation, curiosity, experimental willingness, emotional intelligence, having an open mind towards change, criticism, others, and an Agile way of working and open, mutual, and transparent, and direct communication.

From the process-oriented viewpoint, having an Agile mindset encourages incremental and iterative development, effective and long-term application of Agile approaches, continuous adaptation, flexibility, and adjusting agile practices according to the specific needs and contexts. All these are needed because there is no "book of truth" for how to be agile [46]. Consequently, after these all, it brings more influencing power to inspire, facilitate, lead, and direct people, productivity, performance, project success, possessing an appropriate culture, better management methods and approaches, and competitive advantages to organizations that may require challenge the status quo. It facilitates the transition to agility with a holistic view and awareness of surroundings and others.

Nevertheless, Agile Mindset is an abstract, vague, intangible, and latent (invisible) construct, thus, difficult to measure, even to observe, and demonstrate [3, 17, 21, 23, 46], which makes the transformation it the most difficult part [21, 23]. Agile mindset transformation and development is not a clear, straightforward, and painless process. For reasons like these, organizations and teams experience difficulties or fail to enable an Agile Mindset of individuals [60]. One of the main reasons for this is that the transition between causes and consequences is **contingent** upon several factors, independent of context. Thus, we assert that Contingency factors have a determining effect on the relationship between Causes and Consequences.

The contingent factors include strategic, management, leadership, personal qualifications, process, communication, transformation, and behavioral aspects. From the **strategic** perspective, it demands value, goal, solution, and customer orientation. For **behavioral habits**, it requires changing behaviors, reflecting on actions, making quick and correct decisions, proper intent, continuous learning, getting, and providing feedback, continuous improvement, creativity, innovation, focus, taking risks, proactive view, trust, empathy, respect, taking responsibility, equality, pragmatism, authenticity, possibility thinking, curiosity, experimental willingness, attention to details, continuous adaptation, teamwork, sharing and collaboration. Although it is difficult to observe, not only the outcomes of the behaviors but also the person's intentions should be considered. Agile Mindset also demands open, mutual, and transparent, and direct communication.

In terms of **personal qualifications**, certain qualifications, prerequisites, and attitudes are critical for people to have. They include having an open mind towards change, criticism, others, and new ways of working. Other personal qualifications include attitude of inquiry, positive attitude, commitment, self-confidence, self-respect, determination, motivation, courage, resilience, sincerity, willingness to take initiatives, resourcefulness, a sense of pride, assertiveness, mental flexibility, honesty, emotional intelligence, and humility.

From the **process** point of view, Agile mindset requires a holistic view, awareness of surroundings and others, role elasticity, flexibility, incremental and iterative development, continuous delivery, steady pace, simplicity, and quality.

A supportive environment, **management and leadership** providing people orientation, acquired people with agility orientation, equality, shared understanding, sense of security, a nurturing culture across the organization and empowering the teams and individuals are critical. This calls for no hierarchies, cross-functional and self-organizing teams, teamwork, and leading Agile Mindset transformations by the management.

In Agile Mindset **transformations**, ensuring an accurate understanding of the need for agility, perception management, respect for the nature of transformation, team-specific caring during the transformations, providing permanent training and coaching, progress observation are mentioned.

5   Discussions

The study's findings demonstrate that there should always be a driving factor behind Agile and Agile Mindset transformations, which is the motivation behind the question "Why". "Why" should be the first question to ask, before the question "How" or "What". The transformations also ought to be based on people. It is important to acknowledge the human factors and their transformations. The human-centered transformations should also be supported by mutual and transparent communications across the organization. Especially while transforming to Agile Mindset, organizations need to be persistent and patient. It is crucial to organize the transformation well and observe results of it in practice and behaviors of individuals and teams including the leaders. It is required to allow people and teams to create their space and freedom. Therefore, it should be normal and even expected for practices of teams to go beyond the classical Agile methods such as Scrum [40]. Like in every transformation, the leaders should first be transformed, and their support should be obtained.

Humans, with their equally sophisticated talents, are faced with managing the complex world of reality and its contextual changes. Processes, documentation, and plans are examples of human-made proxy entities that are unable to compensate either reality or human capabilities. Thus, as one of the most powerful attributes of people, a person's mindset is something that organizations and leaders should and will always invest in.

According to our results, **individual personalities** have a unique place and capacity to support Agile Mindset. To investigate what kinds of companies and individuals are better equipped to apply Agile Mindset, it would be fascinating to integrate studies on Agile Mindset with research on personality, social elements [34], and experiences and maturity of practitioners [45, 46]. It is recommended that practitioners and managers should pay greater attention to candidate selection processes, with a particular emphasis on personality traits, cognitive abilities, beliefs, and attitudes toward change by applying proven tests and customized interviews used to evaluate these qualities [53]. Moreover, agility could be emphasized in job advertising to draw applicants with more Agile personalities and mindsets [53]. Further research should be done on job rotation, job expansion, and job enrichment initiatives in agile organizations [47].

Like in the job-related **flexibility** forms, investing in the invisible—that is, the flexibility that fosters agility—is equally essential. Static structures, team utilization, and other inward-looking technical debt issues are examples of factors that should be examined in addition to the outward-looking viewpoint to the customer.

We note that internalizing the Agile values and principles is essential to becoming agile [57], as recognized by the Agile community and practitioners. The Agile Manifesto [4] and many others underline the importance of people and human factors [9]. However, it seems from our study that the increased interest in Agile in the academic field focuses more on **tangible entities** like practice, method, and frameworks; the addiction of Agile to the **concrete** has been proven again. Numerous studies have been conducted to explore the technical aspects of agile development even though such aspects are on the "less valuable side" of the Agile Manifesto. The interesting thing is how little attention has been paid to the social facets of agility and Agile Mindset [19]. Thus, it is obvious that further research is necessary to examine the "soft aspects" of Agile including Agile Mindset.

Many elements found in our study associated with Agile Mindset remain at the practical level. Instead of investigating the Agile Mindset itself, there is a focus on elements circling around and relating to it. In this sense, the sociological and psychological dimensions of Agile Mindset have not yet been explored. This may be because Agile emerged from engineering fields such as software and manufacturing sectors, not from **social sciences**. However, there are novel studies that go beyond these areas in terms of context. We think that there will be more studies towards these dimensions of Agile Mindset in the future. Although the "What" about Agile Mindset has mainly emerged, it would be beneficial to make room for more studies on "How" and even "Why" they should be achieved.

Value and collaborating with clients who are closest to the point to represent value are the cornerstones of having an Agile Mindset. As a result, the goal is to be as close as possible to customers, who are more aware of their needs and demands. Being close to customers means that customers and end users are real owners and users of systems to be developed, which serves as a reminder to keep the focus on customers, value, quality, and goal at the center.

As the similarities at the level of practices increase and Agile practices equalize across different organizations, it will become more difficult to distinguish between a successful Agile transformation from an unsuccessful one. In this and all other similar cases, the distinguishing feature will be about the change in **value orientation**, value production, and focus on goals by individuals, teams, and organizations. Agility, and Agile Mindset should serve a greater purpose—value creation—rather than encouraging aimless behaviors [51]. Otherwise, agility may become a matter of "How", rather than serving for a greater whole (What) and purpose (Why). Regarding the question "How", after a while, when Agile practices will be largely equalized for organizations, organizations will make a difference with people [2] and with their mindset, not with practices, but with the value creation. Thus, the focus on the people side and having a proper Agile Mindset will be more important and the predefined practices will have less place in the future [23], which requires the intellectual capabilities of people's minds to make practices evolve more originally and organically.

Like development in every context, it is important to nurture the question **"Why"** for the development of Agile Mindset. Every stakeholder who is or will be affected by the change should understand the benefits and rationale behind the change, and they should participate in the transformation processes [17]. Therefore, individuals, teams and organizations should understand "Why" Agile and Agile Mindset is needed, to internalize the agile values, principles, and practices. For instance, teams should get an explanation of why each respective agile practice is helpful and should be implemented to comprehend the vision and rationale behind using an agile way of working [34]. Even though this reason of "Why" can be reasonable for organizations, it should be meaningful and reasonable for the individuals as well (the goals of the organizations and the individuals cannot always be aligned by default).

Keeping this "Why" in their heads, people should adjust practices when needed and combine them with existing elements. Since reality frequently changes based on the **context**, it is necessary for each distinct practitioner to establish a space appropriate for their context and to mold their own agility within it [51]. Agile transformations in general and Agile mindset-specific transformations in organizations are an individual activity as well as a collective one. Therefore, every part in organizations should take a holistic view and awareness of surroundings and others, have open, mutual, and transparent, and direct communication, and collaboration with others.

The results show that changing one's mindset to one that is more agile is a challenging process that calls for perseverance and hard work. Managing Agile Mindset **transformation** requires meticulous, careful, patient, time demanding and complicated leading and management that needs a strong will [53]. It must be carried out in an agile way and concentrate on all aspects of change. During it, adequate coaching, training, transformation progress observations, team-specific caring, perception management, shared understanding, and respecting for the nature of transformation especially in terms of the duration are required. Team dynamics, current situation and way of working should be considered [34]. Structural approaches in Agile mindset transformations also indicate using the classical controlling, redirection, and monitoring activities specific to individuals and teams.

Even while physical acts may be seen, we still need to figure out **how to develop** Agile Mindset or how to observe the minds of people by **measuring** it [19] to make sure that people are fully immersed in Agile Mindset [17], especially when considered that there are not enough studies to measure Agile Mindset in the literature [19]. Organizations should take down the obstacles standing in their paths to having a proper Agile Mindset by the individuals [19]. Further research is required to determine the various stages at which achieving an Agile Mindset can occur, ranging from the individual to the organizational levels [19, 45].

Having an Agile Mindset is not enough; people should reflect their mindset in actions. This is also a unique learning process for individuals and teams. Companies should set up expensive, drawn-out, **ongoing endeavors** (the contingencies) for individuals to have Agile Mindset. For instance, individuals should establish habits of continuous learning, constant feedback, and continuous progress, among other ongoing initiatives. Thus, every distinct person, team, and organization should evaluate the benefits, costs and drawbacks of adopting an Agile Mindset to identify their ideal levels. Specifically speaking for the drawbacks side, for instance, investigations about whether an overly Agile Mindset detracts from performance [3], quality or other factors may be worthwhile to study. Even in the initial stages of the Agile Mindset transformations, organizations might allow for a drop in performance.

While some items of Agile Mindset that are discussed in this study are unquestionably beneficial in the absolute sense (such as continuous improvement), some others have **trade-offs** that must be considered (even though it has not been encountered much in our review). For instance, while cross-functionality lowers communication costs by bringing the required skills together within the team and facilitating quick decisions, self-sufficient (!) teams erode their capabilities overall due to potential alienation of surroundings, which poses a risk to teams operating in a multi-team environment [51]. A focus on agility without a focus on resilience might lead employees to experience increased stress and perform less well as a result [53]. It also serves as a kind of reminder that firms should possess a variety of capabilities (such as resilience, quality, sustainability, etc.) in addition to agility and find a balance between them [29]. Agile Mindset ought to be combined with other constructs in a holistic network [19] while achieving a desired and planned level of it, at a relatively excessive cost. This difficult aspect of Agile Mindset adds to its power; it gives organizations independence and a "safe place" away from the "Agile marketplace".

We conclude that possessing the right Agile Mindset has certain causes and advantageous consequences. Reaching such consequences, though, comes at a **cost**. Agile Mindset is one of the aspects of Agile that is difficult to internalize in organizations [23, 38]. It takes a new way of thinking to adopt it, which makes it difficult to unlearn long-standing habits and adopt new ones [58]. Changing the mindset of employees and management appears to be more difficult than simply implementing Agile practices, which is simpler [34]. Agile mindset initiatives may thus need a significant investment of time, money, and services [53]. Putting an Agile culture in place with an Agile Mindset will take considerable time, patience, and effort, requiring a wide range of discussions, iterations, and a strong will [53].

The findings indicate that for employees to build an Agile Mindset to cope with changing environments, appropriate leadership and management mindset approaches are necessary. The outcomes demonstrate once more how much **leaders** have an impact on Agile Mindset initiatives by being role models and establishing a supportive environment including physical facilitations for meeting rooms and offices, as well as sociopsychological aspects to support Agile Mindset developments, explorative activities, risk-taking, and independent thinking. Throughout a bi-directional (from the top-down, from bottom-to-top) transformation [57], leaders should be role models [34, 57], ambassadors [53, 57], problem solvers [53], core values installers [53], and invest in coaching, training, learning, building, and measuring Agile Mindset. They should empower employees to make their decisions and cocreate change [57]. As a result, we must identify the roles that leaders, talent acquisition and development, and people management play in implementing target-oriented programs and provide means for actors to cultivate an Agile Mindset [13, 19]. Important insights into the attitude of Agile leaders and their impact on organizations are also required [19].

One of the things people need during their learning process to face the complexity is the courage to change, including changing oneself. They also need to feel comfortable and have a reasonably high tolerance provided by their leaders for making mistakes for their **personal safety**. This necessitates mutual **respect** and **trust** across the organization. Respect promotes collaboration, opens avenues of communication, and permits **taking risks**. Respect ensures that every individual has a suitable and secure space for learning and experimentation. **Courage** is necessary to motivate to take risks and veer off course to adjust along the way.

Individuals with an Agile Mindset are expected to **align their mindset with Agile practices** since these practices themselves embody an Agile mindset too. For instance, as a practice, a large amount of development is broken down into smaller functional increments with iterative development in conjunction with frequent delivery. This helps to better understand functionalities that customers demand, control risk, and obtain early feedback from clients and end users. Iterative development also promotes learning and experimentation. Because the system to be developed can produce small steps forward, it can expand organically as needed to adjust to changes. People with an Agile Mindset frequently employ inquiry, observation, improvement, learning, learning from mistakes and feedback loops to learn more about reality. People with an Agile Mindset must embrace these agile techniques to reap their benefits. Seeing such distinct behaviors and methods in practice can serve as a reliable gauge of an individual's Agile Mindset.

Agile processes and people are additionally equipped with quick and accurate **information**. Information in Agile should circulate swiftly both within and between the teams to move quickly and accurately. To be quick, self-organizing and cross-functional teams are ideal for Agile teams. Cross-functionality along with self-organization brings required capabilities closer and together, lowering the cost of communication and transfers to enable quick actions for a variety of complex scenarios. To be accurate, communication is facilitated by transparency. Learning is supported by communication including communication with the developed solution itself. Furthermore, communication with shared goals fosters collaboration and teamwork. As a result of this, quick and accurate information that is updated, rectified, accelerated, and shared to gain experience and generate innovative ideas brings more agility.

The act of putting Agile practices into practice is quite easy compared to changing the mindset of management and individuals which is much more challenging [34]. Assuming that they are put in practice successfully, Kuhrmann et al. [36] investigated how different agile practices and approaches were used and how much agility was influenced by them in software engineering fields. They discovered a minimal correlation between the application of specific agile techniques and a project's level of agility. Consequently, they conclude that other factors must influence the level of agility. Thus, examining the impact of Agile Mindset and studying the covariance correlations for each item in the model we propose would be beneficial.

Researchers and practitioners alike recognize the importance of adopting an Agile Mindset. Despite its well-known significance, Agile Mindset is susceptible to being overlooked in favor of more visible, commercially viable Agile practices. Even if it is undertaken with solid intention, with proper guidance and specific suggestions to make it happen, the process of **changing the mindset** appears to be far more challenging.

One of the most fundamental reasons why Agile transformation is **difficult**(!) to achieve may be the desperate attempt to transform institutions and people without transforming their mindsets. It is a matter of curiosity whether a better result would have been achieved regarding Agile if some of the investments in the practices and the economy surrounding it had been made on people, values, principles, and mindset instead of these (certification, method trading, etc.). But at least we are sure of this; Investments made in the same way will not take organizations that have reached a saturation in the field of practices much further. It becomes evident that the primary success factor and prerequisite for developing Agile is the people-related matters, team members' personal prerequisites and attitudes [34]. Thus, it would be beneficial to give the human related elements (e.g., personality traits) more attention since projects may be improved by concentrating on the individuals engaged in the process [34].

In addition to the mind, the heart of people with **intentions** (in other words ethical and moral values) posing potential paradoxical values, unique interests, a dialectical nature of culture, and conflicting orientations [20] is significant. Despite this, it was surprising not to encounter this phenomenon in such a subject that focuses on people. Similarly, we have seen extremely limited attention to dimension of experience, even though experience is especially important for managing the demands of a complex world.

When it comes to the investigated studies including the term Agile Mindset, like the results from the study of [45] and [49], in our work we have also realized that most of the excluded studies use and mention the term Agile Mindset as a "**fixed term**" without actual definitions, descriptions, elaborations, investigations, details, or explanations. Most of these articles look upon Agile Mindset as a prerequisite [34], one category among many [16], or as a necessary condition for putting Agile into practice.

For many people and companies, Agile Mindset represents a completely **new** way of thinking [38] or a box that has not been opened yet; how the state of having an Agile Mindset can be achieved is described by limited studies [34]. When considering the underestimated position of Agile Mindset in literature and its new developing progress, it is recommended and worth researching the construct in terms of practice and theory. It appears that much remains to be discovered about this subject. In our study, our goal was to create a comprehensive representation of Agile Mindset through a model. Utilizing the data from most of the well-known studies on the topic to date, we hoped to make the analysis comprehensive and complimentary. Additionally, we hope that the results can guide in transformation processes of Agile Mindset.

There are too many social, psychological, emotional, and individual aspects at play about this topic rather than a clear path to success [34, 37]. For further studies, in the initial stages of the research on this topic, it is recommended to consider studies that examine mindset in a broad sense and benefit from findings of related fields of study. Further research in the fields of learning (as opposed to teaching), cognitive science, behavioral science, and multidisciplinary studies will likely be needed to advance this still-emerging construct. In this way, for instance, lessons from historical accounts of notable mindset transformations can also be applied to studies of Agile Mindset development, providing motivation and direction.

Working with an Agile mindset presents certain challenges because almost everything that is related to Agile is impacted by people, and nearly everything related to people is influenced by the mindset. As a result, it is challenging to identify boundaries for Agile Mindset. Such boundaries need to be clarified using scientific and systematic approaches. For instance, such a clarification might make a distinction between the external variables (environment, leaders, processes, etc.) and the internal components of the Agile Mindset of individuals (goal, personality, motivation, etc.). Furthermore, a differentiation between individuals who may possess an Agile Mindset in the future and those who already possess it can also be considered.

As a result, it is a matter of question to see what trajectory the construct of Agile Mindset, which is new but necessary, necessary but difficult to obtain, difficult to observe but should be observed, easy to ignore but at an excessive cost, will follow.

6 Conclusions and Limitations

Beyond the prescribed set of practices that guarantee no assurance for successfully implementing Agile methods, firstly individuals require an Agile Mindset. Even implemented in a successful manner, there are certain basic constraints to the practices provided by the Agile methods. This requires correct understanding and locating the Agile mindset before the practices. Interestingly, the construct of Agile Mindset is underestimated in the literature, even though numerous research and individuals have acknowledged its significance. Most of the research involving Agile Mindset uses it as a fixed term, thus, it would appear necessary to further dissect the construct which is worth researching in terms of practice and theory. We need more knowledge and wisdom beyond stating that Agile Mindset is important and required for various aspects.

In our study, we aimed to deal with the Agile Mindset construct comprehensively, by using sources from many disciplines. We aimed to unbox this construct by providing comprehensive data from the literature modeled within the Six C's model by Glaser [24]. Our research incorporates the data currently accessible in the literature on Agile Mindset and offers a model that encompasses all this data, making it simple to acquire pertinent facts at one time and providing guidance on how to develop an Agile Mindset based on the model's recommendations. In the future, we will study further development and measurement of Agile Mindset for individuals in organizations.

The procedures used in our study and the nature of our study have limitations in several ways. Many items stated as contingencies in the study could also be a consequence of Agile Mindset. For instance, although trustworthy relationships are necessary and supportive of Agile Mindset, their existence is also a result of Agile Mindset. The obtained Consequences can also provide inputs to the model as Contingencies. We included these items in our analysis under only one category where we think they are prevalent to keep the model simple. Our study also does not purport to be exhaustive or finished to offer a list, model, or framework for cultivating an Agile Mindset, either in its entirety or in part.

Limitations of search terms and search engines coverage can lead to an incomplete set of primary sources obtaining only those written in English and the peer reviewed. A single researcher extracted the data from the included studies. The data obtained from the sources is prone to bias. Also, the values of the quality assessment criteria are subjective but based on field experience. Moreover, the primary studies' results are context-dependent and have thereby limited generalizability. Agile mindset is a strong and abstract construct that touches on a wide range of topics. Because of this, even though it subtly influences many aspects, such data is ignored if this effect is not clearly linked to Agile Mindset in the studies. However, when these processes were unclear, a consensus session was applied with the first and second authors. To ensure the reliability of our study, the entire pool of the sources was analyzed carefully, and the data were reviewed, extracted, and synthesized in iterations according to the research protocol and guidelines applied. However, since most of the research in the literature ignores the outcomes of Agile and many beneficial consequences of agility are hypothesized [53], the validity of data used in our study from the identified sources needs to be evaluated.

References

1. Ahuvia, A.: Traditional, interpretive, and reception based content analyses: Improving the ability of content analysis to address issues of pragmatic and theoretical concern. Soc. Indic. Res. **54**, 139–172 (2001). https://doi.org/10.1023/A:1011087813505
2. Alexander, C.: Beyond the Agile manifesto: epoch of the team. Crosstalk: J. Defense Softw. Eng. **29**(4) (2016)
3. Asseraf, Y., Gnizy, I.: Translating strategy into action: the importance of an Agile mindset and Agile slack in international business. Int. Bus. Rev. **31**(6), 102036 (2022). https://doi.org/10.1016/j.ibusrev.2022.102036
4. Beck, K., et al.: The Agile manifesto (2001). https://agilemanifesto.org/
5. Benaben, F., Vernadat, F.B.: Information System agility to support collaborative organisations. Enterp Inf. Syst. **11**(4), 470–473 (2017). https://doi.org/10.1080/17517575.2016.1269367
6. Bider, I., Söderberg, O.: Moving towards agility in an ordered fashion. In: Hammoudi, S., Maciaszek, L.A., Missikoff, M.M., Camp, O., Cordeiro, J. (eds.) ICEIS 2016. LNBIP, vol. 291, pp. 175–199. Springer, Cham (2017). https://doi.org/10.1007/978-3-319-62386-3_9

7. Calafat, A.L.M., Mas, A., Pacheco, M.: Fake Agile: what is it and how to avoid it? IT Prof. **24**(2), 69–73 (2022). https://doi.org/10.1109/mitp.2021.3139826
8. Cambridge Dictionary: Meaning of mindset in English (2023). https://dictionary.cambridge.org/dictionary/english/mindset. Accessed 16 May 2023
9. Cockburn, A., Highsmith, J.: Agile software development, the people factor. Computer **34**(11), 131–133 (2001). https://doi.org/10.1109/2.963450
10. Conboy, K., Coyle, S., Wang, X., Pikkarainen, M.: People over process: key challenges in Agile development. IEEE Softw. **28**(4), 48–57 (2011). https://doi.org/10.1109/ms.2010.132
11. Cooke-Davies, T.: The real success factors on projects. Int. J. Proj. Manage. **20**(3), 185–190 (2002). https://doi.org/10.1016/S0263-7863(01)00067-9
12. Corbin, J.M., Strauss, A.: Grounded theory research: procedures, canons, and evaluative criteria. Qual. Sociol. **13**(1), 3–21 (1990). https://doi.org/10.1515/zfsoz-1990-0602
13. Crnogaj, K., Tominc, P., Rožman, M.A.: Conceptual model of developing an Agile work environment. Sustainability **14**(22), 14807 (2022). https://doi.org/10.3390/su142214807
14. Çelik, H., Başer, N.B., Kılıç Memur, H.N.: Nitel veri analizi ve temel ilkeleri. J. Qual. Res. Educ. **8**(1), 379–406 (2020). https://doi.org/10.14689/issn.2148-2624.1.8c.1s.16m. (in Turkish)
15. Denning, S.: What's missing in the Agile manifesto: mindset. Forbes (2016). https://www.forbes.com/sites/stevedenning/2016/06/07/the-key-missingingredient-in-the-agile-manifesto-mindset
16. Dikert, K., Paasivaara, M., Lassenius, C.: Challenges and success factors for large-scale Agile transformations: a systematic literature review. J. Syst. Softw. **119**, 87–108 (2016). https://doi.org/10.1016/j.jss.2016.06.013
17. Durbin, M., Niederman, F.: Bringing templates to life: overcoming obstacles to the organizational implementation of Agile methods. Int. J. Inf. Syst. Proj. Manage. **9**(3), 5–18 (2021). https://doi.org/10.12821/ijispm090301
18. Dweck, C.S.: Mindset: The New Psychology of Success. Random House Publishing Group, New York (2006). ISBN 978-0345472328
19. Eilers, K., Peters, C., Leimeister, J.M.: Why the Agile mindset matters. Technol. Forecast. Soc. Change **179**, 121650 (2022). https://doi.org/10.1016/j.techfore.2022.121650
20. Fang, T.: Yin Yang: a new perspective on culture. Manag. Organ. Rev. **8**(1), 25–50 (2012). https://doi.org/10.1111/j.1740-8784.2011.00221.x
21. Fronza, I., Wang, X.: Revealing Agile mindset using LEGO® SERIOUS PLAY®: experience from an online Agile training project. In: 34th International Conference on Software Engineering and Knowledge Engineering, pp. 428–433 (2022). https://doi.org/10.18293/seke2022-117
22. Geffers, K., Bretschneider, U., Eilers, K., Oeste-Reiß, S.: Leading teams in today's dynamic organizations: the core characteristics of Agile leadership. In: Hawaii International Conference on System Sciences (HICSS) (2024). ISBN 978-0-9981331-7-1
23. Gelmis, A., Ozkan, N., Ahmad, A.J., Guler, M.G.: Perspectives on the sustainability and future trajectory of Agile. Systems, software and services process improvement. In: 29th European Conference, EuroSPI 2022, pp. 443–458 (2022). https://doi.org/10.1007/978-3-031-15559-8_32
24. Glaser, B.G.: Theoretical sensitivity. The Sociology Press, Mill Valley (1978). ISBN 978-1884156014
25. Gouda, G.K., Tiwari, B.: Ambidextrous leadership: a distinct pathway to build talent agility and engagement. Hum. Resour. Dev. Int. 1–9 (2022). https://doi.org/10.1080/13678868.2022.2163101
26. Gregory, P., et al.: Onboarding: how newcomers integrate into an Agile project team. In: Agile Processes in Software Engineering and Extreme Programming: 21st International Conference

on Agile Software Development, XP 2020, pp. 20–36 (2020). https://doi.org/10.1007/978-3-030-49392-9_2

27. Gregory, P., Barroca, L., Sharp, H., Deshpande, A., Taylor, K.: The challenges that challenge: engaging with Agile practitioners' concerns. Inf. Softw. Technol. **77**, 92–104 (2016). https://doi.org/10.1016/j.infsof.2016.04.006

28. Hajjdiab, H., Taleb, A.: Adopting Agile software development: issues and challenges. IJMVSC **2**(3), 1–10 (2011). https://doi.org/10.5121/ijmvsc.2011.2301

29. Hoda, R., Noble, J., Marshall, S.: Balancing acts: walking the Agile tightrope. In: ICSE Workshop on Cooperative and Human Aspects of Software Engineering, pp. 5–12 (2010). https://doi.org/10.1145/1833310.1833312

30. Hoda, R., Noble, J., Marshall, S.: The impact of inadequate customer collaboration on self-organizing Agile teams. Inf. Softw. Technol. **53**(5), 521–534 (2011). https://doi.org/10.1016/j.infsof.2010.10.009

31. Hohl, P., Klünder, J., van Bennekum, A.: Back to the future: origins and directions of the Agile Manifesto—views of the originators. J. Softw. Eng. Res. Dev. **6**(1) (2010). https://doi.org/10.1186/s40411-018-0059-z

32. Joskowski, A., Przybyłek, A., Marcinkowski, B.: Scaling scrum with a customized Nexus framework: a report from a joint industry-academia research project. Softw. Pract. Exp. (2023). https://doi.org/10.1002/spe.3201

33. Kitchenham, B., et al.: Systematic literature reviews in software engineering–a systematic literature review. Inf. Softw. Technol. **51**(1), 7–15 (2009). https://doi.org/10.1016/j.infsof.2008.09.009

34. Klünder, J., Trommer, F., Prenner, N.: How Agile coaches create an Agile mindset in development teams: insights from an interview study. J. Softw.: Evol. Process **34**(12), e2491 (2022). https://doi.org/10.1002/smr.2491

35. Kramer, R.: From skillset to mindset: a new paradigm for leader development. Public Adm. Issues, **5**, 26–45 (2016). https://doi.org/10.17323/1999-5431-2016-0-5-26-45

36. Kuhrmann, M., et al.: What makes Agile software development Agile. IEEE Trans. Softw. Eng. (2021). https://doi.org/10.1109/TSE.2021.3099532

37. Leeuw, R.T., Joseph, N.: Reciprocal influence between digital emotional intelligence and Agile mindset in an Agile environment. Adm. Sci. **13**(11), 228 (2023). https://doi.org/10.3390/admsci13110228

38. Lindskog, C., Netz, J.: Balancing between stability and change in Agile teams. Int. J. Manag. Proj. Bus. **14**(7), 1529–1554 (2021). https://doi.org/10.1108/ijmpb-12-2020-0366

39. Macmillan Dictionary: Definition of mindset in English (2023). https://www.macmillandictionary.com/dictionary/british/mindset. Accessed 16 May 2023

40. Masood, Z., Hoda, R., Blincoe, K.: Real world scrum a grounded theory of variations in practice. IEEE Trans. Softw. Eng. **48**(5), 1579–1591 (2020). https://doi.org/10.1109/tse.2020.3025317

41. Melo, C.O., Santana, C., Kon, F.: Developers motivation in Agile teams. In: 38th Euromicro Conference on Software Engineering and Advanced Applications (2012). https://doi.org/10.1109/seaa.2012.45

42. Mikhieieva, O., Baumgartner, R., Stephan, K., Lipilina, E.: Agile mindset competencies for project leaders. In: IEEE European Technology and Engineering Management Summit (E-TEMS), pp. 208–213. IEEE (2022). https://doi.org/10.1109/e-tems53558.2022.9944538

43. Miler, J., Gaida, P.: Identification of the Agile mindset and its comparison to the competencies of selected Agile roles. In: Przybyłek, A., Morales-Trujillo, M.E. (eds.) LASD/MIDI -2019. LNBIP, vol. 376, pp. 41–62. Springer, Cham (2020). https://doi.org/10.1007/978-3-030-37534-8_3

44. Miler, J., Gaida, P.: On the Agile mindset of an effective team—an industrial opinion survey. In: Federated Conference on Computer Science and Information Systems (FEDCSIS) (2019). https://doi.org/10.15439/2019f198
45. Mordi, A., Schoop, M.: Making it tangible – creating a definition of Agile mindset. In: 28th Conference on Information Systems (ECIS2020) (2020)
46. Mordi, A., Schoop, M.: Scaling with an Agile mindset-a conceptual approach to large-scale Agile. In: AMCIS (2021)
47. Muduli, A., Pandya, G.: Psychological empowerment and workforce agility. Psychol. Stud. **63**(3), 276–285 (2018). https://doi.org/10.1007/s12646-018-0456-8
48. Ozkan, N., Gok, M.S.: Definition synthesis of agility in software development: comprehensive review of theory to practice. Int. J. Mod. Educ. Comput. Sci. **14**(3) (2022). https://doi.org/10.5815/ijmecs.2022.03.02
49. Ozkan, N., Gok, M.S.: Investigation of Agile mindset elements by using literature review for a better understanding of agility. In: Turkish National Software Engineering Symposium (UYMS), pp. 1–6. IEEE (2020). https://doi.org/10.1109/uyms50627.2020.9247073
50. Ozkan, N., Erdogan, T.G., Gök, M.Ş.: A bibliometric analysis of Agile software development publications. In: 3rd International Informatics and Software Engineering Conference (IISEC), pp. 1–6. IEEE (2022). https://doi.org/10.1109/iisec56263.2022.9998291
51. Ozkan, N., Gök, M.Ş., Köse, B.Ö.: Towards a better understanding of Agile mindset by using principles of Agile methods. In: 15th Conference on Computer Science and Information Systems (FedCSIS), pp. 721–730. IEEE (2020). https://doi.org/10.15439/2020f46
52. Ozkan, N., Eilers, K., Gök, M.Ş.: Back to the essential: a literature-based review on Agile mindset. In: 2023 18th Conference on Computer Science and Intelligence Systems (FedCSIS), pp. 201–211. IEEE (2023). https://doi.org/10.15439/2023f6360
53. Petermann, M.K., Zacher, H.: Agility in the workplace: conceptual analysis, contributing factors, and practical examples. Ind. Organ. Psychol. **13**(4), 599–609 (2020). https://doi.org/10.1017/iop.2020.106
54. Ryskowski, J.: Revealing the unobvious social norms and traditional development fantasies that impede Agile adoption. In: 2018 International Conference on Computational Science and Computational Intelligence (CSCI), pp. 829–834. IEEE (2018). https://doi.org/10.1109/aero.2019.8741796
55. Sathe, C.A., Panse, C.: Analyzing the impact of Agile mindset adoption on software development teams productivity during COVID-19. J. Adv. Manage. Res. (2022). https://doi.org/10.1108/jamr-05-2022-0088
56. Senapathi, M., Srinivasan, A.: Sustained Agile usage: a systematic literature review. In: 17th International Conference on Evaluation and Assessment in Software Engineering, pp. 119–124 (2013). https://doi.org/10.1145/2460999.2461016
57. Sommer, A.F.: Agile transformation at LEGO group: implementing Agile methods in multiple departments changed not only processes but also employees' behavior and mindset. Res. Technol. Manag. **62**(5), 20–29 (2019). https://doi.org/10.1080/08956308.2019.1638486
58. Thangasamy, S.: Lessons learned in transforming from traditional to Agile development. J. Comput. Sci. **8**(3), 389–392 (2012). https://doi.org/10.3844/jcssp.2012.389.392
59. Van Manen, H., van Vliet, H.: Organization-wide Agile expansion requires an organization-wide Agile mindset. In: Jedlitschka, A., Kuvaja, P., Kuhrmann, M., Männistö, T., Münch, J., Raatikainen, M. (eds.) PROFES 2014. LNCS, vol. 8892, pp. 48–62. Springer, Cham (2014). https://doi.org/10.1007/978-3-319-13835-0_4
60. Wang, Z., Pan, S.L., Ouyang, T.H., Chou, T.C.: Achieving IT-enabled enterprise agility in China: an IT organizational identity perspective. IEEE Trans. Eng. Manage. **61**(1), 182–195 (2013). https://doi.org/10.1109/tem.2013.2259494
61. Weinberg, M.G.: Secrets of consulting: Dorset House (1985). ISBN-13: 978-0932633019

62. Yang, H., Antunes, P., Tate, M.: Towards a unified conceptualisation of IS agility. In: IEEE 20th International Conference on Computer Supported Cooperative Work in Design (CSCWD), pp. 269–275 (2016). https://doi.org/10.1109/cscwd.2016.7566000

63. Zablah, A.R., Brown, B.P., Donthu, N.: The relative importance of brands in modified rebuy purchase situations. Int. J. Res. Mark. **27**(3), 248–260 (2010). https://doi.org/10.1016/j.ijr esmar.2010.02.005

64. Ziegler, A., Peisl, T., Ates, A.: The future of Agile coaches: do large companies need a standardized Agile coach certification and what are the alternatives? In: Yilmaz, M., Clarke, P., Riel, A., Messnarz, R. (eds.) EuroSPI 2023. CCIS, vol. 1891, pp. 3–15. Springer, Cham (2023). https://doi.org/10.1007/978-3-031-42310-9_1

Author Index

E. Ziemba et al. (Eds.): FedCSIS-ITBS 2023/ISM 2023, LNBIP 504, pp. 283–284, 2024.
https://doi.org/10.1007/978-3-031-61657-0

Printed in the United States
by Baker & Taylor Publisher Services